99 FOR 1

by Will Cravens

Second Edition
September, 2020
Endurance Leadership, Inc.
Ashburn, VA 20148
99 for 1, Copyright © 2017

Dedication

This book is dedicated to my best childhood friend, Ed Pelzner.

Our time together growing up and incredible memories have contributed to the man that I have become.

Thank you Ed for adding to the adventure of my life and daring me to take more risks.

All throughout the course of this journey, you have added to the richness of my life without even knowing it.

If you hadn't been lost on the streets of San Diego, I would never have met so many extraordinary men and women who live there. I want to thank you for your friendship. And, I pray that the Living God brings restoration to your life in such a way that you become significantly more than you ever dreamed possible. On that day, it will be clear to everyone that God worked a miracle.

I love you brother,

Will

Special Thanks

First off, I want to thank my dedicated friend Steve Bowman. Although he didn't know Ed personally, he joined me on nine trips. Steve spent his own money and time, walking over 300 miles on the streets of San Diego to help me search, while loving countless homeless individuals along the way. He is an incredible friend and sacrificial leader. Thank you, Steve, I could not have done this without you!

I am also grateful to the 42 men, women and children who have accompanied me on the homeless trips in search of Ed. They cared for many homeless souls along the way and loved them well!

In addition, I want to thank my friends who helped me with the creative and editing process of writing and publishing this book. That list of individuals includes, but is not limited to Sandra Cravens, Gene & Linda Davis, Jane & Gary Ellrod, Lily Jourdan de Hidalgo, Dustin Holliday, Elaine Sales, and Suzanne Vel.

Lastly, I want to thank my unbelievable wife Sandra Cravens, for supporting me throughout this journey. She was also extremely understanding each time I announced that I was headed back to the West Coast in search of my friend. Sandra was my biggest cheerleader, even though it meant that I was gone for a total of ten weeks all together. She even joined me on four different trips and never stopped believing in the cause. Sandra's love and support for me throughout this emotionally-taxing six-year process has served to keep me going and I'm grateful to God for giving me such a caring wife and best friend to do life with!

Trip Log

Trip 1: (*2/9-13/15*) Will Cravens

Trip 2: (*9/14-20/15*) Will Cravens, Brian Carruthers & Steve Bowman

Trip 3: (*2/7-13/16*) Will Cravens, Steve Bowman & A.G. Ukwa

Trip 4: (*3/23-28/16*) Will & Sandra Cravens

Trip 5: (*10/9-16/16*) Will Cravens, Steve Bowman, Dave (Gumby) Houston, Trevin Frame, Tom Pounder, John Costello, Georgia McGowan & Audie Hall

Trip 6: (*2/12-18/17*) Will Cravens, Steve Bowman, Jason Bruce, Dave (Gumby) Houston, Georgia McGowan, Ben Atkinson, Evan Reyle, Connor Sarant & Courtney Cravens

Trip 7: (*8/14-20/17*) Will & Sandra Cravens

Trip 8: (*9/17-23/17*) Will Cravens, Steve Bowman, Eric Locklear, Connor Sarant, Ben Skriloff & Laki Atanasov

Trip 9: (*2/11-17/18*) Will Cravens, John Morales, Ben Skriloff & Semisi Tipeni

Trip 10: (*8/29/18 – 9/4/18*) Will & Sandra Cravens, Eric Locklear, Ed Hidalgo and Lily Jourdan de Hidalgo, Capri & Skye Cravens

Trip 11: (*9/17-22/18*) Will Cravens, Steve Bowman, Georgia McGowan & Andrew Beall

Trip 12: (*12/30/18 – 1/5/19*) Will Cravens, Steve Bowman, Holly Bowman, Kara Bowman, Clay Whitley, Georgia McGowan, Hawley Hansen, Peter Hong, Randy Stenson, Melanie & Enzo Uribe

Trip 13: (*8/12-19/19*) Will & Sandra Cravens, Lily Jourdan de Hidalgo, Hailey, Capri & Skye Cravens, Dustin & Lisa Holiday

Trip 14: (*1/12-18/20*) Will Cravens, Steve Bowman, Kara Bowman, Hawley Hansen, Peter Hong, Emil Short, Bill Bryson, Brian Silvestri, Betsy Jones, Maria Arevalo

Regarding the Book

The details of this book are true and without exaggeration. All photos were taken by trip participants with the consent of those who were being photographed.

It is my hope that the details of this journey would inspire others to pursue those who have lost their way. True love is demonstrated and is not limited to words. The world is in dire need of people willing to leave the comfort of their surroundings to pursue and to care for those who have lost the ability to help themselves.

The journey of leaving 99 who are in a safe place to search for the 1 that is in trouble is a noble assignment, one worthy of our time and resources.

<u>Note</u>: A percentage of all the profits of "99 for 1" are donated to the continued mission efforts which benefit the less fortunate and often over-looked in today's culture! Through the vehicle of Endurance Leadership and Leadership Excursions, we continue to organize and lead medical missions, homeless excursions and other trips meant to get people out of their comfort zones. We seek to create opportunities for individuals to love others by serving practical needs and caring for others as we would want to be cared for if the roles were reversed. Such trips have proven to be life changing.

<u>Reference</u>: The concept of "99 for 1" comes from a passage found in the Bible (reference: Luke 15:3 – 7).

- Will Cravens, author

Contents

Foreword

By Steve Bowman

(9-Time Trip Participant)

(Left to right: Steve & Will in Ocean Beach, CA)

Who exactly is this friend of Will's by the name of Ed Pelzner? That was what I wanted to know after I heard Will Cravens stand in front of the church congregation in August 2015. He asked an entire auditorium full of people if anyone wanted to go to San Diego to help him locate his childhood friend, Ed. Apparently Ed had suddenly left all he had behind--possessions, friends and family--to live on the streets of San Diego, California.

Will explained that he had already been to San Diego once in search of Ed, to no avail. During his first excursion, he had been challenged by a homeless man named Ted, to actually live on the streets himself in order to find Ed and learn more about Ed's new chosen way of life. So, Will being Will, was planning to do just that, and had begun recruiting volunteers for the mission. When I heard the invitation, I thought to myself, "*That's one mission trip I definitely won't be going on.*" However, God had a different plan.

Over the next few weeks my mind kept wandering back to Will's challenge. What would it be like to live on the streets and help Will search for his friend? "*This must be some special friend,*" I pondered.

After taking some time to pray, I became more and more convinced that I should volunteer to join the search party. My next challenge was figuring out how to present this idea to my wife. To my surprise, she was on board from the moment I brought it up. I wasted no time and called Will to make him aware of my decision. I had no idea what I was getting myself into. Nor did Will for that matter. This was going to be a fly-by-the-seat-of-your-pants kind of trip, but something just seemed right about it.

Decisions and trips like this one are far from the norm in my life. The thought of being on the streets and living like a homeless person was completely out of my comfort zone. My naïve idea was that we would explore the streets for the day, and simply locate Ed on a street corner somewhere. This was not the case. It was more like searching for a needle in a haystack. After learning that the number of homeless people in San Diego surpassed thirteen thousand, I realized just how challenging the search might be.

During the nine trips I took with Will, I learned more about Ed and the tight bond of friendship that he and Will forged while growing up in the same neighborhood. I began to feel like I knew Ed as well, which made me all the more motivated to find him. The appreciation Ed's parents expressed before and after each trip and their obvious love for their son, served to fuel my determination to find him.

Our time searching for Ed was never in vain. The homeless souls we met on the streets were unbelievable! Every person we encountered had their own unique story regarding how they landed on the streets. Their backstories ranged from financial loss, drug and alcohol addiction, the desire to escape society and a myriad of other assorted circumstances.

While I was on my fifth trip with Will, I came to the realization that this mission had grown bigger than Ed. We found that the homeless we meet on each trip actually enjoy our company and have come to realize that we love them too. The individuals who we have been fortunate to know by name are always eager to see us every time we return. Not to mention that the friendship I've developed with Will is something that I'll cherish for life. You definitely get to know someone when facing significant challenges together; such as walking countless miles each day, sleeping outside in the freezing cold or rain, waking abruptly in a field of sprinklers, or some other memorable trial.

It's hard to forget being awakened by police flashlights in your eyes. What also comes to mind are the many laughs and tears we've shared along this path. I'm convinced as you read this book, you too will develop a concern for those who are less fortunate, like Ed. You're sure to be inspired by the lengths Will Cravens has gone to in order to search for and love his childhood friend.

So, I want to challenge every single person who reads this book, to honestly consider leaving the ninety-nine and go search for the one that is lost and struggling. It is a journey entirely worth taking!

Steve Bowman, (Participant on 9 trips)

Foreword

By Eric Locklear

(2-Time Trip Participant)

(Eric Locklear cycling in Maui)

I was a reluctant Christian when I walked into Bridge Community Church one Sunday evening in 2016. I say reluctant because I wasn't ignorant of the Lord, nor was I enthusiastically against religion, I just wasn't a cheerleader, lukewarm at best. I was born in Robeson County, North Carolina, a hot bed struggle between Pentecostals, Baptists and sin. Even though I grew up in Reston, Virginia, I had heard and seen plenty. Mahatma Gandhi summarized my thinking best when he said, *"I like your Christ, I do not like your Christians. Your Christians are so un-like your Christ."* However, when my wife drew my attention to a story on Will Cravens' Facebook account, I saw the posts and photos which described his search for Ed Pelzner on the streets of San Diego.

My life momentarily froze in place. You see, I knew Will and I knew Ed from the time we attended Hunters Woods Elementary School until we graduated from South Lakes High School many years later. Our lives would again become inextricably linked after a 30-year gap from the last time we had each seen each other. Who besides God would have known that approximately one year after I stepped into that church in 2016, that I would be walking the streets of San Diego? Only He could have known that I would be living amongst the homeless, and propelled by an invisible force, through heat and headwinds to meet Ed Pelzner the following year, on a street corner in Paia, Maui in late summer of 2018. I was no longer a reluctant Christian and skeptic, I was committed.

I attribute this profound change to the Living God of the Bible, which my friend Will Cravens led me to see. When I say that he led me to experience a significant change, I should add that he didn't preach about it as I was expecting, rather, he simply loved God and the people who came across his path. While you may attribute my thinking to something else, what is indisputable to me, are the lives that I've witnessed positively transformed since I re-engaged with God. The stories written in these pages only scratch the surface of the thousands of other lives which were impacted in a positive way. I use the figure of 'thousands' since the actual number would be inestimable, but calculable anecdotally. I say this because it's impossible to set aside the comforts of a loving family, shelter, and food to walk the streets of a distant city, talking to the homeless, and living amongst them, without the experience significantly impacting your world view, Christian or not.

After my trip to San Diego in 2017, I found myself seeing people differently, and understanding my place in this world with a fresh perspective. One tangible example of the change that occurred in me, led me to buy breakfast burritos from McDonalds on Wednesday mornings and hand them out to the homeless who I encountered at the Washington DC metro station before I went to work. Similar to the burrito man I met in Pacific Beach during my week on the streets there, I was inspired to follow his example.

The narrative that Will Cravens tells of his relationship with Ed on the streets, woods, and fields of Reston, Virginia where we grew up is stunning in its simplicity, and beautiful in its impact. Will walks through this life and loves people along the way. Will goes grocery shopping and loves people in the process. Will rides his bike and loves people he has encountered. My guess is that Will didn't live this way from the time he came to faith as a middle school kid. I imagine that the seeds of his character must have been sown early, albeit hidden under layers of pain and struggle during his formative years.

What Will demonstrates is that there doesn't need to be a committee, there doesn't need to be an organization, nor does there need to be a government agency to impact the world. What I have noticed in my friendship with Will is his steadfast conviction to treat others as he would like to be treated if the roles were reversed. If each one of us lived out that simple yet profound practice on a daily basis, it's inestimable what impact and ripple effect it would have in this world in which we live.

"*99 for 1*" completes the mission to find Ed, but doesn't finish the journey. God doesn't come in and out of our lives randomly, and there is still so much more life left for me, Will, and Ed that is left to be discovered. Even you, dear reader, if you never walked a street in San Diego or rode a mile in Maui, are just as much a part of this saga as Will, Ed, and myself. Don't be surprised if you find yourself doing something kind for someone after you complete this spectacular, real-life account of what it means to love your neighbor, as seen in Will's quest to find Ed Pelzer in "99 for 1."

Eric Locklear, (Participant on 2 trips)

Introduction by Will Cravens

I was seated in a fancy restaurant in downtown Quito, Ecuador, enjoying the conversation and awaiting the first course, yet somewhat distracted. While trying to focus on my friend and what he was sharing, there were two secret service agents buzzing around the perimeter of our table. Todd and his wife moved to Ecuador after accepting his appointment as the US Ambassador of Ecuador. I was already impressed when we got stuck in traffic earlier that evening, which the security detail viewed as a potential risk. They handled it by turning on the blue lights and eluding traffic by driving in the median. We averted the jam and made it to dinner in no time. While Ambassador Chapman may have become accustomed to the constant presence of Secret Service agents, I was somewhat distracted.

I was visiting in the spring of 2017, and in the midst of planning a medical mission trip to Ecuador. Todd had helped by introducing me to some tremendous contacts who agreed to coordinate our excursion later that summer. I had spent a few days in the capital and also in Cuenca where we planned to host our medical team. Our dinner was our final meal before I had to fly back to the States later that evening. I simply figured we would enjoy a nice meal together before I took off and had no idea that the conversation would impact my future.

Todd caught me off guard when he asked me a question, "*So, when are you going to write the book?*" I'm fairly sure that my eye brows furled as I replied, "*What book are you talking about?*" Todd responded, "*The book about your homeless friend Ed.*" I sat there for a minute processing his indirect challenge. I asked, "*Why would I write that book? I've made a few trips and I haven't found him, which makes the quest feel like a failed mission. Why would people want to hear about that?*" He was unfazed by my response and said, "*You've lived on the streets with the homeless and that's remarkable. ABC News San Diego ran a story on you and that's no everyday occurrence. Lastly, you haven't given up, and even now you're planning more trips. That's inspirational!*" He allowed his comments to sink in before he added, "*The story needs to be told.*"

We chatted more about the idea and importance of capturing the story and in late September I completed my first draft of "*99 for 1.*" The problem was, the story wasn't finished yet. Every time we took another trip, I'd need to update the material. When you're writing a true account based on real-life events, how do you know if and when the story is complete? I toyed with writing a sequel to the first draft and even out-lined a trilogy before settling on what I have compiled in this book. I had a sense that it was time.

It is my hope that this story serves to inspire you on your life jour-ney. Although I kept random notes concerning the lessons I learned throughout this journey, the idea of writing a book never crossed my mind until Todd brought it up. Now that I've taken the time to complete it, I'd like to say at the onset that I believe people are the number one investment that we can ever make in this life. They are worth taking risks for and investing our time. Pursuing a fellow human who is in trouble, even if they caused it themselves, demonstrates value that can be a catalyst for change. Offering grace to those who have been told they are beyond repair, is something that is in dire need in the world we occupy.

It is my hope and prayer that this book causes you to question what real love looks like. This journey began for me when I realized my friend was in trouble and I dared to ask one simple question. "*How would I want to be loved if the roles were reversed?*" That single question and the answer that came to my mind propelled me on this life-changing jour-ney. I never stopped to consider how many trips it might take, how much money it might cost or how my own life might be impacted as a result. I simply knew that loving another person the way that I would want to be loved if I were in his place, was the right thing to do.

I pray that the true stories found on the pages you are about to read serve to encourage, inspire and motivate you to love others in ways that stretch you to your core. If you dare to love someone who is a significant risk regardless of the outcome, you will be changed in the process even if they are not. What kind of world would we live in if everyone lived in such a way? I don't claim to be an expert, but I feel blessed by what I've learned along the way. I wouldn't trade this experience for anything and pray that it serves to impact your life beyond what you could ever possibly imagine.

Will Cravens, (Author & Participant on 14 homeless trips)

Chapter 1
The Phone Call

One afternoon, in early October of 2014, my phone rang. I had no idea that the conversation would change my life forever. The caller was my childhood best friend's mom and she got right to the point. *"Ed's in trouble!"* Her voice was shaky as she continued, *"He's given up on his business and decided to live on the streets. Can you believe that?"*

I was speechless as I tried to process the disturbing news. *"Maybe she's wrong?"* I thought to myself. At least I hoped she was.

Ed's mom, knowing that Ed and I had managed to maintain a friendship from our early teen years until the present (despite living on opposite coasts for a majority of that time), knew I would take her concerns seriously. She had just returned from a week on the West Coast and I was one of the first people she called.

Ed and I had grown up in a town called Reston, Virginia. Today, Reston is a bustling suburb of the nation's capital, but in the 1970s (when we were growing up), the neighborhhoods were only just beginning to spring up amongst a few cattle farms.

Ed moved to the West Coast in the late 1980s, settling in the city of San Diego, California. He told me that he loved it there and swore that he'd never leave. On most of my trips out west I would visit with Ed and he always appeared to be fairly happy. I couldn't imagine what would have caused him to quit his business and take to the streets.

Ed's mom speculated that perhaps he was wrestling with some form of mental illness. She reasoned, *"Normal people don't just give up on life and become homeless, do they?"* Her motherly intuition, knowing that something wasn't right when she last spoke to Ed via telephone, caused her to book a flight to California without delay.

Ed's mom was not the only one to sense that something wasn't right. After her week-long stay trying to organize Ed's belongings, she learned that two of Ed's best friends (Mason and Brett), showed up to help Ed move his things. They had known Ed since high school. Although they were all there to help, what really worried them was the fact that Ed had rejected their offers of assistance. When they were packing, Ed didn't stick around to offer his opinion regarding what to do with his things. He told Mason and Brett that he needed to get a haircut and then he took off.

Mason and Brett did their best to offer Ed help and couldn't understand why he refused it. When they realized he was being evicted from his work facility, they quickly organized a storage container to salvage his heavy woodworking tools. They stored his smaller possessions with a local friend by the name of Stephanie. Ed's tools represented his livelihood and together with his road bikes were easily worth more than $25,000. Ed's mom and his friends were trying to make sense of it all.

The validity of his mom's concerns became even more evident when she declared, "*I don't believe that this is a temporary thing. Ed told me that from now on, he plans to live on the streets!*"

She was not asking me to take action when she called, but was coveting the prayers of local churches for her son's well-being. Before hanging up, she commented that Ed had even abandoned his cell phone and Facebook account, leaving us no way to contact him.

It was hard for me to reconcile her words with the fact that I had just seen Ed, on my last trip to the West Coast, only ten months earlier.

Because of our life-long friendship, I always made a point of contacting him whenever I had a trip planned to Southern California. Continuing this habit for the last thirty years had allowed us to remain close friends.

On one of my trips out west with my wife Sandra, I contacted Ed and arranged for us to have dinner. He brought his girlfriend Lori along. We spent the better part of an evening catching up and getting acquainted with Ed's girlfriend. We swapped old stories, (his version always made him sound better, and mine was probably just as biased in the opposite direction). We laughed, ate food, played catch up, and enjoyed spending time together as couples.

At the end of the evening, Ed's girlfriend Lori commented, "*You two have been friends since you were kids. Not many people have this kind of bond or stay in touch. You two should cherish your friendship.*" Lori's comment shifted the mood to a very serious one, but we joked to ease the tension. We spent another hour reminiscing before calling it a night.

The following morning, before we left for the airport, Ed joined us at our hotel for breakfast. He said, "*I have been thinking about what Lori said, and I believe she's right. I value our friendship and want to do a better job of staying in touch.*"

Then he thanked me for making the time to reconnect whenever I was out west. I was moved by his response and was appreciative of Lori's warning not to take our friendship for granted.

The following year, my wife and I returned to the Anaheim area for business. I let Ed know that while I was not going to be in San Diego, he was welcome to make his way to Anaheim and crash at our hotel. Our hotel was a suite, with a separate room that contained a sleeper sofa. I honestly didn't expect Ed to make the trip, yet I was pleasantly surprised when he decided to take me up on my offer.

Ed caught a train to Anaheim, with his bike in tow. Then he rode his bike from the station to our hotel. I was thrilled to see him. Sandra had just gone to bed, so Ed and I took some time to catch up, while sampling the local recommended craft beer. Ed didn't bring his girlfriend this time (not because she didn't want to make the journey, but because they'd recently broken up). He didn't seem anxious to talk about that, so we settled for small talk instead.

As was our custom when we hadn't seen each other in a while, one of us would bring up a past shared adventure to reminisce about. I'm not sure which one of us brought it up, but before I knew it we were re-living the memory of a random Saturday when we chose to kill time at the National Zoo. Somehow, we wound up at the Primates House and were taken with a large group of monkeys who were playing in the outdoor portion of their cage.

This particular breed had long black hair, with a big pointy tuft shooting from the crown of their heads. They somewhat resembled those freaky-looking blue flying monkeys from *The Wizard of Oz*, although these were black. While the sign clearly stated, "*Do not feed the monkeys,*" Ed saw no harm in offering them popcorn. One enormous black monkey with a large tuft of hair on his head, similar to *The Grinch Who Stole Christmas*, became extremely interested in Ed's popcorn. While Ed began by tossing pieces of popcorn toward the edge of the cage, the monkey got braver and closer with each bite.

However, as the monkey grew bolder, so did Ed. Before long, we had a small audience of interested people, closely watching Ed bond with the large primate. When Ed ran out of popcorn, the monkey stretched his furry arm through the bars and extended an open hand to Ed. We were all touched by their connection and watched with interest as Ed offered his index finger, in the monkey's direction. Just as Ed rested his finger in the palm of the monkey's hand, a few people pulled out cameras to capture the moving moment. If you and I looked at one of the photos, we might believe that they were copying Michelangelo's famous fresco hanging above the Sistine Chapel. However, that peaceful exchange was soon to change. Without warning, the monkey clutched Ed's finger more tightly while yanking it toward his open mouth, revealing large white fangs. The popcorn was the appetizer for the beast who was clearly ready for the main course, Ed's "finger food."

I never knew Ed had such lightning fast reflexes until I witnessed him jerk his hand away from that cage. The audience who had gathered roared with laughter, myself included. Ed seemed to find it less than humorous at the time. Reliving the memory on that particular evening in the lobby of the Embassy Suites in Anaheim, we both found it hilarious.

The conversation took a sharp turn when Ed became dead serious. He shared with me that he had made the long trek via bike and train, because he wanted to share something. This was unlike Ed, so I listened intently. He went on to say, "*I have been watching you on Facebook lately, and I've observed the trips you lead to serve the poor in different coun-*

tries. I've always wanted to do something like that and even contemplated joining the Peace Corps."

He confessed a sense that his life had been lived too selfishly up to that point, and that he was ready to make a change. He solicited my advice as he tossed back the end of his beer. After listening to my friend's remorse and his desire to make a change, I was moved by his candor. I invited him to join me, later that spring, on a medical trip that we had planned to Ghana, Africa. Ed confessed that he didn't have enough money to cover the trip.

I didn't want the lack of funds to be a hindrance to my friend's desire to serve. The window of opportunity can close without warning, and there is no guarantee that it will reopen. In my opinion, when any human expresses the desire to truly make a significant life change, it is a moment that needs to be taken seriously. I know how rare that type of moment is, and I realized that it was time to act.

I felt compelled to offer Ed a free trip, so I did. I said, *"I'll go and find the money for your trip so that you can join us, but you'll need to make sure that you have a valid passport before I can purchase your ticket. Ghana requires a visa, so I'll need your passport to acquire your visa from the consulate's office in Washington, D.C."* Ed seemed incredibly moved by the gesture and said, *"You don't have to pay for my trip with your money."* I replied, *"I don't have the money to pay for your trip, but God is not short on cash and something will work out. When you do the right thing, it always does."* Ed informed me that his passport had expired, but he appreciated the offer and assured me that he'd apply for a new one right away.

He promised to keep me updated via text concerning the process. We exchanged a few more stories for old time's sake and then headed upstairs to the room. We stepped into the suite, and I showed him where the pullout sofa was.

What Ed did next came as a complete shock to me. He said, *"Will, before you head off to bed would you please pray for me?"* Ed had never asked for prayer since the day we met, so I was moved by his humility and desire for God's help. I said, *"Of course"* and then we prayed and asked God to bless Ed and his desire to make a change.

God was clearly moving in Ed's heart. I felt that he wanted to share more, but that was as much as he was willing to divulge on that particular evening. We called it a night, and then I headed off to my half of the suite, where my wife Sandra was fast asleep.

The next morning, Ed joined Sandra and me for breakfast. He expressed his appreciation and excitement about the upcoming trip to Ghana, yet again. My wife Sandra was thrilled to hear that Ed would be taking part, as we caught her up on the plan that we had concocted the previous evening. Ed let us know that he had to start his bike ride back to the train station and we were in a hurry to head to the airport. Then he pulled something out of his backpack, and slid it across the table.

"*I made this for you,*" Ed commented as I removed a wooden box from the plastic bag it had been wrapped in. It was a handcrafted mahogany box, with a black iron handle on the lid. I thanked my friend for his thoughtful gift, and Sandra suggested a quick photo of the two of us before he departed.

(Left to right: Will & Ed in Anaheim, November 2013)

She snapped the photo just before we said our goodbyes. Ed thanked me again for the generous offer and also for my commitment to our friendship for so many years. I hugged him and thanked him for the handmade wooden box. With that, he was off. Sandra and I packed up and left for the airport. It had been a great visit with my old friend, full of unexpected surprises.

I left our exchange excited to help Ed get his passport rolling, and to raise the necessary funds so that he could join our medical team in Ghana. We exchanged phone calls and Facebook messages over the following months, as he assured me that he had submitted an application for a new passport. I realized that the deadline was approaching for me to submit the group passports for the necessary visas, so I checked in with Ed. He sent me a reply, although he never mentioned his passport. The last message I received from Ed simply read, "*Love you Will – Ed.*" I responded by letting him know that I loved him as well. I was somewhat puzzled by his Facebook message. I wondered more about what was going on in Ed's life at the time. And, I was left to wonder, since he failed to reply after that exchange.

I was curious regarding the catalyst which compelled Ed to go to great lengths to see me months earlier in Anaheim. He had expressed a sincere desire for change in his life at that time and even asked me to pray. I also wondered what had transpired since the evening that Ed had come all that way to see us? I tried to call his phone to see if he was still open to the Ghana trip, but I never received a response.

From that point on, Ed's life took a serious downturn; one that mystified his family, as well as his close friends (myself included). When I received the call from his mom in October telling me that he was homeless, none of it made sense.

In just under one year's time, Ed had gone from desiring change in his life to disengaging from his friendships and his occupation.

Why hadn't he just applied for his passport and come with me as we had discussed? I wondered if he had applied for a new passport at all. What was going on in his mind? I was so confused and had more questions than answers. And yet, what could I do about it? I lived on the opposite side of the country.

I began to pray and ask God for answers. I replayed our last conversation in my mind, searching for clues. Had something traumatic happened that caused his sudden change of heart? The curiosity was too great, so I called Ed's mom back, looking for answers.

It was clear from the second phone call that Ed's mom wasn't taking the news about her son's chosen street life very well. If your child suddenly ends up homeless and rejects your help, it doesn't matter what their age is or the circumstances that caused the unfortunate situation, it's still devastating news.

Mrs. Pelzner gave me a few more facts and let me know that she had befriended a close friend of Ed's who ran a dog walking business in San Diego. Her name is Stephanie and she made regular rounds in the neighborhood that Ed frequented, known as Ocean Beach. Stephanie agreed to keep his parents abreast of his latest whereabouts and condition. As a friend, she was also confused by his sudden break from his business and residence. She agreed to watch his personal belongings (that he left behind), in case he should decide to return to reclaim them.

After speaking with Ed's parents and with Stephanie, who kept an eye out for him, I had a better idea of where Ed was spending his days. However, I still had no answers regarding why on earth he made the break. There were too many unanswered questions for me to make sense of it all. Unsure of my next step, I simply hoped and prayed that Ed would have a change of heart and call for help. What else could I do?

Chapter 2
Crazy Ted

I began praying for Ed on a daily basis. On one particular day as I finished praying, the second greatest commandment came to my mind: "*Love your neighbor as yourself.*" (Luke 10:27). I spent some time contemplating this command, which is sometimes referred to as "*the Golden Rule.*" The question that came to mind as a result was, "*How would I want to be loved if I were suddenly thrust on the streets?*" Without much thought I concluded that if I became homeless in a city somewhere, then I would hope that someone would come looking for me. I certainly didn't want to be written off and forgotten.

Shortly after that revelation, I made plans to take a trip to San Diego and search for my friend. I asked a couple close friends if they might accompany me on the journey. A friend by the name of Dustin Holliday agreed to join me. He had previously been a police officer, so I thought his skills and street smarts would come in handy. I asked other friends to pray about joining us. Then I booked a hotel room, and made flight preparations.

About a week before my trip, Dustin called to tell me that a family emergency had arisen, therefore he would not be able to join me on my quest to find Ed. I asked a few other people to consider taking his place, but it was to no avail. When it came time to travel, I made the journey alone. I stayed at an Embassy Suites which is located in the downtown area, not far from Coronado Island. Sandra and I had stayed at the same hotel when we double dated with Ed and Lori two years earlier.

I'm not sure what I was thinking, but I was clearly not prepared for what lay before me. I arrived at the hotel just before midnight, and after checking in, I began asking locals where the homeless population congregated.

I naively thought that I would arrive in San Diego, find the park where the majority of the homeless people hang out, ask a few people about Ed, and then locate him. I imagined that we would have a conversation in which I planned to talk some sense into him, and then I would bring him back east. If it had worked out that way, you wouldn't be reading this book. I couldn't have been more wrong about the complexity of the journey before me.

Early the next morning, I walked the streets, looking for Ed amongst the homeless. With minimal effort, I found a homeless man on the seafront and showed him a picture of Ed, to see if he recognized him. The man said that he didn't recognize him, so I looked for another likely person to ask. It wasn't hard because there were homeless people all along the seafront of downtown San Diego. They were as common as seagulls, and probably viewed as a similar nuisance. Many were sleeping on sidewalks or in grassy areas. I interviewed any that were awake and willing to engage me.

I approached a security guard, near the enormous retired aircraft carrier (the USS Midway), which draws countless tourists each year. He was friendly and willing to help. He told me that there were more than 12,000 homeless in the San Diego area at that time. The number hung in my mind, but the figure didn't register. "*Is there a nearby park where they hang out?*" I asked. "*Many,*" he responded. "*They're everywhere.*"

What does "*everywhere*" mean? Then he proceeded to share a list of places that he thought I should explore. He mentioned: Balboa Park, the parking lot in the downtown area near Padre Stadium, Saint Vincent's Catholic Church shelter, Ocean Beach, the stadium area near Arena Boulevard, the Riverbed... I couldn't keep up. I wasn't familiar with the city, so I decided a better idea would be to call Ed's friend Stephanie, with the dog walking business. I asked her where she thought I should concentrate my search. She directed me to Ocean Beach, without hesitation I hopped in my rental car and resumed the hunt there.

Dustin called to check in and see how things were progressing. I gave him an update and told him that I was showing Ed's picture around. He asked me if I was using a photo that showed Ed and me or just Ed? When I responded "It's just Ed," Dustin suggested that I use a picture that showed the two of us together. This would demonstrate the fact that I actually knew Ed and am not an undercover cop or debt collector. Great advice, since many of the homeless I had questioned appeared to be suspicious of me.

I was grateful to my wife Sandra for suggesting that Ed and I pose for a photo when we'd seen him in Anaheim on our previous trip. I was able to locate the image on my phone and began using that picture of the two of us.

That afternoon, I passed a few homeless hipsters along the seafront in Ocean Beach. I showed them the photo on my phone. After passing it around, they commented, "*He looks familiar and it's very cool what you're doing.*" One young gal covered in piercings and tattoos exclaimed, "*I wish someone was looking for me!*"

I was moved by her remark and wondered about her family and the journey that led her to the street. Then, a tall, slim man, with sun baked leather skin, asked me, "*Where are you staying while you're in town?*" The question caught me off guard. I considered saying, "*The Embassy Suites downtown,*" but that response felt awkward to make when addressing a crowd of young homeless individuals. Pointing in the direction of downtown I answered vaguely, "*Over that way, toward the city.*"

They let it go, as did I. I felt shame for a brief moment about staying in a nice hotel downtown. If I had announced my nice digs, would they have asked to join me? Would I have refused? All questions and ideas which I hadn't considered prior to that exchange.

I was only in town for three days so I covered as much ground as I could, as quickly as possible. I had numerous conversations in hopes of finding useful information or a clue that would lead me to Ed. I spoke with one homeless man near the baseball park in Robb Field, while he sat near the dugout. He had no idea who Ed was and said that he was new to the area. He was a homeless drifter from the northwest, where the weather had taken a beating on him.

His name was Phil and he had recently arrived in San Diego to soak up the sunshine and make a fresh start. He was not alone. According to a police officer I met in the Gas Lamp District, he said that there are approximately 13,000 homeless in San Diego, 50,000 in San Francisco and 90,000 in Los Angeles. I checked his figures when I returned home to discover that according to Google, the numbers are not quite as high as he said. Google estimates approximately 5,000 in San Diego, 10,000 in San Francisco and 70,000 in Los Angeles. I suppose it depends on who's doing the counting. Regardless of the precise number, I came to realize that the incredible weather in California seems to serve as a homeless magnet. I'd never seen so many people living on the streets in my life.

(Phil behind a baseball dugout at Robb Field Park)

We talked near the backstop fence line where Phil told me, "*The streets can be an addictive place to live.*" "*What do you mean by that?*" I prodded. "*Well, when you feel as though you have let people down and suffered failures at work, home, in marriage or with your kids, the trauma is enough to break your spirit. Out on the street, I have no one left to disappoint.*"

He continued, "*Out here, I'll never be late for work, I'll never miss an important meeting or stress out if I fail to meet someone else's expectation of me.*" He took a long pause, staring off at the riverbed that separated Ocean Beach from Mission Bay. "*The thought of returning to society and applying for a normal job is terrifying to me, because I'm so tired of failure.*"

I digested his words, wondering how many of the homeless masses feel the same way. Was this part of what caused Ed to live on the streets? Phil and I chatted a bit more, then he asked if I might be willing to pray for him. I had mentioned the fact that I was a pastor when he asked me about myself. Phil apparently felt comfortable enough to make the request. We offered up some prayers to God before I headed back toward Ocean Beach.

As I walked away, Phil warned me, "*Be careful, the streets can also be extremely dangerous. While I like the chill atmosphere and absence of expectations, you have to be careful if you want to stay alive.*" My mind immediately went to Ed, wondering about his safety after living on the streets for almost half a year.

Where was he sleeping each night? I thought back to camping trips that Ed and I had taken and the discussions we had as teenagers about living off the land. Maybe it had prepared him for the streets in some regard.

I was in high school when the movie *First Blood* came out and I recall seeing it with Ed. The story of a drifter and broken Green Beret veteran who had been trained to "*eat things that would make a Billy Goat puke,*" was inspirational to Ed and to me. If an army recruiter had been outside the theater that evening, he would have signed up two fresh recruits. We were ready to scribble our names on the solid line and be sworn in, if we could be trained like John Rambo. We shared a similar crazy streak and a desire for the extreme. We wanted to take part in things that challenged our survival skills.

The movie inspired us to plan a camping trip in the mountains of southwest Virginia. We took off one weekend with fishing poles, BB guns, and a trap, but brought no other food to eat. We reasoned, "*If we are going to learn to live off the land like John Rambo, then we'd better get some experience."* We went fishing and caught nothing. We loaded our BB guns and hunted for squirrels but came up empty. We set a trap that we also found empty. As the sun set in the distance and the woods darkened around our tent, we realized that it was going to be a long night.

We built a fire and hoped that our luck might change. At one point, an eastern box turtle wandered toward our campsite and we noticed him in the dancing light of the fire. We named him Tommy and commented, "I hope for Tommy's sake we find something else to eat." For animal lovers, I must apologize in advance and wish I could tell you that Tommy survived the night. He did not. We ended up having roasted a turtle kabab over the fire, which I do not recommend. We charred the meat and forgot to bring salt for seasoning. In addition, as one might imagine, there isn't a whole lot of meat on a small box turtle. Finally, it's difficult to fill your belly with only two turtle legs each. I recall waking the following morning with an awful burnt turtle taste in my mouth, which caused me to regret eating our little friend Tommy all the more. Live and learn.

I thought back to that period of our lives when Ed and I camped out, feeling quite confident that Ed would not resort to eating turtles. But what was he eating? Surely our experiences growing up had somewhat prepared Ed for his current reality, navigating the perils of street living. I muttered a prayer for my childhood friend and for his protection. I was fairly sure that our experiences had prepared Ed, and I could only hope that they had also prepared me. If I was to spend more time amongst the homeless searching for Ed, I needed to develop some street smarts.

The next homeless man I approached looked to be in his late 50s, had long unkempt hair and a thick, scruffy dirty-blond beard. He sat at a picnic table in the grassy area of Ocean Beach. He introduced himself as Ted. His life possessions were tied up and bundled on top of a medium size suitcase which he dragged on rollers. He was sporting an old military jacket and wore faded jeans with a hole in one knee. I asked him about Ed and showed him the photo of the two of us. He responded, *"Yeah, I know Ed, but how do I know you aren't a cop or out here to get him?"* My heart raced as this was the first person to tell me that he knew Ed. I mentioned the fact that we are together in the photo, and Ted replied, *"You could have doctored that photo."*

I let him know that I was a pastor and hoped he might drop his guard. He responded, *"Prove it!"* What does one do to prove he's a pastor? Should I preach a sermon and do some Bible trivia? I contemplated his challenge for a moment and then asked, *"Would you believe me if I pulled up a link online of me preaching at a recent church service?"* He pondered my response and then said, *"Yeah, I suppose that would do it."* In a matter of minutes, I showed him a video of myself preaching at a church back in Virginia. Ted said, *"OK, that'll do. Your friend Ed hangs out at a coffee shop in the downtown area of San Diego."* With some hesitation, I offered to drive Ted downtown in hopes of locating Ed.

We loaded Ted's belongings into the trunk of my rental car and then climbed in the vehicle to head downtown. Ted was seated in the passenger seat up front to my right and I was feeling somewhat nervous. Have you ever given a homeless stranger a ride? It wasn't a normal occurrence for me, and I was adjusting to my homeless co-pilot. I kept my left hand on the steering wheel and my right hand free, in case I needed to defend myself. Perhaps I've seen too many movies, or then again, maybe simply driving around with a stranger off the streets is reason enough for apprehension.

As Ted was chatting, I imagined him trying to rob me, so my mind drifted to a scenario of me slamming on the brakes and punching him with my right hand. Don't judge me, I'm simply trying to share honestly so you have an accurate understanding of my frame of mind during the ride. My mind tuned back to Ted's comments, as he directed me to an open parking place near a Starbucks in the historic Gas Lamp district. As I parallel-parked my rental car, Ted commented, *"Yep, this is where Ed hangs out."* My heart began to race a bit and I grew nervous wondering if I was about to find my lost friend.

31

My nervousness shifted to excitement wondering if Ted might be right, and my hope began to build. What if Ed is actually here? As we approached the front door, a few homeless people lounged out front on the sidewalk, holding up the building with their backs. My eyes scanned the surrounding area, in hopes of spotting my friend.

Ted and I made our way toward the front of the line, and the barista greeted Ted by name. I figured that was a good sign. Then he asked the gal at the counter if she had recently seen Ed, as he proceeded to place his drink and sandwich order. The young gal responded, *"I'm not sure who you're talking about, who's Ed?"*

It was at that moment that I realized I might have been hustled. Ted turned to me as we stepped away from the counter to wait for our order to be filled. I paid the bill and joined him. He remarked, *"I don't think the employees are allowed to tell us the names of the street people who they serve."* Maybe there was some truth to his comment. However, the barista's face showed true confusion and she didn't appear to be lying as far as I was concerned.

We made our way back to the car, and I told Ted that I planned to resume my search for Ed back in Ocean Beach. He thanked me for the coffee and food, then asked me if I wanted to get high. He said, *"I realize that you're a pastor, but the plant is natural and I use it for medicinal purposes."* I declined but thanked him for the offer, and said that he would have to wait to light up until after I dropped him off at the beach.

When we were a couple of miles from Ocean Beach, Ted looked in my direction and challenged me. *"You know pastor, if you really want to find your friend, why don't you live on the streets like us? The homeless would be more likely to trust you, and you'd see what it's like for your friend if you were willing to walk a few miles in his shoes."* His words lingered in the air, as I allowed them to soak into my head and even further into my heart.

I pondered, *"What would it be like to live on the streets? How different would my quest for Ed be, if I were actually willing to live with the same conditions that he was facing?"* I must admit that Ted got me thinking.

There was something so right about what he had suggested. Of course, the probability of finding Ed would be greater, and I'd gain insight into those who made the streets their way of life. As I dropped Ted off, I offered to pray for him. As I'd prayed with Phil earlier in the week, many of the homeless who I met welcomed the invitation. Ted was different.

"No thank you, you can't pray for me. Do you want to know why?"
"Sure Ted, tell me why."

He then proclaimed, *"Because I am the Lord."* Not having a good poker face, I'm confident that my expression revealed what I believed about Ted's confession. He carried on, *"In fact, I'm a descendant of the line of David from the Old Testament and I am the Lord."* I remained silent for a moment, trying to think of the appropriate response. Ted had certainly surprised me with his revelation. Then I replied, *"If you are the Lord, why couldn't you locate Ed?"* He shuffled away without responding. I lifted my hand to wave and offered a brief prayer on his behalf. When he heard my prayer, he began to shriek and run as fast as his legs would carry him. That was the last I ever saw of Ted.

Then the idea occurred to me, *"While this man was obviously not Jesus in the flesh as he had conveyed, I wondered if God had used him to convey a message?"* His words didn't reveal Ed's location, but Ted's challenge did strike me to the core. I couldn't help but imagine that Jesus would stay on the streets with homeless people if He were in my place.

As I saw Ted disappear around a street corner dragging his entire life possessions, I couldn't shake his challenge from my mind. Ed had been living on the streets for half a year. I reasoned that I could do it if he could. Or could I? I suppose I was about to find out.

Chapter 3

Does Anyone Have a Screwdriver?

On the flight home, I had more time to think about my friendship with Ed. We met when I was in the eighth grade, before I entered high school. I was one grade ahead of Ed in school, and while I had seen him on the school bus, we were yet to become friends. In fact, when I share the story of how our paths crossed, you may wonder why we became friends at all.

Middle school is not the sort of phase that most want to repeat. To make matters worse, I was born in late August, which made me one of the youngest people in my grade. I remember my weight as a freshman in high school because I tried out for the wrestling team. I weighed all of ninety-eight pounds, and while I did have muscle, I was lean. Although I climbed trees and liked to wrestle, my small stature didn't help me much during my middle school years, or when I entered high school.

Being fairly insecure at the time, I stuck to my close friends. My best friends at that time didn't live far from my house, and they were twin brothers, named Ricky and Barry Rosenzwieg. I would often head over to their house after school while both my parents and their parents were usually still at work. On one particular day in September, I was almost to the Rosenzwieg's home when I spotted a group of guys standing in front of the house next door. As I was about to pass the crowd, the ringleader, a freshman from high school, said something to me. His name was Joel and he was a gymnast. I thought Joel was a cool kid, and looked up to him as an athlete as well as an upper classman.

However, Joel stepped out in front of me and began to make some ridiculing comments about me in front of the small audience that was present. They, of course, played their part and began to laugh and encourage him. Then he gave me a slight shove and said, "*Why don't you get out of here Cravens?*" This brought more laughter, and I was faced with a choice. Should I put up with the scorn and head toward my friend's home, or should I choose another course of action? My mind was processing options as my heart began to race.

Let me add that I'm the youngest of four children in my family. My father died before my third birthday and my mother remarried within a year. My stepdad was a great provider and very loving with my mom. However, he had very little patience when it came to raising four step kids. He worked for the IRS in Washington, DC and was a decorated World War II veteran. He served as a medic in the Battle of the Bulge and had seen things that no human should have to see or experience. As a result, he wasn't the soft and warm cuddly type, which led to trickle-down tension and an atmosphere of fighting in our home. Being on the low end of the totem pole amongst my siblings, I got pummeled by everyone. I learned how to take a beating and give it back, not fearing an altercation.

When Joel shoved me, I wasn't about to walk away. I decided instead to catch him off guard and shoved him right back. Since I was a grade younger and much smaller, he didn't anticipate my response. Joel lost his footing and he fell backwards onto the ground. This caused the small band of spectators to laugh even louder as they witnessed this David and Goliath style triumph. I was bright enough to know that it may not be wise to wait for him to get up and make matters worse. A bruised ego can cause a person with an audience to go past the point of friendly retaliation, if there is such a thing.

While I may have been small for my age, I was very fast, especially when adrenaline was rushing through my veins. I sprinted from the street in front of Joel's house, straight for Ricky and Barry's home next door. Knowing that his parents would still be at work, I opened the front door without knocking and ran straight up their stairs.

The shouts of the boys followed behind me and I imagined Joel was gaining on me. Their cries said it all, *"Fight! Fight! Fight! Fight!"* This only served to increase my pace, as the pack followed me straight into the Rosenzwieg's home and right up the stairs.

I dashed into the bathroom and locked the door behind me. The sort of interior door locks used in the early 1980s required a small screwdriver or key to unlock the door. Joel pounded on the door and demanded, "*Come out of there Cravens!*" I responded, "*Nope, I'm fine right here.*"

Then he asked a surprising question, "*Does anyone have a small screwdriver?*" I was leaning against the door and figured I was safe. After all, what kind of middle or high school kid goes around carrying a pack of screwdrivers in their pocket? To my surprise, I heard a single voice pipe up to say, "*I have a pack of small screwdrivers you can use, right here in my pocket.*"

"*Who invited that kid?*" I wondered. Without hesitation, Joel was fumbling with a screwdriver, attempting to get the door open. My heart raced as I heard him attempting to get the lock open. I was contemplating my next move. There was no window to escape through, so I stood with my back pressed to the door, hoping my weight was enough to keep it shut.

Just as it swung open, another voice shouted, "*What the heck are you all doing in my house?*" It was Harris, Ricky and Barry's older brother. He was a senior in high school and big enough to intimidate the crowd. Harris responded to the scuffle and demanded that the boys leave immediately. He saved the day and as they all filed out, I took note of the neighborhood kid with the pack of screwdrivers.

That kid just happened to be Ed Pelzner. Later that year, I saw him in the neighborhood and asked him why on earth he carried a pack of tools in his pocket. He told me that he had been building a cage for a snake he caught in the woods. By some odd coincidence, he was carrying them in his pocket on the day that Joel asked for them. I chose to believe Ed and was curious about the cage he mentioned.

I was interested in snakes as well, so his cage comment caught my attention. My interest originated as the result of my childhood allergies. Our family doctor suggested to my mom that we consider a pet with no hair. I didn't know at the time that there was such a thing as a Mexican Hairless dog, so I settled for snakes.

This was the start of our adventurous friendship. In addition to searching for reptiles, we fished, climbed trees, and enjoyed pranks involving risk and some form of challenge. We were never bored.

One day, we stood on the edge of the Potomac River with a full day ahead of us. Ed's dad had dropped us off on the Virginia side of the river, in an area known as Great Falls National Park. We weren't crazy enough to enter the river near the falls, so we hiked about a mile north until we arrived at River Bend Park. The Potomac River separates the states of Virginia and Maryland, and runs south from the falls, winding its way just past our Nation's Capital.

The sun was hot, and the water looked refreshing. About 20 feet out into the enormous river there was an island. We were preparing to head in that direction when we noticed a sign which read, "*Caution, No Swimming!*" Just below the warning on the very same sign was the statement, "*An average of eight people drown here each year.*"

This type of warning is meant to prevent people from stepping foot in the water. I suppose I should preface that by saying, most *normal* people. However, if you thrive on risk and love an adrenaline-induced challenge, then this sign seems more like an invitation. I glanced at the words on the sign, and my brain processed the caution in different terms.

Turning to my best friend Ed I said, "*I bet the people who drowned here each year were children or perhaps they weren't strong swimmers. I'm sure we'll be fine!*" With that, Ed nodded in agreement, and we plunged into the river.

We trudged through the water and were quickly in up to our waists. The current was not a threat, and we made it to a small island in a matter of minutes. We spent some time exploring and turning rocks in search of snakes. We grew bored in a matter of minutes and decided to cross the larger portion of the river located on the northeast side of the island. After all, the river on the southwest side was like walking through a calm creek. However, as we attempted to cross the next stretch of river, we quickly realized that we were in over our heads.

No one would realize the rapid pace of the current by looking at the surface of the water. Once we were about ten feet away from the island, the deceiving current began to sweep us rapidly downstream.

We entered the Potomac at River Bend Park, just one mile upstream from Great Falls Park, named for the tremendously powerful water falls there. Let's just say they don't call them "Great" Falls for nothing. We watched as the stretch of land we were swimming toward didn't seem to be getting any closer. Instead, the land we were swimming toward was passing before our eyes as we continued to be propelled by the undertow. Panic ensued and I started swimming as hard as my body was able. I looked back at Ed who was laying on top of a log and flapping his arms as fast as they would move.

(Great Falls National Park, Virginia)

By looking at the land on each side, I began to wonder if we were going to make it. Then the thought occurred to me, "*Perhaps those eight drownings each year weren't children, on the contrary, they were foolish teenagers like us?*"

I actually began screaming for help. Ed laughed out loud and said, *"No one can hear us, we're separated by islands on both sides!"* He was right, and adrenaline swept through my body as I imagined the two of us headed straight for the raging falls.

Realizing that shouting for help was futile, we both encouraged one another to swim faster, understanding that we had very little time. I had no idea I could move that fast in the water until my life depended on it. Thankfully, we both reached the Maryland side of the river before it was too late. We had survived crossing the Potomac River, so our names wouldn't be listed on the river sign in the following year's statistics.

As a matter of reference, we crossed the river in the summer of 1982. This was long before anyone had invented electronic devices such as cell phones. The video games of that time period didn't have graphics that made people look at all like real humans. We played a video game called Pong, which consisted of two paddles and a small ping-pong like ball that bounced back and forth. What I'm saying is that kids growing up in those years had to be creative to find something fun to do. Parents would kick their kids out of the house, telling them to go play and not to watch much television.

Unshackled from iPhones, Netflix, tablets, the Internet, and computers, we were left to create our own adventures. For Ed and me, this was not a problem. We were not like many of our friends, which is probably the reason we got along so well. Days such as the Potomac River crossing were common-place, although not always as life-threatening as that particular one.

Whether we were camping, hunting snakes, crossing rivers or climbing trees and cranes, Ed and I lived for the thrill. We were constantly pursuing the next adventure and for some odd reason, we had little to no fear. The more I thought back on those memories, the more convinced I became, that Ed was doing fine on the streets. Near-death experiences have a way of preparing you for survival. At least I hoped they did. I was committed to the mission of finding my friend, which motivated me to accept Ted's challenge. Streets of San Diego, here I come!

Chapter 4
Homeless in San Diego

Talk is cheap and I was tired of just talking about going back to search for Ed. In addition, context means everything.

Just a short time after my trip to San Diego in search of Ed, my friend Mark Powell recommended I read a book titled *Chasing Francis*, by Ian Morgan Cron. Mark had recommended other books in the past and never steered me wrong, so I read it. I had no idea what kind of impact the book would have on me and my journey to search for Ed!

The book is packed with insight, but what really captivated me was the little man who Cron magically brought to life on the pages of his book. Cron's primary character was inspired by an Italian man born in 1182, by the name of Giovanni di Pietro di Bernardone. Most would recognize him as Francis of Assisi and he was a truly remarkable individual. Francis had been so impacted by God, that he decided to sacrifice his family inheritance and position to serve the poor. Who does that?

The Mother Teresa of his day, Francis discovered a new type of riches as he chose to live on the streets just like those he was hoping to impact.

I was so inspired after reading *Chasing Francis*, that I visited the Umbrian town of Assisi in March of 2015. Apparently I was not alone, as thousands of pilgrims make the journey each year. Why do so many want to learn more about an impoverished man who led such a humble life of servitude? Why are so many churches, towns and even cities such as San Francisco, named after this man?

Francis loved the homeless of his day and he wasn't afraid to be identified with them? His life dramatically influenced my journey and I reasoned, "*If Francis could do it for the majority of his life, I could cer-*

tainly live on the streets for five days." Timing and context play a part in our formation and it just so happened that Ted had challenged me in February of 2015, one month before I made the trip to Assisi. As I pondered the idea of living on the streets, Francis helped to seal the deal.

Our plane was about to touchdown at Lindbergh Field, more commonly known as San Diego International Airport, and this time I was not alone. The date was September 14, 2015, seven months after my previous trip.

While about twelve people had expressed an interest in the mission, only two actually bought plane tickets and embraced the vision. My first recruit was Steve Bowman. Steve co-owns a plumbing business with his brother, and I knew his family from the church I'd worked for years previously.

My second recruit was also a business owner. He heard me speak about the trip and contacted me afterwards to express his interest. His name is Brian Carruthers and he simply felt compelled to join me. We all flew out on a Sunday evening flight from the east coast and headed for a hotel in the historic Gas Lamp district of downtown San Diego. We selected the same Embassy Suites that I had stayed in on previous trips. We all headed straight to bed after arriving, with a plan to wake early the following morning to get a fresh start. We left our valuables, wallets, and identification with the hotel manager during our week on the street, with the intention of reclaiming it on the following Friday.

The next morning, we shared a complimentary hotel breakfast before heading out on the street.

We had established a few rules for the road and I suggested that we each read the book, *Under the Overpass*, written by Mike Yankoski.

While *Chasing Francis* had impacted my heart and mission to the homeless, *Under the Overpass* had specific details about living on the streets.

My friend Kathleen Rumford had suggested the book as it features two men who decided to live on the streets, in different cities around the

USA. Kathleen was correct, as this book was a tremendous help when planning this sort of trip. After all, I've never run across a book titled, "*How to Live on the Streets: A Travel Guide for Homeless Living.*" The book had some helpful nuggets and even a chapter about the men living homeless in Ocean Beach, San Diego. I treated it like a blueprint for our pending trip!

The rules that we agreed upon for the week were a compilation of ideas I gleaned from reading three books; *Chasing Francis, Under the Overpass* and the *Gospels* found in the *New Testament* of the *Bible*.

Our rules/packing list was something like this:

1. Do not bring anything of value that could put us in danger.
2. Bring an old backpack, a sleeping bag, a raincoat, and a camping pad.
3. Do not pack any food or snacks. In seeking to relate with those on the street, we could only eat what we were willing to beg for or find.
4. Pack a couple of old outfits and a good pair of walking shoes, with no expensive name brands or labels.
5. Bring a cell phone and an extended life battery charger.
6. Do not pack any money or credit cards. We wanted to depend on God and our wits to survive.

This was our agreed upon allowance for the week, and with that we hit the streets.

Steve, Brian and I left the hotel that Monday morning after leaving our valuables at the front desk. Our homeless adventure felt all too real as we crossed the street toward the wharf, just west of the Gas Lamp district.

(Left to right: Brian, Will & Steve)

In addition to formulating a packing list, we each carried copies of a photo of Ed and myself. It was the same photo that I'd used on my previous trip, taken the morning Ed had breakfast with Sandra and me in November of 2013.

We did not try to deceive anyone on the street by saying that we were fully homeless. We simply approached street people and showed them the photo of Ed and myself. We asked each individual if they recognized him. They would often ask who we were and why we wanted to locate him. I would say that Ed and I were life-long friends and then let them know that we had chosen to live homeless for the week in the hopes of finding my friend Ed.

We would also mention the fact that we had no money or even a credit card to fall back on. We were living on the street, and if we didn't find money or food, we wouldn't eat. Most homeless people responded very favorably and usually offered us some insight or key places to search for Ed.

We usually began by asking about Ed, although after they responded, we would always ask, *"What's your story?"* We stood and listened to countless stories of those willing to share their path to street life. Some confessed addiction. Others blamed a job, relationship or the government for their misfortune.

Some expressed the desire to leave the streets, while others said it was their chosen way of life, similar to Phil, who I met on my previous trip. After asking about their stories and listening to those who decided we were worth trusting, we would ask if we could pray for them. About nine out of ten of those we asked, answered "*Yes*," without hesitation.

We would pray with them and then ask them which direction they might advise us to go. Once they pointed the way, we would walk in that direction and follow their advice. We were also trusting that God would direct our path, using those who we met along the way to provide guidance.

We met one homeless man that very first morning immediately after we crossed the street from our hotel. He had a bushy black perm and a thick beard to match. He was wearing a long sleeve fluorescent green shirt, which read "*Trust Jesus*" in bold letters across his chest, and "*Cry to God*" down his left sleeve. He told us that his name was Brian and said, "*Hello.*"

(Left to right: Will & Brian)

Brian had been quick to greet us when he noticed us walking in his direction. His voice was what made him so unique. It was so incredibly high that I wondered if he had an addiction to helium. We approached him and asked if he had seen Ed, showing him the photo.

He introduced himself as Brian and he was extremely friendly. He confessed that he hadn't seen Ed and then asked us if we would pray with him. He expressed tremendous paranoia about his belief in a looming apocalyptic tidal wave that he believed was coming to sweep us all away. Just before praying, Brian reached out his hands toward us, hoping we could all hold hands during the prayer. A quick glance at Brian's hands revealed the fact that they were covered in grime and his finger nails looked as though he had used them to scrape the bottom of an oil can. Regardless, Steve and I took his hands to pray.

I peered over my left shoulder to locate our third teammate, Brian Carruthers. He was standing about ten feet behind us, praying from a safe distance. After the prayer, we resumed our walk, heading north up the coastline. Brian confessed to having a germ phobia and being a bit of a clean freak. I asked how he planned to deal with a germ phobia while living on the streets with people who rarely shower.

Brian mentioned that he brought an ample supply of disinfectant gel. He shared this as he squeezed the clear goop into his hands and rubbed it around thoroughly. The smell from the bottle hung in the air as we walked a few steps behind Brian.

It was at that point that it occurred to me that I really didn't know much about these two men. Although they had kindly agreed to accompany me on the journey, we barely knew one another. Living on the street for the first time ever with two people you hardly know makes for an interesting trip.

In addition to the trip rules I listed, we also decided against rental cars and taxis. This choice seemed to match our desire to live as genuine homeless people for the week, as well as allowing us to meet any homeless man or woman that we passed on the street. We were headed toward Ocean Beach, about a six mile walk from downtown San Diego.

We had time on our hands, and there was no rush, so I suggested the idea that we each take turns sharing our life stories. Brian began, and Steve followed. I was curious to know their backstories and to understand what motivated them to join me on that unique trip. After all, neither of them knew Ed, yet they were willing to pay their own way and live on the streets to help me search.

Brian mentioned his desire to write a book about helping others and said this trip could serve as good material for his book. Steve stated that he had seen his daughters serve on mission trips, although he never felt like participating in one himself. Both Steve and Brian said that the day they heard me share in church concerning this opportunity, they both felt strongly that this was the trip for them. I will forever be grateful for these two men, who each took a risk accompanying me on this life-threatening excursion.

(Left to right: Brian & Will walking toward Ocean Beach)

Several of the homeless people we met along the way had lost their mental ability to verbally express themselves. We were eager to get to Ocean Beach and were overwhelmed by the sheer volume of the homeless population in the San Diego area. Twelve thousand plus people is a lot of people, even if they are scattered throughout the entire city.

We arrived at Ocean Beach and hit the waterfront. We wasted no time, meeting as many homeless people as we possibly could. We asked questions about Ed, their lives and how we might help them. Many mentioned seeing Ed, but none of the sightings had been recent.

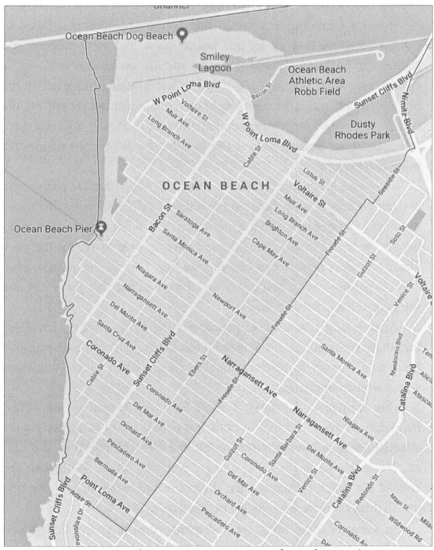

(Ocean Beach, San Diego. Courtesy of Google Maps)

We began to get hungry in the late afternoon, and Brian started checking soda machines and underneath park benches for loose change. He scored a few coins, but it became evident that if we wanted to eat, we better begin asking people for money or food.

It was then that I realized I was the lone extrovert surrounded by two introverts. This meant that I was going to have to do the begging. I stood on the corner of Ocean Front and Cable Street, and looked for likely prospects who might seem more willing to donate some money.

It was a humbling exercise in case you are wondering. I failed to mention that we had all let our beards grow and were wearing old clothes and backpacks. Looking sloppy and disheveled can work for or against you when begging. My stomach was growing hungrier by the minute, which was a tremendous motivator. I planted myself on the corner and looked for my first potential investor. Part of my reluctance to engage those passing by was the fact that I was procrastinating this humbling exercise.

Steve and Brian egged me on, "*Come on Will, ask these people who are approaching!*" Some ignored me, others said, "*No*," but a few asked me what I planned to spend the money on. I shared the truth. "I'm looking for my friend who is homeless and have decided to live for the week like a homeless person and beg as they beg. One young woman said, "*This is really wrong if you are lying.*" I assured her that I was not and she gave us a ten-dollar bill.

After asking a number of people passing by for money, I realized that there really are generous people out there. Most of those who had been kind enough to give us donations were either older couples or young women in their 20s or 30s.

One woman said, "*Sorry, I don't have any money on me.*" How many times have I said that to homeless people who I've passed on the street? Just when I thought my request had met with rejection, she added, "*So let me go to the ATM and get you some cash.*" With that, she crossed the street, withdrew a ten-dollar bill and came back to give it to us. All three of us were moved by her generosity.

In a matter of an hour, we had managed to beg forty dollars and change. We went to purchase food and figure out where we might sleep for our first night living homeless. We purchased three large burritos and a few drinks, then sat down to savor our first meal since breakfast. It felt so wonderful to sit down after walking all day.

We inhaled our burritos and then walked south on Sunset Boulevard. The author of *Under the Overpass* mentioned sleeping on Sunset Beach, not far from where we were. He did warn of wharf rats, which made the location less appealing. All three of us were clearly nervous about sleeping outside for our first night on the street. We shared some of our expectations for the week as we watched the sun disappear into the horizon. We decided to set up camp right there on the sandy beach. It seemed safe enough, and we were exhausted due to jetlag and our pace that first day.

I was discouraged that our day hadn't yielded a single solid lead. I faded off to sleep, asking God for direction and success on our quest to locate Ed.

(Front to back: Brian & Steve on Sunset Beach)

I felt as though I had barely closed my eyes when I was abruptly awakened three hours later. Brian nudged me to wake up. There was a man standing directly above us, shining a bright flashlight in our faces. I realized quickly that it was a San Diego police officer, although I couldn't see anything but his silhouette with that light blinding my eyes. I was trying to make sense of what was going on, still getting my bearings, as I'm a heavy sleeper.

He began by asking, "*Can you read?*" Somewhat confused by this police officer's question, I responded, "*Yes, I do.*" And then he asked, "*Then why did you neglect reading the sign at the top of the hill which clearly states, 'No sleeping or camping on the beach?'*" I told him that we entered the beach from a different direction and had never actually seen the sign. Then he asked what we were doing there.

I told him that I was looking for my homeless friend. I went on to share the fact that we had travelled from Northern Virginia to live on the streets and search for my friend who had gone missing 11 months earlier. He asked what city we lived in and I responded, "*Ashburn, Virginia.*" The interrogation concluded with one final question, "*If you really live in Ashburn, then tell me what county Ashburn is in?*"

We answered in unison, "*Loudoun County!*" The officer eased up when he heard our answer and responded, "*No way, my brother is a police officer in Loudoun County.*" He went on to say that he would allow us to sleep there, but he advised us to move along before 5am, when the next group of "*not so friendly*" cops would make their rounds. We thanked him and laid back down to sleep.

I recall hearing an old 1973 song by Albert Hammond, "*It Never Rains in Southern California.*" I came to realize that the chorus simply isn't true. The song should have been titled, "*It Rarely Rains in Southern California.*" Shortly after the officer departed, we began to feel the first drops of rain. Unsure how long or hard the rain might fall, we decided to pack up and look for a place to sleep with some form of covering. We wandered from the cliffs back toward Ocean Beach. It was around 2am when we noticed a fire on the beach.

We walked toward the bonfire and met a young homeless man by the name of Gino. Gino was an excited, fast-talking, extrovert who welcomed us with open arms. He began by offering us Doritos, bread, and other items that he told us he had scored from a local dumpster. He made the comment, "*Can you believe people throw this stuff away?*"

Gino's gesture was generous, but we decided to pass. As Gino was walking through a description of how he acquired every coat, shirt and random item in his possession, we were interrupted by another cop. His name was Sergeant Lu, and he was familiar with Gino. He started by asking, "*Gino, why do you have a fire going at this hour, it's illegal after midnight?*"

Gino tried to answer and was chastised by the officer, barking, "*Don't give me an attitude or I will lock you up!*" Sergeant Lu then turned in our direction to inquire as to what we were doing there. I told him our reason for coming to San Diego, and he responded, "*Well if that is even true it doesn't matter, because you all need to leave immediately!*" We complied and walked north on the beach, as Gino rolled his belongings into a blanket and headed in the opposite direction.

Our first night on the street was filled with these sorts of interactions. We were quickly receiving an education regarding how to cope with the night life. We soon learned that it was perfectly legal to be outside during the night, but against the law to be found sleeping or to have a fire on the beach. If a homeless person is to make it, they must find a hidden place to nest or sleep during the day without distraction. If you were unable to locate a suitable place to sleep you would be left to wander throughout the night.

And so, we wandered. We found ourselves in an area called Robb Field just past Dog Beach. The rain had returned and was picking up momentum. We were fortunate to find a thick Holly Tree on the edge of Robb Field to camp under. The bushy branches provided some protection from the heavy rain. We were not bothered by another police officer that evening, and tried to get some sleep amidst the dripping rain. We awoke to the noise of sports teams arriving to use the busy park fields. While the rain had subsided, threatening clouds were still looming. We packed up in a hurry and began to move.

A kind homeless man told us that the Salvation Army, together with a local church partner, provides lunch for the homeless at 11:30am, every Monday to Friday. He also mentioned that the meal takes place at Mission Bay (also known as Mariner's Point), due north of our location. We began walking in that direction. We crossed a bridge, and then took some time to sit and journal our experience in a park across the street from a Hyatt Hotel. We prayed together and then carried on toward Mariner's Point.

(Steve resting at a picnic table beside Mission Bay)

"*What if Ed shows up at today's meal?*" I wondered. As I paused to process our first twenty-four hours on the street it made me think of Ed and what his first twenty-four hours were like? How had he adapted and survived without money? Would we run into him or get a substantial lead? I was reminded of our mission and hoped it would be productive.

We crossed over one more bridge before descending a large hill and arriving at the pavilion shelter in Mission Bay Park. There were numerous homeless characters already assembling and ready to be fed. We began to ask a few there if they had seen Ed. Some said he looked familiar but there were no solid leads. One person asked if he may be using a different name. We learned that many of the homeless take on a street name in place of their given legal name. Some use the name as a sort of alter identity, while others are perhaps hiding from an abuser, debt collectors or the law. We were clearly rookies on that turf, so our presence caused some suspicion. Some of the regulars were reluctant to speak with us and we noticed their stares.

About ten minutes before the food cars arrived, the rain returned with a torrential force. The homeless who had congregated on nearby picnic tables, all rushed for the shelter of the pavilion. In a matter of minutes, the small area which provided covering overhead was jam packed with homeless individuals attempting to stay dry. We met a man who referred to himself as Crazy Billy. He wore a cyclist shirt with a picture of Bob Marley on the front. He had bleached blond hair and a dark brown tan.

Crazy Billy had a contagious smile and shared with us the details of his painful failed marriage back on the East Coast. He confessed that the broken relationship had been the catalyst for moving west. Billy decided to hit the streets in San Diego, never to return. When cars carrying food finally arrived, the rain was too heavy to bring the food to the pavilion. Everyone stayed put and waited for the downpour to slow down.

(Rainy day at Mariner's Point)

When there was no break in the storm, Crazy Billy's hunger got the better of him. He took off running in the direction of the parked cars, despite the downpour. Volunteers who had taken shelter in their vehicles saw him coming. A couple of them exited their cars and loaded him up with food and an umbrella to use as he carried the supplies in our direction. His actions seemed to compel others. With the pavilion serving as an oversized umbrella, the homeless began working together along with the volunteers. Everyone did their best to assemble lunch under the shelter, while the rest of us joined Billy to carry the remainder of food that was meant to be distributed.

Everyone seemed to know the drill, so we mimicked our new street friends, grabbing Styrofoam plates, napkins, a fork and waited in line. I was told by one of the volunteers that the food had been provided by a church in La Jolla and that the coffee was from the Salvation Army.

It was my turn for the volunteers to load up my plate on the buffet line so I stepped forward. I shared with one woman who was serving that I'm actually a pastor from the East Coast. She looked directly at me from across the table and quickly sized me up, holding her large spoon full of baked beans. After taking a look at my puffy sleepless eyes, dirty skin, and unkempt beard she responded, "*That's nice, honey. More beans?*" It was obvious to me that she didn't believe a word I said. To her, I was another homeless man with some outrageous story. As we had quickly discovered, everybody had a story.

I wondered how many times I had volunteered to serve food at Franklin Park in Washington D.C., when the roles were reversed. Many homeless people tried to share their stories with me, while they waited in line and I held the serving spoon. Had I looked at them in disbelief as this woman had done with me? With the tables turned, I didn't like being treated with suspicion and assumed a liar. I also didn't appreciate the feeling of being distrusted by the bean slinging woman, nor by Sergeant Lu the previous evening. We were clearly guilty by association.

You can feel a person's insincerity and a condescending look is hard to miss. I was not judging those who had been kind enough to serve. I was merely humbled by the exchange and was left to consider my own actions when I had served others.

We were grateful for the hot lunch and spent more time talking with a gal by the name of Candace Barrett. Her street name was "*Gypsy.*" Gypsy and her friend Joaquin Tuttle were very helpful in offering suggestions for other places that we might search for Ed. We weren't in a hurry to resume our search in the pounding rain, so we continued chatting with Gypsy and Joaquin even after we finished our meal.

Joaquin had an interest in making specialty beach bicycles and said he had hopes of growing his own business, which he has already started. Gypsy shared with us her journey from Gainesville, Virginia (not far from our home). She had left the East Coast to be a live-in caregiver with an older gentleman in San Diego. The job lasted no more than three weeks, so she was forced to find another career path or return home. She decided to stay and enjoy the weather for a time. That decision led to some partying on the beach, which evolved into an indirect path to the homeless lifestyle.

We told her our story and reason for the street life on that given week. Candace responded, "*I knew something didn't fit when I saw your large backpack.*" I had purchased the pack from a Good Will store back in Virginia, along with some used clothing before the trip. I replied, "*You can have it when I leave on Saturday, if you want.*" She was quick with her response, "*Hell yeah!*" "*OK, meet us this Friday evening at Ocean Beach, and it's yours.*" She agreed to the rendezvous with excitement.

Ocean Beach served as our base area for the search, since Ed's friend Stephanie told us that was the last place that she'd spotted him. The crowd and subculture of the unique homeless populations seemed to vary from town to town. Ocean Beach was a local haunt of the Bohemian-like homeless. The rain had slowed down a bit, so we put on our ponchos and headed south toward Ocean Beach to resume our search.

When we arrived at the seafront, the rain ceased all together, so we sat on the wall and chatted up the homeless who passed by. We met an older, well-spoken homeless man by the name of Clay, who asked us if Ed had a drug problem. I knew Ed drank and perhaps dabbled in weed, but I told him that I didn't believe him to be an addict. I said, "*His family thinks that perhaps his mind is failing or that he chose a life on the streets due to the shame and loss of his business.*"

(Left to right: Will & Mo in Ocean Beach)

While we remained on the seafront, we met a young woman named Mo. Mo had come to play her guitar and sing for the homeless. She wasn't panhandling, although with her musical ability, she would have made some money if she had been. Mo simply wanted to bless the homeless with music.

We met numerous caring people willing to help the homeless, as well as many homeless willing to offer assistance to others. It was inspiring to meet individuals scattered throughout the community who were eager to help us on our quest. There were others who stumbled by us, either drunk or in a drug-induced stupor. Some had mental health issues that made it difficult to carry on a conversation.

(Left to right: Brian, Will & Tony)

One young guy by the name of Tony, wearing only board shorts and drinking a homemade concoction that he had mixed himself, offered a few suggestions. He encouraged us to attend the homeless dinners offered on Sunset Boulevard in Ocean Beach, by the churches there. Tony told us that the Episcopal Church had one later that evening, so we should look there. He offered to walk with us and show us where the church meals take place. We took him up on his offer and were grateful for his help.

As we walked toward Sunset Boulevard, Tony offered us a sip of his powerful potion. We declined but thanked him for his assistance and advice. He replied, *"Not a problem dude, it's cool what you guys are doing."*

With Tony's guided tour of the area, we were quickly becoming familiar with the Ocean Beach vicinity and headed back to the seafront to keep an eye out for Ed.

There was a commotion just up from the main street, where we noticed an ABC News van which had erected their satellite dish and deployed a reporter. There was apparently a breaking news story. We came to find out that a row of new multi-million dollar condos on the beach front had flooded during the torrential downpour and the owners were not happy.

We watched the stir of excitement when the homeless man next to me (Clay) turned and said, *"Hey man, let's go tell the reporter about what you're doing. If they pick up the story, perhaps it'll lead to some clues as to where Ed is."*

"Not a bad idea," I replied. Moments later we were heading that direction. It was inspiring to see homeless individuals moved by our search and willing to offer their assistance. Clay was right there at my side when we reached the young female news correspondent. She was preparing to go on camera and report about the flooded condos.

I approached her to ask if we could talk for a minute and see if she might be interested in a local story. Her name was Bree Steffen and she was the correspondent responsible for running around town to report the latest hot stories for ABC 10 News in San Diego. Within a matter of minutes, we gave her the lowdown about Ed, and she seemed more than intrigued.

She said, *"Even if my supervisor doesn't like this story, I'm in!"* Bree asked for my phone number and where we might be in an hour or two. I told her that there was no telling where we would be, but she could call us, and we could sort it out from there. Brian and Steve were also excited about potential tips that a news story might yield. It was clear that the homeless endeavor was taking its toll on all three of us. Our clothes were wet and our bodies exhausted and yet we still had zero promising leads.

Our quest for information from the homeless usually yielded the exact same response. They'd glance at the photo of Ed and me, and say something like, "*He looks familiar.*" "*That's all?*" I thought, "*Somebody around here must know something about Ed or have seen him recently, right?*" Perhaps they simply didn't trust us. A few had no doubt ingested enough substance that they were unable to recall seeing Ed, even if they had.

A few who'd obviously been on the street too long would say, "*I've definitely seen that guy.*" Each time this happened, just as we thought we had a lead, the person would point at me in the photo. Apparently, I looked familiar to them. One guy even added, "*Yeah I've definitely seen him but I'm not sure when.*" It took everything in me not to say, "*Perhaps you saw him in the last minute or two because you're pointing at a photo of me!*" Rather than respond with sarcasm or insensitivity, I'd simply say "*Thanks for your help.*"

A couple of hours later, I received a call from Bree. She seemed excited and told me that her supervisor granted her permission to pursue the story. We told her what street we were on and noticed a Denny's restaurant in the Point Loma area, just across the street. Bree replied, "*That's perfect! I'm headed your way now.*" Twenty minutes later, we were in the Denny's parking lot giving her the low down. Bree scribbled down notes as we spoke and then asked where we were headed next. I told her that I was on my way back to Hancock Street, where Ed's woodworking shop used to be.

Bree offered to drive us there, but first, she wanted to film a short piece and use it as a teaser for the evening news. And so, she did. Once the four of us squeezed into her car, she held up her phone and shot a selfie video. "*Here I am in the car with Will, Steve, and Brian, three men looking for a long-lost friend who is homeless right here in San Diego...*" She dropped us off on Arena Boulevard and promised to meet up later with her film crew.

In the meantime, she posted her self-made video online and we resumed our search for Ed. Walking the streets of Ed's old stomping ground, I began to recall many times when I had come to his shop to pick him up for dinner. We crossed the street and ran into a gal in her mid-twenties. We greeted her and she introduced herself as Russo. She was with a young Hispanic man, who looked to be about nineteen or so. We went through our usual line of questions, and Russo seemed engaged. Her younger friend was not interested judging from his body language. He stood a few feet away while we chatted with Russo.

When I began with the reason of our quest, she said, "*That's cool, do you have a picture?*" As soon as I showed it to her, she piped up, "*I know Eddy. My boyfriend and I partied with him recently!*" "*You know him?*" I responded in shock. "*Could this be our first real lead?*" I wondered. I asked Russo to describe how tall Eddy is and what his personality is like, and she nailed it.

It was what she said next that caught me off guard. I prodded, "*When you said that you 'partied with Ed' do you mean drinking or smoking weed?*" She replied, "*No, we were using.*" I showed my street ignorance by asking if Ed had become a "*mether.*" Russo laughed out loud, with a raspy smoker's cough depth to her laugh.

"*They're not called 'methers,' they're called 'tweakers,' and hell yeah, Eddy is a tweaker!*" I felt like someone punched me in the stomach. Ed's mom had told me that the last time she'd seen him, before he hit the streets, he acted extremely paranoid. She wondered if Ed was suffering from Schizophrenia.

I came to learn later that day, that methamphetimine addicts known as 'tweakers,' have the same symptoms as those who suffer with Schizophrenia. I was beginning to believe that it may not have been a mental condition that was responsible for sending Ed to the streets, rather a hidden habit. Russo's words still danced in my mind as I stood speechless.

She asked if she could use my cell phone. I went ahead and gave it to her as I was frozen, trying to process the unexpected news. How might this new revelation impact our journey? Ed was still my lifelong friend, and I began to wonder if this was what he wanted to share with me on the night he visited our hotel in Anaheim.

(Left to right: Will & Russo)

Russo finished her call and offered us a few places that we might try looking. Despite the negative news concerning Ed's habit, we were encouraged that we were in the right area. She commented, *"This is where Ed likes to hang out."*

As we walked further up the street, Steve and Brian could tell that the news of Ed's situation had left me feeling low. They did their best to encourage me. The news of Ed residing in close proximity caused us to pick up our pace. We scoured the area, checking in two local Denny's restaurants on both ends of Hancock Street.

One of the workers said that Ed often frequents the restaurant late at night. The Denny's off of Rosecrans, was also promising. The manager said that he had recently seen Ed, so we knew that we were close!

My cell phone rang, and it was Bree. She announced, *"I'm on my way to you with a film crew to do a live shoot. Where can we meet?"* We decided on the parking lot of the Denny's at the corner of Camino Del Rio West and Greenwood. Bree showed up with her camera crew and began setting up on the edge of the parking lot.

(Left to right: Will, Bree & Brian)

Bree warned us that we were going to do a live shoot. She wanted us to walk alongside her through the parking lot as she made comments about our quest. She planned to ask us a few questions about our search and seemed excited when we brought her up to speed on the new insights. Bree said that we would do one practice run before shooting live.

We began walking through the parking lot with the camera man about ten feet ahead of us. I was lagging behind and making jokes about what not to do on live TV, during our practice run. Brian turned around and said, "*Will, this is the live shoot!*"

I wasn't sure if he was joking or not, so I quickly joined the three of them and began answering Bree's questions. About thirty seconds later

Bree said, "*Well, that's it.*" She turned to the camera man to ask him if the take had been successful. "*Was Brian joking with me?*" I asked Steve. "*No, at the last minute, Bree said that they needed to go live due to a time crunch.*" Apparently, I was the only one to miss her comment and must have looked a bit silly running up to the group after they had begun walking. Now we needed to wait and see if the story would turn up any more promising leads once it aired on the 6pm news.

Bree very kindly set up a way for people to post leads on an ABC News webpage. She would text or call me with each new lead, after which Brian, Steve and I would race to search those particular locations. The leads began coming in and we raced around town to chase each one. We chatted with owners of cheap taco joints, the managers at Denny's, as well as alcohol shop owners. Almost every person we interviewed mentioned seeing Ed within the past few months.

The leads were helping, but we were growing tired. Not to mention the fact that more rain was in the forecast. We didn't want to be ill-prepared for another downpour. I took my place on Main Street back in Ocean Beach until we panhandled enough money to purchase three blue plastic tarps for the night. We headed back to Robb Field, and began to set up camp under the same large Holly Tree. With soft wet mulch under our camping pads, this seemed like the perfect place to bed down for the second night.

Both Steve and Brian were bolder than I was in embracing the authentic homeless journey. I say that because each of them simply packed a blanket and found a used piece of cardboard as a bed mat. I seemed like some homeless prima donna, pulling out my insulated sleeping bag and camping pad from my backpack. I felt guilty for the miscommunication when I realized that it was difficult for them to sleep well. My guilt was assuaged when I had been successful raising all of the money to purchase three rainproof tarps.

(Brian and his makeshift cardboard sleeping pad)

Our tarps served as rain protection and insulation for each of us, as we rolled up like blue burritos for our second evening on the street. The night was long, with bouts of heavy and soft rain under the cover of that bushy tree. We saw the rain was a blessing since it kept the cops and homeless neighbors from waking us from our much needed slumber.

During the third night, our trio decided to stake out the Denny's, where we had been told that Ed was a frequent late-night visitor. Brian had only been able to commit for three days, due to his job. We had appreciated having him along but he needed to head back to the airport.

We said our goodbyes late Wednesday evening, before Brian hopped in an Uber outside of the Denny's. He made his way back to San Diego International Airport, while we did our best to take turns getting rest and keeping a watchful eye for Ed.

(Anna at Denny's)

A kind graveyard shift employee by the name of Anna, told us that Ed was a regular at that particular restaurant. She recognized his photo and told us that she would warn us if he walked in. We had begged enough money earlier that afternoon to purchase coffee, a sandwich and still leave her with a generous tip. We did not want to take our helpful waitress for granted.

When Brian left for the airport, Steve and I moved to an inconspicuous corner booth near the back of the restaurant. We trusted that Anna would wake us if Ed showed up. She was very kind allowing us to sleep in the booth which was a gift since we were both exhausted and wanted a break from the rain.

Steve woke me numerous times throughout the night to tell me that I was snoring loudly. He was afraid that customers might notice us sleeping and get us bounced. I felt bad, as I didn't want to cause any trouble for Anna, although I had little control over my snoring. Anna never woke us that evening because Ed never showed up.

The next day I will always remember as the day we spent the afternoon with Kyle.

Chapter 5

Kyle's Coffee

The two of us pressed on from Denny's the following morning. The sun was rising and the air was crisp as we hiked west toward Ocean Beach. Steve and I were exhausted by the time Thursday morning arrived. Homeless nights cramped in a restaurant booth or being awakened by rain, police officers, and random outdoor noises, left us feeling like zombies from the Walking Dead. We found an area of turf near the sandy beach and decided to rest under the shade of the palm trees above.

We'd been careful all week concerning what we pulled out of our backpacks in public, not wanting the homeless to covet the contents and attempt to rob us. However, the week was winding down and we only had one fine night left to sleep outside, so we threw caution to the wind.

We no longer cared if anyone saw what was in our bags. We yanked out our belongings, sleeping bags and other contents, and made ourselves cozy on the plush green grass near the beach. We figured that with only forty-eight hours left on the streets, what could go wrong?

With our gear strewn out around us, we noticed two homeless men who began to take an interest. One approached us with an offer. He said *"How are you guys doing? Have you been for a swim today? The ocean water is so refreshing."* I replied, *"No, we haven't."* He proceeded to tell us how wonderful the surf was before offering to watch our bags while we went for a swim. We thanked him but declined his offer.

He was persistent and asked us where we planned to sleep that evening.

During my trips to San Diego, I realized that people who live on the street tend to be extremely private about where they camp. This was generally not a topic openly discussed among fellow homeless individuals, especially not strangers. We heard numerous stories of street people being robbed by other homeless individuals, even by those who they previously considered to be friends.

Steve and I knew better than to share our camping location. In truth, we never actually made up our minds about where to crash until it was dark.

I responded to the man's question, "*It's difficult to say, every night it differs.*" Then I shot back, "*Where are you sleeping tonight?*" He remained guarded and replied, "*Yeah, I'm never sure where I might sleep either.*" Most homeless find a place to camp every night and then stash their belongings in a hidden spot during the day, hoping to find them when they return.

Our exchange concluded the discussion and he wandered away. While we met plenty of generous and kind people on the street, you can never relax completely. Street smarts and precaution serve you well when you're living outside. I heard one man say, "*A meth addict will steal your things and then offer to help you look for them.*" We were doing our best to adjust to our new surroundings.

I arranged my camping pad and sleeping bag on the grass near the sand, while Steve made a nest on his blanket. He didn't bother to find another piece of cardboard. We were no longer concerned about personal appearances. We were beginning to identify with the other homeless in terms of exhaustion and appearance and realized that when you're that tired you can sleep just about anywhere.

We were both attempting to nap and on the edge of drifting to sleep, when we heard a group of young people making noise. They looked to be in their late teens or early 20s. We spotted Kyle, a good looking young man who we'd met earlier in the week.

By the looks of it, they were passing some form of substance around and rocking to the music from a boom box. We heard the bass thumping and watched as Kyle stumbled away from the crowd, headed in our direction.

He staggered forward and appeared to be in bad shape. We watched in silence as he hunched over and began retching and gagging loudly. What followed next was grotesque, as he vomited several times onto the grass. Just when it seemed that he was finished, he froze above his vomit, with his hands plastered on his thighs. Kyle balanced his body above the mess below as he stared directly at his puke.

Then he did the unthinkable. Our eyes were fastened on Kyle's every move, as he stretched out his right hand and scooped up some of his own vomit. Unsure of what he planned to do with the puke in his hand, I was disgusted to see him raise it toward his face and put it back into his mouth. We had been quiet up until that point, but his actions forced me to break my silence.

"*Is he eating his own barf?*" I asked Steve. "*No, I think he puked up whatever pills he'd ingested to get high, then scooped them up to attempt swallowing them again.*"

Steve was dead right! Kyle forced himself to gobble down the same puke coated pills he'd taken at the beach party, just before he'd thrown up. His body wasn't having it! We watched as Kyle vomited yet again. Then he stumbled forward into his own puke, with his bare feet.

It was difficult to watch, an unforgettable scene that remains in my memory to this day.

I thought to myself, "*How badly must someone want to escape reality by getting high, if they're willing to swallow pills from their own vomit? How difficult does life have to get for a person to want to remain wasted that badly?*"

We continued to watch the heart-wrenching state of that young man as he staggered forward. I wanted to help, but wasn't sure how.

I called out his name, "*Hey Kyle, what's going on?*" Oblivious to everyone and everything around him, he perked up and looked our direction. His feet followed his mind, and he began to walk toward us. When he eventually reached us, I asked, "*How are you doing, Kyle?*"

His answer was an honest one, "*Not well, I just puked.*" I shot back, "*Yeah, we saw that. It was pretty gross. Would you like to sit down?*" He responded, "*Thanks,*" as he plopped down right then and there. He crossed his legs and sat in front of us, looking quite comfortable.

A kind older man walked up to the three of us carrying a large bag of bologna sandwiches. He tossed a few at our feet, saying, "*Here you go guys, I thought you might enjoy some dinner.*" We said 'thank you' and he took off up the beach to bless other homeless individuals with the remaining sandwiches in his bag. I honestly had lost my appetite after having front row seats to Kyle's puking incident. I handed mine to Kyle as did Steve, both realizing that he needed them more than we did. He thanked us, then removed one from a cellophane wrapper and took a bite. *"This sandwich is disgusting!"* he insisted, putting it down as though it was covered with mold.

I processed his remarks, considering they came from a man who just ate pills out of his own vomit. I decided that if these sandwiches were not acceptable for Kyle's goat-like taste buds which could stomach his own vomit, then I had no plans to try one later.

The three of us sat on the turf, enjoying the calm. The sun would be setting soon, and the beach was full of couples strolling hand in hand. I broke the serene moment by telling Kyle what we were up to. I told him that we decided to travel west and live on the streets to search for my friend Ed, who we believed to be addicted to methamphetamine.

Using the street term for a meth addict, I told him that my friend Ed is a *"Tweaker."* Kyle piped up, *"I'm a tweaker!"* *"You are?"* I asked. *"Yes, I am,"* he replied as though that was something to be proud of. I chose not to pursue his response.

Rather, I asked, *"Do you think anyone is looking for you, the way we are looking for Ed, Kyle?"* *"Hell no!"* he shot back, and it took him no time to consider his response. *"Where are you from?"* I inquired. As the conversation carried on, we learned that Kyle was from Irvine, California where he attended a well-to-do school and played rugby. I tried to dig deeper, *"Do you think your parents are concerned about you now?"*

"I don't have any parents, I was a foster kid," he replied with anger in his tone. *"Were they abusive?"* I asked as a matter of digging deeper into his story. He nodded in the affirmative but fell silent. *"It must have been rough."* He nodded again, another *"Yes."* Once again, we sat in silence.

I gazed at Kyle as he stared into the distance. He was wearing jeans that looked as if they were a few inches too short. The lack of socks and shoes on his feet only drew more attention to his *"floods,"* as we use to call them in middle school. When Kyle first walked over, he had no shirt on, and was wearing only a black, unzipped winter coat.

We offered him a t-shirt which he was quick to accept and pull over his head. Then he put his winter jacket back on over his new shirt. He shared with Steve and me a bit about his life. He told us that he had recently turned twenty-one years of age, but it looked as though the streets had added some wear. He sported a thick black beard, and his lips were semi-swollen and weather-worn. I imagined him at the preppy West Coast high school wearing an expensive striped rugby shirt.

What had happened to this good-looking kid to send him to the streets at such a young age? What memories of pain and abuse did he carry that drove him to want to be high so badly? Steve and I simply sat with him and listened to the painful details of his past, which somehow formed a path to the streets of San Diego.

(Kyle sitting in the grass at Ocean Beach)

We had been living like the homeless all week on the streets and had no money or identification on us, but it occurred to me that I did have a Starbucks app on my phone. The app contained credit and I noticed a Starbucks just around the corner from the seafront in Ocean Beach. *"How would you like a drink from Starbucks?"* I asked Kyle. *"That would be awesome!"* he replied.

Steve glanced my way, perhaps wondering how I planned to pay for the high-priced caffeine of suburbia. I shoved my sleeping bag and pad back in my pack, and Steve did the same. We'd become skilled at packing up in a hurry - a skill that every homeless person should acquire.

We slung our packs back up over our shoulders, and walked with Kyle toward the Ocean Beach Starbucks. He was slow moving due to his bare feet and his quest to find half-smoked cigarette butts, known as *"blunts."*

In fact, he stopped multiple times to pick them up and examine each butt for any potential tobacco left to smoke. I finally said, *"Kyle, let's just get a coffee, and then you can resume your hunt for cigarettes later."* He agreed, yet still required extra guidance to get him from the beach to the café at the corner Newport Avenue and Bacon Street.

Steve and I eventually accomplished the task of getting Kyle through the door and in line for a drink. I asked Kyle what he wanted to drink, and he responded, *"I'll have a venti caramel macchiato with whip!"* He made the order with a large beaming smile, and didn't order the typical homeless man's strong dark coffee with twelve packets of sugar.

This was clearly the selection of a kid who grew up in the wealthy part of Irvine, California. How his path led him to Ocean Beach was a mystery to me. I asked Steve to wait with Kyle while I used the bathroom, since the line was quite long. There was a combination lock on the door at the Starbucks, and one had to order a drink to obtain the combo.

I was excited to use a clean bathroom and returned to the line after washing my hands. We were next up to place our order when I rejoined Steve and Kyle, as I had timed it perfectly.

Just as I stepped in line, a man standing directly behind us piped up, "*Hey buddy, you can't cut in line!*" I turned to face my accuser. He looked as though he was in his late 50s and was not a happy camper. I said, "*I'm sorry, but I was actually in line before I stepped out to use the bathroom, and now I'm back with my friends.*"

My response had no effect as he continued, "*You still can't just walk away and expect to jump back in line.*" I looked at his face, contemplating a few different possible responses. We always have a choice in situations like that, and I took a long pause to consider mine. I offered a quick prayer for wisdom and then said to the man, "*Hey, how about I buy you a drink?*"

His face displayed shock as his eyebrows spiked. "*You don't have to do that,*" he responded with a total change of demeanor. "*I know, but I want to, so go ahead and tell the barista behind the counter what you'd like to drink.*"

He shot back, "*But my drink is expensive.*" "*Dude, go ahead and order your frou-frou drink!*" (Not my exact wording, but it was my thought as I encouraged him to place his order). He did order some over-sized venti sugar-induced dessert drink. I should add that he was a different person after that interaction. The man thanked me emphatically and introduced himself as Chris. He waited for his drink to be made and stood off to the side observing our interaction with Kyle.

It was clear that once Kyle had his drink in hand, he was ready to jet and possibly resume his search for blunts. Before he took off, I asked, "*Can we get you anything else?*" His answer caught me totally off guard, "*Can I get a hug?*"

I looked at this young man, with remains of vomit still on his black winter coat. Should I give him a safe right-arm side hug to remain clean?

Of course not! I wondered if any foster father had ever really hugged Kyle or loved him the way that he deserved to be loved. I hugged Kyle with a full bear-style hug, as though he were my own son. He actually held it for an extended period, enough to make bystanders feel awkward.

Keep in mind, we were standing in the middle of a bustling Starbucks. We were surrounded by a large group of people who were either waiting in line to place their orders or standing around while their orders were being filled. It's an awkward place to have an extended man hug with a homeless friend, yet it was the perfect place and time for a tangible act of love.

I was moved by his request for a hug and savored the moment. He even embraced Steve after me, just before he disappeared out the front door. I missed him as soon as he left.

(Left to right: Steve, Kyle & Will at Starbucks in Ocean Beach)

With drinks in hand, Steve and I noticed Chris, who'd been impatient with us just moments before we had ordered. When Kyle hit the street, we saw Chris sipping his drink and patiently waiting to speak with us. "*Who are you and what are you two doing here?*" he inquired. I suppose his curiosity got the better of him.

We told him about our mission and what we'd been up to all week. The place was crowded, so we moved our conversation out to the sidewalk on Newport Avenue. There was a lot of pedestrian traffic, with people drifting up and down the street, no doubt considering where to grab dinner. Newport Avenue in Ocean Beach is a good place to do that, since there are so many options.

Chris seemed eager to share a bit of his own story, despite the busy crowd. After hearing our reason for traveling across the country, he shared candidly. "*My son is homeless on the streets here.*" He continued, "*I helped him get a college degree and even his Masters, and now he and his girlfriend have decided to throw it all away and live homeless.*" He was clearly broken up over his son's decision. What loving father wouldn't be?

"*Perhaps you two met him this week? His street name is 'Fire Walker.'*" I was moved by his story and replied, "*No, I don't believe we have. How did he get that nickname?*" Chris answered, "*He was partying on the beach one night, when a drunk girl fell into the fire. My son instinctively stepped right onto the burning coals to pull her out. He has been called by that name ever since.*" We hadn't heard that story nor had we met his son, as I'm convinced that we'd remember a name like "*Fire Walker.*"

Chris shared his pain with us and the difficulty associated with having your child live homeless on the streets. He was just concluding his comments and about to walk away, when off to my right I noticed two women kissing. This was not a simple peck, but they were doing some serious smooching. I was distracted by what I witnessed, since that type of interaction isn't commonplace in Northern Virginia, where I'm from.

One of the woman's eyes met mine, so I quickly looked away. I didn't want to appear rude, yet she must have caught me momentarily staring based on her reaction. Just as I looked back toward Chris after he had turned to leave, I heard the woman shout something and I hoped she wasn't speaking to me.

What is worse, in my peripheral vision I noticed that she was moving in our direction and shouted once more, "*Hey you, I saw you!*" motioning my way.

As she and her girlfriend headed toward Steve and me, Fire Walker's dad had faded into the sidewalk crowd. I wanted to do the same. I tried not to make eye contact with the woman as she approached and pretended that I hadn't heard her. However, she was closing in fast.

The woman stood directly in front of me and said, "*I saw you!*" "*Did you?*" I asked, with no idea where this conversation was headed. Then she added, "*Yep, I saw you on ABC News. You're the guy who has been living here on the streets in search of your childhood friend, right?*"

"*Yes, I am that guy, and this is my friend Steve, who has been helping me look.*" I was so relieved that she wasn't referring to seeing me looking in her direction when she kissed her friend. She introduced herself as Sharon, then went on to say, "*I want you to know that I think what you are doing is incredible!*"

"*Not only that, but my son was homeless, and I searched for him for more than a year. Would you like a tip?*" She asked. She clearly identified with my situation and genuinely wanted to help us on our quest. I responded, "*Absolutely, what would you suggest?*" She answered, "*When I was at my end and just about to give up, I went down to the beach. Then I lit a candle and I cried out to Jesus for help. Do you know that it was within the next day that I found him? Perhaps you should turn to Jesus for help?*"

Having no idea that I was a pastor, she began to tell me about the importance of prayer. A smile found its way to my mouth, and I asked, "*Would you like to pray with us right now?*" She responded, "*Of course!*"

The next thing you know, there we were standing in front of Starbucks, the four of us all holding hands. We prayed together, asking Jesus for another shot at finding my friend Ed and to restore him to full health.

(Left to right: Sharon & Will on Newport Avenue)

We thanked Sharon for her advice, hugged each of the ladies, and then wandered back toward the beach. So much had happened in the last hour that was still turning in my brain. Life is messy. Many of the homeless we met had stories, very similar to Kyle's. Some were just looking for a genuine hug or someone who believed in them. It's under-standable, after being bruised and burned by the adults who should have treated them with dignity.

Many have suffered abuse from a parent, an uncle, a neighbor, a teacher or another person in authority who should have protected and cared for them. The scars of the past drive many to find sources of med-ication on the street, even if it means eating pills coated in vomit. We witnessed raw desperation that made our hearts hurt for each individual.

The week had run its course and we were spent. We slept behind an elementary school storage trailer in Point Loma. It was a different type of risk to sleep in the wealthy neighborhood. It was a risk we were willing to take because neither of us wanted any more drama in the middle of the night.

The miles of walking didn't seem as laborious on that final morning. We discovered a new-found energy, knowing that we'd complet ed our final night on the streets. Home was not far away, yet we still hadn't found Ed.

For our final evening, we checked back into the hotel where we'd begun the journey five days earlier and got cleaned up. It felt pretty good taking a shower after going without one for so many days. The night was young and we wanted to take a final walk through Ocean Beach to say our farewells, as well as making one final pass for Ed.

After a speedy Uber ride from downtown, we were back in Ocean Beach. It felt odd to no longer be carrying a heavy backpack and five days of grime on my skin. We wanted some closure with our new homeless friends and looked for Kyle and others we could connect with before heading back east.

We ran into Joaquin. Candace was unable to make it that evening so she sent Joaquin to retrieve the backpack that I had promised her.

We told Joaquin that we wanted to buy a bunch of pizzas to bless our homeless friends on the seafront. He led us to the Ocean Beach 7-11, and advised us that they had the best pizza deal in town. We purchased ten pies and waited as they heated them in the oven. We left Joaquin with a pizza as well as my backpack for Candace. We wished him well with his custom bike venture and thanked him for his help earlier in the week. Joaquin expressed his gratitude before peddling away on his bike while wearing my backpack and precariously balancing the pizza box with his right arm.

(Left to right: Joaquin & Will at 7/11 in Ocean Beach)

We hit the streets near the seafront to have some closure with the friends we had made there. We walked up just as they were passing around a joint. I announced, "*Nobody move, San Diego Undercover Narcotics!*" Everyone froze, until I said, "*Just kidding, pizza party!*" They turned around and saw that it was Steve and me and seemed relieved. We said our goodbyes and thanked them by name for their help in searching for Ed.

We met several kind-hearted homeless individuals who are not addicts, nor did they have a history of mental illness or abuse. There are some who for whatever reason, have decided to call the street their home.

It's difficult to hear stories like Kyle's. There are so many who appear trapped by addiction and yet, they may simply be seeking something to medicate the pain of their past.

One man who volunteered at the Episcopal Church in Ocean Beach told us that he'd been helping serve the homeless for just over twenty-five years. He commented, *"I've seen a pattern repeated time and again. First, they lose their job, then they lose their home, then they lose their dignity, then they lose their mind."*

While there are obviously variations to that pattern, every person who we meet on the street has a story of what landed them there. I've personally listened to hundreds of stories during our trips, which has made one thing abundantly clear to me. That is, there is no one-size fits all homeless person or solution.

With every trip, we have attempted to keep in mind that *"Every person we meet is another person's 'Ed.'"* While we were unable to locate my friend Ed on that particular trip, I'm convinced that individuals like Kyle were also worthy of our time. I certainly gained more insight and leads concerning my childhood friend. However, even if that intel didn't help us find my friend in the immediate future, I saw a change in the homeless people we attempted to love along the way. I also began to witness a change in my own heart. With that concept in mind, I wondered when we might return. I hoped it would be soon.

Chapter 6
Back for Another Round

Five months later, Steve and I were airborne yet again. Following the same pattern, we headed out on a Sunday evening, February 7, 2016 for my third attempt to find my friend. We were ready to resume our search early the following morning.

Instead of Brian, we had a new recruit by the nickname of AG. AG had previously served in the U.S. Marines. After hearing the stories Steve and I shared about our trip to San Diego, he was ready to join the team.

Having a U.S. Marine on the team is a perk when living on potentially dangerous streets. We resumed our search where we left off, right back at Ocean Beach. Steve and I arranged to meet up with AG at the Starbucks on Newport Avenue, where we had shared a drink with Kyle. It seemed like a smart place to pick up where we left off.

As we stood on the sidewalk in front of Starbucks, we couldn't help but notice an increase in the homeless population there. In addition, we were struck by the fact that we didn't recognize a single face!

(Left to right: Steve, Will & AG)

Once again, in preparation for our week on the street, we had allowed our facial hair to grow and did our best to look the part. However, AG won the prize when he removed his sweatshirt and appeared to be wearing an old torn polo shirt. He was so convincing that one of the local homeless men actually offered AG a shirt to wear! AG thanked the older gentleman and chose to stick with his torn shirt instead.

Our backpacks were jammed with the usual gear for our journey. We immediately started walking the streets in hopes of spotting Ed. We had hundreds of cards printed this time, with a photo of Ed and me, along with a local Google phone number I registered for with an area code from San Diego.

It felt surreal to be back on the streets yet again. I began wondering where we might sleep. As soon as the sun set, I would get an uneasy feeling about where we might end up sleeping. We learned to keep a watchful eye for potentially quiet and safe places to set up camp. Of course, most of our homeless friends were looking for the same thing. On more than one occasion I checked behind a crop of bushes only to find other homeless individuals who would holler something like, "*Hey buddy, this space is taken! Look somewhere else.*" They never hung a "no vacancy" sign, so we were left to do some exploring to locate the right place.

AG, Steve, and I canvassed the surrounding Ocean Beach vicinity and then pushed east toward Hancock Street. We checked out the Denny's restaurant where Ed had been sighted on our previous trip. The waitress we questioned told us that she hadn't seen him recently, and that Anna was no longer employed there. We made our way up Hancock, walking right past Ed's old wood shop.

The shop had been taken over by a surfboard business that seemed to stay busy constructing fiberglass boards. You could smell the resin in the air. We had been walking for hours without yielding a single lead. The three of us were tired, so we stepped up our search for a safe place to bed down.

About a football field away from Ed's shop, Steve noticed an abandoned building that had suffered a serious fire. In front of the building there was a small parking lot where someone had parked a lengthy moving truck. The gap between the moving truck and the vacant building provided the perfect space to camp without being noticed.

I contemplated climbing up on the roof to make camp and AG was up for scaling the building. However, Steve wanted nothing to do with sleeping on a roof. It was important that we all agree on the same space and not separate. We settled for the space between the truck and the abandoned building. We began unpacking our sleeping bags and camping pads. It turned out to be the perfect place, although it grew unseasonably cold for San Diego, dipping into the 40s.

We hadn't scored any dinner on day one. I believe our empty stomachs were what woke us the following morning. The mid-day meal at Mariner's point seemed like our best option, so we headed in that direction.

We arrived just before they began to serve and people were lining up for the meal. As we scanned the crowd for familiar faces, it appeared that our homeless friends had been replaced by an entirely different group of men and women. Was that the norm in San Diego? Was the homeless community so transient that we couldn't recognize a single person after only five months? Where had our friends gone? Was it safer to keep moving?

The pressing question in my mind was, "*Had Ed moved on or was he still living on the streets of San Diego?*"

A homeless man by the name of Ray told us that the weather played a big role in the decision to move on. He let us know that there had been an unexpected amount of rainfall that year, which caused many to search for a dryer location.

We managed to run into our bleached blond friend who referred to himself as "*Crazy Billy.*" We asked him how he was doing and he told us that his bike had recently been stolen. He said, "*It was a bummer man, cause I had to walk everywhere.*"

I happened to notice a bike just to the right of where Crazy Billy was sitting. I commented, "*It looks like you found one.*" He replied, "*Oh *yeah, God blessed me with this bike."* I inquired about the *"blessing"* that he referred to. Billy answered, *"I was walking past a nice home this past week and happened to notice this beauty parked in the backyard."* He went on to share that the bike's placement at that precise time must have been a blessing from God, because God knew that he needed a bike. The concept of stealing was never mentioned. I'm not so sure that the bike's previous owner considered the exchange as much of a blessing as Crazy Billy had.

We ate lunch at Mission Bay and began showing Ed's picture around. The church from La Jolla was back in full force with a fresh crew of volunteers serving lunch. The Salvation Army was also present, pouring strong dark coffee with plenty of sugar packets to add. I surveyed the crowd as I sipped coffee from my Styrofoam cup.

AG and Steve were eager to continue the search. We wanted to search an area not far from there, known as *"the riverbed."*

The riverbed is known as a local haunt for "tweakers," (those hooked on Methamphetamine). We'd been warned that some of the more progressed addicts grow too paranoid to congregate in populated areas, they seek refuge along the riverbed.

We spoke with a few San Diego Police officers who warned us concerning the dangers associated with the riverbed. Crazy Billy cautioned us, 'I've heard of tweakers living in the riverbed who won't think twice about killing an unsuspecting stranger for ten bucks, desperate for another fix.

Understanding that this was not a safe place to wander around while wearing our backpacks, Steve kindly volunteered to remain at Denny's, while AG and I explored the riverbed. I had briefly explored the riverbed with Steve and Brian on the previous trip, but no one was thrilled about the potential risks associated, so we cut it short. I figured that if there was a chance that Ed could be camping in the riverbed, then I wanted to spend some time searching. I reasoned that traveling with a former US Marine was a much safer option.

The riverbed was full of winding paths, makeshift shelters in thickets and under bridges. There was plenty of mud, tall brush to provide cover, loads of trash strewn out along the river and hundreds of acres to hide in. We found several abandoned campsites tucked in the middle of the brush, often littered with drug paraphernalia and empty liquor bottles.

The deeper we wandered into the brush, the faster I could feel my heart racing. I decided to pick up a good size rock to carry just in case I came face to face with an angry addict. Not sure what I'd really do if such an altercation occurred, but it gave me a slight sense of safety, when AG and I split up to cover more ground. My mind drifted to thriller style movies that always create suspense when the main characters split up. It's usually at that point in the movie when one of the characters encounters something unfortunate or even deadly.

(The "Riverbed")

Despite the potential for risk, AG and I escaped without anything unfortunate happening. I only ran into one older homeless man, who saw me and took off running in the opposite direction. Realizing it wasn't Ed, I didn't bother to follow him.

AG and I returned to Denny's, and caught up with Steve who had been faithfully guarding our packs. We took a short break and plotted our next move.

(Left to right: AG, Will & Steve at Denny's)

The afternoon spent walking the streets yielded no more leads, and so we headed back to Ocean Beach. We had been told that the Sacred Heart Catholic Church on Sunset Boulevard was hosting dinner that evening. Supper at the church was also another opportunity to look for Ed and gather clues. We searched the faces, always hoping to spot him, but he was nowhere in sight. I spoke with one of the church volunteers and asked about Ed. They didn't recognize him from the photo but seemed willing to help.

I also let him know that we were willing to help out if they needed an extra few sets of hands. He took us up on the offer and allowed us to sidestep the crowd, assigning us all tasks.

After the final preparations for dinner had been made, a man by the name of Jack circled the volunteers together to thank them for their hard work. He led the group in prayer before opening the church doors. Jack turned his attention toward Steve, AG and me, saying, *"We had been short a few volunteers this evening and prayed, asking God for more help. God answered our prayers and provided these three men from the East Coast."* He thanked us for being an answer to their prayers.

Jack was obviously a veteran of that kitchen and a master chef to the homeless. He addressed his troops, *"In just a few minutes the doors will open, and I want you to love these people like family. Let's serve them with dignity, shall we?"* Jack concluded his pep talk and it was clear that he was a gifted leader and motivator. He possessed an authentic heart for those who were hungry and needed more than just a meal.

Like professional staff serving in a renowned Parisian restaurant, Jack's team took pride in their service. He offered one final prayer before welcoming his hungry patrons in to dine. Once the doors were thrust open, workers rushed to their assigned positions, and welcomed their guests.

The dinner drew quite a crowd. Their faces looked tired, and the clientele were all too pleased to fill their plates in the buffet line. Steve, AG and I were each assigned a set of metal tongs and told to give one piece of chicken to each individual until everyone had been served. We greeted our homeless friends with smiles and did our best to make Jack proud.

The line was efficient, and the church filled close to a hundred hungry stomachs that evening. Once again, there was no sign of Ed.

We enjoyed serving, as well as dining, after everyone had been fed. Many of the guests shovel down their meal as quickly as possible, and then form the seconds line. When everyone had made a first pass through the line, they reopen the buffet for seconds.

A homeless man by the name of Paul commented, *"You develop a certain mindset after living on the streets for a time. One never knows when you might get another meal, so you tend to eat as much as you can when it's offered, similar to a squirrel packing away food for the winter."*

After the second line piled on more food, a few stragglers returned hoping for thirds. Our team was given mops and a broom to make the floors shine again after the homeless returned to the street. Steve and AG worked the mops while I pushed the broom.

I was swinging my broom on the far end of the room, along with another man who looked familiar with the routine. I asked him if he had been attending the church for long. He smiled and replied, *"I'm actually a priest here."*

He introduced himself as Father Joe Coffey, and added that he was serving as a military chaplain. I commented, *"I wouldn't have known you were a priest since you never spoke up during the preparations, and are not wearing a collar."* He replied, *"I figure that Jesus was a servant first, so I try to serve in a similar fashion. I wanted to support Jack's leadership and not attract attention to myself."*

I was inspired by Father Joe's attitude. We exchanged contact information and he took a sincere interest in our mission. We left that evening, so encouraged by inspirational servants like Jack, Father Joe and the others who we'd been fortunate enough to meet that evening.

(Left to right: AG & Steve mopping at Sacred Heart)

When we left the church that evening, we headed back toward Hancock Street to make camp in the same spot as the previous evening. We were immediately struck by the cold temperature. It was 45 degrees, which feels much colder when your body gets accustomed to the mid-70s during the day. It's hard to acclimate to a thirty-degree variance. We walked as fast as possible, trying to get our blood flowing.

I was discouraged with zero Ed sightings. I was suddenly entertaining the fear and idea that my friend could have died. I confessed my fear to Steve and AG, and we stopped to offer up a prayer for God's guidance and protection of my friend.

Once we resumed our walk, I said, *"I'd love to find a police officer who would be kind enough to help and could perhaps search their database to see if Ed had shown up on their radar."* I wanted to know for sure if Ed was still alive. Certainly, the police could answer that question and would have access to that sort of information. I offered another prayer asking God to provide us with a kind cop who would be willing to help.

AG said, *"A cup of hot chocolate or coffee would be amazing right about now."* Once someone plants an idea like that in your mind, it's difficult to shake. On that cold night, it was even more appealing. We searched our Starbucks app to find the closest location. Steve realized that there was one enroute if we picked up the pace, since it was scheduled to close in 15 minutes.

As our pace quickened, motivated by the mental image of a venti cup of hot chocolate, topped with whipped cream. I could almost taste it and kept an eye on my watch, calculating our pace. We were sure to make it in time, until we realized we had a choice to make.

Just across the street, to our right, we noticed two police cruisers parked and in the middle of a situation. I was reminded of my prayer to locate a kind officer who might be willing to assist or search. I realized that the diversion to speak with the police across the street meant no hot chocolate. Obviously, we abandoned the hot drinks for our mission. We were there to find Ed and were not about to miss an opportunity to pursue comfort. We crossed over West Point Loma Boulevard to speak with the officers.

We arrived to witness two police officers arresting a man who was on his knees, with his hands cuffed behind his back. This was taking place in a gas station parking area. One of the cops noticed us standing there and asked, "*What do you three want?*" I began sharing our situation when the officer interrupted saying, "*We're busy man, you need to talk to the guys in the car behind us.*"

We walked around the situation and approached the vehicle parked behind them. Another cop saw us coming and asked us what we needed. I began to fill him in our quest to find Ed when he interrupted me. "*Wait a minute, I know you guys!*" It just happened to be the same officer who woke Steve, Brian and me on our previous trip, when we were sleeping on the beach at Sunset Cliffs. What are the odds?

"*You all are back? Did you ever find your friend?*" I brought him up to speed with what we knew about Ed, but told him that the trail had grown cold. I confessed my fear that Ed may have died and asked if he might be willing to help us out. He agreed to access his database to find out what he could. After a quick search of Ed's name and date of birth, there was no news to report. He said, "This database won't tell us if Ed has died, but the coroner's office would have that information since Ed does have a prior arrest, so his fingerprints are in our system.

Not only had we run into the exact same officer from our previous trip, but his partner on that particular evening was a police chaplain. He stepped out of the car and introduced himself. He was kind enough to give me his personal cell phone number and encouraged me to call the county coroner's office the following day. He added, "*They may not be willing to share information, but mention that you're a visiting pastor and friend of mine and the chaplain on site will do what he can to help.*" Talk about an answer to prayer, this beat any hot drink on a cold night. Now I needed to focus my prayers on a positive report from the coroner's office.

The two officers could not have been more helpful. The chaplain left me with a final word of encouragement, saying, "*I'll call my friend at the coroner's office to let him know to expect your call. In addition, I'll be praying for you guys and for your friend Ed.*"

We left the scene and gave thanks to God for answering our prayers in such an unexpected way. As we once again were reminded of the cold, Steve announced "I just realized that there is another Starbucks that is open later than the other one. If we leg it, we can make it in time before they close. So we did.

Using our Starbucks app to make the purchase, we ordered three hot chocolates to go and boy did they hit the spot! Feeling warm and encouraged, we made our way back to our camp spot behind the same truck.

We were all so thrilled to find our site vacant once again. We rolled out our pads and sleeping bags, hoping they would keep us warm in the cold of the night. I was quick to brush my teeth, take a "bathroom" break and slide into my sleeping bag with a full set of clothes on for extra warmth. I pulled my winter hat over my bald head, since that was the only part of my body left uncovered.

(Left to right: Steve & AG in our camping spot)

AG argued that he was colder than we were, since he was originally from Nigeria and accustomed to extreme heat. I argued that my bald head meant that I had one less layer of insulation on my crown than they had. Steve had no dog in the fight and was snoring within minutes. It's amazing how well you sleep after walking all day in the hot sun.

I am a heavy sleeper. Steve on the other hand, is a very light sleeper. On the street, it's helpful to have at least one person who wakes easily on your team. They can sound the alarm if trouble appears unexpectedly as it did that night.

Steve woke AG and me twice to tell us that a homeless man had walked by and peeked under the truck. He said, "*The guy is watching us. I wonder if we are in his space?*" We had found a grocery cart behind the truck a few used clothing items, along with a cardboard sign used to panhandle money. I asked if the man appeared to be a threat. Steve didn't think so, which was all I needed to hear before drifting back to sleep.

The third time Steve woke us, it was serious. I awoke just in time to witness a squad car turning the corner beside the truck. The officer turned his flashing lights on, as well as a spotlight, which he directed in our eyes.

As the officer exited his car he asked, "*What are you all doing here?*" I said, "*We're sleeping,*" trying not to sound disrespectful. I let him know that we were looking for a friend who was lost and homeless. We simply needed a place to stay for the night and weren't making any trouble.

He was kind but stern. He made us aware that he had received a call that we were sleeping in that space and asked us to move on. "*Where can we sleep legally?*" I asked. "*The only legal place to sleep on the streets is downtown near Saint Vincent's,*" he replied. I said, "*I've been to that place and it's dangerous during daylight hours. I can't imagine sleeping there at night!*" He smiled and agreed with me. Then he added, "*Look fellas, I'm not sure where you should sleep, but since we received a complaint about you here, I need to ask you to leave.*"

We didn't want to make any trouble. We packed up our bags and were walking away within five minutes. Steve was convinced that the homeless man who peeked under the truck must have called the cops. Many homeless are territorial and we must have been in his spot. If I had been obnoxious, I would've called the cops to go back thirty minutes later to rouse the new occupant. I chose to let it go.

Where does one go in the middle of the night, when you are tired, freezing and in dire need of rest? Forced to leave the comfort of our sleeping bags, we felt the bite of the cold. Denny's was lit up brightly and looked cozy and warm inside. We found a booth in the back and ordered hot drinks with what little money we had managed to beg for earlier that day. I was unable to sleep so I sat up to keep watch, hoping for a potential Ed sighting. Steve did his best to get a few more hours of sleep in the corner booth, while AG selected a couple of chairs to stretch out on.

I rested my head on the table and drifted in and out of consciousness for what was left of the night. I kept imaging Ed walking into the Denny's and began to wonder, *"How would Ed react if he walked through the front door and saw me here?"* I hoped I would soon find out.

Whenever Steve or AG would begin to snore loudly, I'd give them a nudge as a reminder to keep it quiet. A different sort of clientele visits Denny's in the wee hours of the night and I didn't want us to get kicked out. It was difficult to sleep, but it was warm and cozy. I wanted nothing to do with sleeping outside until the sun came up.

(Steve sleeping at Denny's)

I looked at the two men sleeping and couldn't imagine that AG was very comfortable on the three chairs that he strung together. Perhaps his training in the U.S. Marines equipped him to sleep in such a way. Anything was an improvement now that we were out of the cold.

(AG sleeping at Denny's)

When I noticed the morning breakfast crowd filling the booths around us, I knew that it was time to go. I woke my friends and we were quick to pay the bill, grab our packs and head toward the beach. It was difficult to keep our eyes open as we headed for another spot to get more rest. The sun rising was a welcome sight, and would soon provide some warmth.

With the absence of humidity on the West Coast, a sunrise makes an immediate difference! By the time we reached Ocean Beach at our lethargic pace, the sun was up and the temperature was increasing by the minute. Realizing that it is completely legal to sleep outside during daylight hours, we spread out our camping mats on the elevated portion of the sand dunes, not far from the shoreline.

93

The three of us arranged our camping pads parallel to the beach with our backs to the sun. I watched the morning surfers dance on the waves as I faded off to sleep, lulled by the sound of Seagulls and breaking waves. The shivers that convulsed my body subsided as the rising sun worked its magic on my back. With the dawn, we had the freedom to rest without legal interruption in a public space, so we exercised that right.

After a few hours of rest, we headed toward Pacific Beach for some free lunch. I was not much in the mood for eating and wanted to call the coroner's office. I told the guys that I wanted to split up for a short time, so I could make a call. In truth, I was worried that the news I was about to hear may not be positive and I didn't want anyone else around while I made the call. I gazed off at the waves after dialing the number.

I was strolling slowly down the boardwalk at Pacific Beach while I waited for someone to answer. *"Hello, can I help you?"* the voice inquired. I asked if I might speak with the chaplain who works at that location and waited on hold while they tried to locate him. *"This is the Chaplain speaking, how can I help you?"* I asked him if he might be able to look up the records of my friend Ed Pelzner, to see if he had turned up dead. I referenced the police chaplain who'd given me his name the previous evening. *"Sure, he mentioned that you might call. I'm happy to assist. Can you give me Ed's full name and date of birth?"* I provided the information he requested and waited in fear, as he put me on hold.

Was this the end of my journey? Had Ed become a casualty of the streets? I waited patiently while the chaplain searched the database for Ed. I wondered why the waiting process seems to feel so much longer when the potential news is more serious or life threatening?

His voice was back, *"Hello, Will?"* *"Yes?"* I answered in a quiet tone. *"I have good news. Your friend has not turned up dead."* This was tremendous news and my spirit lifted immediately. Then he added, *"We would know, even if Ed died in a different state, since we cross reference our system."* What amazing news! I thanked him profusely and then went searching for Steve and AG to tell them the news. When they heard the news, we thanked God for Ed's continued safety and protection. We spent the remainder of the day searching the Pacific Beach area, encouraged by the fact that he was alive.

On our final day we decided to head back downtown, since our hotel was in that direction. We decided to spend the day searching in the Padre Stadium area.

(Left to right: Steve & AG next to Dog Beach)

We stopped at a park near the water's edge and sat around a picnic table. AG said that he wanted to share a song with us, which he played on his cell phone. The song was titled, *"No Longer Slaves,"* by Bethel Music. His voice grew soft as AG said, *"I've been praying for Ed and pleading with God to set him free from his enslavement to drugs."* As he shared his prayer with us, he began to weep for Ed. Steve and I were moved by AG's heartfelt words spoken through tears.

As the week came to an end, I was saddened by yet one more trip without any sign of Ed. We had leads, but I wanted a face-to-face conversation with my old friend. I was grateful to have received confirmation that he was still alive, and moved by the support and commitment of my two friends, Steve and AG.

Steve and I said goodbye to AG, since he didn't share the same flight itinerary. As the two of us boarded the plane back east, I took my seat and offered up another prayer for my friend. As the city faded out of view, I began to consider the unique impact that the three trips had on me. I felt as though I never returned feeling the same.

Having no idea when I might return, I decided to get some rest. The journey was clearly not over, but I was unsure when we might return.

Chapter 7

9 Miles and a Pregnant Wife

After returning from my third trip to the streets of San Diego, my wife Sandra said, "*I'm going with you next time you search for Ed.*"

That may sound like a logical desire of hers, but I was unsure how safe the streets would be for a woman. No, I'm not being sexist, but I did question the safety of living on the streets, as my wife was pregnant at that time. Sandra was about five months pregnant when she asked about returning with me to San Diego.

I was able to convince her that we should stay in a hotel rather than on the street. We planned a brief three-day trip. I figured that would be enough time to take a few long walks, explore some of the trails, and search as a couple for Ed. In addition, Sandra wanted to meet some of our friends from the street, who we had talked so much about.

I used to view San Diego as a beautiful place to visit. My street trips have forever tainted the way I view the city now. Don't get me wrong, it's still a beautiful city. My problem is that I imagine Ed on every street corner, and I'm all too aware of the homeless population scattered throughout the entire city.

Having walked from downtown San Diego to Pacific Beach and many miles to the east, I decided on a hotel in Pacific Beach, not far from the Mission Bay lunch location. Before leaving for the trip, I contacted a woman by the name of Cathy from a church in La Jolla. Cathy was responsible for starting the homeless meals that we took advantage of every day in Mission Bay and I was interested to hear more of her story. She agreed, and we set up a date for Sandra and I to meet up with her and her husband Bill.

Being a person of action, Sandra was ready to see it all for herself. I wasted no time once I heard her express the desire to go. We landed back in San Diego exactly 40 days after I had departed on the previous month with Steve and AG.

Soon after arriving and getting checked in at our hotel, we walked around the Pacific Beach area to get a lay of the land. The sun was setting before long and we only had two full days to cover a lot of ground. We decided to call it an early night to help our bodies adjust to the three-hour jetlag.

The following day we got an early start. We walked south to Ocean Beach. We spent some time chatting with the homeless population there before heading east toward Hancock Street, where Ed's shop had been. I gave her a play-by-play tour, acting as the guide and showing her where we'd been awakened by police, where we camped in Robb Field and where we met Kyle. I even showed her the booth where we slept at Denny's. As we walked past each memorable spot, we continued searching for Ed.

Along the way, we carried the same information and photos cards to distribute, hoping for a nugget of new information or perhaps that we'd actually find Ed.

We'd been walking for so long that we lost track of time. Sandra asked me how far we'd travelled, since she was growing tired. I was amazed when I checked the application on my phone, which recorded a distance of nine miles. Granted, we had no backpacks, although Sandra was carrying a little baby in her belly.

When she said, "Enough is enough, I'm tired," I called an Uber and we made our way back to our hotel. The journey had exhausted her, but she was glad to have seen so many of the places she heard me mention from previous trips.

We concluded the day by going to the homeless meal at the Methodist Church in Pacific Beach. I introduced Sandra to as many of my homeless friends as possible. We had a wonderful visit with them before calling it an early night.

The highlight of the following day was meeting up with Cathy and her husband, Bill. We hadn't rented a car, so they picked us up in route to dinner. We headed to a seafood restaurant near the wharf in the downtown area. Cathy said that the restaurant was known for their tasty seafood.

It felt odd actually dining in a restaurant. I noticed a few homeless individuals sitting along the pier as we walked from the parking lot to the front door. How strange it felt to be in a different role. At the same time, I'd been looking forward to meeting with Cathy and Bill for some time.

Cathy was the woman responsible for launching the lunchtime meals, which took place at Mariner's Point five days a week. Our teams had been taking advantage of them ever since we discovered they were an option.

For more than ten years she'd been responsible for faithfully coordinating the meals enjoyed by thousands of homeless individuals. It's difficult to say precisely how many homeless men and women had benefited from that service. I was anxious to hear how it all began.

When I asked the question, Cathy replied, "*It began by simply offering lunches as an occasional service opportunity. I never imagined that this would become such a staple at Mariner's Point, feeding so many people.*" She went on to share how blessed she felt to know the countless souls who made sandwiches, donated food items and most importantly, took the time to be present with the homeless Monday through Friday, every single week.

Cathy explained her partnership with the Salvation Army and how they coordinate their weekly efforts. It was an inspirational story that had met with its share of adversity.

(Left to right: Will, Sandra, Cathy & Bill)

One story that was extremely unsettling took place just as the feeding program began to get off the ground. Cathy said that a few police officers showed up one day during the lunchtime meal. They informed the volunteers that they needed to cease from serving food at that very moment. Furthermore, they were told that the City of San Diego had decided that the lunches were attracting far too many homeless people. For that reason, they were being shut down.

Cathy asked, "*On what grounds or formal charge are we guilty of transgressing?*" The officer in charge stated that due to the unnecessary crowd of homeless occupants, the city had made the decision to cancel all future park meals. This meant that it would no longer be possible to hold the daily lunch at Mariner's Point.

Cathy encouraged her team to comply with the officer's instructions at the time. However, Cathy knew in her gut that this mandate seemed unjust. She obtained legal counsel and filed suit against the City of San

Diego for wrongfully shutting down a meal service, which had been responsible for feeding countless hungry individuals.

Cathy's huge heart to feed the homeless is an inspiration. Not only did she take the time, energy and resources to establish the service, she had the tenacity to take on the City of San Diego. And she won!

After battling the city in a courtroom and once again obtaining the right to feed the homeless, she coordinated the meals on a daily basis. In fact, the additional publicity helped her to recruit more groups and volunteers to assist with the meals. Presently, Cathy allows others to run the incredible service that she established so many years ago.

Sandra and I enjoyed hearing about the streets from the perspective of those who focus on providing meals for the homeless. It was an insightful evening and I left inspired by her resilience.

Living on the streets of San Diego has allowed me to meet some unbelievable people - both those on the street, as well as those who care for the homeless there. Over the course of my three trips I can think of Cathy, Jack, the cook at the Catholic Church in Ocean Beach, Father Joe Coffey and countless others.

In similar fashion to Cathy's resistance from the authorities in San Diego, Jack told us about the hate mail he receives on a regular basis, written by local residents. Despite the opposition, Jack has persevered for years and there are hundreds of volunteers just as dedicated as Jack, Cathy and Father Joe. The individuals working in the local churches and other non-profits throughout the city are making a difference, even if some find it bothersome.

I don't claim to have the solution to solving the homeless epidemic. However, I applaud the men and women who are doing something about the problem.

On our final day, I took Sandra to Old Town San Diego to spend some more time looking for Ed. With a feel of the Wild West, we walked the unpaved streets chatting up a few homeless individuals congregating on the lawn in the center of the park. There are always a few scattered there on the grass, either napping or seated around the picnic benches.

When we approached the end where most tourists enter the historic area, we found one of my favorite homeless friends by the name of Tom Williams. Tom was seated on a bench near the entrance to Old Town, doing his best to panhandle some money.

We greeted him when we were a few feet away, as a matter of courtesy. Since Tom was unable to see us, we didn't want to startle him. I first met Tom on my previous trip with AG and Steve, while we were dining at the Episcopal Church on Sunset Cliffs Boulevard.

At the end of the meal, when we had volunteered to help, I had been asked to assist an old blind man as he gathered his belongings. He instructed me as I carefully packed his possessions into a tall narrow upright cart. I wheeled the cart with my left hand, as I guided him with my right. We headed to the parking lot behind the church to load his stuff into a camper that was parked out back.

While helping assist Tom, I began to consider his situation. Afterall, he was the first blind homeless man who I was fortunate to meet. Learning to trust people on the street is a matter in itself. However, add to that complexity: Tom's age as an elderly man of 82 years, his lack of vision and his slow pace, and I was left to wonder how he had survived at all. Tom was extremely polite and spoke with a sweet elderly southern gentleman's drawl. He told me that he was from Bluffton, South Carolina, not far from Hilton Head Island. I was familiar with that town, as I had actually driven through it with Ed's family when we were in high school.

I told Tom that I had been to his hometown on more than one occasion when traveling to Hilton Head Island. He told me that he was well acquainted with that entire area as well as their rich history.

Tom spoke a bit about his own journey and his path from South Carolina to the West Coast. He had no tale of a broken marriage, and he'd never had children of his own. He was alone and had chosen to live out west after he visited there years earlier for work. Tom loved the cool air and absence of humidity. The only tragedy he spoke of was losing his eyesight.

While he shared about his life, I quickly noted the fact that he never complained. In the midst of his rather unfortunate circumstances, he was grateful to be alive and wanted to move on from his story to discover more about mine. Tom was selfless in nature and expressed sincere concern for me when I mentioned my quest to locate Ed.

With his belongings safely packed onboard, Tom turned to me and said, "*Please take down my phone number so we can stay in touch regarding your friend Ed.*" We exchanged numbers and I typed mine into his phone, wondering how he might dial it or locate my name.

Tom's friend who owned the camper was clearly ready to go. He had been more than patient while we conversed.

I told Tom that it had been a pleasure meeting him. Tom simply responded, "*I want to help you locate your friend Ed, so I'll pass along the word and see what we discover.*" I had no idea that I'd see him again a month later.

I was thrilled to introduce Tom to Sandra and have the opportunity to visit with him before we headed home.

(Left to right: Tom & Will in Old Town San Diego)

While Tom had been living in the camper with his friend during my previous trip, I came to discover that his friend moved away from San Diego two weeks after we left. Without a camper to sleep in, Tom had to find a new place to bed down each night. We met a number of homeless who lived in their cars, trucks and campers similar to Tom. We always referred to them as the "upper class" homeless. The vehicle certainly comes in handy on rainy nights.

I was curious as to where Tom was camping. After asking him a few questions, we learned that he was sleeping under a bridge in close proximity to Old Town. I could tell that Tom expressed some shame concerning his new residence, yet he never complained about it. When I discovered his precise location for sleeping, I hiked there later in the evening and snapped a photo, to see for myself. Curiosity got the better of me, and I was still trying to process how he could have such an amazingly positive attitude while living in such a difficult place.

(Tom sleeping under the bridge near Old Town)

Sandra and I relaxed on a bench in Old Town with Tom, savoring the conversation with such a sweet man. Feeling inspired by his attitude, I asked his permission to video him about his journey. I had no idea how blessed I would be by his answers to my questions.

The following is an exact transcript of that interview I conducted with Tom. You can watch it yourself at the following Vimeo page web address: https://vimeo.com/188167852

Video Transcript:
Tom is homeless. He is from Bluffton, South Carolina. Tom is 82 years of age and legally blind. At present, he lives under a bridge near Old Town San Diego.

I asked Tom how he feels about his current situation…

<u>Tom's Response:</u>
"OK, being in San Diego is great! This is where I want to be. I've enjoyed every minute I've been in this city, and I'm not anxious to go anywhere. I'll be 83 next month. Um, living on the street, well it saves a lot on rent. And wherever there's people living on the street, there are people to help. And there are people that will help. They have helped me. So, no big deal, it's just that if your roof is covered with beautiful stars, then you can really enjoy it."

I asked Tom about living under a bridge…

<u>Tom's Response:</u>
"The bridge I've been under before, and it's very nice and convenient when it rains. It's dry."

I commented, "You seem to find the silver lining, don't you?"

Tom's Response:

"Well, it's always there. It's been my experience in life that whatever happens, however horrendous you may consider it, there is always something good that comes out of it. But all you have to do is wait, and look for it. It'll show up."

I asked, "Have you always been this positive?"

Tom's Response:

"No, I haven't, certainly not. But you know what? Looking back, it just wasn't any fun. There is nothing God made more available to all of us than an attitude. We can pick and choose our own, and they're free, so why not pick a good one?"

I asked Tom, "How are you doing presently?"

Tom's Response:

"Today is the best day of my life. And I hope it is you all's too. Yesterday is gone forever. It is never coming back. And nobody, but nobody has promised us tomorrow. It might not get here. But we've got today. In the game of survival, we're all winners. This morning, we all woke up on the right side of the dirt and we are still sucking air."

(End of Interview)

Sandra and I felt incredibly blessed to have some time with Tom before we left. At the conclusion of my fourth trip, I came to realize how many treasures there are on the street. Listening to stories and attitudes like Tom's, meeting others like Cathy and Bill, I left feeling inspired.

Imagine how many homeless people we walk past or step over in our lifetime. Each individual has their own hopes and dreams, and in most cases, loved ones somewhere who are praying for them.

While the trip with my wife was shorter than the rest, it served to deepen my appreciation for those who serve the homeless. In addition, even though I was yet to stumble into my old friend Ed, I became grateful to him for opening my eyes to the streets. If he hadn't gone missing, I would have missed out on such an incredible opportunity. I hoped that when I finally find him, we could sit down and talk all about it. Imagine what stories he has to share. I look forward to that day and pray God brings it sooner rather than later.

Chapter 8
A Pizza Party for Drug Dealers

In August of 2016, five months after Sandra and I journeyed to San Diego, Ed's mom and dad traveled there for a commemorative World War II event. Ed's father is a World War II veteran, who fought in the Pacific arena. Joining Ed's mom and dad was their daughter Diane, along with her husband Doug.

While Ed's parents were busy with the celebration, his sister and brother-in-law spent some time looking for Ed. Ed's mom contacted me after she returned home to pass along a few nuggets of information concerning Ed's whereabouts.

She mentioned a conversation they had with a homeless man who steered them to a San Diego homeless Facebook page, which is only available via invitation. The man posted a photo of Ed on their behalf, and asked the homeless community if anyone had seen him.

The intel they received led them to an area known as Mission Gorge, east of the coast and farther up the riverbed. Ed's parents walked as much as a couple in their late 80's and early 90s could. Together with Ed's sister, they scoured the area on foot. What family wouldn't make the journey for their child/brother? Mr. and Mrs. Pelzner love their son Ed dearly, and asked a number of homeless people questions concerning his whereabouts.

Their conversations led them to a man, named Israel, who was living in the drain area, behind a motel in Mission Gorge. He told them that he knew Ed and had even seen him recently.

They were unable to actually locate Ed despite their efforts. However, their intel inspired me regarding where to concentrate my search on my next trip.

On October 9, 2016, two months after Ed's family searched for him, I landed in San Diego. This was my fifth trip looking for Ed, and we had grown our team to a search party of eight dedicated individuals. Of course, my faithful friend Steve was back for his third round. What an amazing man Steve is, taking more time away from his successful HVAC business! Not only was he willing to return and look for my friend, but he even agreed to lead a team of two men so we could double our efforts.

The two men who I assigned to Steve's team, were Trevin Frame and John Costello. Trevin was a police officer from Prince William County, Virginia, and John was a 60-year old gym teacher and varsity basketball coach from a high school in Loudoun County, Virginia.

John shared with us that he took the week off from school, as a matter of demonstrating to his students the value we should place on those who are in trouble. Trevin confessed that he desired to grasp an understanding of the homeless mindset, walking a mile in their shoes. He believed that the experience would help him to be more caring when he encountered homeless individuals in his jurisdiction. Both Trevin and John were tremendous assets to our team!

My team consisted of two old friends who had heard enough stories about the trips that they wanted to see it for themselves. Tom Pounder serves in a church back in Virginia and Dave (also known as "Gumby"), owns a few local radio stations. I have known Dave since 1987 and Tom since 1990, so we had been friends for 26 - 29 years.

Lastly, we had two female recruits. After my wife Sandra demonstrated that a pregnant woman could handle the streets, my mother (Audie Hall), registered for the trip at the age of 79. Serving alongside my mom, was a native of San Diego, who I had met at church. Her name is Georgia McGowan and she was kind enough to pair up with my mom, although our two ladies were not planning to camp out with the rest of us.

(Front left to right: John, Georgia, Audie, Gumby & Will.
Back left to right: Steve, Trevin & Tom)

A kind woman by the name of Beth, from Cathy's church in La Jolla, offered to put our ladies up in her home during the week. We were not ready to have women live on the streets with us, especially with my mother close to the age of 80.

Our team arrived late on a Sunday evening and headed straight to a downtown hotel to get some rest. The next morning, we reconvened before dividing up into our three respective groups. As usual, we had everyone leave their valuables, money and a fresh change of clothes back at the hotel before trekking out for the week. My mom and Georgia were the exception, since we rented them a vehicle to get around in and they were staying in La Jolla with Beth.

While my team and Steve's team launched into the search early on Monday morning, Georgia and Audie had a different plan. They took their rental car to each meal that we planned to go to and volunteered with the evening churches and the daily lunchtime meal at Mariner's Point.

Steve and I were both acclimating to having to train our groups. Showing them the busiest homeless population near Saint Vincent's Church and Padre Stadium was always a great place to start.

I employed a *"throw them in the deep end"* approach by taking my team to the most dangerous area at the start. I wanted to encourage a cautious attitude in each new recruit before we split up later in the week.

Walking through the downtown area near the train station early that morning, was all it took to open everyone's eyes to life on the street. We saw people using drugs, others selling them and some individuals who looked as though they wouldn't think twice about hurting you.

After our introductory walk, I broke away with my team. As a larger group we agreed to meet up at dinner time. We discovered a meal being offered later that evening by a local non-profit in a drug store parking lot.

My team began walking toward Balboa Park, since a few homeless individuals suggested that we start there. We met a few characters along the way and prayed with one young man by the name of Terrance. He had a disabled arm and expressed his desire to get off the streets.

We prayed with Terrance on a sidewalk across the street from a police station before resuming our path to Balboa Park.

(Left to right: Terrance, Will, Tom & Gumby)

We didn't spend much time in Balboa Park since all I wanted to do was press on toward Mission Gorge, where Ed's parents heard that he had been sighted two months earlier. Afterall, that was the best lead I had received in three trips.

Georgia and Audie located the volunteers serving dinner in the city and joined their ranks. Most days we had no clue where we might eat dinner until we canvassed friends on the street to find out who was offering supper. On that particular week, Georgia and Audie did the research so that they knew where they might be able to volunteer. In turn, they let the two other teams know where to meet up late in the afternoon.

Every church and non-profit organization they contacted welcomed their assisstance with open arms. No one refused two extra sets of hands to serve. We appreciated Georgia and my mother Audie for their part on the trip. In addition to serving meals, the two ladies would carry our heavy backpacks in the rental vehicle during the daylight hours. That may seem like a small thing: however, it made a tremendous difference to walk miles while traveling light.

(Left to right: Georgia & Audie)

Along the way to Mission Gorge, we stopped at a Denny's, since I had been told that Ed made frequent visits to the one on West Point Loma Boulevard.

The manager was extremely helpful and said that he had seen Ed before at their restaurant. His name was Roberto and he inquired about Ed's situation.

After hearing the basic details of Ed's story, he asked, "*What do you plan to do if you find him?*" I honestly didn't have a major plan, other than letting Ed know he's loved and offering to help.

Roberto pressed further, "*But what's your plan to help him get clean?*" Roberto seemed to have some experience dealing with addicts, so I asked, "*What do you suggest?*" He went on to tell us that his brother had been a tweaker. He shared that after his family located him, he invited him to celebrate in Tecate, Mexico. He generously purchased his brother as much booze as he wanted to drink. Once his brother was fairly inebriated, the family hired a couple of men to come pick him up and take him to a treatment facility.

Roberto went on to explain that in Mexico, a family member can call a rehabilitation facility and ask them to pick up a friend or family member who suffers with a serious addiction. If the family or friends pay for the service, they will keep the person in treatment until they are completely clean. In the United States the addict must willingly seek treatment. That was not a factor in Mexico. All it took was a concerned friend or family member willing to pay the associated fees.

That may sound harsh to some, but to those with family members who have lost the ability to make healthy choices, and who may be a risk to themselves, it could be a godsend. Complying with HIPPA laws and restrictions in the USA makes it almost impossible to obtain a shred of information concerning their suffering relative.

Roberto said that the facility does not permit family members to visit during the first three months, but encourages visitation after the initial detoxification period. He concluded, "*My brother is now completely clean after spending a year in rehabilitation. He has remained clean for more than two years.*" I appreciated Roberto's willingness to take the time to share with us, which had been insightful.

Roberto gave me his phone number in the event that we located Ed. We left Denny's with more than a Grand Slam! I wasn't so sure that Ed would be willing to go party in Tecate, Mexico, but Roberto certainly got me thinking about my options beyond simply locating Ed.

I pressed on with my team toward Mission Gorge, and called Steve to see how his team was doing. He said that he and Trevin and John were in Ocean Beach meeting homeless individuals and searching for leads. They had no Ed sightings to report. Although, he mentioned some significant conversations with new friends they had met.

(Left to right: Trevin, Bear & Steve in Ocean Beach)

Steve, Trevin and John wandered around between the Ocean Beach and Mission Bay areas, chatting up those who wanted to talk and pray.

Trevin met a man who said, "*I lost my shirt last night and have nothing to wear.*" Without hesitation, Trevin removed his shirt and handed it over. The man was moved to tears and thanked Trevin for his generosity. They spent a few minutes praying with him.

They also took some time to pray with a man who went by the street name of "Bear." Bear confessed to making a living as a general contractor until his alcoholism got the better of him. He'd been living on the streets of San Diego ever since.

(Left to right: Trevin, Jake & Ned)

In the afternoon, Steve's teammate Coach John Costello needed a break. His ankle was in pain so he decided to sit in front of the Pacific Beach Library and talk with the homeless men and women who congregated there. Meanwhile, Trevin and Steve met Jake. Jake had been battling a nasty meth addiction and had recently chosen to get clean. He'd been sober for just over a month and was attempting to get accepted into a Teen Challenge program to help him get clean for good. He was grateful for the time that Steve's team invested in him.

I arrived at Mission Gorge in the early afternoon. Tom and Gumby helped me locate the motel where Ed's parents and sister met a man by the name of Israel. He was the one who mentioned knowing Ed. We began canvassing the area and immediately found evidence of homeless campsites in the drain area behind the motel.

(Left to right: Gumby, Tom & Will in Mission Gorge)

While no one was present, the storm drain area was littered with homeless debris; blankets, used clothes and empty liquor bottles. We felt like we were getting close, so we searched for someone living on the streets who might offer more clues.

Back on the street we met a young homeless couple who told us their names were Bill and Marla. They confessed that they had been battling addiction. We showed them Ed's photo, and they said they hadn't seen him. *"However,"* they remarked, *"you may want to try the Home Depot just up the street. A lot of addicts and drug dealers hang out in the riverbed located just behind their parking lot."* We appreciated their tip and prayed with them before taking off in that direction.

(Left to right: Gumby, Will, Bill, Marla & Tom)

As we walked away, they warned us that the riverbed was dangerous. This was a different section of the riverbed than we had searched on our past trips, yet we received the same warning. We wasted no time. Home Depot is only a three-minute walk from the drain area.

When we arrived at the Home Depot parking lot, we spotted an older gentleman serving as the security guard there. He was a friendly man by the name of Jeff, who told us that his job was to keep the homeless and the day laborers from bothering the shoppers. He'd held that job for several years and knew the area extremely well.

When I showed him Ed's photo, he responded without hesitation, *"Oh yeah, I see that guy every couple of days."* He added, *"Your friend walks straight through the parking lot, then ducks through the fence over by the garden center."* He added a word of caution, *"The riverbed is full of drug dealers and dangerous crime, so be careful!"* We thanked Jeff for the information and for the warning. I was encouraged by the new intel and was ready to plunge into the riverbed behind the parking lot.

When we reached the far end of the parking lot, we noticed a hole in the fence that the homeless used to go in and out. We watched a few suspicious characters as they disappeared through the hole and into the riverbed.

Keep in mind, while this was my fifth trip, it was day one of trip one for Tom and Gumby. Hoping to get them motivated to join me in the riverbed wasn't an easy task. They both expressed healthy caution, but after a little cajoling, they agreed that the lead was too important not to pursue. They were hesitant, yet kind enough not to make me go it alone.

We slid through the opening in the fence and began to navigate the trail. There was a maze of paths and a tent set up to our right. We examined the tent, but no one was present. I could tell that my team was anxious. My adrenaline was fueling me with the hope that Ed could be around the next corner. As we walked a bit further, we saw a large metal fence which someone had erected. The fence stood as a barrier to keep strangers away, with an enormous homeless encampment on the opposite side.

As we closed in on the gate, we were startled suddenly by a short Latino man with a machete strapped to his side. He confronted me while standing his ground on the opposite side of the gate. "*Who are you and what do you want?*" I moved closer to speak with him. "*Lord, give me wisdom,*" I prayed internally, knowing this would be a crucial interaction.

I said, "*I'm actually a pastor from the East Coast and I'm looking for my friend.*" He looked nervous when I reached for my pocket, but eased up when I withdrew a hard stock postcard with the pic of Ed, along with my contact information.

His eyes bulged when he saw Ed, and he responded, "*Yeah, I know him, what do you want with him?*"

I said, "*I want him to know that I'm here and would love to see him. If he needs anything, I'll be here all week.*"

I motioned to my phone number on the card and asked him to have Ed call me.

(Left to right: Gumby, Juan & Will in the riverbed)

I asked the guard his name, and he answered, "*It's not important.*" However, we discovered the following day that his name was Juan. He simply wasn't ready to trust us after we'd only just met. I asked if I could pray for him and he responded abruptly, "*No!*"

I asked God for wisdom and immediately had a thought come to mind. I inquired, "*Do you have a daughter?*" "*Yes, I do,*" he exclaimed. "*Can I pray for her?*" "*Yes, please,*" he answered. "*Her name is Gabriela and she is six-years old.*"

We prayed for Gabriela, that she would be safe and know that her dad loves her. We asked the Lord for provision for their entire family. Just as I said "*Amen,*" Juan added, "*I have a son too.*"

It was clear that he wanted us to pray for his son as well, so we did. Juan's demeanor changed and he warmed up to us. I thanked him for his time and thanked him in advance for passing along my message to Ed.

As we walked away, we each expressed our excitement concerning the positive encounter with Juan. After walking about twenty yards, I noticed an opening in the fence line.

We were still navigating the riverbed area when I spotted the hole. I couldn't resist, so without consulting my team, I stepped through the opening and began exploring the other side.

There was a trail that led deeper into the homeless encampment. Tom and Gumby followed my lead, although none of us spoke a word. As we moved farther up the trail, we noticed a blond surfer-looking guy who was fast asleep in a cot, near his belongings.

He woke at the sound of our steps so I said, "*Hello.*" He appeared to be freaked out at the sight of three complete strangers. If his job was to guard the open hole, then he should have been fired.

I showed him the picture of Ed and asked if he'd seen him. He took one look at Ed's face and blurted out, "*Fast Eddie!*" I wondered if that was his street name. Gumby asked our surfer friend a few more questions which must have spooked him, because he instantly changed his tune and said, "*I've never seen that guy in my life.*" "*That's interesting,*" I thought, "*a moment ago he blurted out Ed's nickname.*"

In my frustration, I said, "*Thanks anyway,*" and walked away. I decided to press farther down the trail. I motioned to Tom and Gumby to follow, and they did.

Wandering deeper into the populated encampment, a voice suddenly shouted, "*Stop! What do you think you're doing?*" We turned in the direction of the command and noticed Juan standing before us. He didn't look happy.

I said, "*As I mentioned earlier, I'm looking for my friend Ed.*" He replied, "*This is our camp! You can't just go walking back here.*" In a non-threatening way, he added, "*You'll get yourselves killed if you continue down this path.*" Regardless of his gentle tone, the warning was clear. My crew was ready to roll. Gumby responded, "*Alright, thanks for the heads-up.*" We turned around and headed back the way we came.

Once we were back in the Home Depot parking lot, we discussed everything that had just transpired. Gumby and Tom were in high spirits, while I experienced a sinking feeling in my gut.

Tom and Gumby asked me what was wrong. I said, "*I feel like our initial interaction went well. However, when we pushed past the surfer guy, we must have violated their trust.*"

I became convinced that Juan was going to tell Ed that we were hunting for him and this would only serve to make Ed more paranoid and send him deeper into hiding. We prayed together and then decided to wander the streets of Mission Gorge, hoping to catch a glimpse of my friend.

We ducked into a few local stores and taco shops, to no avail. We must have found at least three more local store employees who each recognized Ed in the photo. We were hot on his trail, but the sun was setting and we needed to catch an Uber to meet up with the rest of the group downtown.

We failed to factor the additional time needed to navigate rush hour traffic, and arrived 45 minutes late. Everyone on our team was engaged assisting the volunteers who were responsible for supplying the meal. Thankfully, we arrived in time to still get a plate of food.

It was refreshing to see everyone working together. I was proud to be part of such an incredible group of people. I looked forward to swapping stories later that evening when the meal was over.

(Left to right: Georgia, Gina & Trevin)

After helping clean up the tables and parking lot, we decided to call some Uber cars to taxi the group over to Robb Field. The women carried on toward Beth's house in La Jolla. Making camp with our largest group yet took a little creativity so as not to attract attention to ourselves. We decided to spread out along the fence line of one of the baseball fields and hide in the shadows.

Four of the men seemed a little freaked out by our first night sleeping in a public park, while Steve and I had no problem falling asleep within minutes.

At one point around three in the morning, Steve woke me. He was speaking in a whisper and said, "*Hey Will, there is a squad car in the parking lot that is shining a spot light around the park. What do you want to do?*"

I was still trying to wake up enough to think clearly. "*The cops don't seem to be bothering us, so let's all stay low to the ground and not attract any attention to ourselves.*" With that, I laid my head back down and fell fast asleep.

We woke early the following morning to pack up before someone noticed us. We hiked at a leisurely pace toward Mission Bay, knowing that there would be lunch and coffee delivered at 11:30am. We had also designated that time and place each day to meet up with Georgia and Audie. They served alongside the La Jolla Community Church and Salvation Army workers all week. We also knew we could offload our heavy packs into their rental car at that time.

(Audie in the glasses & Georgia holding the box)

While our ladies helped serve, our men scattered amongst the plethora of homeless huddled around the park. Steve and I encouraged the team to break up in an effort to meet more homeless. I was encouraged as I looked around the park area to witness a number of conversations taking place between the homeless and our new-to-the-streets team members. What a tremendous example of caring for others on their turf!

While I was inspired by our team, my mind drifted to consider the next step with the men who we'd met in the riverbed behind Home Depot.

After lunch, we coordinated our efforts and agreed to meet up in time for dinner at the Episcopal Church back in Pacific Beach. Once everyone knew the time and place to meet, we prayed together and broke huddle.

As we began walking back toward the bridge over Mission Bay, Tom and Gumby asked me about our plan for the day. I wasn't yet clear on the precise plan, but I knew we needed to get back to Mission Gorge. I said, "*I'll let you know when we get there,*" and then ordered an Uber ride.

While we waited for our ride, I asked God a question, "*What would it look like to love the crew of intimidating men in the riverbed area?*" One idea came to mind immediately after I uttered my silent prayer, "*Throw them a pizza party!*"

What a great idea, I thought. It was unique and unexpected, and seemed like the perfect next step! Fear began to creep into my thoughts, and I hadn't yet shared the idea with my team. I was afraid that they may try to talk me out of it, since one of them had already commented, "*You're not going to make us go back to the riverbed, are you?*" I chose to keep my mouth shut.

I knew that the riverbed wasn't a safe place to go, so I continued praying silently as we drove toward Mission Gorge. During my prayer, a passage from the Bible came to mind which I believed to be inspired by God's Holy Spirit. The actual words were, "Do not have any fear; they cannot harm one hair on your head unless I allow it," (a reference from Luke 21:18).

This thought was encouraging and yet I am a bald man, so I wasn't sure what harming hairs on my head meant, given my situation. At the same time, my internal fear had been replaced with peace. The ride from Mission Bay to Mission Gorge was almost over, so I had the driver drop us off at the 7-Eleven just across the street from Home Depot.

Once we disembarked from our ride, I shared the plan with Gumby and Tom right there in the parking lot. I gave them a few minutes to allow the plan to sink in and to field any questions. They were certainly shocked but willing to trust me and give it a shot.

I had suspicions that Gumby had not complied with our "*no money on the street policy.*" I asked him if he might perhaps have any loose cash or a credit card on hand. Just as suspected, he did. Then I asked if he might be willing to purchase five pizzas and some drinks for our friends in the riverbed. Gumby replied, "Of course, let's do it!" With that, we headed into the convenience store to get what we came for.

While we waited for the man behind the counter to heat up five pizzas, we reviewed the plan. Soon enough our pizzas were hot, boxed up and ready for delivery. We packed the cold drinks into a bag, picked up the hot pizza boxes and headed out the door!

We crossed the street made our way across the Home Depot parking lot, waving to the security guard who we met the previous day.

When we reached the edge of the fence, we were all feeling a bit uneasy. Gumby suggested the importance of prayer for protection. Tom and I agreed and so we devised a plan. Each of us texted five to ten people and asked if they might be willing to pray for us in that precise moment. We decided not to give any particular details, but to simply ask people back at home to pray. After each of us had received at least five or more texts back, confirming that people were indeed on their knees in prayer, we knew it was time for us to proceed.

With that, we made our way through the fence. In no time, we were back at the front gate, which had been guarded by Juan on the previous day. There was no one in sight, so I hollered, *"Hello?"* Instead of Juan, another man approached to meet us at the gate. He looked as though he was from the Middle East and we hadn't seen him before.

He introduced himself, *"My name is Israel."* We were face-to-face with the man that Ed's parents and sister had met two months earlier. This was the man who knew Ed!

I asked Israel about the shorter Latino man who we'd met the previous day. He replied, *"Oh, you mean Juan, he's around here somewhere."* As Israel glanced around to look for Juan, so did we. I couldn't help but notice makeshift tents, loads of bike parts, tarps, and a path that curved out of sight. The bike parts appeared to be inventory for a chop shop of sorts. In addition, we'd been told by local homeless individuals that this was also the headquarters of a booming drug business. For that reason, we had been warned to exercise extreme caution. A pizza party was cautious, right!

Just then, Juan came walking toward the fence. He asked us the reason for our return. I spoke on behalf of our group. *"Well, we were praying for you guys after meeting you yesterday, and felt that the Lord wants you to know how much He loves you. We decided to treat you all to lunch today and brought you pizza and drinks!"*

Juan just stood there in shock as Israel threw the gate open and walked out to greet us. *"This is awesome!"* he said, as he planted his backside on the ground, ready to eat. Juan was clearly a little less convinced, although he followed behind Israel. As Israel picked up his first slice, I began to share the details regarding our search for Ed. He seemed to recall meeting Ed's family back in August and commented, *"This is the first time a pastor has brought us lunch back here, but it's cool."*

As we broke out the napkins and paper plates, Juan decided that he was hungry as well. However, just before I could serve him a slice, the entire atmosphere of our picnic took a sharp unexpected turn.

A new character, unknown to us, emerged from the encampment behind the gate. We heard him coming, at which point everyone's head turned in that direction.

From the heart of that small tent metropolis, the obvious alpha leader made his way directly toward us. He was not wearing a shirt, which revealed his lean, muscular, tattoo-covered body. He was bald like me, but devoid of any smile whatsoever. He wasted no time speaking his mind, *"What the F... is going on here?"*

Israel was quick to respond in our defense, *"These guys are cool man, and they showed up with free lunch."* Their leader was clearly not impressed, nor did he request a piece of pizza.

Israel continued, *"Can you believe it man? Free lunch! And one of these guys is a pastor!"* That was enough; their leader shouted in response, *"I don't care if he's the F-ing Pope! They'd better get the hell out now, or they'll wind up dead!"*

Israel still had the courage to stick up for us, although I could take a hint and we all knew that we had overstayed our welcome. As we stood to leave, Israel carried on, *"Hey man, this isn't cool, those who are for us can't be against us."* I'm not so sure that Israel was aware that he had quoted a reference from the Bible, but it was obvious that his furious leader didn't care. As we walked away, Israel picked up the pizza boxes and drinks and followed us.

The bald alpha male disappeared out of sight, when he saw that we were leaving. I was following closely behind Tom and Gumby as we all made our way toward the Home Depot parking lot. Israel was just behind me and still had the guts to holler, *"This is messed up man! I'm going to eat pizza with my new friends."*

When we reached the edge of the parking lot, we all sat down just inside the fence line. Israel joined us and said, *"I'm sorry about my friends treating you guys like that. It's not right!"* He took a seat on the ground and said, *"Let's eat!"*

Just as we began to eat, Juan resurfaced, but he didn't take a seat. He seemed less interested in a slice of pie and was pacing nervously back and forth. He said, *"You guys should split, man. Our boss is really pissed off."*

Juan told Israel that it wasn't cool of him to be eating with us. At that point Israel spoke directly to Juan. *"Dude, I don't care about this place anymore, if this is how we treat people who are nice to us."* He went on to say, *"I've been here a lot longer than you, and you can take my place if I leave, so just relax."*

It was clear that we had created serious tension with the unexpected pizza party. Apparently, they weren't accustomed to the riverbed delivery service, especially by a church pastor. They could not agree how to respond or interact with us. The three of us watched like spectators to a family argument. Juan wandered back to the gate, most likely to check on his tattooed boss.

Israel apologized once again, as we continued eating our lunch. I began to inquire about Ed when Juan returned again. He interrupted our lunchtime banter, addressing me this time. He said, *"Look, I'm going to have to ask you guys to leave. I appreciate you all coming by and bringing lunch, but you have to understand that this just isn't normal. I mean, stuff like this never happens. Nice people don't bring us lunch."*

I responded, *"Well, maybe they should! How else will you realize how much God loves you?"* He replied, *"You guys are going to get hurt if you stay.*" With that, I was reminded of what came to mind earlier during my prayer time, and I felt inclined to stand up and speak those words very clearly to Juan. "*Juan, I want you to know that you can't harm a single hair on our heads unless God gives you permission to do so. And, we are not afraid of you or your boss.*"

I told him that we'd leave out of respect, but at the same time, I wanted to convey something. Understanding that Juan had most likely known fear his entire life, I wanted him to understand that it's possible to live without fear of man, when you're in close relationship with God. Living without fear doesn't guarantee that we won't get hurt. The source is not rooted in our protection from pain, but the confidence of knowing that we're doing what we believe God wants us to do, regardless of the circumstances. With that, Juan thanked me and disappeared back toward the encampment.

Israel asked if we might pray with him before we took off. Of course we did. After which we said goodbye and headed back to the parking lot.

We left with a sense of peace and texted all of those who had been praying for us back home. We wanted to express our gratitude for standing with us in prayer. I sent a group text and asked, "*Did any of you get a word from the Lord or have any thoughts come to mind while you were praying for us?*" One friend by the name of Linda Davis replied, "*All I heard was, 'You should not fear, for they cannot harm a single hair on your head without God's permission.'*" I showed her text to Tom and Gumby, as the hair was standing up on my arms.

There are times when I wonder if I'm really hearing from God when I ask Him a question and an immediate thought comes to mind. I'm aware that I'm sure to get it wrong sometimes. Despite the potential for error on my account, I love when God confirms an answer to prayer. I don't believe for a second that the fact that Linda and I heard the same exact word from God in prayer was a coincidence. Yet she responded with the exact same word I had heard, knowing nothing about our situation. How amazing is that, when two people praying on opposite ends of the country both hear the exact same response from God? It was a powerful moment as the three of us stood in the Home Depot parking lot, staring at Linda's text message.

Steve pulled up a Google satellite image of the area behind Home Depot. We were able to see part of the enormous homeless encampment from an aerial view.

(Image of encampment, courtesy of Google Maps)

We wondered how many people were actually living in the encampment area behind Home Depot. Was Ed hiding in one of the makeshift tents? My mind was full of questions and I couldn't help but believe that we were extremely close.

I was considering our next move, since Israel had been so responsive. Although his boss had threatened our lives, we could see that both Israel and Juan were warming up to us. The day was coming to an end, but it felt as though each encounter brought us closer to Ed. What would tomorrow bring?

Chapter 9
Perspective Matters

The evening meals hosted by non-profits and churches are always a welcomed treat. We are inspired by the volunteers who serve. We enjoy sitting across the table from homeless friends and hearing their stories while sharing a meal, and we appreciate the break at the close of every tiresome day. It's also a gift now that we no longer need to panhandle for the meal itself. We are grateful in each and every regard.

As I carried my plate of food to the table that evening, I happened to notice a familiar face. Tom Williams, my blind friend from Bluffton, South Carolina. I'd last seen Tom on my previous trip six months earlier with Sandra. I made Tom aware of my presence and said hello.

Tom asked how our search for Ed was progressing. I gave him an update and he suggested that I ask the senior pastor of that church if he might be willing to make an announcement and find out if anyone there knew Ed. "*Great idea,*" I thought and went to follow through on it. The pastor agreed and invited me up to make the announcement myself and distribute photo cards to anyone interested in helping.

After making a public plea, I returned to my seat hoping someone would come forward with new information, but no one did. After a minute or two, Tom suggested that I talk to his friend Paul, who may be able to help. He mentioned that Paul seemed to know almost everyone in the local homeless community and is a tremendous support.

With that, Tom handed me his cell phone and asked me to open his contacts and look for Paul Arnold. I located his name and number and pushed the call button before handing the phone back to Tom.

A moment later, we heard a phone ring just a few seats away. Paul glanced down at the incoming call and then hollered in our direction, "*Hey Tom, why are you calling me when I'm only a few seats away?*" It was humorous, and a good reminder of Tom's inability to see those around him.

Tom invited Paul to join us before soliciting his help. Paul was 60 years of age and had an obvious gentle spirit. He greeted us before asking to have a peek at Ed's photo. After studying the image, he commented, *"Ed looks familiar, but I haven't seen him in quite a while."* Paul agreed to keep an eye out for him, so we exchanged contact information. He agreed to keep us informed if he heard or saw anything.

(Left to right: Georgia, Gumby, Paul, Steve, Trevin, Audie, Will, Tom & John)

Paul lived in a Ford truck, equipped with a roof over the bed, which doubled as his home. For the homeless living in their vehicles, which we referred to as upper-class homeless, the struggle had to do with where to park. We were told that Walmart stores allowed cars with homeless occupants to sleep in their parking lots without harassment, but I wasn't sure if that was true. Most vehicles housing occupants had all of the windows covered with paper so no one could see inside.

If a police officer suspected that someone was sleeping in a vehicle on a side street, they could wake them up, and ask them to move on.

There was apparently an art to remaining hidden in the vehicle and not moving or making a sound when they heard a knock. In Paul's case, he had hung a mix of fabric and paper to block the windows on his truck. If a police officer can't see you, then he can't ask you to leave.

Tom and Paul had a special relationship, and I watched as Paul helped his blind friend gather his belongings after the meal. Paul was a veteran of the United States Navy. In addition, he had served as a beach life guard in San Diego for many years. While Paul had a significant share of beach rescues, he wrestled with periods of drowning in his own life.

Back in 1991, Paul recalled a time when he was seated in a chair with a bottle of whisky in one hand and a loaded revolver in the other. Although he came horrifyingly close to taking his life, he never pulled the trigger.

When I met Paul in February of 2016, he was serving others on the streets of San Diego. Although he held no formal degree in theology, many of the homeless who knew him, referred to him as 'Pastor Paul.' I was moved by the way he cared for Tom, and learned that Tom was not the only recipient of Paul's service. I appreciated his offer to begin keeping an eye out for Ed.

I said goodbye to Tom and Paul, and joined my team members who were busy helping the church staff get the room back in shape. When we finally exited the building, everyone began asking where we planned to bed down for the night. I had some good news to share.

Earlier that day, an old friend of mine texted me when they noticed via Facebook that I was back in San Diego. She was familiar with our mission and said, "*My nephew lives in Pacific Beach and when I told him what you are doing, he said that your team can sleep in his backyard.*" When I let the other five guys know about the invitation to sleep in a local yard surrounded by a fence, they were thrilled. In fact, our dinner that evening had been hosted by a Pacific Beach church, located only half a mile from the man's home.

Our band of tired bodies headed in the direction of the vacant yard, looking forward to a night of uninterrupted sleep. Strolling along, I envisioned lush green grass and a secure tall fence to keep intruders out. I was correct on one account, as it was surrounded by a tall wooden fence. However, instead of a soft bed of green grass, the "*yard*" was actually a large rectangular slab of concrete. While we would be able to sleep void of distractions, the idea of comfort was not in the cards. Steve and I were still grateful for a place to sleep with no threat of danger.

After everyone rolled out their sleeping bags, I remarked, "*Isn't this awesome?*" I wasn't being sarcastic. John, our 60-year old physical education teacher responded, "*Are you kidding me, my back is killing me on this pavement. This sucks!*" He was half joking and half serious. We all laughed and chatted under the stars before fading off to sleep.

The next morning, John commented, "*We've got to find another place to sleep or head back to Robb Field, since my back is in bad shape after sleeping here.*" A few of the others joined John in his sentiment. Attempting to keep things positive, I agreed and we packed up to vacate the "yard."

On our way to find some coffee, we happened to notice a couple sleeping in a parking lot behind a building. It was timely passing those two people sleeping on the hard pavement, just as a few on our team were complaining about our night on the yard of concrete. I said hello to the couple and we stopped to introduce ourselves.

The difference between our group and this couple was the reality that they sleep there every night. Their names were Eric and Michelle, and Eric was laying on a mat next to his wheelchair. When we stopped to hear their story, Eric shared about his chronic back pain and the difficulty of living on the streets in a wheel chair. Michelle and Eric's relationship was strictly platonic. She enjoyed helping him and he clearly appreciated the assistance.

We offered to pray for them and they were so grateful. Michelle was moved to tears as was Eric. After the prayer, Eric told us about a man by the name of Robert Laffoon, who provides breakfast burritos every Wednesday morning at the lifeguard house in Pacific Beach. We thanked him for the tip and hoped to see them there.

*(Front to back: Michelle, Will, Gumby,
Eric, Steve, Trevin & John)*

Gumby was so moved by Eric's pain and plight that he gave him his inflatable camping pad right there on the spot. Another team member sacrificed their pad for Michelle. The couple thanked us for the pads and the prayers as we turned to leave.

Our team walked in silence, clearly processing the unexpected exchange with Eric and Michelle. Finally, John piped up and made a confession. *"I feel like a selfish jerk! I've spent the better part of the morning complaining about one night on the pavement, when these two individuals have to live this way."* Two other team members admitted to feeling the same way.

It's worth considering how important our perspective is. Just when you begin to feel that life has dealt you an unfair shake, you meet someone who has it worse than you. Those moments serve as significant reminders of the principle that "our circumstance could always be worse." Giving thanks for what we do have, rather than focusing on what we lack is an important mindset to cultivate in life. Personally, living homeless two weeks out of the year has done wonders when it comes to me fostering a deeper sense of appreciation.

All six of us were reminded to count our many blessings as we made our way to the Pacific Beach boardwalk. Eric and Michelle had told us to be at the life guard stand before 8am, so we took their advice.

As we strolled up the meeting place, we noticed about 12 homeless individuals who had beat us to it. We stood around waiting with the rest of them and saw Eric wheeling his way over about five minutes after we'd arrived.

I was getting hungry listening to people around me talk about the coveted breakfast burritos. As we waited with great anticipation, Eric parked his wheelchair near our group and began telling us about his life as a sailor. He spoke of his great love for the sea and his desire to live on a sailboat. Eric's tales made for easy listening with the serene sound of seagulls and crashing waves to create atmosphere.

A hungry homeless crew continued to assemble and I began to wonder if Mr. Laffoon would bring enough warm burritos to go around. When the regular crew saw him peddling in our direction, the disorganized line quickly took form to establish order. Those who'd been waiting the longest were salivating at the front of the que. We waited our turn. When I was finally face-to-face with Robert, I introduced myself and thanked him for breakfast. He replied, *"It's great to meet you too, stick around so I can hear your story."* He handed me a warm foil wrapped breakfast burrito and I went and sat down near a homeless man that I wanted to speak with. After I visited with him, I returned to speak with Robert Laffoon.

We swapped stories and he mentioned battling addiction in his past. Robert said his faith in God and some grace-filled people at a local church were the catalyst he needed to turn his life around. I asked about the breakfast burritos which he delivered from a large basket mounted to his bike. He replied, *"The local church I attend pays for the ingredients. I'm responsible for cooking and delivery. I like it because it allowes me to serve others and to stay in touch with people who battle the same demons that nearly destroyed my life.*" After meeting Robert, we always made a point to be at the life guard stand in Pacific Beach on Wednesday mornings. After all, who would want to miss out on those tasty hot breakfast burritos?

(Steve & Robert Laffoon with his breakfast burritos)

After breakfast, the team rallied to discuss how everyone was holding up. John's ankle was causing him more pain and he needed to rest it. Everyone else seemed to be feeling physically and emotionally drained, yet willing to keep going. Gumby and Tom wanted a break from the riverbed area, so I invited Trevin to join me as I resumed my search there. As a Prince William County police officer back home, he was excited to explore the area he'd heard us share about.

We strategized and divided into teams for the day. Then we gave everyone some alone time to read, pray journal and relax. If you are an introvert, the trips can be draining since we are constantly surrounded by people. After about 90 minutes, we rallied and then walked toward Mariner's Point for the midday meal. Our plan was to split into the designated teams after lunch, when we dropped our packs back in the rental car.

When we arrived, Steve and I were thrilled to run into Candace. We'd met Candace on our second trip when we were stuck under the same park gazebo in the torrential downpour. We hadn't seen her since, so it was nice to catch up. She goes by the street name of Gypsy, but prefers her friends to call her Candace.

We inquired about Joaquin and she replied, "*He's well, and has been working hard on his dream to build custom bicycles.*" We were encouraged to hear that and then turned our attention to Candace. I asked, "*How have you been?*" The moment I asked the question, her eyes welled up with tears and she whispered, "*Not good.*" I invited her to tell us about it and she did.

Most of the team wandered over to meet Candace but when they noticed her sharing, they listened quietly. She confessed a great deal of difficulty related to the street life she'd chosen and desperately wanted God's help. She was vulnerable about a few specific accounts and then asked if the team would be willing to pray for her. My mom took the lead and placed her hand on Candace's back as she prayed. Candace said later how much she appreciated a maternal figure demonstrating that kind of love to her.

Our team rallied and circled up, with everyone joining hands. We began to lift up her concerns to God and ask Him to bring healing and restoration to her life. Some prayed for her provision and others for her protection. It was a moving experience.

By the time we said, "amen," Candace was in tears again and turned to embrace my mom. She took a moment to collect herself and then thanked us profusely for the time we'd taken to be present.

After praying, Candace asked if she could share a poem with us. We answered, "*Of course,*" so she did. It was a powerful poem she'd written, memorized and delivered as a rap. I was struck by her willingness to share so openly with our group. She commented, *"I'm never sure who I can trust on the streets. I recently prayed and asked God to send someone who might help. You all are an answer to my prayer, so thank you!"*

(Left to right: Gumby, Georgia, Candace, Audie, Will, Steve & Trevin)

We assured her that we were equally blessed and grateful that we had been able to catch up with her. She had to get going and gave us all hugs before departing.

After eating some lunch and praying with Candace, our team was ready to split up and resume the search. Steve had some pain in his knee, so he decided to remain in the Pacific Beach area, while Trevin joined my team. While Gumby and Tom didn't want to return to the riverbed, they did want to continue searching in the Mission Gorge area. The four of us boarded an Uber and headed straight for the Home Depot parking lot. I wasn't sure what our next move should be, but I was convinced that we needed to head back to that area.

Tom and Gumby decided to watch for Ed near the Denny's restaurant in Mission Gorge, after a waitress told us that she'd spotted him recently. I spent a little time prayerfully considering my next move, and decided to write Ed a letter. I figured that if Ed was in hiding, I could search for Israel and ask him to deliver it for me.

At that point, the manager showed up at our table. She was a heavyset woman who I guessed was in her mid-40s. Judging by her demeanor and the scowl on her face, she wasn't thrilled about three men loitering in a booth and only ordering coffee. She inquired, *"Is there anything else you boys need?"* Her body language with one hand on her hip seemed to be code for, *"Hit the road!"* I wondered how we might be able to encourage her.

I looked at her and asked, *"Would it be possible to get a piece of paper and a pen?"* Her facial response appeared to reflect a new level of annoyance with my question. I continued, *"You see, my best friend is homeless and we've been living on the streets this week in hopes of finding him. I want to write him a letter and let him know that he is loved."* At some point while listening to my reason for needing a pen and paper, her hardened expression melted away. Her entire mannerism changed when she understood the reason for our being there. Once again, our perspective matters. Making assumptions about people we don't know (and even the ones we do), often leads to serious misjudgments. As she stood beside our table, she became emotional and teared up. With a sudden sense of urgency, she said, *"I'll be right back!"*

She returned in a flash with paper, pens, and she'd even brought me an envelope. Then she added, *"Please let me know whatever you gentlemen need. I'll do what I can to help."* *"Wow! What just happened?"* I thought to myself. We transformed from boys to gentlemen in a matter of minutes once her perspective of us changed. I was inspired by her support and willingness to help.

I took a sip of my semi-cold coffee and attempted to look to God for inspiration regarding what to write. When I put the pen to paper, the words seemed to flow and I finished writing in a matter of minutes. I sealed the letter in the envelope she provided and headed out the door.

Trevin and I took the letter to search for Israel in the riverbed, while Gumby and Tom walked the streets of Mission Gorge.

Just as Trevin and I were preparing to plunge down into the riverbed, Tom and Gumby hustled over to the Home Depot parking lot and shouted, "*Wait a minute!*" We waited for the two of them to catch up. I figured they had a change of heart and decided to join us. I was wrong.

When they arrived, Gumby said, "*I feel uneasy about the two of you going down there today and believe we should pray first and ask God for direction.*" That wasn't a bad idea, so we joined hands and prayed right then and there. "*Lord, if it's unsafe for us to return to the riverbed today, please bring Israel to us, so we can deliver these letters directly to him without stepping in harm's way.*"

I'm not exaggerating when I tell you that immediately after we concluded our prayer, we looked up and saw someone on a bike headed in our direction. You guessed it! It was Israel and he rode his bike until arriving right in front of us. We must have said "*amen,*" just before he hit the brakes. I was encouraged by the instant answer to prayer, and decided to tell him about it.

"*Israel, we were just in the middle of praying and asked God if He might help us find you. We literally just muttered an 'amen' to the prayer as you peddled up. So, here you are my friend.*" I handed him the envelope and told him about the letter I'd written for Ed.

Israel responded, "*Awesome man, I'll leave Ed's letter with his stuff.*" He stayed and chatted with us a bit more about his life and thanked us again for the lunch we'd delivered. After a few more minutes of banter, he took the letter and peddled away. The four of us stood there amazed at what had just transpired. Trevin asked if I might still give him a brief tour in a different section of the riverbed. As a cop, he wanted to at least see the riverbed we'd spoken of and didn't want to feel as though he'd come all that way for nothing. I took him down a path on the opposite end of the parking lot so he could get a sense of the place. We met back up with Tom and Gumby later that afternoon so we could all catch an Uber to meet up with the other teams.

(Left to right: Gumby, Will & Israel at Home Depot lot)

We rendezvoused with Steve, John and the ladies at a meal back in Ocean Beach. It was nice to sit down and share a meal with friends. Everyone was fairly exhausted as we had been covering a lot of ground and going hard all day. When the meal ended, there was the matter of where to set up camp. We settled on spending the night back at Robb Field, since it was situated only a few blocks from the church. While we agreed on the place as a group, we couldn't agree as to where to actually bed down in the field. The fence line had worked well for us on the first night, but people wanted to scatter around the field. I didn't feel like squabbling over where to lay my bag, so I picked a spot in the middle of the baseball outfield and arranged my sleeping bag for the night. I'm not sure about the rest of the group, but I was out within a matter of minutes.

Anything can happen when you're living on the streets and sleeping under the stars. Just before 3 a.m. that night, a homeless man came striding right through the center of the field, where we were sleeping. He was quiet, yet made enough noise that I woke up when I heard him approaching. He turned in our direction and simply announced, "*The sprinklers go off in ten minutes.*" I was groggy but heard what he said. I turned to Steve and said, "*Do you think that guy knows what he's talking about?*" Steve responded, "*I don't know.*" With that, we both fell right back to sleep.

Like clockwork, approximately ten minutes later we all heard the unmistakable noise. A number of commercial grade sprinkler heads sprang from the ground like angry groundhogs. They immediately began dousing a large portion of the field. Trevin was the first victim. With cop-like reflexes, he shot out of his sleeping bag and relocated, escaping with only a partial spray. The rest of us were thrilled to see that there was only one casualty.

When the excitement passed, everyone tried to get back to sleep. What we failed to consider is the fact that most sprinkler systems are arranged in separate zones. As soon as the first set of heads disappeared in the ground, another set sprang up to saturate a different area.

Round two took Coach John by surprise. Unlike Trevin, he wasn't so quick to move. In defiance, John hollered out with his thick Long Island accent, "*I'm not moving!*" His resilience was short lived once his sleeping bag became completely drenched. It was clear that no one was safe and that every zone was going to eventually get soaked. Everyone packed up in a hurry, knowing that we didn't have much time. We also had no clue as to which zone would be next.

If only we'd heeded the homeless man's warning! Hindsight and regret made no difference, as we all moved to the dry dugout and began laughing about what had happened.

We spent our final days making new homeless friends and catching up with old ones. I'd left a contact phone number in my letter to Ed, and decided to leave the situation in God's hands for the remainder of the trip.

As had become a tradition, we usually treated a homeless person or two to dinner on our final evening. On that particular week, I called Tom's cell phone and invited my blind friend to dinner. We made reservations that Friday evening, at the old historic hotel restaurant in the town square of Old Town, San Diego. Tom seemed ecstatic to be our guest of honor. He accepted without hesitation. We met him in the square, close to the bench where Sandra and I found him panhandling on the previous trip.

We guided him to the restaurant and gave him the seat at the head of the table. We read him the menu, and placed his order. He selected a juicy ribeye with a few tasty sides. To wash his dinner down he requested a large glass of milk. If milk had been beer that night, Tom would have been too drunk to walk. Every time he emptied his milk glass (which seemed to be within seconds), he'd ask the waiter to bring him another. I've never seen a man drink so much milk.

Tom shared with us a bit of his backstory, and periodically asked more questions about our group and about Ed. He was a blessing to be with, and it was a wonderful way to conclude our week on the streets. Paul was kind enough to meet Tom after dinner to make sure that he made it back to his nest under the bridge. We said our goodbyes and offered a prayer for him before departing.

(Left to right: John, Georgia, Audie,
Will, Tom, Gumby, Tom & Steve)

We concluded the trip feeling encouraged. While we hadn't seen Ed, we had certainly made progress. I was hopeful that my hand-written note would be delivered to him. It was time to patiently wait on his response. Would Ed be willing to write back or to call? Time would tell.

Chapter 10
Whitey & Breakfast Burritos

While I shared many of the details of our fifth trip, I neglected to share about one memorable interaction. It took place on the same Wednesday morning that we sat at the life guard house waiting for breakfast burritos. Robert is scheduled to arrive at 8:30 a.m. each week, and our team arrived almost 30 minutes ahead of schedule. We waited patiently with the rest of the crowd, and struck up conversations with Eric, Michelle and others.

One man's arrival changed the entire atmosphere, although I'm not referring to Robert Laffoon, the burrito man. The man was probably about my age, although his years on the street made him appear older. He went by the street name of "Whitey" and he arrived mounted on a skateboard.

Whitey popped the back of his board using his right foot and caught the front with his hand. He clearly wasn't a boarding rookie, nor was he a stranger to the streets.

Whitey commanded a certain presence and seemed to know everyone. Eric greeted Whitey from his wheelchair and Whitey responded by berating him, using a number of derogatory terms.

Whitey was not a friendly character, although he was an obvious leader. He reminded me of a middle school bully who called all the shots on the playground and ruled with intimidation. The other homeless who were present acknowledged his authority as the alpha, and no one dared challenge him. He barked a few orders before taking his place near the front of the line.

Whitey wore his baseball cap to one side, had extra-long board shorts and looked like he'd never lost his middle school fashion sense. He barked out a few more snide remarks, each directed at different homeless individuals who were present. He was clearly letting everyone know who was boss.

I felt like I was watching a National Geographic special about wolves. The alpha dog entered the pack and his presence caused the other wolves to cower away and give him whatever he demanded.

Whitey didn't know the six of us, although my guess is that we were the only people that he didn't know. Our group was spread out amongst the other homeless, so it would have been difficult to know that we were all together. I could tell he was aware of our crew and kept an eye on us. However, he was reluctant to comment or acknowledge anyone on our team. Whitey was a wise wolf, observing the new members of the pack and waiting for the right moment to assert himself.

It was about that time, when Robert arrived via his bike, with a basket full of burritos. Trevin handed me a warm foil wrapped breakfast torpedo, and I decided that it was time to make my move.

Spying a strategic place to sit, I noticed an opening between Whitey and a younger man to his left. I quickly moved in that direction. I turned in the direction of the non-threatening young guy and asked, "*Is it alright if I sit here?*" I realized that Whitey could object, but before he was able to respond, the other guy said, "*Sure, man.*"

I dropped my backpack down and sat directly on it. It's more comfortable than the pavement. I noticed Whitey paying full attention to my every move as he unwrapped his burrito. I wasn't trying to be disrespectful or to annoy him, I simply wanted to meet the alpha in the crowd.

I decided to engage the younger guy on my left. Laying beside him was an acoustic guitar that clearly belonged to him and had its fair share of use. To his right, sat a tiny Chihuahua he called Ace. I introduced myself and discovered that his name was Chris. Chris yanked a can of Pringles out of his pack and was enjoying the chips and burrito combo, which he shared with the pooch. I asked him a bit about his life and how long he'd been living in San Diego.

It was obvious that Whitey was eavesdropping, and trying to gather some intel on me. I asked Chris, "*Have you been playing for long?*" motioning toward his guitar. "*Ever since middle school,*" he responded. Chris was only 20 years-old, so I figured he'd been playing for about eight years. He asked, "*Do you play?*" I replied, "*Not like you, I only know a few chords and mess around when I'm bored.*" With that, he handed me his guitar and I strummed a bit of the only song I could recall how to play, "*Free Falling*" by Tom Petty.

After a minute or two, when I reached the full extent of my guitar knowledge, I thanked Chris and handed it back to him. I didn't want to embarrass myself. At that point, I glanced in Whitey's direction and he was completely locked into our exchange.

Most of his skin was covered in tattoo ink which told a story. His face was leathery and baked to reveal countless hours in the sun. The worn wrinkled skin is common amongst the California homeless. Sunscreen isn't at the top of their shopping list, so skin cancer is a common problem and is often left untreated.

As I contemplated what to say, my mind went back to my training when I served on the staff of an organization known as Young Life. As a ministry that focuses on adolescents, I was expected to visit the high schools in my area and meet teenagers on their turf. This was an intimidating part of the job.

I recall a staff leader training me when I was new to Young Life. His name was Jerry Kasberg. Jerry was from Ohio and it was obvious by his enormous size, that he'd been an unstoppable force back in his college football days. He coached me concerning certain skills that are necessary when meeting intimidating kids. I recall him stressing the importance of remembering that almost every teenager wrestles with some level of insecurity. He said, "*Teenagers are usually thinking about themselves, not you, so don't worry about what others think when approaching them.*"

Jerry taught me to be observant of the way kids interact socially. One evening while we were standing on the floor of a basketball game played at Carlyle High School in Pennsylvania, Jerry gave me an assignment. He had me look up into the bleachers and try to pick out "the alpha" leader in each pack of students. Then he told me, "Take note of which kids demonstrate leadership. Those are '*key kids.*' If you can reach the key kids, you can reach the group.

I looked at Whitey and thought to myself, "He is the key kid on this turf and I'm sure he battles some level of insecurity." I asked God for wisdom and then turned to engage him. I turned into his direction and asked, "*How's it going, man?*" Whitey responded, "*It's all good.*" I pressed in deeper, "*Are you from this area?*" He said, "*No, but I've been here for years now, so this is home.*" He mentioned growing up on the East Coast. I told him that I was from the Washington, DC area, trying to establish some common ground.

Whitey continued, "*Yep, most of the homeless drift this way for the weather, if they're smart.*" According to the sheer numbers, he had it right. The homeless population living on the West Coast made them the leader in the United States. The numbers seem to be even greater in the beach towns.

Referring to his comment, I pried, "*So, is that what brought you here, the weather?*" "*No, I left after my marriage blew up.*" Perhaps going too far, I asked, "*What broke up your marriage?*" So as not to seem superior I added, "*I have a failed marriage as well.*" "*Are you a cop?*" Whitey asked, ignoring my question. "*No, I'm a pastor looking for my best friend who is homeless in this area. I'm just here for a week, and chose to live on the streets to increase my chance of finding him.*" He looked my way and said, "*That's cool, what's his name?*" I handed him one of the cards with Ed's photo and my contact information. He studied the image before responding.

(Left to right: Chris, Will & Whitey)

After a moment staring at the card, he shared with a bit more candor. "*I was an angry drunk, that's what broke up my marriage. I realized that I was a horrible dad to my kids, so I got out of the way for a better man.*" I asked him if he loved his kids, and as almost every dad would respond, he said, "*Of course I do! Hell, who doesn't love their kids?*"

I decided to press on further. "*When was the last time you spoke with them?*"

"*It's been years,*" Whitey replied. "*I don't believe my son wants to hear from me,*" he added. His tone grew somewhat emotional.

I decided that it might help to share vulnerably as well. I said, "*My dad was an alcoholic and he overdosed before my third birthday. I wish I could have known him, even though I've been told that he was far from being a model father. I actually believe that most every son and daughter desires to hear from their dad, especially one who is willing to admit his mistakes.*" Whitey took another bite of his burrito, and we sat in silence, both reflecting on the complexities of parenthood.

I wondered about Whitey's life story, with regard to his own parents. His gears were clearly turning, but I had no clue as to what he was thinking.

He broke the silence with a question, "*You want to know what has never let me down and has always been faithful to me in my life?*" "*Sure, tell me,*" I responded. I wasn't sure exactly what to expect, but I figured he would most likely say, "God," after hearing that I was a pastor. I was wrong.

Whitey paused before answering his own question, allowing the suspense to build. Then he proceeded, "*The one thing that has never let me down in my life is Meth!*" He continued sharing as though he was trying to make a sale to a potential client. "*When I'm tweaking, I can stay up all week, I don't need to eat, I feel incredible, and I don't do stupid things like I used to do when I was drunk!*"

In the middle of his pitch regarding the benefits of using Crystal Methamphetamine, he added, "*In fact, I can't think of a single negative side effect.*" At that point, his sidekick Chris interrupted, "*That's not true Whitey. Why, just last week you passed out high on Meth in the bushes in front of the library. You lost your wallet and woke up with nothing left.*" Whitey shook his head in disagreement and finished his presentation, "*Meth is the only thing I can really depend on in this life.*"

I sat between these two men, processing through Whitey's declaration. According to his statement, Meth was truly dependable and his primary drive in life. I wondered if Ed would say the exact same thing. Perhaps Ed was sitting back in Mission Gorge making the same speech to Israel and Juan? I had no clue, but his remarks caused me to wonder.

I was still struck by Whitey's stated reason for abandoning his son, "*to make way for a better man.*" I also sat considering the power of the drug that seemed to be influencing Whitey's life, as well as Ed's. I'd heard firsthand the toll it took on Whitey's relationships and speculated that it was the catalyst for causing Ed to abandon his. How do you help an addict break free from such a powerful substance, and reconsider their choices? I sat processing our interaction, as I crumpled up my empty aluminum burrito shell.

On several occasions throughout this homeless journey, I've run into situations when I'm uncertain about what to do or say. This was one of those times when I was speechless. I offered up a brief, yet heartfelt prayer to God. Silently in my mind I prayed, "*God, is there something I can say or do, to convey to Whitey that he is loved?*"

I've never actually heard the audible voice of God. However, when I pray like that, I usually have a thought or two come to mind, that I believe is inspired by Him. The thought that came to mind in that instance was, "*Offer to pray for his son.*" I went ahead and asked, "*Whitey, would you like to pray for your son?*" He immediately responded in the affirmative, "*Yes!*" I asked, "*What's his name?*" "*James,*" he replied.

His entire demeanor changed as he removed his baseball cap that had been positioned sideways on his head. I cleared my throat and began to pray for James. I poured out my heart in prayer for Whitey and his son. I asked God if He might grant them a fresh start and reconcile their broken relationship. I pleaded with God to give Whitey the confidence he needed to be the dad he wanted to be, before alcohol left him defeated. When I concluded the prayer for my new friend, I looked in his direction. It was clear that God had been at work on that hardened street leader's heart. Whitey was wiping tears from his eyes. He thanked me for praying and softened up for the remainder of our conversation.

A few moments later, he jumped up, dropped his skateboard on the ground, and prepared to jet. Before rolling away he turned to me and said, "*Good luck on that search for your friend.*" I replied, "*Thanks Whitey. I hope you're able to reconnect with your son.*" With that he mounted his board, and rolled away.

My conversation with Whitey made an impression on me. When I first laid eyes on him and saw how he treated others like Eric, I wasn't too fond of the guy. He came across as cruel and intimidating. Covered with ink and barking commands at those around him, he reminded me of the type of character you might see playing a hardened street thug in a movie. I suppose he looked that way because the actors were trying to portray someone just like Whitey. However, none of the movies I'd seen ever seem to reveal the soft side that was evident when Whitey dared to open up. Everybody has one - some just do a better job of keeping them buried under layers of scar tissue and pain.

I'd only been privy to a partial glimpse of Whitey's story, and I left feeling burdened for him. I was amazed at how quickly he transformed from a gruff, angry addict, into a soft vulnerable friend. All I did was take a genuine interest in his life. It wasn't rocket science, but it did force me to move out of my comfort zone. It would have been much easier to have sat off on the side, stayed out his way, enjoyed my burrito and hit the road. But then I would have missed the blessing of meeting Whitey.

I wasn't completely sure about the reason for his abrupt departure after our prayer. I suspect that showing emotion and tearing up is not part of his everyday routine. I prayed that perhaps he departed in a hurry to find a quiet place, where he could call his son. I wondered if God had sent any individuals into Ed's path, to ask him about his life. On both counts, with Ed and Whitey, I decided to hold onto hope and continue asking God for a miracle.

Chapter 11
Fever on the Trail

Georgia was ecstatic! She spoke with me several times after our fifth trip and expressed her desire to return to San Diego. However, this time she had no intention of sleeping back in La Jolla. As kind as Beth had been to open her home to my mother and Georgia, she wanted to have the full experience. I let her know that if she was willing and ready, understanding the risks associated with living on the street, then she was welcome. She thanked me and began making plans.

Shortly after my conversation with Georgia, my 26-year old daughter Courtney, phoned me. "*Dad, I want to join you on the trip to San Diego.*" I couldn't say, "*We don't allow females on the trip for safety reasons,*" because I'd just said "*Yes*" to Georgia. "*Alright, but you'll have to be on my team!*" I responded. As a protective dad, I figured that I could watch out for her if she was close by my side.

I've had a number of interested individuals call me to inquire about joining us for a homeless excursion. They usually ask something like, "*Can you assure me that living on the streets of San Diego will be completely safe?*" How would you answer that question? Just because we've never been harmed on the streets, is not a guarantee that we never will be. I try to convey that fact, responding, "*We live on the streets amongst 13,000 other homeless men and women. We can't possibly be certain that no harm will come to us. It's a risk you must be willing to take if you want to join the team.*" In most cases, that response is all they needed to hear to decide against the trip. My intent is not to turn people away, but to be honest and open about the potential danger of living on the streets of any city.

When we finished assembling our sixth team, we took the largest group to date. In addition to the two ladies, we had four new male recruits: Ben Atkinson, Jason Bruce, Connor Sarant and Evan Reyle. I was also thrilled to have two returning veterans: Steve Bowman and Dave

(Gumby) Houston, back for another round. While I was thrilled to have nine people on board, I wondered where we might sleep such a large crew.

We arrived on Sunday evening, February 12, 2017. Eight of us rallied at the airport for a group photo, before heading to our hotel. Since Georgia was originally from San Diego, she'd flown out early to catch up with some old friends.

With an able-bodied search party of nine volunteers, we divided into three teams. Since three of us had one to five trips under our belts, it made it easy for me to designate team leaders. Steve led our two millennials: Connor and Evan. Gumby's team included Ben and Georgia, while I took my daughter Courtney and Jason. Everyone seemed eager and ready to roll. The atmosphere was positive and devoid of fear. I was encouraged and thought, "*Perhaps this will actually be the trip when we come face-to-face with my old friend Ed.*"

(Left to right, front row: Courtney, Evan, Connor & Will.
Back row, left to right: Steve, Gumby, Jason & Ben)

We split up early Monday morning and directed all three groups toward the downtown area near Padre Stadium. We unintentionally developed certain trip rituals that we'd grown accustomed to. Similar to concluding each week by taking a homeless person or two out for dinner, we liked to take the rookies to one of the most intimidating areas on the first morning of the week. This served as an orientation of sorts, allowing everyone to catch a glimpse of how large and diverse the homeless population truly is. They appeared wide-eyed, and perhaps a bit frightened.

I've had trip participants share with me after the fact, their thoughts when walking through that part of town on day one. In the middle of the week Connor confessed, *"When I saw all those intimidating people standing around the train stop and scattered around Father Joe's Village, I thought, 'I want to go home!' I wasn't so sure I'd make it through the week."* My belief was that if I exposed the team to one of the most frightening areas in San Diego on day one, it would only get better from there.

The teams went their separate ways from that point on. I'd met with Steve and Gumby before the trip to brainstorm strategy and make sure that we as leaders, were on the same page. Each knew where they wanted to search, and where to meet up each evening for dinner. We'd done our homework and discovered which churches hosted meals on each night of the week.

I led my team just up the street from St. Vinney's. I wanted to explore the county facility there, known as the Neil Good Day Center. I'd discovered the center on my very first trip, and someone mentioned seeing Ed at the center.

We entered from the main entrance off of 17th Street and Imperial Avenue. The center provides a wonderful service to those living on the streets. A homeless individual can receive their mail, do laundry, take showers, rest, and even watch TV while they are there. Just as I entered the indoor portion of the facility with Jason and Courtney, a large naked Latino man poked his face around the corner of the bathroom. He timed his exhibition just as we were walking past the open bathroom door. It seemed like a good idea to keep moving.

Knowing that no one would give me information concerning Ed due to HIPPA laws, I approached the mail counter and said, *"I'm here to check for mail."* The woman behind the counter said, "Name please?" I replied, *"Ed Pelzner."* Without asking for identification, she said, *"Just a minute,"* and turned to check the mail bins. I got excited, wondering what leads I might receive. She returned to the counter and said, *"Sorry honey, nothing today."* I wasn't sure if that meant Ed had already checked it, or if he never receives mail. *"Oh well, it was worth asking,"* I thought.

We decided to leave the downtown area and head in the direction of Balboa Park. A large number of homeless congregate in the parks, so it seemed like a good place to get some potential leads and make some new homeless friends in the process.

As we walked down the busy sidewalk, populated by at least 50 homeless individuals, I noticed a police cruiser parked on the side of the road. I decided that it was worth showing them Ed's picture and asking if they might be willing to run his name through their system. After all, we'd been helped before by police officers, why not ask these two officers? Surprisingly, one of the cops said, *"Yes, I've seen Ed and I spoke with his parents when they were here about six months ago."* Go figure, what are the odds that I run into the same cop who spoke with Mr. and Mrs. Pelzner half a year earlier? I was thrilled about the connection and asked if he would be willing to check his database for any current news regarding Ed's whereabouts.

The officer said, *"Sure, give me his name and date of birth,"* and I did. He was kind enough to check his computer screen and punched in Ed's details. He looked at me and asked, *"Can you call Ed's parents?"* I got nervous and asked, *"Why?"* He advised me, *"Call them and ask them to file a missing person's report regarding Ed with the San Diego Police Department. They may be able to give his parents some useful information."* With that, he gave me the phone number they needed to file a report.

(San Diego police officers who assisted our search)

I wasted no time and had Ed's mom on the phone minutes later. I explained to her exactly what the officer told me, and Ed's mom wrote down the number. She agreed to follow up and proceeded to ask me what they knew? I responded, "*They haven't told me anything specifically, but apparently if you call, you may discover something.*" With that, she thanked me and hung up to work on the potential lead.

Our team continued on to Balboa Park. Courtney and Jason had loads of questions about past trips. We met a few homeless along the walk, and scoured Balboa Park for potential leads. After searching the park and speaking with anyone willing to talk with us, we decided to Uber to Mission Gorge. They'd heard me share stories of our previous trip and the pizza party with drug dealers, but wanted to see for themselves. I was curious as well, regarding what the cops had seen on their computer screen and who we might find back in the riverbed of Mission Gorge.

(Left to right: Courtney, Jason & Will)

We took an Uber to Mission Gorge to resume the search where it had concluded four months earlier. I showed Courtney and Jason the drains where Ed's sister had first met Israel, before we then made our way to the Home Depot parking lot. We prayed a prayer for protection before plunging through the fence back into the riverbed area. My heart was racing, thinking of the threats I'd received on the previous trip. We came right up to the gate, but there was no sign of Juan or Israel. I hollered, "*Hello*" before moving forward through the gate.

A young homeless man who I'd never seen before, came out and inquired, "*Can I help you?*" I asked him if Israel or Juan were around. He responded, "*Who are they?*" I clarified, "*The guys who lived here when I was here back in October.*" He laughed, "*Dude, a lot can change on the street in just one month, let alone four months.*" I stood there, digesting what we'd just been told.

"*What do we do now?*" I wondered. I asked if he'd heard of Ed or "*Fast Eddie.*" He responded, "*Oh yeah, I know Fast Eddie.*" With that, he welcomed us back into his makeshift home. He was not living alone. A young woman was sitting on the floor of the shelter when we arrived. The place consisted of some cardboard boxes, a tarp, and a few boards held in place with two large branches. The ground was covered with old mildew-stained carpet fragments, which provided a buffer from the dirt. They welcomed us to sit down, so we did. We were anxious to hear more about "*Fast Eddie.*" When I sat on the carpet, I noticed a stench in the air and fruit flies that rose from the floor the moment we sat down.

I took the lead in the conversation and began asking about Fast Eddie. The woman, who went by the street name of Butterfly, responded to my inquiry. "*He'll be so glad to know that you're here! He's been going through such a difficult time.*" I wondered what difficult situation he'd been facing and got excited when Butterfly told us that he'd be happy to see us. Then she added, "*He's been fighting with his parents lately and they refuse to speak with him. He's battling depression, if you ask me.*" At that point it occurred to me that we were talking about two different "*Fast Eddies,*" unless of course, he'd lied to them about his parents. I decided to inquire about his approximate age and height. Butterfly replied, "*He is about five feet, seven inches, in his mid-twenties.*" Apparently, the nickname 'Fast Eddie' belonged to Paul Newman in the movie *The Hustler*, as well as my friend Ed Pelzner, and some complete stranger in his mid-twenties.

I thanked them for their willingness to try and help. My daughter Courtney suggested that we pray for their friend Eddie, before leaving, so we did. As we exited that portion of the riverbed, I was trying to get my head around the fact that the entire group who occupied that space only months earlier, had changed hands. Where had Juan and Israel relocated and what were the circumstances of their eviction? I'd been looking forward to asking Israel how Ed responded when he gave him my letter. I assumed the search would resume where it ended. Instead, it appeared that the trail had gone cold.

We wandered around the area, hoping for a clue. That's when we ran into Jose. Jose is an older Latino gentleman from Mexico. He has done construction work his entire life. You can usually find Jose standing in front of the Home Depot parking lot, soliciting work. Gumby, Tom and I met him on our previous trip. It was refreshing to see a familiar face. I asked him what had happened to the people who had been living in the riverbed on my previous trip. He replied, "*The police showed up in late December and raided that area. There'd been too many complaints about it getting dangerous, so they cleaned the entire place out and arrested everyone who wasn't fast enough to escape!*" He added, "*They do that from time to time.*" I wondered where Ed had been during the raid. Would his parents find out after calling the number I gave them? I hoped to hear back from them soon.

I asked Jose how he'd been doing and decided to shift the focus onto him. He seemed to appreciate the question and was in no hurry when it came to answering. One of the things I love about the San Diego trips is not feeling rushed. I have no meetings to attend or deadlines to keep. We know when lunch and dinner are served, but apart from that, we're free to focus on people without rushing everywhere.

Jose told us about his life and thanked me for praying with him on my previous trip. After sharing in detail about of his life and family, Jose asked, "*How would you three like to see my home?*" I'd never seen his home, but was aware that when a homeless friend offers to show you where they camp, it's a big deal. The invitation is a sign that they trust you. I responded on behalf of our team, "*We'd be honored to see your home, Jose.*"

He replied, "*Great, let's go!*" He immediately spun around and began walking on a trail which led us back into a different area of the riverbed. We dropped down into unchartered territory, and Jose commented, "*It's not far from here.*"

As we approached Jose's casa, he leaned toward me and whispered, "*I want to play a joke on your daughter, so go along with it. I'm going to scare her with the 'oso' back in my tent.*" The word 'oso' is Spanish for bear. I played along as Jose stopped and became very serious and animated. He looked directly at Jason and Courtney and warned, "*I have a* pet oso (bear) who lives in my tent and he is very, very dangerous." He went on about how he'd tamed the bear, but warned that it may still try to bite. I wondered if he was referring to a dog that looked like a bear, curious to see what Jose was actually preparing to pull from his tent. He finished his attempt at building suspense until we arrived at the edge of his small red tent. Jose lived about twenty yards down a trail off of San Diego Mission Road. His tent was situated behind a patch of tall bamboo trees, with a gentle creek on the opposite side. He seemed proud to show us his home.

Jose said, "Wait right here and remain very still. Any sudden moves may cause my oso to attack." He reached into his tent to extract the "bear." And there it was... an amusement park-sized, gigantic, white stuffed bear. He began laughing and wanted Courtney to give his bear an 'abrazo' (hug), which she was happy to do. We all laughed and thanked Jose for sharing his home and his pet oso with us.

(Left to right: Courtney, Oso & Jose)

We were entertained by his warm welcoming spirit. Jose offered us some hard candy from his tent. He was a true host. We thanked him again and took a few minutes to pray with him before resuming our search. We decided to follow the unfamiliar trail farther back into the riverbed to explore new territory.

We ran into some tall bush that served as camouflage for another homeless campsite. Although we couldn't see into the makeshift tent, constructed with tarps, cardboard and sticks, the occupants must have heard us outside their dwelling, because one of them hollered out, "*Are you here to buy product?*" "*No, I'm looking for a homeless friend of mine by the name of Ed.*" The rapid response back was, "*If you're not here to make a purchase, then get the hell out!*" It was his way of saying, "*No loitering,*" I suppose.

The words were not spoken directly to us; rather, they were shouted from deep inside a campsite, hidden by extremely thick brush or bush. We heeded their advice and turned our search party around. As we backtracked, we passed by Jose's tent again, and said one more "*good-bye.*" We each stopped to give him an 'abrazo,' (hug) before heading out of the riverbed area.

When all of our leads had been exhausted, we decided to head toward Old Town. We caught an Uber in that direction and decided to search the historic Old Town area for fresh information. Upon reaching the town square, I took a quick bathroom break. When I emerged, I didn't see Jason. I asked Courtney, "*Where did Jason go?*" She replied, "*He's helping Tom.*" "*Tom my blind friend?*" I inquired. "*Yes, dad,*" she responded, "*We'd both seen him in the video you made on YouTube, featuring Tom. Not to mention, he's in his 80s and blind, which made him easy to spot.*" Sure enough, Tom and Jason were just coming around the building at the end of the courtyard. We walked over to greet them.

Tom shared with us that he'd just been released from a hospital downtown, where they'd operated on his toe. A taxi had been paid to drop him off in Old Town, and he was trying to find his way with a wounded foot. That's when Jason and Courtney spotted him. Apparently, the timing of our arrival had been perfect, since Tom added, *"I'm so thankful y'all showed up when you did. I wasn't exactly sure where that taxi driver had dropped me off, he was in such a hurry to leave."* Jason noticed a blind man struggling on the side of the road, then he and Courtney quickly realized that it was Tom. We helped him make his way across the street to the light rail station, once he told us that he needed to get on the bus to Pacific Beach. We got him situated on the right bus and let him know that we'd be at the Pacific Beach dinner later that evening. He thanked us and said, *"I hope to see you there."*

(Left to right: Courtney, Tom, Jason & Will)

Later that evening at the meal, we spotted Tom and Paul. I spent the meal catching up with Paul, while Courtney thought the world of Tom and stayed by his side. She helped him with his food and learned more about his life.

My conversation with Paul was enlightening. He shared the back-story of how Tom ended up in the hospital. Apparently one week earlier,

Tom had been losing feeling in his right foot. During that time, he accidentally dropped a heavy object on his foot, which crushed his large toe. Unable to feel the pain, he continued walking on it until it became severely infected. Paul realized the seriousness of Tom's situation when he was helping Tom change his socks. Paul commented, *"Tom doesn't care for doctors, although I was able to convince him to see one."*

Paul actually told Tom that they were headed to the library, then pulled a fast one and detoured to the hospital before Tom realized what was happening. Sure enough, the doctors admitted Tom and had to operate on his infected foot to save the badly damaged appendage. After spending five days in the hospital to recover from the operation, the medical staff determined that Tom was ready to be discharged. The hospital gave Tom the medicine and instructions to care for the toe that was on the mend, then called him a cab and sent him on his way. We located him just after he'd been delivered to the street corner in Old Town.

(Left to right back: Connor, Paul, Gumby, Will & Steve
Left to right front: Courtney & Tom)

Even with Tom's blindness, foot surgery and homeless condition, he remained positive and selfless, asking me for an update concerning Ed. I feel blessed to know Tom and Paul. Paul expressed his appreciation for being there to help Tom make it to the light rail. I believe that was God's doing, since we prayed before getting in the Uber and felt that we should head for Old Town. Go figure.

After dinner, our team volunteered to help clean up at the church. A kind man by the name of John Jay Owens, introduced himself to me and told me that he is the custodial worker for two separate churches on the same street. Someone on our team told him what we were doing and he felt compelled to make an offer. *"If your group would like to take a break off the streets for the night, you're welcome to crash on the gym floor of the church once I lock up. Besides, there is rain in the forecast tonight."* We were grateful for a safe, dry place to sleep, and accepted his thoughtful offer. I'd been wondering where to park nine bodies that were in dire need of rest, and this came as an answer to prayer.

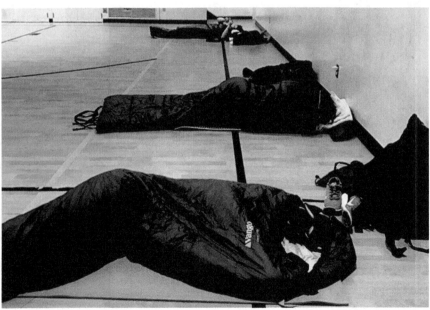

(Sleeping on the gymnasium floor of the church)

The night felt long and the floor was hard, but no one complained. I felt a head cold coming on and wasn't excited about another twelve-mile hike the following day. Moving from Pacific Beach to Ocean Beach and then toward Mission Gorge was no minor stroll. Our groups legged it and racked up between ten to fifteen miles per day. However, when we needed to get somewhere fast or far, we utilized Uber.

When morning arrived, we made our way to a local coffee shop in Pacific Beach looking for a cup of Joe. We used the early hours to journal, read and relax before hitting the pavement. When you meet countless individuals, who pour out their life stories and ask for prayer and help, it begins to take a toll. It's natural to feel drained at the end of each day. To combat that, we intentionally start each day looking to God for inspiration. Although we never have a clue what each day may hold, I'm confident that God does, so I attempt to encourage the team to focus on Him and not me.

(Left to right: Courtney, Georgia, Jason,
Gumby, Connor, Evan, Ben & Steve)

Our group was growing hungry. We circled up, prayed, and then walked close to four miles south towards the 11:30 a.m. meal at Mariner's Point. Everyone chatted as we walked and spirits were high.

(Route from Pacific Beach to Mariner's Point,
Image courtesy of Google Maps)

There were loads of homeless friends lined up and ready to eat. Our team joined the crowd. However, I lost my appetite and used the mealtime to rest. I laid down on the green grass, hoping the break would give me a second wind. I'd never been sick on the streets before, but I was feeling worse by the minute. Where do the homeless go when they have a bad cold or fever? I wondered how many times Ed had been ill since his journey on the streets began. He'd been homeless for two and a half years at that point, and I was curious how he managed situations like that.

When everyone finished eating, Courtney roused me from a nap. My daughter knew it wasn't like me to sleep at midday, especially while leading a trip. She asked if I was alright and I told her I was fine. I stood up and shrugged it off, praying that God would give me the energy I needed to make it through day two. I had a quick team leader meeting before we all split up, to find out where Steve and Gumby each planned to take their teams.

My team settled on Hancock Street, where Ed used to run his business. The afternoon was a bit of a blur for me. I allowed Courtney and Jason to do the majority of the talking and praying with those we met. I was spent and just tried to make it to dinner without having to rest. I was thrilled when 5:30 p.m. finally came around. We rendezvoused at the Methodist Church in Pacific Beach, where a crowd of hungry homeless was congregating.

I saw a familiar face while I waited on the lawn in front of the church. It was our pal Whitey and he'd apparently traded his skateboard out for a beach cruiser. Gumby approached him to say hello while I waited for the two to finish chatting. I didn't want him to feel outnumbered, as I recalled our conversation from the morning when we ate breakfast burritos. Whitey remained perched on his bike in front of the church, never making a pass through the buffet line. I noticed one of his underlings brought him a plate piled high with food. I approached him as he began to consume his meal, right there on his bike.

"*How have you been Whitey?*" His gaze darted my direction. I could tell by the confused look in his eyes, he was trying to figure out how he knew me. I reminded him, "*We met four months ago on the boardwalk at the burrito breakfast. We talked about your son and prayed for him.*" "*Oh yeah, I remember now,*" he replied as he nodded.

169

(Left to right: Gumby & Whitey)

I continued, "*I went home and asked my entire church to begin pray-ing for you.*" "*You did?*" he asked in shock. "*Yep, and I was hoping I'd run into you this week. How have those burritos been treating you?*" I asked, trying to make small talk and lighten the mood. He told me that he'd been banned from the boardwalk by the police, and was unable to show his face there anymore. I let him know that I'd continue praying for him, as well as for his son James. He thanked me, clearly not used to that sort of interaction. We chatted for a bit more before I left to connect with the rest of our team.

After the meal, we headed north toward La Jolla. Georgia had spo-ken with Beth, the kind woman who'd allowed my mom and her to sleep at her home on the previous trip. She invited Georgia to bring our entire team of nine to sleep in her backyard. Of course, I inquired if Beth's yard was actually grass or another concrete slab. Georgia assured me that I wouldn't be disappointed. I wasn't complaining, I simply wanted to know what to expect. Realistic expectations have a lot to do with disappointment. Steve and I had never gone as far north as La Jolla. I hoped we might discover something new. We didn't realize until the Uber dropped us off, that La Jolla didn't have a very large homeless community. In fact, we didn't even see one. Every home we passed as we walked through town was beautiful and each was surrounded by its own well-manicured lawn. The yard we were invited to sleep in was no exception. We used Google maps to navigate our way. While Google showed us the distance we had to hike to arrive at Beth's home, it didn't reveal the fact that it was situated at the top of a very steep hill, three miles from the city center.

Apparently, their neighborhood wasn't accustomed to seeing hikers marching through the streets. I suppose the sight of nine people dressed in homeless-style attire walking in a pack and laughing was enough to create a stir. One, if not more neighbors called the cops. By the time we finally reached the top of the hill outside of Beth's home, we had a police helicopter circling above with a spot light shining directly on us.

Georgia called Beth to let her know we'd arrived and to make her aware of the helicopter circling above. She said, *"I'm sorry, I'll call the police now to let them know you all are here by invitation."* It was kind of her to allow all nine of us to sleep in her backyard. Everyone scattered around her swimming pool, setting up camp around the artificial turf. Next to the pool there sat a large cabana, equipped with its own bathroom which Beth said that our team could share. A bathroom in close proximity can make a significant difference when you're camping on the streets.

(Group sleeping in backyard, Courtney on the pool deck)

We'd never camped in an elevated area, situated so high above sea level. The noticeable difference didn't come until we woke up the following morning. We were surrounded by a thick fog-like cloud, which soaked our sleeping bags with dew. It was not the way you want to wake up if you're already feeling sick. I woke with a sore throat and pounding headache. I attempted to shrug it off. We stuffed our wet sleeping bags into their sacks and were quick to order a couple Uber cars back to Pacific Beach.

We rendezvoused in front of a coffee shop with picnic tables, making use of their bathroom. We chatted with a few familiar homeless friends, who had the same idea. We ran into our wheelchair bound friend Eric, from the previous trip. He turned to Gumby and said, "*Hey man, I still use the camping pad you gave me every night, and ever since y'all prayed for me my back has been better.*" He was grateful and brought us up to speed on the details of his life. Michelle was no longer traveling with him, but he said that she was doing well. Eric was excited to meet our new team members and share his dream to live at sea.

(Left to right: Connor, Evan and Cheryl)

Connor and Evan invited a kind woman by the name of Cheryl to sit with them. In addition to sharing the details of her life, she attempted to teach them a clapping game. It never caught on but was amusing to watch.

I appreciated the relief that the hot tea provided on my throat, although it didn't take the pain away for long. I was feeling sicker as the day went on, but didn't want to let my team down. Everyone broke into their teams and scattered as usual, and within one hour, Gumby called me to share a tip.

His team spoke with a police officer, who mentioned finding Ed on the street late one night and driving him to a mental health facility. He added, "*I'm not so sure when that was exactly, but I remember that Ed was clearly disoriented.*" He mentioned that it was cold out and that Ed was getting around in bare feet, wearing nothing but a pair of board shorts. The officer was worried about him and was successful getting him checked into a warm facility.

I called Ed's parents to find out if they'd heard back from the San Diego Police Department. Mrs. Pelzner said that she'd received a call from a kind police officer who said, "*We know where Ed is but all we can tell you is that he's in a good place.*" Taking into account what the other officer shared with Gumby, we assumed that Ed was still in treatment. Due to HIPPA privacy laws, the police couldn't divulge his whereabouts, but at least they could confirm that he was in a 'good place.' They also added that Ed was not in prison, since prison records are public.

I was grateful to get the update about Ed from a reliable source, which also meant that the remainder of our week no longer needed to be a frantic search. We decided to focus the rest of the week on loving homeless friends and trusting God's leading.

After the Wednesday night dinner in Pacific Beach, our custodial friend John Jay Owens, invited us to crash at his church. I was glad we took him up on his offer, due to my physical condition. John Jay asked our group to relocate from the gymnasium to a classroom in the basement. This kept us from being visible to any church visitors who may not have been as welcoming as John Jay.

(John Jay Owens reading us a poem he wrote)

On Thursday morning, I woke up with chills and a fever of 103 degrees. As soon as I sat up, I put my head right back down and acknowledged that the teams would have to press on without me. As much as I hated to admit it, I didn't have the energy to join them.

I sent Courtney with Steve's team and Jason with Gumby. While they were gone, I spent the day resting, curled up in my sleeping bag on the basement floor. The room had a cold cement tile surface that I laid on. While the tile may have been less than comfortable, the cool basement temperature provided some relief. Steve made sure that John Jay was aware of my presence. I was grateful to him for making the church floor an option. I can't imagine what my day would have been like, if I'd been forced to spend it recovering on the ground in a park somewhere.

My mind drifted back to considering what the homeless must suffer when they get sick. I wondered again how many times Ed had been sick over the last two and a half years. Who was there for him? Without a warm bed or anyone to take care of you, it would be exponentially worse.

As I laid on the floor hoping for a rapid recovery, I began to feel frustrated by the reality that I wasn't able to join our team. I asked God, "*Why have you allowed me to be sick, when I'm needed by our team?*" I managed to drift back to sleep and slept until the group returned, later that evening. Everyone returned in high spirits, and began retelling the accounts of their day. I eavesdropped on the conversations while I remained tucked in my bag. I fell back to sleep, but woke on and off all night long. My body alternated between shaking with cold chills, to feeling as though my skin was burning up. Gumby heard me making noise and felt my forehead. "*Dude, you are burning up and covered in sweat!*" He selflessly left to find an all-night drugstore to purchase some Nyquil. Courtney was also a comfort, checking up on me throughout the night.

When I woke the next morning, I was not 100%, but I was on the mend. It was clear that my fever broke and I was ready to finally emerge from the church basement. I reunited with my team and realized that my absence for a day had been for the better. Not only was I able to get some much-needed rest, my absence allowed others to step up and truly lead in my stead. Everyone on the trip was more than capable and the stories from the previous day were confirmation of that fact. I had an answer to my prayer from the previous day. God knew what He was doing. He happens to have a knack for taking something we view as negative and using it for the good. Nothing has to go to waste if we remain teachable.

While the two teams had been out caring for the homeless on the previous day, they found out about a meal in Presidio Park. We decided to make that our final location for dinner on the streets. We arrived at the park, just as the sun was setting. We came to find out that the Thursday evening meal was hosted by Hope Christian Fellowship Church located in Ramona, California, 34 miles away. They'd been serving the homeless faithfully in Presidio Park every Thursday night for 21 years.

(Left to right: Victor & Evan)

The volunteers from the church strung up some Christmas lights and two of their people began playing the guitar and singing. The songs were from an old-style worship genre, and I'm not so sure that the homeless were familiar. The live music was followed by a pastor preaching to the crowd about salvation. He challenged them to consider what it might take to get off the streets. I was curious what some of my street-hardened friends thought as they listened. It didn't seem to matter what anyone thought, since it was a captive audience. Whether or not anyone was moved by the presentation, you had to sit through it if you wanted to get a plate of food. I wondered how many would stay, if the service took place voluntarily on the backend of the meal?

We made our rounds that evening, visiting with friends like Tom and others who we'd met throughout the week and on previous trips. Once the sun had set, the temperature dropped significantly. Despite the cold, our group had clearly bonded with each other as well as with friends from San Diego. It was a memorable evening together for our last night living on the street.

(Left to right: Steve, Connor, Ben, Barb & Georgia)

Our trip ended abruptly that Friday, without the delight of treating a few of our street friends to dinner. There was a severe storm advisory that threatened everyone's travel plans. According to the airlines, you needed to either book a flight out that day or be stuck in San Diego until Sunday or Monday.

After receiving the news, everyone grabbed their packs and headed straight for the San Diego International Airport. Everyone did their best to re-book earlier flights in a hurry to avoid being stranded. The place was packed with people desperately trying to leave town before the storm hit.

(Left to right: Steve, Will, Connor, Courtney,
Ben, Evan, Jason, Georgia & Gumby)

It was a privilege hunting for my friend Ed with this amazing group of people! Steve and I began to recognize the impact that the trips were having in our hearts and lives, including the bonds formed between the team members. Being part of such a unique experience, and facing adversity together, had become a life-changing adventure. Not to mention the added humor and tears shared throughout the journey.

Despite receiving the news that Ed was in a 'good place,' I didn't believe that it was time to call it quits. I must confess that at the conclusion of trip six, I was unsure how to carry on the search without more intel. What I wasn't aware of, was that I was about to receive a phone call that would change everything. A woman named Ruth was soon to provide just the intel that I'd been waiting for.

Chapter 12
Aloha Ed

My phone rang one evening in late June, just as our family was sitting down to dinner. I ignored the call until the same person called a second time, immediately following their first attempt. I picked up my phone to see if I recognized the number. I realized that the call was directed to my San Diego Google phone number. I'd set up that number specifically to receive information concerning Ed's whereabouts and had it printed on the cards that we distributed during each trip. This seemed like a smart idea, as an alternative to giving every homeless person we met in San Diego my actual phone number.

I immediately took the call and found myself speaking with a stranger. It was a woman's voice and she began by asking me a question. *"Is this the Will Cravens who's been looking for homeless Ed Pelzner?"* I replied, *"Yes, it is. How can I help you?"* Then she announced, *"I found your friend Ed."* It took a minute for her words to register. Understanding what she said, I hoped this wasn't a bad joke or another mistaken identity as we experienced with 20-year old, Fast Eddie.

She continued, *"I'm actually a social worker and my name is Ruth. I had a run in with your friend Ed that wasn't positive."* As I listened, I was trying to understand how Ruth's encounter with Ed transpired if he was in a 'good place?' I assumed that perhaps Ruth worked at a treatment facility where Ed resided. I stopped trying to guess and tuned in to what she had to share.

Ruth went on to tell me that she had an exchange with Ed in the middle of the road in which he stood directly in front of her moving car. When she stopped to ask him what the problem was, Ed's temper got the better of him and it evolved into a heated altercation. She got back in her vehicle and drove away. She noticed in her rearview mirror that he did the exact same thing to the car behind her, so Ruth decided to take action. She pulled her car over and called the police.

When the officers arrived to deal with the situation, Ruth brought them up to speed regarding what she had witnessed. The policemen confronted Ed, and quickly realized that he was having a mental breakdown. After speaking with a few more witnesses, and hearing about his suicidal behavior, jumping in front of moving vehicles, they decided to take him to a local hospital.

As a caring social worker, Ruth wanted to help Ed. Wondering if he had any family or friends in the area, she did some research. Ruth Googled "*Searching for Ed Pelzner*" and came across the ABC News story from San Diego, recorded back in September of 2015. She read the news piece by Bree Steffen and with a bit more research, she located my San Diego Google phone number.

When she finished explaining her interaction with Ed and detective work that led her to me, my mind was buzzing with questions. First things first, I wanted to verify that we were talking about the same Ed. When I asked her to identify Ed, not only did she give me his height and weight, but she even told me his date of birth. As a witness to the incident, Ruth was privy to Ed's complete information, just in case she wanted to press charges. The information that she shared with me was proof positive that she had indeed seen my friend Ed.

Sandra was wondering why I took a call just as we were sitting down to dinner. Judging from the surprised look on my face, she knew that I was on an unexpected call. She whispered, "*Who is it? What's wrong?*" I looked at her and whispered back, "*Someone found Ed!*" She looked just as shocked as I was, as her jaw dropped. I stepped out of the room to focus on the call.

"*Where in San Diego did the car incident take place?*" I asked, wanting to know where Ed had been hiding. How had he been able to avert us for six trips? I was extremely familiar with the layout of the city and often speculated about his whereabouts. I was about to hear the answer.

Ruth shocked me when she replied, "*I'm not in San Diego, or even California for that matter.*" "*Huh? Where are you?*" I asked, totally confused. She went on to say, "*I'm calling from the island of Maui in Hawaii. Ed is living homeless here.*" I gazed out my back window as I digested the surprising turn of events. I wondered when Ed actually left San Diego and how he'd traveled to Maui. Ruth went on to say that after researching Ed's situation, she discovered that he had a caseworker helping him on the island. She gave me the name of the woman and the name of the local mental health clinic where he'd been taken.

With all this new information, my mind was overwhelmed with un-answered questions! I speculated that this was the "good place" the cops had referred to four months earlier. I would certainly describe Hawaii as a good place.

Ruth concluded by saying, "*And that's all I know about your friend.*" Wow, that was more than I could have asked for. I thanked Ruth for tak-ing the time to hunt me down and pass along the valuable information. I asked, "*If my wife and I fly to Maui, can you show us where Ed is?*" She replied, "*I'm sorry, no I cannot. To be honest, your friend's demeanor frightened me, so I am simply giving you this information to allow you to take it from here.*" I made one final request, "*Are there any other clues you might offer to help us locate Ed in Maui?*" She said, "*I've seen him working in a local bike shop.*" I inquired, "*Which one?*" She said, "*I'm sorry, that's all I can say. You're going to need to take it from here.*" Simi-lar to a witness of a crime who is fearful about sharing too much, Ruth said, "*Good luck, I've got to go!*" And with that, she ended the call.

Sandra was waiting patiently in the kitchen, to hear about the call. I brought her up to speed and took a step toward a calendar, which hangs on our kitchen wall. I began searching for the first open opportunity for us to travel to Maui.

Everything in me wanted to purchase a ticket, pack my bags and head straight to the airport. That just wasn't practical. In fact, the very next day I was scheduled to lead one of our group excursions to Limat-ambo, Peru. We work with an orphanage there known as Casa del Aguila. Not long after the trip to Peru, I was leading a hiking expedition with a group in British Columbia. Believe it or not, I was slated to coor-dinate a medical trip in Cuenca, Ecuador within a week of returning from Canada. Our summer calendar was jam-packed.

A trip to Maui wasn't remotely possible until the middle of August. The idea of having to wait for two months to pursue this incredible lead drove me bonkers! I was afraid that Ed may no longer be there if we waited too long. I wondered if this was going to turn into a multi-trip manhunt to locate my friend in the Hawaiian Islands. While I had certainly learned how to navigate the streets of San Diego, I wasn't familiar at all with Hawaii.

The thought occurred to me, "*I sure am glad that my friend Ed has chosen such beautiful places to be homeless in. I can't imagine how we might have managed a similar journey if Ed had been lost in a northern city, such as Chicago or Minneapolis.*" Searching Maui wouldn't be all bad.

The next day, I sat waiting at Dulles International Airport for our departing flight to Peru. I couldn't stop thinking about Ed in Hawaii. It felt like a cruel joke, "*We finally know where your friend Ed is, but you'll have to wait more than two months to search for him.*" I wanted to send the Peru team off with someone else who could serve as an impromptu leader. If I could find such a person, I could purchase a ticket to Hawaii and leave right now. After all, I was already packed and sitting at the airport.

When the distraction impaired my ability to be present with the team, I wandered away from our departure gate. I called a good friend by the name of Todd and asked him to give me some counsel. Once I'd brought him up to speed on the facts, he did his best to calm me down. "*Would it be wrong to send this group off without me?*" I asked, already aware of the answer. Todd began by reminding me that God is in control. He added, "*God was aware of your schedule, long before the Hawaiian social worker told you about Ed.*" He speculated, "*Perhaps Ed needs more time before he's ready to be found?*"

Todd's words were helping. He continued, "*What would it look like for you to trust God with the fact that His timing is perfect?*" I expressed my frustration, "*Yeah, but it's not only the Peru trip! When I get back, I'm only here for a brief time before leading a trip to Canada.*" Todd replied, *"I know, I'm signed up for that trip with my daughter, remember?"* *"Of course, I do, but then I've got to lead the medical trip in Ecuador. Why did I receive this information during our busiest season?"* Todd listened patiently, as I expressed my frustrations like an immature middle school kid.

When I finished my rant, Todd paused, allowing my words to settle before asking, *"When can you feasibly go to Maui without any schedule conflict?"* Putting it that way, I looked at the calendar on my phone while he waited. *"The first possible date I could travel west, given the six-hour time zone differential, is August 14th."* He calmly responded, *"Well then, run it by Sandra and book your tickets. I think you'll be more at peace when you have a plan."* Todd wasn't telling me anything that I didn't know. However, there are times when having a friend help us process emotionally-charged decisions, is a good idea.

Before hanging up the phone, Todd offered to pray for me. He asked God to replace my frustration with excitement about leading the team to Peru. He prayed for me and my family, as well as for Ed. Todd concluded his prayer and said, *"Will, God wants you to trust Him with Ed. Don't waste time worrying, because it won't do you any good. Go enjoy Peru and trust God's timing, because His timing is always perfect."* I thanked Todd for taking the time to listen and pray, before returning to the gate.

Sandra had remained at the gate with our group, so I brought her up to speed on Todd's suggestions. She felt a similar tension, understanding that I wanted so desperately to be in Hawaii searching for Ed. We both agreed on a mid-August trip. I impulsively booked two tickets for Sandra and me to Maui on my phone, before boarding our flight to Peru. I had peace of mind to at least have the trip booked and scheduled to depart on August 14, 2017.

We decided to keep this trip off the grid, and didn't feel that recruiting participants would be a smart idea. We put zero information on social media concerning the trip, just in case Ed was monitoring Facebook. In addition, we only told a short list of friends about our plans, and invited them to pray for a successful mission. Those we did tell were extremely supportive. One couple from our church even offered us a free timeshare on the island, so we could save some money. Another couple gave us $300 toward our flights. The rest committed to pray for us every day during that week. We sent a private email to keep our short list of supporters informed and on their knees.

Those two months seemed like an eternity to me. I have no idea why it feels as though time moves at a slower pace when you're truly excited about something in your future.

When Monday, August 14th finally arrived, we departed as scheduled. I was afraid to get my hopes up on the flight, so I brought along some work to keep me busy. The morning of our departure, we received a message from United Airlines. The email stated that our outgoing flight had been delayed by almost two hours. This created a problem, since our original connecting flight in San Francisco only allowed us sixty minutes to change planes. In other words, we wouldn't make the flight to Hawaii!

In my frustration, I immediately called United Airlines to find a solution. The reservation agent was understanding and began searching other possible options. She was working as fast as she could, since time was limited. She asked, "*Can you two make it to the airport in the next twenty minutes?*" I replied, "*No ma'm, that isn't possible, since the drive alone is about 20 minutes.*" Then she offered us two alternatives, both of which had us arriving a day late. I was growing frustrated, and offered a prayer to God, asking Him to find a way.

I wasn't willing to give up a day of searching since I knew we needed as much time as possible. After another few minutes waiting on hold, the United reservations specialist came up with another option. "*I can book you two on a flight that departs in two hours for Hawaii, with a one-hour layover in Los Angeles. That option would have you in Maui late this evening.*" That was clearly the best possible itinerary so I said, "*Great, please book it!*" Before securing our tickets she added, "*I need to let you know that the flight from Washington Dulles to LAX only has two random middle seats left in economy, so I can make the booking, but wanted to make you aware that you will be seated ten rows apart.*" If you

185

are over six feet tall, as I am, middle seats in economy are never a comfortable option. However, we were desperate and wanted to get to Maui as quickly as possible, even if that meant sitting ten rows apart in the middle seats.

(My knees on our flight across country in the middle seat)

We traveled on that flight for close to six hours, from Washington Dulles International Airport to Los Angeles. After a brief layover, we boarded another similar sized aircraft and traveled for approximately the same amount of time before arriving at our destination. We'd finally made it! Our bodies were well aware of the six-hour time differential. Even though the clock behind the rental car counter read 9pm, our bodies weren't fooled (it was actually 3am to us).

Based on Ruth's tip, she mentioned that Ed had been seen working in a bike shop somewhere on the island. I did my research before the trip and compiled a list of every bike shop listed on the island. I'd often wondered if Ed had ever made money utilizing his woodworking skills, although it never crossed my mind that he might be working on bikes.

We arrived at our timeshare, picked up the keys to the room, and headed straight to bed. We wanted to get some much-needed rest so we could begin our search early the following morning. I awoke with the sun shining in my eyes and tried to get my bearings. When you're running on limited hours of sleep, and wake in an unfamiliar bedroom, it's disorienting. I made my way to the kitchen to get some strong coffee brewing. Sandra followed me to the kitchen table and we began making plans for the day. We had a number of bike shops to visit, although none seemed to be open until 10am. Since it was only 8am, we decided to get some breakfast and map out a logical order for visiting every bike shop.

We found a well-rated breakfast joint on the main street in Kihei, situated directly across from Kalama Park. We placed our orders and found a couple of seats facing the street, so we could keep an eye on people passing by.

(Homeless men in Kihei, near Kalama Park)

It didn't take us long to spot some of Maui's homeless population. We'd decided against staying on the street this time, even though Sandra was no longer pregnant. I was eagerly watching the homeless men walking by and hoping to see my friend Ed. I also wondered how the Hawaiian homeless differed from the California crew who I'd become so familiar with.

After polishing off an omelet and downing two more cups of coffee, I was ready to roll. We crossed the street and engaged a few homeless individuals. We had a wonderful conversation with an articulate older gentleman who introduced himself by his street name, 'Stoybs.'

(Left to right: Will, Sandra & Stoybs)

Stoybs sat with us on a park bench, with a wheelchair beside him. He shared with us a bit of his story. He'd been a landscaper for most of his life but was no longer able to do so while confined to a wheelchair. He told us of a failed marriage and about his children and grandchildren, who he was rarely able to see.

Stoybs admitted to having a problem with alcohol as he sipped a tall can of Miller Lite just before 9am. He seemed to appreciate having people to chat with, who were willing to take an interest in what he had to say. We told Stoybs about our mission, then prayed with him before resuming our search. We walked along a trail that snaked through the park between the main road and the shoreline. We surveyed the town for about an hour in hopes of spotting Ed.

Once 10 a.m. rolled around, we entered the first bike shop on our list. It was situated just across the street from where we had enjoyed our breakfast. We entered the shop, and I said hello to a young man across the counter and asked, "*Who are the mechanics you use to repair bikes at your shop?*" I asked that question, because Ruth told us that she believed Ed was making money as a part-time bike mechanic. The man behind the counter asked, "*Why, what's wrong with your bike?*" I showed him a photo of Ed and said, "*Actually, I don't have a bike issue, but I'm looking for my friend who repairs bikes in Maui and I'm not sure which shop he works at.*" He took a glance at the picture and replied, "*He doesn't look familiar, but there are a bunch of other bike stores on the island.*" I pulled out our list and laid it on the counter. I asked, "*We made a list of shops we found online. Are there any more you know of that we may have neglected to put on the list?*" He was kind enough to survey the names and addresses we'd written down and said, "*Actually, you're missing a few. I know of at least one in Lahaina that you don't have listed.*" He provided us with a few more names of shops to add to the roster. As we headed out the door he hollered, "*Good luck!*" We thanked him and headed for our rental car (a Nissan Juke). We were ready to explore shop number two.

When I crossed the parking lot toward our car, I noticed a police cruiser parked outside. I looked for the driver and spotted two officers eating breakfast in a small diner next to the bike shop. With that, I went inside and asked them if they had a minute to talk. They motioned for me to take a seat, so I did. I showed them Ed's photo and gave them a brief version of the story. The older of the two officers said, "*I'd be hap-*

py to check our database and can call if anything comes up." I gave him one of the photo cards with my San Diego Google number on it. I also asked where the homeless tend to congregate on the island, soliciting their advice. The officer told me about three locations that we should check and warned me to be careful. I thanked him before returning to the car. We figured that if the bike shops didn't prove successful, we could try the other three locations that they gave us.

We headed to the next bike shop on our list. I began to wonder if this was going to be one more man hunt with no sign of Ed. I imagined a tiny island with very few places to check before we arrived in Maui. The actual size of the island overwhelmed me. I thought, *"He could be anywhere!"* I decided to stop worrying, and instead offered up a prayer to God, requesting His guidance and help. I could feel discouragement creeping in, every time we struck out at another bike store.

We hit the next bike shop and then another, with no sign of Ed. We drove past a homeless shelter to have a look and also took a walk through their local library. I'd learned that many homeless use computers in libraries to check email and Facebook accounts. Ed was nowhere to be found. How many bike shops could there actually be? Certainly, someone knows something, right? We decided to take a lunch break and dine on some fresh fish tacos. We used the break to collect our thoughts and cross off the leads that turned out to be dead ends. With each failed attempt, my heart sank a little more. I was trying to remain positive, but could feel hope slipping away.

We went to one more bike shop after lunch. While I spoke with yet another mechanic who had never seen Ed, he did have a lead. He said, *"I've heard of a guy by the name of Ed who works at a bike shop in the next town over. It's called Paia."* I didn't want to get my hopes up only to end up disappointed. He said the shop in Paia is called 'Maui Cyclery.' And we were off! Could this possibly be the place? Within fifteen minutes, we parked our car in Paia, to locate Maui Cyclery on foot.

The shop wasn't hard to find. We noticed the bike rental sign and saw assorted bicycles parked out front. Two men were working at the counter as we entered the store. Hank and Will were their names, and I tried to size them up quickly. We asked them if they had an employee by the name of Ed. Hank responded, "*Yes, we do. Ed runs our island bike tours. Are you two interested in a tour?*" "*Could this actually be our Ed?*" I wondered.

I asked a few more questions about Ed's age and height, to clarify if this was indeed Ed Pelzner, and let them know that Ed was a friend of mine who I wanted to reconnect with. They answered, "*Ed is short and stocky, an ex-military guy in his mid-50s.*" Once again, another dead end. No one describes a man who stands six feet, three inches tall as "short." I was discouraged. I said, "*Nope, it's not him. The Ed I know is very tall and had the desire to join the service, but never followed through. Thanks for your time.*" I wasn't sure where to go from there, since we were running out of bike shops.

(Left to right: Will & Hank at Maui Cyclery in Paia)

In a last-ditch effort before walking out the door, I reached into my pocket for the information card with Ed's picture on it. I slid the card across the counter and asked, "*Have you ever seen this guy? His name is Ed Pelzner.*"

Their eyes grew large when they saw Ed's photo. "*Oh, yeah, we know that Ed, but he's not an actual employee here. Donnie pays him to wash bikes when renters return them.*" Hank went on to say, "*Ed makes five dollars per bike, which gives him some spending money.*" I stood there in complete shock. We finally located Ed! What should our next move be?

I needed more information, so I pressed on, "*What is his weekly or daily routine? How often do you guys see him?*" They answered, "*We see Ed almost every day. Sometimes in the morning, but almost always in the afternoon.*" I looked at my watch, and it was 2:30pm. We had a couple of hours to kill before we might finally see Ed face-to-face. Was this really happening? It was surreal to consider that after seven trips we had finally located the place where my friend Ed was living.

We chatted a bit more with Hank and Will, and I inquired about Ed's state of mind. Will shared about living with a roommate who had wrestled with drug addiction. They confirmed that Ed had some of the same behavioral quirks. Will said, "*Ed is friendly on most days, although there are times when he has severe mood swings and can become hostile.*" Irrational, erratic behavior is typical for someone using methamphetamine, just as it is for someone battling mental illness. I gave the two of them my number and pleaded, "*Please call me if you see him today or this week for that matter. We flew all the way here from the East Coast, hoping to see him.*" They agreed to text or call me at the first sign of Ed.

We thanked them before heading out to the main street, known as Hana Highway. Sandra and I figured that we may as well get acquainted with the small town, if this was Ed's home. Even though we hadn't seen him yet, we were ecstatic. Being able to locate the town where he lived and people who he knew within the first twenty-four hours of our search was a true answer to prayer. We walked the streets, poked our heads into shops, and then wandered into a tattoo parlor. We were basically killing time and hoping to either see Ed or get a call from the shop. Once again, in the same way that time seemed to move at a slower pace when we were waiting to fly to Maui, it had slowed to a crawl. We were both anticipating something big, but when?

While we were chatting with a local tattoo artist by the name of 'Jimbo,' my phone rang. I didn't recognize the number, but picked it up hoping it was Hank or Will and not a sales call. "*Hello?*" It was Hank from the bike shop, as I'd hoped.

At precisely 4:15pm on August 15th, Hank called me to say, "*I just saw Ed on his bike in front of the shop! He didn't enter the store, but he's riding through town right now.*" I thanked him for the call and told the tattoo artist at the counter, "*Sorry, we've got to go!*" As I turned for the door Jimbo asked, "*Do you want your wallet?*" In haste, I left it on the counter after purchasing a Paia sticker. Sandra, realizing the significance of the moment, said, "*I'll get it, just go and I'll catch up!*"

I took off. I ran out of the store and began combing the street for a tall bleached blond man, riding a bike. There was no sign of him. Sandra quickly joined me as we searched frantically. We separated to cover more ground. I made my way back to the bike shop. "*Which way did he go?*" I asked Hank. He replied, "*I saw him riding to the right, headed in the direction of the beach.*" He pointed in the direction of the beach and we were off!

The two of us legged it down the sidewalk along Hana Highway to Baldwin Beach Park. We immediately separated to cover more ground. We scoured the beach area and public restrooms. There is a clubhouse and a skatepark as well, so I raced around looking for Ed. I wasn't sure where Sandra was, but just kept scanning the faces and praying that he hadn't peddled away.

"*Was he already long gone?*" I wondered. My heart began to sink at the idea of being that close, yet missing him once again.

As I circled around a small building, I poked my head in the public bathroom to see if Ed was present. It didn't seem likely, with no sign of a bike out front. I decided to head back toward the basketball courts where Sandra and I had originally divided our search efforts.

I spotted Sandra across a field between the beach and the main road. She was walking across the basketball courts when I noticed that she was looking at me. She had an intense facial expression and began pointing toward the beach. I looked left in the direction she was pointing, and I saw him.

His frame was definitely tall enough to be my old friend, but I couldn't see his face clearly. As I got closer his face came into focus. He was walking up from the ocean up over the sand dunes towards a bike parked in the grass. He had black bike shorts on and wasn't wearing a top. He'd just taken a dip I suppose, to cool off before returning to his bike.

At that moment, I knew without a doubt... That was my friend Ed!

Chapter 13
Fish Tacos and Tattoos

I did a double-take when I realized that Ed was walking in my direction! My heart began to race. What should I say? What if he runs? I quickened my pace, realizing that he hadn't noticed me yet. I tapped the record button on my phone, although I held it at my side. I figured that if he ran away, I should at least capture some video for his family to see, since they hadn't seen him in three years. I imagined telling his parents that I finally saw their son, knowing they would ask if I had taken a photo. I couldn't dare return empty- handed after my 7th trip.

When I came within fifteen feet, I spoke to Ed. *"No way, I can't believe it's actually you!"* Ed looked as though he was in shock. He was clearly attempting to process the event, as was I. His eyes darted toward my phone, so I immediately stopped videoing and slipped the phone in my pocket.

Then his eyes darted toward Sandra. He looked frantic, as though we were boxing him in. You could sense he was nervous and I didn't want to spook him. *"You remember my wife, Sandra, right?"* I said, motioning in her direction. Ed responded, *"Of course I do."*

Then I commented, *"What are the odds of us running into each other* here?" He shot back with quick wit, *"Not likely. In fact, I'd say borderline suspicious!"* I tried not to laugh at his comment although a smile crept across my face. That was the funny Ed that I remembered.

Attempting to shift the direction of our conversation and lighten it up, I said, *"How are you doing? You look good."* Ed thanked me for the remark and returned the compliment. Then I inquired, *"So what brought you to Hawaii? Have you been here for long?"* There were so many questions I wanted to ask, and yet I didn't want to scare him off with a conversation that subtly turned into an interrogation.

He appeared to ease up a bit and began chatting. He shared with us that he arrived at the decision that he was finished with San Diego and purchased a one-way ticket to Hawaii. Then he added, *"You know, I should have paid better attention in geography class, because when I purchased my ticket, I thought Hawaii was one big island. I thought that Maui was just one city on a large island called Hawaii, so I purchased the cheapest fare with that false assumption."* The three of us laughed.

While Ed was open and willing to answer my question about moving to Maui, he was vague regarding to when the actual trip took place. He merely said, *"Oh, I've been here a while."* That made me more curious but I held my tongue.

Sandra asked how he was enjoying the island compared to San Diego. Ed said, *"I don't care much for the island, but it beats San Diego, so it's alright for now."* His eyes were constantly darting here and there. It was obvious that he was clearly nervous about our unexpected meeting.

I let him know where we were staying in Kihei and mentioned the fact that friends from church had generously given us their timeshare for the week. *"There are two large bedrooms if you want to use one while we're here."* He politely declined, saying it wouldn't be necessary. Then we asked him if he would like to be our guests at dinner. He declined that offer as well. It wasn't like the old Ed I knew to turn down a free dinner. He was clearly suspicious of our presence.

We visited for about fifteen minutes before he told us that he'd better get going. I offered to give him my phone number in case he had a change of heart. He told us that he didn't care for social media and no longer owned a phone. We repeated our address and let him know that the invitation would remain open until we left on Saturday.

We told him that we loved him and he responded, *"I love you too."* Sandra offered to take a picture of the two of us, for old time's sake. I was glad she asked, because I feared he would decline if I'd suggested it. He agreed, so I handed my phone to Sandra and we posed for the photo.

Just before she snapped the pic, I asked, *"Do you remember when we took our last photo together at the hotel in Anaheim?"* Ed replied, *"Of course I do. I remember that you pointed at me just before Sandra took the picture. So, this time I'll point at you."* And he did. (The photo I'm referring to is in chapter one). Although it had been almost four years since that time, Ed's mind was sharp enough to recall the specific details.

(Left to right: Will & Ed at Baldwin Beach Park)

Sandra snapped the photo, we exchanged hugs, and again, I told him that I loved him. Without hesitation, Ed replied, "*I love you too. You two are good people.*" With that, he hopped on his bike and rode away.

It was a surreal moment! It happened so quickly. Seven trips looking for Ed, and there he was, living in a small beach town on the northern coast of Maui. We were so grateful for the chance to finally see him, and have a chance to speak with him. Three years and nine months after our previous meeting with Ed in November 2013, we were able to see him again.

Soon after Ed's speedy departure, I began thinking of all the things I wish I'd said. Hindsight is a funny thing. All of a sudden, a flood of clarity hits you, and you wonder why you didn't have it earlier, when you needed it most.

Sandra and I walked back to the car, so grateful for that unforgettable encounter. We were replaying the conversation to savor the moment. We began to analyze every comment, attempting to understand Ed's frame of mind.

While I was thankful to God for granting us an encounter, I also wondered, "*Was that all?*" I wasn't complaining, yet I still had so many unanswered questions buzzing around in my mind. How long had Ed been in Hawaii? How did he get the money for a plane ticket? What type of identification did he use to travel? Where was he camping? How does he eat? Are there local churches that host nightly dinners, as we experienced in San Diego? Hopefully, I'd have the opportunity to see him again and find out how we might be able to help.

We returned to our little rental car and began driving back toward Kihei on the southside of the island. Just then, Ed whizzed past us on his bike. His arms were outstretched, free as a bird. I asked Sandra to video him while I drove faster, attempting to catch up. She managed to capture about 12 seconds of footage and then we decided to re-park the car. Perhaps he would turn around and cycle past us, as we were hoping for a second attempt to connect with him.

(Ed biking at the intersection of Baldwin Ave. & Hana Hwy.)

After parking the car, we kept an eye out, hoping Ed might turn around in our direction. We noticed that he parked his bike in front of a convenience store, and was peering through their window. He looked as though he was contemplating whether or not to enter the store. He decided against it and mounted his bike again. When Sandra saw him headed in our direction, she announced, "*Will, he's riding back on our side of the road.*" She wanted to be sure that I was looking in the same direction, so as not to miss him.

We did our best to act naturally, so as not to stir up any paranoia and look like a couple of stalkers (that we were at the time). I tried some reverse psychology as he approached us, "*Are you following us, Ed?*" He smiled and then stuck out his right hand while passing me, to give him a high five. I hollered, "*Come have a drink with us!*" He turned and smiled and said, "*Not today,*" as he continued peddling away.

Observing Ed randomly drifting through town, got us thinking. We decided to settle into one of the many small-town restaurants at the end of Baldwin Avenue. We reasoned, "*If we request outdoor seating, perhaps Ed will spot us with a table of food and drinks, and have a hungry change of heart.*" We hoped the sight of a full table would be too irresistible for him to turn down. We ordered our food and ate slowly, constantly looking up and down the street. However, after an hour with zero Ed sightings, we decided to call it a day. After all, this was day one of our search and we'd already seen him twice. Why not pace ourselves? Besides, the time in Maui was 6 p.m., but our body clocks knew it was midnight. We paid our bill, returned to the rental car, and headed back to the timeshare.

Sandra and I chatted at length about the interaction we had with Ed on the beach. It was still so surreal. Despite the major time difference, I called Ed's parents to let them know the news. Mrs. Pelzner confessed having a difficult time sleeping, knowing that we were following our strongest lead to date. She was thrilled to hear the news. Like me, she also had a myriad of questions, but I had to confess that we simply didn't have answers. My second call was to Steve Bowman, my friend who had accompanied me on all four of the homeless excursions. He had also given me permission to call at any time, if we had positive news to share. Steve was fully invested in the journey and deserved to hear the exciting breakthrough.

We were exhausted but running on adrenaline from our interaction with Ed. If the men at the bike shop were correct, then this was only day one, and we had three more days in hopes of seeing him before we had to head back east. I was determined to be better prepared next time and gave more thought to what I planned to say and what questions I wanted to ask.

We were spent and when the adrenaline finally wore off, we faded into a deep sleep. Although we didn't feel the pressure to get an early start as we had on day one, we still woke early because we were on East Coast time. We tried a different breakfast spot that had rave reviews. We realized through social media that a couple we knew were vacationing just a few miles away, so we decided to invite them to breakfast. The couple manages a non-profit similar to ours, so we thought it might be nice to connect. Their names are Eric and Barbara Johnson.

They run a successful company known as The Radford Coffee Company, and use the profits of that business to fuel their non-profit to care for orphans. We had talked a few times about getting together back east, but were never able to make it happen, since we lived four hours apart. Why not take advantage of the 'coincidence?'

We enjoyed our time hearing a bit of their story, and we told them about our mission in Maui with Ed. It was a pleasure to meet others in the same line of work and exchange ideas. They encouraged us in our pursuit of my friend and prayed with us before departing.

(Left to right: Will, Sandra, Barbara & Eric in Kihei)

We left breakfast feeling encouraged, well-fed and ready to resume our search. As we drove back toward the north side of the island, we chatted about our interaction with the Johnsons. I believe God is aware when we need people to encourage us. In the midst of our quest, what may have seemed like a random chance meeting, turned out to be a much-needed blessing. At the precise time we needed someone to say, "*Keep going!*" God provided the Johnsons.

On our way across the island we began to think that perhaps we should give Ed a little space. After all, the staff at Maui Cyclery said that they tend to see Ed every afternoon. We decided to explore different areas of the island and head back to Paia in the afternoon.

When the time arrived, we made our way back to the little Bohemian town in hopes of another engagement. We quickly found a parking space and began walking the sidewalks. We played the tourists that we were, exploring shops, drinking coffee, and taking a stroll back

201

to Baldwin Beach. We walked past the spot where we had spoken with Ed on the previous day, but there was no sign of him. We were early and yet hopeful.

As the afternoon progressed, we decided to select another roadside restaurant with outdoor seating. Our table provided us with a decent vantage point to keep a watchful eye on the primary intersection. We waited, watched, and sampled some appetizers to kill the time.

At around 4:30 p.m., it began to rain. We had a canopy overhead which served as adequate cover for us. Although, we watched those who were less fortunate to be walking the streets, caught off guard by the storm. Everyone who was unable to find cover or duck into a shop or restaurant was getting completely soaked. Having lived homeless on the streets of San Diego in a downpour, I said to Sandra, *"Ed isn't going to show up if the rain continues."* We checked the forecast and realized that the rain was going to continue into the night. Realizing the slim chance of a day two encounter with Ed, we paid our bill and made a mad dash for the car.

Perhaps Thursday or Friday would give us a better show of sunshine and bring my friend out of hiding. The weather app made the forecast look promising. We were scheduled to depart on Saturday, so I started to get worried. I wondered, *"What if we don't see Ed again before it's time to fly home?"* Again, I was grateful for the opportunity to finally see him, but I wanted to speak with him. The reality of that possibility forced me to consider exactly what I wanted to say to my friend if I was given another chance.

On Thursday, we expanded our search up and down and around Paia, walking farther than we had before. I was trying to guess where Ed might spend his time during the daylight hours.

We returned to Maui Cyclery and I was able to meet the owner. His name is Donnie Arnoult and he was able to offer a little more insight into Ed's history on the Island. He told us that Ed had been there for close to a year. He mentioned that Ed was not very social with the local homeless crowd. I always wondered who Ed befriended while living on the streets. Israel claimed to be friends with Ed, although Ed had severed all of his relationships that predated his life on the streets. There were so many mysteries surrounding Ed's change of heart and new chosen lifestyle. I hoped to see him again and get the chance to ask him in person.

Discovering from the shop owner that Ed had become a loner was sad to hear. I'd been told by one addict in San Diego, that the constant suspicion and paranoia associated with meth use shrinks your circle of trusted friends until the only person you trust is your pusher. Although, you have difficulty trusting him as well, so you end up feeling isolated and alone. Based on the bike shop employees and a few others we met who knew Ed, this sounded like Ed's pattern was one of solitude. However, the one exception was his loose relationships with those who worked in the shops, like Donnie.

Donnie also mentioned that he'd heard that Ed had recently picked up some work swinging a hammer on a short-term construction project farther up Baldwin Avenue. As we had heard on our first day, Ed also made five dollars per bike cleaning up the rental returns. I had no idea Ed was still finding work and carrying on part-time jobs. It made me wonder where he worked when he was living back in San Diego.

I asked Donnie if Ed had held any other jobs while living in Paia. He replied, *"Oh yeah, Ed worked for a while cleaning dishes at Flatbreads, the local pizza restaurant next door."* We paid them a visit to find out what the manager could tell us about Ed. He was kind and willing to co-operate. The manager said, *"Ed was always punctual and hardworking. He struggled from time to time, saying that he was hearing voices in his head. He wasn't able to keep it together, so he stopped working."* He also concurred with the fact that Ed had been residing in Paia for a year at that point.

I was reminded once more of the police officers who told Mrs. Pelzner that her son was in a 'good place.' After chatting with the manager at Flatbreads and with Donnie at Maui Cyclery, we decided to beat the streets again, hoping to find Ed. We had no luck and when the sun finally began to set, we realized that we only had one more day to search. As we drove back toward our timeshare, we both agreed that we would spend the entire final day on stakeout in Paia. Afterall, Ed was the reason we were there.

I laid in bed that evening, feeling the bitter-sweet emotions related to finding my friend, yet not truly being able to connect with him. We had assumed wrongly after finding him on day one, that we'd see him back in Paia every day. We speculated that perhaps Ed was in hiding until Sunday, since we told him that we would be in town until Saturday.

We were praying for one more interaction. We invited our friends back home to pray fervently to that end. We were asking God for a significant conversation and there was only one day left for God to answer our prayers. As I was drifting off to sleep, I begged God, *"Please soften Ed's heart and allow me a chance to speak with my friend."*

Friday, our final day to search had arrived, and were ready to make it count. It was a team effort. We'd enlisted loads of people to stay on their knees praying throughout the day, while we scoured that little town in hopes of having a meaningful exchange with Ed. Realizing that time was of the essence, we began our search from the car, and tried to drive every street in and around the town of Paia. When that yielded no sign of Ed, we continued the hunt by hiking every path that was inaccessible by car. By around 2:00 p.m,, we had woven a path throughout the town by car and by foot and we needed a break. We stopped for some Mahi-Mahi fish tacos at one of the same roadside restaurants that we had visited earlier in the week while keeping our eyes on the road in front of us.

After eating, we hiked up Baldwin Avenue and made our way back into town. We were left to continue canvassing the town, and trust that God would grant us one final opportunity to see Ed.

My wife is very unique, in the sense that many women would caution their husbands against ever getting a tattoo. Sandra, on the other hand, had asked me a question on several occasions that struck me as odd, *"When are you going to get a tattoo?"* My usual response was, *"When I can think of something that I want to have on my skin for the rest of my life."* I'd seen too many friends and acquaintances get tattoos during a period of life, only to regret them later. However, during that particular week, the answer came to mind. Was it perhaps the fact that I'd spent so much time in a small town that had a tattoo shop on every corner?

The inspiration for my tattoo was wrapped up in my entire homeless journey. My mind returned to the very first trip that I made to San Diego to search for Ed. I recalled my memorable ride with crazy Ted as my co-pilot and passenger. While his intel promising that Ed was hanging out at a downtown Starbucks had been a bust, his challenge had impacted me profoundly. My understanding of this mission altered significantly after Ted asked, "*Why don't you come and live on the streets among the homeless to search for Ed, and find out for yourself what it's actually like to be homeless?*" Understanding Ed's world required my willingness to walk a few miles (or more) in his shoes.

Ted's challenge seemed to resonate with the Golden Rule, to love others the way you want to be loved. I knew I'd want someone to search for me if the roles were reversed. What seemed to follow the same line of thinking was something Jesus said, after a group of religious thugs judged him for associating with the outcasts of his day. Perhaps the religious people were wondering, "*Why on earth would Jesus eat with the filth of humanity?*" Jesus had an answer.

In Luke chapter 15, Jesus told three stories to make his point: the story of a lost sheep, a lost coin and a lost son. While all three stories were meant to communicate the same point concerning the importance of grace, one seemed to stand out in my mind.

When Jesus said that a good shepherd is always willing to leave the ninety-nine safe, comfortable sheep, in hopes of finding the one that lost its way, I imagined Ed as the figurative lost sheep. I reasoned that if God was willing to leave the comfort of Heaven to love humanity, then I could certainly leave the comfort of my home on the East Coast to live homeless and search for my friend. It seemed like a healthy example of love, that I would want if I were homeless like Ed.

The concept of leaving the 99 for the 1 served as a reminder that I should always be willing to leave comfort, when there is an individual who is in trouble. Even if the individual is considered an outcast by all, and I might be judged as Jesus was, it is a price worth paying. Furthermore, it served to remind me that when a shepherd left his flock to search beyond the comfort of his own pasture, he was putting himself in harm's way. Loving and searching for someone who has lost their way may put me in danger, yet every single human has value, regardless of poor choices and a checkered past. Even those who others devalue or dehumanize are worth going after. I happened to learn that lesson on the streets when I became homeless myself, and experienced the world from their perspective.

I decided that I wanted to get a tattoo that served as a reminder of those valuable life principles. I considered simply having the phrase "99 for 1" tattooed on my arm, but I wanted to be a bit more creative than that. With a little research, I happened to discover that there was an 'Interstate 99' in the state of California, as well as a 'Route 1.' I used the images of each street sign to portray the numbers from Jesus' example of a loving shepherd. The California street signs are also a daily reminder of the weeks that I've lived on the streets of California.

(Will's Tattoo: "99 for 1," by Tattoo artist Jimbo in Paia)

I located a well-known artist in Paia by the name of Jimbo. He was actually the man who we'd met earlier in the week, when the bike shop called to inform us that Ed was outside their shop. I was pleased with Jimbo's artwork and the design we had come up with. My appointment took place around 3:30 p.m., as Sandra kept watch for Ed in town. As soon as Jimbo gave me my aftercare instructions, I resumed the search with my wife.

Donnie and the guys working in his shop were aware that this was our final day, so they were on lookout as well. Just as they had called me on day one when they spotted Ed, they called immediately after I left the tattoo shop. Donnie announced, "*I just saw Ed walking through town carrying a bike innertube.*" Sandra and I began moving rapidly in the direction of Maui Cyclery. I inquired, "*What was Ed wearing?*" Donnie said, "*He's wearing a baseball cap, board shorts and a long sleeve shirt.*" I thanked him and then we raced down the street as our eyes scanned the faces populating the sidewalks.

Sandra and I were thrilled to hear about the first Ed sighting since our arrival, but worried we might miss him. We were all present in the small town of Paia, yet somehow managed to miss him. "*Why did I get a tattoo today of all days?*" I thought shamefully.

We sat down in front of the Flatbread's pizza joint, where Ed had worked as a dishwasher. We hadn't been sitting there for two minutes when Sandra elbowed me in the side. I looked in her direction and saw what she saw. There was Ed, strolling in our direction wearing the precise outfit that Donnie had described to me. He was sporting a nice long-sleeved yellow surf shirt, name-brand board shorts, flip-flops, and a baseball cap turned backward to polish off his look. He was cleanly shaven this time around and looked like he was ready for a night on the town.

Ed was still carrying what looked like a spare innertube tire for his bike as he walked within inches of us. Just as he stood above us on the narrow sidewalk in front of Flatbreads, he glanced our way. As soon as he noticed Sandra and me seated to his right, he covered one side of his face with his hand, as if to slip by unnoticed.

Sandra spoke up first, "*You aren't going to walk by without saying 'hello' are you?*" "*Of course not,*" Ed shot back, as he extended his hand to shake hers. "*How are you two doing?*" he asked politely. In spite of his words, he continued to walk slowly away from us in the same direction he'd been traveling in before he took notice.

While we had been frantically searching for Ed over the past week, his sudden appearance still caught me off guard. Here he was and looking quite honestly like his old self. I spoke up, "*Hey Ed, do you want to join us for dinner or grab a drink?*"

For a moment, we noticed that he was hesitant as though he was contemplating the idea. He went so far as to begin setting the bike tire down. And then, as abruptly as he had paused, he snatched up the inner tube and replied, "*No, I can't, but thanks. I really have to get this tire changed!*" With that, he turned and started walking away without saying goodbye.

I stood up and said loudly, "*Ed, we leave tomorrow morning and haven't hung out in almost four years. At least stay and have one drink with us!*" He said, "*Sorry, I have to repair my tire, but thanks,*" as he continued walking. He was about to slip away, and we'd traveled so far to see him.

I took a few steps in his direction and pleaded, "*Will you at least give me five minutes of your time?*" He turned in our direction but kept walking and hollered, "*I just can't do it. Sorry, it's not you, it's me.*" I thought, "*Seriously, you're going to use a lame male-female breakup line on us?*"

I made the decision right then and there to pursue him. Realizing that this could possibly be my last opportunity to connect with Ed, I went after him. It's an interesting endeavor to physically chase an addict who struggles with paranoia. When Ed turned around and saw me headed in his direction, he decided to cross the bustling Hana Highway. Keep in mind, he was still carrying the bike tire, as well as the rim. I took off after him across the busy roadway and hollered, "*Is this like the war games we used to play, where you hide and I come after you?*"

I was trying to say something that might jog his memory regarding our friendship since middle school, and perhaps lighten the atmosphere that was growing more intense by the minute. It didn't work because Ed made no attempt to slow down. In fact, he picked up his pace and yelled, "*Stop following me!*" There we were, two grown men playing chase, in the middle of a crowded parking lot. I almost got hit by a car that didn't see me coming.

Ed turned around when he reached the end of the parking lot to see if I was still coming. I attempted to hide my frame behind a parked car. He spotted me and then vanished behind a large advertisement in the grass. I saw him turn left behind the sign and picked up the pace.

For the past four days, Sandra and I had clocked hours exploring that tiny town. It seemed to have paid off, since I'd become so familiar with the geographical layout. I knew that there was one paved lane that was a shortcut between Hana Highway and Baldwin Avenue. When I took that road and looked left, sure enough, Ed was jogging at a brisk pace up the road.

Ed was already half way to Baldwin Avenue, so I started to run and hollered, "*Wait up, just give me a minute to talk!*" He screamed back, "*I can't!*" as he continued moving. I was somewhat disturbed by the fact that Ed was outrunning me. I do my best to stay in shape and exercise on a regular basis. "*How's it possible for a tweaker to outrun me?*" I wondered.

It had become clear to me, that his days on the bicycle had paid off. One of the guys at Maui Cyclery had mentioned that there isn't a day that Ed fails to ride his bike. Considering his daily cycling routine, riding up and down the hilly terrain of Maui, it made me feel a little bit better. However, I was unable to catch him. I noticed that he peeked over his left shoulder one final time before disappearing, to see if I was still following. While I tried to move my legs at a faster speed, the chase seemed futile. In my frustration, I cried out to God.

Alone on the road, I prayed outloud. "*God, this is ridiculous, should I stop chasing him?*" The immediate thought that came to mind was,

"No, I pursue you because I love you, so you should pursue Ed." So, I did, and I pleaded, *"Then make me faster, God!"*

In a moment of reflection, while jogging up the hill, I thought back to the numerous flights I'd taken to search for Ed. I considered all the miles that I walked, along with others during seven separate weeks. I thought of how many nights we'd slept under the stars, as well as the nights that we got very little sleep. I began thinking of all of the men and women who had joined me in the pursuit. How many miles had we covered and how much money had been spent to let Ed know that he is loved? Ed was the "one" worth searching for, and we had left a whole lot of "99" to pursue him. Giving up wasn't an option!

Just as I began to accept the realization that catching Ed on foot was not possible, a thought came to mind. *"Our rental car is parked near here!"* Realizing that the car keys were in my pocket, I spotted our car just as I reached Baldwin Avenue. Within no time, I'd unlocked the door, hopped in the driver's seat and pulled a fast U-turn to drive up Baldwin. The thought occurred to me as I raced up the hill in my Nissan rental, *"The Lord had answered my prayer and made me fast!"*

I hadn't seen Ed since he turned right at the corner, probably four minutes ahead of me. I just hoped that he stayed on the main road without diverting down a side street or even worse, into the woods.

As I rounded the next corner, there he was! When I spotted Ed, he was walking backwards on my side of the road with his left hand clutching the bike wheel, and his right arm extended with a thumb pointed to heaven. Ed was trying to hitch a ride to get away from me. He would've never imagined that I had a car parked mid-route along the road.

I slowed the car down and lowered the electric window on the passenger side, *"Do you need a ride?"* I shouted as he approached the passenger door, about to open it.

The second he peeked in the window and realized it was me, he said, *"Stop messing with me, Will!"* There was anger in his voice now, generated by fear, no doubt.

"Lord, give me the words, please," I offered a brief prayer and then with my window down, I began to share what was in my heart as Ed walked beside my car.

"*Ed, I've traveled to San Diego six times to search for you. I've been worried about you living on the streets.*"

"*I don't care!*" he shouted back. "*I love you Ed and want to help,*" I exclaimed. "*I don't want anyone's help,*" he replied.

"*Can't you just give me the courtesy of five minutes to chat with you?*", I pleaded. "*No, I can't!*" he shouted as he stomped furiously up the hill, still carrying the bike wheel.

Ed continued making excuses as he stormed up Baldwin Avenue. I wondered how the years on meth had messed with his mind. What wrong ideas or lies had he begun to believe that made him so scared of people from his past? What fear, shame or pain did he suffer that contributed to his delusional thinking? Why didn't he want to connect with any of his family or friends? His behavior seemed erratic and his anger misplaced.

When it was completely evident that Ed was finished with our exchange, he crossed to the other side of the road and began walking downhill. I made a U-turn, and shouted out the window, "*I will leave you alone, but I want you to know that I love you and will continue to pray for you.*"

Then I added, "*If you ever want to take a trip with me, I have your passport. Why didn't you ever tell me that you actually got it renewed after we met? Your friend Stephanie back in San Diego gave it to me, so if you ever want to take that trip that you asked me about back in 2013, I'm still game!*" He responded, "*That's great,*" in a sarcastic tone. He gave me a thumbs up, yet the spirit behind it felt as though he had chosen the wrong finger. I sat in my parked car and watched him disappear. With that, I coasted back down the hill towards town.

I'd left Sandra back on the bench in front of Flatbreads, where the pursuit began. My heart was racing. I knew it was because of my thwarted efforts to engage Ed on trip number seven. Ed had done his best to keep up a barrier and communicate that he desired little to no contact with people from his past. I was processing the emotional pain lingering from our exchange and the feeling of being rejected by a friend I loved.

I grabbed my cell phone and called Sandra. I was trying to hold back my tears, as they flooded from my eyes. It made steering difficult. So much emotion was brimming, like lava cresting one of the Hawaiian volcanos, I had difficulty containing it.

Sandra answered her phone, "*Where are you? Are you OK?*" She asked with a shaky voice. There was an obvious element of fear in her voice that reflected her worry. When I looked at my phone while I sat at a red light, I realized that she'd sent a group text which I'd been copied on. It read, "*Please pray right now! Will ran off chasing Ed and I don't know where he is.*" Sandra's mind recalled the warning we had received from Ruth, the social worker. She was the one who tipped me off concerning Ed's whereabouts in Hawaii, and about his temper. She was afraid of Ed after watching him jump in front of her moving car. In fact, she warned me to be careful, stating, "*He may not be the Ed that you remember.*"

While it was true that he'd changed, I was convinced that the real Ed was still under the surface somewhere. Perhaps he was buried by years of emotional scar tissue and shame. It was clear from his eyes that there was an internal struggle, even in the moment when he contemplated having a meal with us. Despite his initial actions and verbal distancing, I believe that he was simply not sure who he could trust and who was out to get him.

I picked up Sandra, and we agreed that this excursion had run its course. We made a final call to Ed's family to bring them up to speed. After that, we received an encouraging call from Gumby and his wife Becky, who'd been praying for us all day long. We put them on speaker and processed our thoughts and emotions with them as we headed back to our hotel. I made one more phone call to Steve Bowman, since he was anxious to hear about Ed too.

We hung up and drove in silence. Emotions were running high, adrenaline was at a tipping point, and the gears in my head were still turning. I pondered, "*What do you do when the friend you've pursued for years comes face-to-face with you and rejects your help? What does a shepherd do when the one lost sheep evades coming home?"* The logical answer is perhaps to turn around and walk away. Since when does God make decisions based on logic? I had no idea what the way forward would hold, but I knew that our journey to locate Ed had concluded. Our first miracle was finding Ed. The second miracle involved getting him home and he simply wasn't ready.

Sandra and I decided to get dressed up and enjoy a final dinner to celebrate finding Ed. Not only that, we also wanted to celebrate the fact that God had answered our two prayers. First, that we would see him again, and second, that I could share with him the fact that he's loved, and that help is available if he ever wants it.

While Ed didn't express a desire for help or to reconnect, that decision was not ours to make. It is up to each of us to choose whether to love, or to withhold love. However, the recipient also has a choice, regarding whether or not they want to receive that love. Ed's choice was out of my control, but it did not dictate my decision to continue loving in the face of rejection. Actually, that is how God loves us. Our part is always based in our choice to receive or to reject His love.

During our flight home, I had some time to reflect on my final exchange with Ed. I was reminded of how often I'm very much like Ed when it comes to my relationship with God. God pursues a daily relationship with me that I oftentimes reject. It seems crazy when I think of Ed rejecting the very family and friends who truly love him, and yet how often am I guilty of doing the exact same thing with God? Why would anyone run from sincere love or an offer to help? While drug use may be Ed's excuse, I wonder what mine is? Perhaps you can relate?

I wondered if in Ed's situation, perhaps he's believed a lie which served as a catalyst for keeping others at a distance. I'm told that methamphetamine and similar substances can do serious damage when it comes to altering the way humans think.

Many of my homeless friends in San Diego have spoken with our team members about shame they carry for horrible life choices they've made in their past. If an individual allows their shame to foster the false belief that they are unlovable, then they may never allow anyone close enough to actually love them. Their false belief becomes a self-fulfilling prophesy.

Jesus' model of a good shepherd dedicated to pursuing one lost sheep inspires me. It is often times easier for me to offer grace to another person who has ship-wrecked their life, than it is for me to receive God's love for myself in my own brokenness. In addition to the model inspiring me to love others who are lost, it serves as a reminder, that as a sheep who is prone to get lost as well, I must also be willing to receive God's love and grace for myself, even when I don't feel like I deserve it.

I sat on the flight considering what a shepherd might do in my situation. What happens if he locates the one lost lamb, who in turn doesn't want to be found? My guess is that a good shepherd never gives up, because he sees value in every single sheep. I was left to consider what persistence might look like in the face of adversity.

Our trip to Hawaii was a success in locating Ed, yet it felt like a failure with regard to re-establishing the deep friendship that Ed and I once shared. I sat on that plane grieving the loss of a close friend and looking to God for insight concerning potential future trips. Should we return to Hawaii or to San Diego or had this adventure run its course? I was about to find out.

Chapter 14

It's Bigger Than Ed

A week after we returned home, I received a call from John Costello, the 60-year old Physical Education teacher and basketball coach from our 5th trip. By this time, the news had traveled to all the previous trip participants and he wanted to congratulate me on finding Ed.

John asked a few questions about Ed's state of mind and wanted to know about my future plans. I let him know that while we had located Ed, and had been able to engage him, it left me with a bitter-sweet feeling. Sure, I was thrilled we found him, but the story of the prodigal son concludes with the lost son returning home, followed by an all-out celebration. Flying back east without a banquet feast in Maui or Virginia, left me grieving and feeling a few laps short of victory.

John listened patiently and then commented, "*I believe the story is bigger than Ed.*" "*What do you mean?*" I asked, not following his line of thinking.

He explained, "*I've shared the story with high school students where I teach ever since I returned home. Kids I know are moved by the story and many of them have difficult lives.*" He went on to say, "*I offered a voluntary school assembly for students who wanted to hear more about my week living homeless, and over 250 kids showed up to participate. Lives are being touched, and it's now much bigger than Ed.*"

John asked me a question to drive his point home. "*You've said that every person we meet on the streets is another person's Ed, right?*" "*That's correct,*" I responded. He continued, "*Do you believe we made a positive impact on the homeless individuals who we met when we were in San Diego?*" "*Yes,*" I replied. John summarized what he was trying to convey with a final challenge in the form of a question, "*Then why would you stop?*" I stood with the phone pressed to my ear as I processed his words.

I might as well have been seated on a bench in Coach Costello's high school locker room. His words felt like a halftime pep talk, delivered to a team that had fallen behind. John was saying that if I wanted to win, then I'd better change my mindset and consider some of the great plays that had taken place in the first half. I soaked up the truth in his encouraging words and was motivated to get back out on the court for the second half of the game!

Coach Costello was exactly right. Not only had the multiple trips to San Diego impacted homeless lives there, but the concentric circles from our efforts continued to span even wider. He mentioned the teenagers from Broad Run High School who'd been inspired, as my mind recalled many of the trip participants who said, "*Living on the streets for a week was a life-changing experience!*" On a personal note, John shared what that trip had meant to him, confessing that he'd lost a close friend to drug addiction. He added, "*I took vacation leave for our week in San Diego to demonstrate to my students that helping people is one of the most important things that we can do in this life.*" For that reason, over 250 students and teachers who know and respect coach John Costello, were willing to stay after school and listen to his presentation.

We discussed possible next steps in Maui, now that we knew where Ed was living. Building on the concept that the mission was now 'bigger than Ed,' John asked, "*What are you going to do with all of the friends we've made in San Diego?*" It was a question that needed to be answered. Over the course of six trips to California, we'd come to know and care about friends on the streets, as well as the ones volunteering in the churches. It was true that the mission had begun with my quest to find the 'one,' but the 'one' had expanded to so many more. John nailed it on the head when he stated, "*This is bigger than Ed!*"

Up until that point, I'd been returning to San Diego between two and three times per year. It simply didn't feel right to never return again. The choice I was faced with was whether to make one final trip for closure sake, or to carry on the mission, focusing on the other 'ones' who were still lost on the streets of San Diego. After all, they certainly had their share of homeless individuals who often commented, "*I wish I was Ed and that someone was looking for me.*" Perhaps it was time that someone did.

After hanging up the phone, John's words worked magic. As I contemplated the entire discussion/locker room pep talk, my feelings of defeat were replaced with hope. I even considered the impression that the seven trips had on my own life. As a result of the journey I'd made some amazing new friendships. I felt privileged to share the adventure with selfless individuals like Steve Bowman. My week living on the streets with my eldest daughter Courtney had also been a highlight. She grew up hearing me share about my friendship with Ed and our crazy stories.

John was correct in the fact that there were multi-faceted blessings related to these trips, and that God had indeed used the journey to touch people beyond Ed. The greater mission was no longer limited to Ed, nor was it about me.

There was an entirely different group of people who had inadvertently been impacted. I'm referring to the spectators who followed the journey on social media. A man by the name of John messaged me to say, "*I'd given up on my homeless brother in Nashville. However, I've been inspired by what y'all are doing for your friend, so I'm planning to drive to Tennessee and spend my spring break searching for him. Thanks for leading by example!*" I had no idea who that man was, nor did it occur to me that others were inspired by our posts. I'll bet his brother felt loved when he realized that he hadn't been forgotten on the streets of Tennessee.

I was convinced that at least one more trip to San Diego was necessary. I figured that we could decide if trip eight was a closure trip or if we should continue returning after we gave it a shot. I wasted no time and called Steve to see how he felt about the idea. We had a lengthy conversation on the matter. In conclusion he said, "*I'm willing to go if you are.*" What an incredible guy Steve Bowman is! He'd repeatedly taken time off work, time away from his family and spent his own money to travel and live among the homeless. He did all that even though he'd never even met Ed Pelzner. I couldn't imagine a trip without him.

I picked up the phone to call a few other people who had expressed an interest in a homeless trip to San Diego. I wasn't so sure people would be interested, since we were no longer searching for Ed there. To my amazement, everyone I spoke with said, *"Count me in!"* Before long, we had another trip scheduled for September 17, 2017, just one month after returning from Maui.

We arrived in San Diego with a team of six. For some odd reason, we always seemed to end up with groups divisible by three. It made it easier to divide into teams. Steve and I traveled together and went to grab lunch in the Gas Lamp District before meeting up with the rest of the team. We spent time reminiscing about previous teams and unfor-gettable memories. We even scrolled through the photos on our cell phones, recalling some of the drama surrounding each image.

The following morning was 'go' time. We rallied as a team in the lobby with packs on, ready to roll. Our group was balanced evenly with three young millennials between the ages of 20-25, (Connor Sarant, Ben Skriloff, and Laki Atanasov), and three old men, each just happened to be 51-years old, (me, Steve and Eric Locklear). For some reason no women signed up for trip eight.

That particular week contained an added degree of risk, since San Diego had been declared a severe health hazard due to an outbreak of Hepatitis. One San Diego news article estimated that 400+ homeless in San Diego had been diagnosed with the infection, with fifteen casualties. As a safety measure, city officials authorized funds to have the streets downtown power washed with bleach, in an attempt to stop the spread.

To minimize our risk, I asked every participant to get a Hepatitis A vaccine before the trip. The team complied and was eager to care for the homeless.

(Left to right: Ben, Laki, Connor, Steve, Eric & Will)

Steve took Connor and Ben to form team one, while I started out with Laki and Eric, on team two. Eric Locklear and I had some shared history, since we attended the same elementary, middle and high schools. Although we'd lost touch since the mid 1980's, we had only recently reconnected. Eric also had history with Ed, since we all grew up in Reston, Virginia and the two of them were both on the South Lakes High School wrestling team together. While Eric was aware that the San Diego trip was no longer a mission to find Ed, he'd registered in July before we found Ed in Maui.

Steve took his team in one direction and I took Laki and Eric in another. Since we began our hike in the downtown area, I decided to bring my team to the Neil Good Day Center. We walked past Father Joe's Village, (also known as Saint Vinney's), and straight toward the county building. Without the quest for Ed, we were free to walk wherever we sensed God's Spirit leading. No longer feeling the time crunch that was associated with limited days to find Ed, we could relax our pace.

About 50 yards before we reached the county facility, we were stopped by an older black man by the name of Robert Ivy, Jr. He inquired as to what the three of us were doing in that part of town, so I told him.

When I asked him about his story, he shared openly. He said that he'd been sober and drug-free since November of 1992. Then Robert asked, "*You want me to tell you how I did it?*" We answered, "*Sure, go for it!*" He went on to say that he'd surrendered his life to Jesus and asked for his help. "*I'm telling you, it was a miracle,*" He exclaimed. "*Cuz I ain't never had the desire to return to that crap again!*"

Then he asked, "*You wanna know why the other people on the streets don't get free?*" We nodded in the affirmative, "*They don't want to. They'd get help if they wanted it, but they're not ready to quit. You gotta be ready!*" His unsolicited opinion was encouraging. He concluded, "*You can't help people that don't want help!*"

I allowed his words to settle in as I processed his wisdom. After a moment, we offered to pray with Robert. Without hesitation, he held out his hands to us. The four of us formed a circle as we joined hands and asked God to hear us. I prayed for my new friend Robert, and he was quick to chime in, "*Yes, Lord, hear my brother's prayer!*" His excitement grew as we asked God to bless him. By the time we'd concluded the prayer, Robert had tears streaming down his cheeks and hugged each of us before he was willing to let us go. He was incredibly grateful that we'd been willing to take the time to hear what he had to say, and also to take the time to intercede on his behalf to God.

As I considered Robert's understanding of local addicts, I wondered what it might take for Ed to make the same choice. What sort of situation must someone encounter as a catalyst for the addict to crave freedom, as Mr. Ivy had done? Eric and Laki were clearly moved by the encounter. We pressed on from downtown San Diego and headed directly north towards Ocean Beach. We took time as we walked to share our own life stories and get better acquainted.

As I mentioned, Eric and I shared history back in our formative years. We'd even been in the same first grade class together. While we attended the same schools, we hadn't really been close friends, nor had we kept up since that time. Hearing him share the details of his life journey helped to fill in the gaps from childhood to the present.

In addition to Eric's connection with Ed on the high school wrestling team, Ed also played a unique role in Eric's faith journey. Approximately one year earlier, Eric showed up at the church where I serve on a part-time basis. I recognized him the moment he came through the door and immediately greeted him. I hadn't seen him in years and said, "*Eric Locklear, how are you doing, man? How many years has it been?*" He responded, "*I've no idea, I didn't think you'd recognize me.*" "*Of course, how could I forget you?*" I replied.

Then I asked, "*So what brings you here?*" Where do you usually go to church?" I made an assumption asking that question, to which he responded, "*I don't go to church!*" His answer puzzled me, so I inquired, "*Really, why is that?*" He spoke candidly and answered, "*I've never really been the kind of guy who attends church. I believe most church people are hypocrites, and the leaders are televangelist-types who all want your money.*" As he spoke his countenance was serious and calculated, without so much as a partial smirk.

He paused to collect his thoughts and then said, "*My wife Carolee was on social media one day and happened to discover that her friend Eddy Pelzner from high school had become homeless.*" Eric's wife Carolee was also an alumnus of South Lakes High School in Reston, Virginia. When Carolee told Eric about Ed's status, he was reminded that they had both been on the wrestling team together. Eric continued, "*Carolee also informed me that you had travelled to San Diego in search of Ed, and had been willing to live homeless to find him.*" He reasoned, "*I know Will, and I remember Ed, so I know this isn't a fake-news story concocted by Facebook. I've gotta be honest, I was moved by your willingness to go look for Ed on the streets.*" He cut to the chase and concluded, "*I figured that perhaps I've been wrong. Anyone willing to live on the streets and look for a guy is not playing games. I want to find out more about church, more about Jesus and that's why I'm here.*"

Wow, I'd never been greeted at the front door of a church with such vulnerability in my entire life! I so appreciated his honesty and willingness to come see for himself.

One year later, I found myself walking the backstreets of San Diego with that same skeptic. Although at that time, Eric had decided to pursue faith in Jesus, he'd also chosen to take a week off from work to love the homeless in San Diego. It was another reminder of John Costello's epiphany, *"This journey has grown bigger than Ed!"* He was dead right, the impact of leaving the *"99 for 1"* had far reaching effects, even with Eric who'd witnessed the trip via social media.

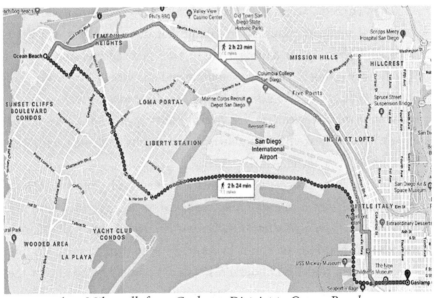

(7.1 Mile walk from Gaslamp District to Ocean Beach,
Image courtesy of Google maps)

Our team rendezvoused with Steve's team in Ocean Beach close to supper time. Everyone was getting hungry so I called my friend Paul Arnold and asked if he knew about a church meal that evening. He replied, *"I don't know of any place that's offering dinner this evening."* I couldn't recall a trip when we were unable to find any food since our very first time living on the streets. I thanked Paul and promised to meet up later in the week.

After the call, I pulled the fellas together to let them know that we had a decision to make... *"We have a dilemma. There are no local churches offering a free meal this evening. We can either beg for money to buy food, or we can go without eating. I'm open to other suggestions if anybody has one. What do you all think we should do?"*

The group didn't seem remotely excited about pan handling. Ben piped up, *"I'd rather fast than beg."* As the guys were discussing potential options, I offered one final suggestion, *"I know of two people who live locally. I can text them about our situation and see if they offer anything, without begging of course. If neither person offers us food, then we can go without."*

The group agreed with the plan, so I sent an identical text to two different women, both in the Ocean Beach area. My text read, *"Good evening, it's Will Cravens and I'm back on the streets this week with a team of six men. We're looking for a homeless meal this evening and have thus far struck out. Do you know of any church food pantries or any other potential options we might consider for dinner tonight?"*

How would you respond to a text like that from someone you know, but are not that close with? One of the women responded saying, *"I'm not familiar with any places that offer food, but if I think of one, I'll be sure to let you know."* I thanked her, and didn't heard back from her again.

The second woman responded, *"How can I help?"* What an amazing response! I asked, *"Do you have any leftovers or canned goods that you want to get rid of?"* Then she texted back, *"Why don't you tell me where you are and I'll come by and give you guys some money?"* I said, *"Thanks for the offer, but I don't feel right taking your money."* She countered, *"Can I bring you pizza?"* That sounded great, so I thanked her and texted her our location. Forty minutes later, she rolled up to the parking lot of one of the churches on Sunset Boulevard with an extra-large hot pizza and a 6-pack of cold, water bottles! We were so grateful! Although we invited her to stay, she had to get going. We thanked her, and she was off.

As we sat in the parking lot savoring every pizza slice, we chatted about the one woman's willingness to serve us without hesitation. Even though the team had been willing to go without, they were extremely appreciative for what had been provided.

Then we discussed the two responses. Having sent the identical text to two different people, with two entirely different responses, we talked about how we might have responded if the roles had been reversed. One detail that I did not mention is that one of the women shares the same faith as me, and the other does not. Which one do you think offered to help?

The woman who responded in kind and asked, "*How can I help?*" to the best of my knowledge doesn't share the same faith. On the other hand, the woman who publicly professes the same belief and has even served in full-time ministry didn't offer any form of help or food. I'm not pointing this out as a form of judgment, and I'm unaware if there had perhaps been some extenuating circumstances. However, I believe the way we respond to others who are in need is a point worth reflecting on.

I was personally challenged by the actions of the woman who asked, "*How can I help?*" I can't honestly say that I'm quick to offer help when I'm sitting at home, relaxing with my family. It's much easier to simply delegate the responsibility to a church, the government or another charitable organization. When the roles are reversed, and I'm the one in need, it provides a very different perspective worth remembering when I'm back home.

While we were finishing up our meal, a police cruiser pulled abruptly into the parking lot. One officer hopped out and stood over us. It became apparent that a local neighbor had reported six homeless men congregating in a church parking lot. When the officer confronted us, he asked if we were setting up camp for the night. I responded, "*No, sir, we were just eating some pizza that a kind friend provided before we move on.*"

Steve asked, "*Was the person who called you the man who lives in that house and hates homeless people?*" Steve pointed at a particular home behind the church where we'd previously seen an older man come outside to yell at any homeless who came within inches of his property. The lead officer answered, "*You know about him?*" "*Yes, we do,*" I replied. I let him know what we were doing there and shared a bit of our story. At that point, both officers eased up. They realized that the allegations of a large group of homeless men camping in the church parking lot were false.

I asked, "*How are you two holding up? I can't imagine what it must be like to police such a large population of homeless in Ocean Beach.*" The taller of the two officers shared candidly, "*One of our biggest struggles in this town is actually related to the fact that we have close to 300 registered sex offenders who live as residents in Ocean Beach. You wouldn't believe the chaos that we deal with as a result. That drama is on top of the thousands of transient homeless who roll through town, with their own set of problems.*" We chatted for a while, thanked them for their service and then pushed on to look for a place to sleep.

Just as they were about to drive away, the shorter of the two officers said, "*I wouldn't sleep in Robb Field Park if I were you. We've recently experienced a rise in the homeless population there, and have responded to calls involving violence there almost every night.*" We thanked them for the tip, since that was precisely where we'd been planning to camp. We walked about a mile past Robb Field and located a spot to crash. There was a small patch of Pine Trees near an exit ramp across the street from Sea World. It was perfect!

We woke up early the following morning, and packed up just after 6:00 a.m. While we were stuffing our belongings back in our bags, I noticed a man walking his dog along the road. He was staring at our group, most likely curious about the large group of homeless campers. I made note of the time and said, "This was a great camping spot. Let's return here tonight, but be sure to set an alarm for 5:30 a.m. tomorrow and depart before the dog walker makes his rounds. Everyone agreed as we packed up.

(Left to right: Eric, Will, Laki & Ben, hiking away from camp)

We decided to mix up the teams, so we traded Laki for Ben, as a way of getting to know different people in the group. We headed southeast toward Old Town and met a kind man traveling with his guitar. He introduced himself as Phil Harrison, and said he was enroute to a gig in El Cajon. He told us that he is the actual brother of George Harrison from the Beatles. He was fairly convincing and bore a resemblance of the iconic figure. However, when we Googled Harrison's family tree after meeting Phil, we learned that George didn't have a brother with that name, nor did the man's age line up with his story.

I found myself wanting to believe his tale, as well as many of the other stories that our homeless friends would tell. Some would turn out to be true, while others, not so much. I want to give people the benefit of the doubt, unless there is a reason to think otherwise. After all, I knew what it felt like to be mistrusted from the first time I'd lived homeless. I recalled the woman who served me beans in a buffet line who asked me to keep moving after I told her that I was an East Coast pastor. No one likes to be treated like a liar.

Later that day, Eric, Ben and I encountered a large homeless man struggling on the side of Arena Boulevard. He looked as though he was in his late 50's and was attempting to stand up. Ben stopped to ask if he needed any help. The man's name was Ward, and he smelled like a distillery. He'd clearly been drinking heavily and as he stood up, we noticed an open wound on his arm. In addition, Ward had a black eye, a swollen hand and a bloody arm. It looked as though there was still fresh blood on his hand, as we helped him to his feet.

He told us that he had recently been released from the hospital as evidenced by the hospital bracelet that was still on his hand. When you stood close to Ward, there was a pungent aroma of alcohol and urine. We offered to pray with him and without hesitation, he grasped our hands and said, "*Yes, please!*" Ben took the lead, and Ward was all too thrilled to receive this sort of care and attention.

After the prayer, Ward teared up and tried to explain what was behind his show of emotion. "*I'd just been released from the hospital where they treated me for wounds inflicted by a group of men who beat me up. When I saw you three approaching, I thought, 'Oh no, here come more thugs to rough me up again.' Instead of pounding me, you all prayed with me. I'm thankful beyond words!*" He was moved by our concern for his well-being and his tears continued to flow as he thanked us and muttered, "*This is one of the best days of my life!*"

(*Ward*)

After expressing his gratitude, Ward confessed, "*I just wish there was a place I could go that had a warm bed, some food and no one that would hurt me.*" In response, I said, "*Ward, we just passed a halfway house a few blocks away. We can take you there now, and they have everything you asked for. However, you'd have to leave your bottle of vodka here, since the shelter is alcohol and drug-free.*"

He answered, "*No, I couldn't do that, but I am very hungry.*" I responded, "*Well, you're in luck! The three of us are headed to a free dinner at Sacred Heart Catholic Church in Ocean Beach.*" He replied, "*Ocean Beach is way too far for me to walk in my condition!*" He said this while leaning on his aluminum crutches. I offered a solution, "*I can call an Uber driver to bring us all there so you don't have to walk.*" He responded, "*I can't go there. I just want to rest on my wall.*" He pointed to a cinderblock wall located across the street from where we were standing.

We offered to help him cross the road, yet once again, he declined our help. As he gathered his belongings to move in the direction of the wall, I wondered how on earth he would manage. He had two crutches, a liter bottle of vodka, some clothes and was badly injured. We watched as he wedged two crutches under his right arm, while in the left hand, he carried the bottle of vodka, and spare clothing.

I turned to Eric and commented, "*That's the picture.*" He looked at me confused as to what I meant by my comment. I added, "*As Robert Ivy, Jr. told us the previous day, 'You can't help someone who isn't ready to change.'*" While Ward expressed his desire for a warm bed, food and a safer environment, he wasn't willing to give up the booze that was crippling him.

As we watched Ward hobble across the street, Eric commented, "*Ward actually has three crutches.*" You could see two aluminum crutches under his arm, although Eric was referring to the third crutch in his left hand, which was the liter of vodka. Life on the street offers a plethora of crutches. One can use alcohol, methamphetamine, crack cocaine, heroin, or any other substance that temporarily medicates pain. While all offer short-term relief, they have a paralyzing effect in the long run.

I thought back to my final conversation with Ed in Maui. He shouted, "*I just can't do it!*" I speculated that perhaps he was referring to his unwillingness to part with his own crutch of methamphetamine. God only knows, but it's heart-wrenching to watch men and women like Ward as they choose to remain alone with their crutch. Until they are ready to get clean, no one can make that choice for them.

We walked from that encounter towards the church dinner, processing the emotional interaction. Ward had wept with us and thanked us with sincerity. He asked us for help, and we offered him a few tangible options, all of which he systematically refused. In the end, we watched him hobble away alone, and return to what he referred to as "the wall." On two separate occasions that week, we returned to Ward's wall, hoping to check in, but we never saw him again.

That evening, we met up with Steve, Connor, and Laki at Sacred Heart. We were hungry after a long day and glad to get a break. We entered from the side of the building, to let their team of volunteers know that we had a team of six men who were ready and willing to serve. I said, "Hello" to Jack and thanked him for his service. He's a true servant-leader in the way he cares for the volunteers and cooks for the homeless. He thanked us for offering to help and asked if our team might stay after the meal to assist with clean-up. We agreed and returned to the front of the church to wait in line with the rest of our friends.

*(Jack – Lead chef at Sacred Heart Catholic Church
in Ocean Beach, San Diego)*

We ran into a friend by the name of Clay, whom Steve and I hadn't seen since our first trip living on the streets. Clay was the man we met on the beachfront who encouraged us to speak with the ABC News film crew. I hollered his name and invited him to join us for dinner. I wanted to catch up, since it had been so long. He filled his plate with food and took the place next to me at our table. He looked rough, with an eye infection and disheveled appearance. I asked *"How have you been doing? What's new since I saw you last?"* He began to catch us up on the details of his life, then shifted topics to inquire about Ed. I filled him in about finding Ed in Maui, although he seemed distracted.

I noticed that Clay's right hand was twitching. I asked, *"What's wrong, can I get you something?"* He responded with intensity, *"Not unless you have a fifth of vodka. I'm having DTs."* "DTs" refers to "Delirium Tremens," a severe form of alcohol withdrawal. The condition is common among individuals who are attempting to detoxify their body from alcohol. The person's body shakes as a reaction to having been dependent on the substance for a prolonged period of time. Clay was trying desperately to hold it together, and bring a cup of water to his mouth, as his right hand could barely hold it still without spilling.

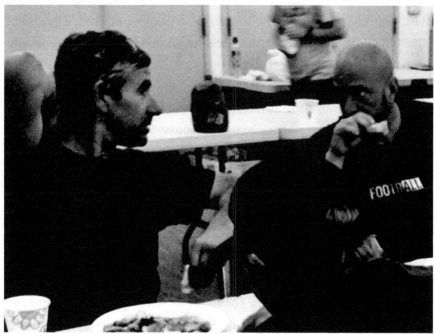

(Left to right: Clay & Will at Sacred Heart dinner)

In his frustration, Clay turned to me and asked, *"I can't handle these shakes, can you watch my food? I'll be right back."* I agreed and he abruptly dashed out the back door. I asked the kitchen staff for some foil to cover his plate. They put it in the fridge with his name on it, but he never did return. It was clear that Clay left to find the only thing that might stop his hands from shaking, giving in to what his body craved. Clay is a great guy. However, similar to Ward stuck on his wall, Clay dashed out to find his crutch. My heart breaks for the men and women we've met who desire to get free, but haven't yet discovered what Robert Ivy, Jr. had come to realize. I prayed that my friend Ed will one day come to his senses, as Robert had, and be free.

On the following morning, our crew drifted back to Ocean Beach for some coffee. While we sat in Starbucks taking a few minutes to charge our phones, we watched an older pusher hand large amounts of baggies to three younger individuals. He gave them instructions about selling and warned them that they better not dare attempt to screw him over. I was amazed at the sheer lack of concern for any surrounding customers. His large container with the packets of drugs was marked, "For office use only." The older boss man was wearing khaki overalls and was dressed like a general contractor.

Perhaps he was a general contractor, and dealing drugs was a side business. It was difficult to say, but it frustrated me to watch the three young people allow themselves to be bossed around by a man that looked as though he could be their father. Why weren't they in college or working in a job that they could be proud of. I wondered what their stories were and how they were recruited by the older man.

Of the three young people, there were two males and one female. One of the men was dressed like a male prostitute, and the girl with him carried herself like an animal that had been abused by its owner. Her eyes darted here and there, and she appeared suspicious of everyone who came near. I struck up a conversation with the other young man, "How are you doing?" He was fairly friendly in his response, and asked me where I was from.

The blond gal across the table was eavesdropping and chimed in when she heard me mention Virginia. She volunteered, "I'm from New Jersey, not far from Virginia." I wondered what kind of family she came from and if her parents were at home emotionally broken, praying for her return? Whose Ed was she? Certainly, someone was grieving her loss, I speculated.

As we began chatting, the older dealer and younger man dressed as a prostitute stepped outside. The young man who was seated at a table on my right suddenly confessed, "*My name is Ray and I'm actually not doing well at all. I've been struggling with depression.*" I responded, "*I'm sorry to hear that, can we pray with you?*" He took my hand and welcomed the gesture, not at all concerned with what his friends might think. We finished praying, and Ray re-engaged with his posse out front.

When we left Starbucks, Connor heard the older man chastising Ray for speaking with us. We headed back towards the beach and found a curb to plant our backsides on. Everyone on our team had witnessed the three young people being treated like slave labor by the older man and they wanted to discuss it. As we were in the midst of deep discussion, a young African-American man made his way over toward us. He was wrapped in a large royal blue packing blanket. His dreads were sprouting out of the top of his wrap, and we invited him to have a seat. He plopped down on my left and introduced himself by his street name, "Chocolita."

He shared, "*I'm from Zimbabwe, and I moved to the USA with my little brother two years ago. I've been living homeless in San Diego for eight months since my brother and I went separate ways.*" We told him our purpose on the streets. He said, "*I was listening to what you all were saying as I walked over, please continue your discussion,*" so we did. At one point he chimed in, saying, "*The drug dealer needs to hear about the love of God as well.*" A truth that we needed to be reminded of, which seemed to resound louder when spoken by Chocolita. He stood up to leave after he'd been with us for about ten minutes, and told us that he'd better get going. I offered to pray for him. With that, he quickly sat back down next to me and responded, "*Yes, please!*"

I put my arm around this young man and began to pray for his family, for his past, for his future, and for his brother whom he'd mentioned earlier in the conversation. When I prayed for his brother, he began weeping. Not a gentle cry, but with deep-rooted sobbing and tears, he buried his head into my chest and squeezed me tightly. I squeezed back, as a father would hold his traumatized son. It was a powerful, profound moment.

I was unsure what God was doing in his heart, but when the prayer was over, he continued clinging to me for a few more minutes. Once we stood to leave, he thanked me profusely for taking time to pray. My shirt was soaked with his tears, which had penetrated my sweater and the shirt I had on underneath that. Then he caught me off guard with an unexpected expression of gratitude. He dropped to his knees, took my hand and kissed it. His gesture humbled me. I'm not the pope, nor am I comfortable with this form of affection, but I received it because it was what he wanted to give. He walked away on that overcast morning as we all stood in silence, still processing the events of that morning.

(Left to right: Will & Chocolita in Ocean Beach)

We were considering the day ahead and how to divide the teams, when I got an idea. I thought it was time to give Connor an opportunity to lead. After all, this was his second trip, and we only had a couple of days left out west. I appointed him leader of the day and gave him charge of the millennial team.

It was great to be on Steve's team once again. The two of us had both been busy leading other teams for multiple trips, so it was refreshing to walk the streets once again with my friend. We were team 51, since that was our age, and we decided to enjoy a more relaxed pace.

Steve turned my direction and asked, "*Where are we off to?*" I responded, "*We haven't been back to Mission Gorge this trip, I say we bring Eric there.*" Both men agreed, and we set off.

We arrived at the Home Depot in Mission Gorge early in the afternoon. This was the location where we encountered Israel and Juan and threw a pizza party for the men hiding in the riverbed. On our previous trip, we met an entirely different band of occupants in the riverbed, and experienced a case of mistaken identity with "Fast Eddy." It was time to return.

We plunged into the riverbed area behind Home Depot and quickly realized that it was completely vacant. We ran into one homeless man and asked where everyone had gone. He replied, "*The cops cleared it out, man. It's been empty for over a month!*" What was at one time a sprawling tent city, was entirely cleared out. We explained to Eric what it looked like before the eviction, and decided to walk farther up the trail to check on my little friend Jose. His tent home wasn't far away and I was convinced he would want Eric to meet his fearsome pet 'oso' bear.

We followed the trail all the way up to San Diego Mission Road, and crossed the busy street to pick up the trail on the opposite side. We were just about to round the patch of trees and bamboo stalks to catch a glimpse of Jose's casa, when I realized that something awful had happened.

In place of the old tent and large stuffed bear, we found a memorial created in Jose's honor. I stood silently reading the memorial sign that was posted next to a sprawling tree on the water's edge. The sign read that Jose Hernandez had passed away on August 19th, 2017, just one month earlier. While it failed to mention the cause of death, it described him as a loving father, uncle, brother, and grandfather to many who would miss him dearly.

(Jose's memorial in riverbed area of Mission Gorge)

I was frozen in shock, recalling our time with him just seven months earlier. My daughter Courtney had even asked me to say "hello" to Jose, since he'd made such an impression on her. I recalled his gentle spirit and silly humor, evident when he introduced Jason and Courtney to his bear.

(Left to right: Jason, Courtney, Will & Jose)

Grieving this unexpected loss, I became filled with curiosity regarding how he passed. We usually didn't venture beyond that area on the trail, which led deeper into another dangerous segment of the riverbed. Filled with sadness, I wasn't concerned with risk, I just wanted to know what happened to my friend Jose. I led Eric and Steve farther down the path.

We worked our way up the quiet trail, and kept our eyes open for any unsuspecting people. We spotted a tent behind a makeshift barrier. The barrier was constructed with a rope strung between trees with a large blanket draped over the rope. The barrier served as a boundary which clearly communicated that visitors were not welcome.

(Left to right: Will & Miles)

I stopped when I reached the obvious barrier and hollered, "Hello." A voice shouted back, "*Who is that?*" I responded, "*My name is Will and I'm a friend of Jose.*" Those ten words were all it took to drive the man in hiding out to meet us. He looked to be in his early 40s as he peered over the rope fence line. He rested his forearms on the rope and asked, "*How'd you know Jose?*" I responded, "*I'm a pastor and I live on the streets a couple of weeks each year, searching for an old friend. I met Jose on one of my trips and we became friends. I stopped by his tent to say hello and see how he was doing.*" He studied my face, deciding if he could trust me or not. I suppose I passed the test.

"*Jose was murdered,*" He stated while his face lost all expression. I'd been wondering if Jose had died of natural causes, since the streets can be hard on a person's body and he was up in years. *"Murdered? Why would anyone want to kill Jose? He was such a sweet little man,"* I asked in shock. He continued, *"Jose was actually partying with a man he knew and tried to joke with him. The man was not one to joke, and became so offended by Jose's sarcasm, that he lost his mind in a fit of rage. He took one of Jose's tent poles and stabbed him in the chest, before hitting him in the head with a rock so hard that Jose's right eye fell out of the socket. Finally, he set his tent on fire and left him for dead."* The three of us stood in shock processing the horror of it all.

The man warmed up a bit and introduced himself as Miles. He went on to share that his girlfriend had dragged Jose's body from the burning tent, before calling 9-1-1. *"Jose was in a coma and lived about a month and a half, before his family decided to pull the plug on the 19th of August."* They caught his murderer who is in jail, awaiting trial.

It was hard to consider such a sweet little man being brutally beaten and murdered. I wondered if there was more to the story as I stood there in shock, pained by the tragedy. I asked Miles if we might pray with him before we leaving. He said, *"Sure."* I inquired to find out if there was anything specific, he wanted prayer for. He responded very candidly, *"I'm sure you know the drill. The usual homeless life struggles: addiction, life change... I'm a mess."*

He understood that a pastor walking the streets becomes familiar with the requests for freedom from addiction, God's provision in their depravity, and His protection. Just before praying with Miles, he said, *"Life is cheap on the streets. You have to be careful who you joke with and never to turn your back on anyone."* We stretched our hands across the rope barrier and prayer together, all four of us. This had previously been an area in the riverbed where Miles, or the people camping in his spot had cursed at us and told us to turn around. Due to the loss of Jose, they were willing to talk and were open to praying.

When we left Miles and dialed up an Uber driver from a nearby parking lot, the three of us waited in silence. Sometimes it's better not to talk. Our Uber driver showed up and I took the front seat. His name was

Ryan, and he asked, "*So what brings you men to San Diego?*" Not really in a mood to talk, I gave him a speedy reader's digest version. He was moved by our story and decided to open up.

He said, "*I'm currently serving in the US Navy as a mechanic and I'm stationed in San Diego with my family. I drive for Uber on the side to make a little extra cash.*" I asked Ryan what he does for fun and he replied, "*My son and I love to take all terrain four-wheeler vehicles riding off road. Life has treated us fairly well. I've been in the service for 22 years and plan to seek a new career path after my retirement.*" We were getting close to our destination so I asked Ryan if there was anything that we could pray for. He replied, "*No, but thanks for asking.*"

After a brief pause he looked in my direction and for whatever reason, said he changed his mind. "*Actually, I could use some prayer in one specific area. My wife and I recently found out that our middle school teenager is addicted to pornography. We had no idea until we caught him and now, we aren't sure how to handle it. Our son isn't a drug addict, but he does whatever he can to look at pornography.*" His voice grew quiet and was filled with emotion.

I took the lead praying, while Steve and Eric extended hands to the front seat on Ryan's shoulder, to let him know that they were present too. We finished praying, exited the car and Ryan popped the trunk to help us collect our backpacks. I extended my hand to bid him farewell, but he rejected it. Instead he threw his arms wide open for a hug. Not your everyday Uber driver's farewell, but his eyes were full with tears, and he wanted to express his appreciation. Although I felt that we hadn't done much, Ryan was moved that we took the time.

Addiction is not exclusive to the streets. It seems to find its way into homes in suburbia as well. Why do we as humans so often desire to medicate, rather than simply face reality? Do we believe falsely that we are stronger than those who went before us and fell prey to the same traps?

It's similar to the insects that fly dangerously close to get a look at the beautiful blue light of a bug zapper. No insect ever stops to take note of the tray below littered with dead bug carcasses. Or perhaps they think, "*I'm stronger than the other bugs, I'll fly away before I get zapped.*" Of course, insects don't reason like that, but it would seem that for a large percentage of humanity, neither do we. An expert I spoke with at one Salvation Army shelter said, "*The chemicals in some of the drugs such as methamphetamine, heroine and crack cocaine, are so strong, that many users report addiction after the very first use.*" After a person gets hooked, only that person can decide when they are ready to quit and get help.

At the close of the day, emotions ran high. After hearing the tragic story of Jose's death, I was reminded that life on the streets is cheap. There are plenty of people who wouldn't think twice about taking a life. I worried for Ed's safety. I hoped that he'd never joke with the wrong person, as Jose had done. I was also left pondering the conversation from our Uber driver Ryan. I'd never been hugged by a driver before and was left to consider what kind of impact our trips had on those with whom we engaged.

Steve and I were up late that evening discussing the merit of making more return trips to San Diego. Should we finalize that branch of the journey to focus on Maui or continue going to both places? We talked about a myriad of options and ideas but couldn't make up our minds either way. We finally decided to sleep on it, and I offered up a prayer to God asking for clarity on the matter.

I should mention that I had a unique experience the week before I left for San Diego. I enjoy public speaking and was delivering a message of inspiration to approximately 300 employees in Charlotte, North Carolina. The event was a staff lunch reception at Joe Gibbs Racing, addressing the NASCAR staff as I do on a quarterly basis there. They are all too familiar with Ed's story and my journey to the streets of San Diego. I shared the thrilling news of finally locating Ed in Maui. I also happened to mention our return trip to San Diego. I asked for their prayers, as I was preparing for our 8th trip back to California, unsure what it would be like without Ed being present.

After I finished speaking on stage, a man by the name of Steve Wesley approached me and introduced himself. He let me know that he'd been battling cancer and asked me to pray. We spent a few minutes asking God to heal his body and invited God to do a miracle. When we finished praying, I began to head for the door, since I had to catch a flight back to northern Virginia. However, all of a sudden before I reached the door, he shouted, to get my attention.

I spun around in Steve's direction. He was pointing at me with his index finger and he hollered, "*Hey Will, I need to tell you something!*" I walked back toward him so he wouldn't have to shout. When I was within five feet of Steve, he said with authority, "*The Lord wants you to go back to San Diego. In fact, there's someone specifically who needs you there. Your work isn't finished there.*" His demeanor was intense and his words were intentional. This was not a general encouragement to return to California. Steve was saying that there was a particular person with a specific need, and that God had made it clear to him that he needed to tell me that. He continued, "*You guys will make an impact when you go back. The trip will not be a waste of your time.*"

(Left to right: Steve Wesley & Will at Joe Gibbs Racing)

Steve's words were in the back of my mind all week long. I would quietly pray, "*God, please reveal to me the person that Steve was talking about, so that I don't miss the opportunity.*"

The evening after learning of Jose's loss, I was feeling sort of low, but did my best to rally and to be an encouragement to my homeless friends at the meal. We happened to be at the Wednesday night dinner hosted by the Methodist Church in Pacific Beach. Ryan had dropped us off a block from the church and my eyes were scanning the crowd of homeless for familiar faces.

I spotted Tom and Paul as we made our way through the line into the dining hall. Paul invited me to join him for dinner. We took two chairs beside one another at a crowded table. When Paul asked me about my day, I expressed my sorrow regarding the loss of Jose. My story seemed to jog a recent memory in Paul's mind and he turned in my direction to share. He began, "*This past month I found a dead homeless man in a public bathroom.*" He had my attention and carried on. "*When the park authority came in to inspect the place, he had difficulty opening one of the stalls, so I volunteered to help. Eventually we were able to force the door open, only to discover a homeless guy sleeping with his body leaning against the wall. I reached over to wake him, and the man was cold as ice and stiff with rigor mortis. The park authority ran to call the police, while I decided to slide the man's hood back, to see if I knew him.*"

Paul continued, "*As soon as I saw his expressionless face, I recognized him. The guy is about my age, my height and my weight. He even has a full white beard like me. In fact, several people have mistaken the two of us in the past.*"

Then Paul's tone grew very serious as he looked straight at me, "*As I stared at that dead man's face, I thought, 'This is me; Dead on a toilet, with no one to mourn my loss.'*" Paul confessed, "*Years ago I battled depression, but it hadn't been an issue until that day. Ever since that moment in the stall, face-to-face with that dead man, I have the nagging feeling that I'm no longer making a difference. I am discouraged by those I have helped get clean from drugs and alcohol, because they often end up right back on them within six months. I've begun to question my own value and purpose."* Paul's demeanor was humble and broken, as though he was searching for a reason to move forward.

As I have stated earlier, there is no one-size-fits-all homeless person. Paul's story is proof to that end. While many wind up on the streets due to an addiction, financial loss, relational breakup, mental illness, or some other life storm, there are others who don't fit those stereotypes. Paul's road to the street is especially unique.

Paul had shared with me that years earlier he'd been reading the Bible, when he was struck by the challenge from Jesus found in Matthew chapter 19, verse 21. Jesus spoke saying that if a person desired to be complete, then they should sell all their possessions and give to the poor, and as a result they'd have treasure in heaven." When Paul read those words, he felt compelled to literally put them into practice. He had a sidewalk sale and then called the Salvation Army to pick up what was left.

Through a myriad of other circumstances, Paul ended up living in his truck and serving other people on the street. After all, my blind friend Tom was the one who introduced me to Paul, saying, *"Paul can help you find your friend, he helps a number of people like me."* While Paul had been living that way for over four years at that time, he had grown tired and discouraged.

As he tried to summarize his feelings he said, *"Ever since I saw the dead man that looked like me, I can't seem to shake the heaviness and depression that my life has lost value and nothing I'm doing is making a difference. In other words, why should I even be alive?"*

As Paul and I sat there considering the heaviness of his words, I had a moment of clarity. It was as if I sensed God's Spirit whisper in my ear, *"He's the one I sent you to encourage."* I felt a smile overtake my face, as my heart was filled with compassion for Paul. I shared with him my experience at Gibbs Racing and the words spoken to me by Steve Wesley before my trip. I confessed, *"I've been praying all week for clarity about who God wanted me to speak to specifically."* Then I looked him in the eyes and said, "*You're the one Paul! If I only came on this trip to tell you that your life is not a mistake or a waste of time, and to reassure you that you're making a difference with Tom and so many others, then it was worth the trip!*" By this time, Paul's eyes were moist with tears, and he began to weep. Although we were in a room surrounded by more than a hundred hungry homeless individuals, we didn't seem to notice. We savored the moment.

As the week came to a close, we made our rounds to see who else we might encourage. We met a man by the name of Fernando earlier that week. We ran into him multiple times throughout the week. He told us that he was 78-years old, and was originally from Monterrey, Mexico. He was missing several teeth and his skin was dark brown revealing years of sun exposure. He was soft-spoken and humble, expressing gratitude every time we'd made time for him that week.

On our final day, we spotted Fernando seated at a picnic table in Mariner's Point Park. Fernando was solving word puzzles and sitting alone. In fact, every time we ran into him, he was alone. We never spotted him at a meal, because he preferred to stay away from larger groups.

Fernando survived by canning. He collected aluminum and plastic bottles all day long. Then he would cart them off in bags and take whatever money they would give him to purchase food. He was particular about his diet since he had so few teeth.

We stopped to chat with him before making the long hike from Mission Bay back to depart on the following day. When we approached him, Steve and I were once again discussing whether or not we should continue returning to San Diego. We chatted with Fernando and offered to pray before leaving. He replied, "*Yes, please pray for me but I have nothing specific.*" Just as we placed our hands on his shoulders to pray, he interrupted, "*I know what I want you to pray for!*" "*What?*" I asked. "*I'm lonely; please ask God to give me some friends. You all are the only people who are nice enough to come talk to me.*"

(Left to right: Fernando & Connor at Mariner's Point Park)

We prayed as he had asked and then gave him a hug before departing. Just as we turned to leave, he asked, *"Wait, you didn't tell me when you're returning?"* I began by saying, *"In the past, we used to come to San Diego every September and February..."* Before I could finish saying that I wasn't sure if we'd return, he interrupted, *"Then I guess I'll see you in February, that's good!"* I thought, "But wait, that wasn't what I had in mind, but I didn't have the heart to tell this lonely, sweet man, who'd only just asked us to pray for friends. Perhaps we would end up being the answer to his prayer request.

Steve overheard my entire exchange with Fernando. I spoke the words we were both thinking, *"Why did this lonely man have to tug on my heart strings? I thought this was our closure trip, but I suppose John Costello was right, 'It's bigger than Ed now.'"* Steve said, *"We should probably bring a set of checkers or more 'find a word' games for Fernando when we return."* *"Of course, we should,"* I replied. We laughed as we began our seven and a half mile walk back downtown, both contemplating what was yet to come.

Chapter 15
Might as Well Jump!

The vast majority of friendships undergo difficult seasons in life. Some friends go their separate ways, while others remain intact, despite a world that's constantly changing. Perhaps one quality of enduring friendships, is the ability to remember. Recalling from a history of stored memories, both positive and negative, is like relational glue. It serves to reinforce the bonds and stay the course.

Monday evening in the spring of 1983, Ed and I were trying to score some free pizza. We heard about a youth group offering an all-inclusive buffet at the Pizza Hut on Wiehle Avenue in Reston, Virginia. Ed and I showed up at the front door with empty pockets and tried to talk our way into the event without paying. Jeff, the adult at the door turned us away and encouraged us to return with money if we planned to join the feast. It wasn't that he was being unkind by not letting us in. Jeff was aware that we both had money, yet we preferred to freeload. For that reason, he told us to pay up or take a walk. We didn't take his rejection personally, and viewed the closed door as an opportunity to do something unexpected.

Realizing that my mom had dropped us off and was already long-gone, we turned around and began walking in the direction of home. Unsure of what the evening would hold, it was nice to have an evening free when our parents thought we were at a youth group pizza party. Ed and I were both high school students, always in search of adventure.

Just after crossing the bridge over the Dulles Airport toll road, we spotted a five-story building that was under construction. We were bored and decided to enter the building and explore. Once we found our way to the top level, we noticed a crane that sprang up another three or four stories higher than the building itself.

We used to play a game we referred to as "dare games." The basic gist of the game entailed daring the friend to do something gutsy, and if he chickened out, then the person issuing the dare had to complete the challenge themself. Ed dared me to climb to the top of the crane. I accepted the task and began climbing the ladder rungs in the center of a square cage which ascended high above the building. For adrenaline junkies, climbing to the highest height was enticing and Ed didn't want to miss out on the adventure. He immediately began climbing behind me. I'm not sure that it was about the competition, since we both accepted the same challenges. What was clear was the fact that neither of us had any desire to back down.

When we reached the top, we gazed down the extremely long arm of the crane. The floor was constructed of a cage-like grate and the sides were thick steel bars that formed a triangular top. If you wanted to make your way toward the end of the arm, you had to duck down a bit and try not to focus on the ground that was so clearly visible through the grate plank.

After arriving at the top, it was only logical to complete the dare by making our way to the end of the long arm. I was in the lead so I hunched over and began moving rapidly toward the end of the crane. Once we arrived at the absolute end of the arm, we both took turns peering over the naked edge. We were approximately 10 stories above the ground below, when I got the idea for Ed's dare. I had completed my challenge so I gave him his, "*You have to lay down on the end of the crane arm with your head hanging over the edge.*" Ed agreed and then finagled his way around me, where he laid down on the narrow passageway with his head hanging over the edge.

As the two of us were gazing at the ground far below, we both noticed a construction worker who exited from an office trailer in the dirt parking lot. He just happened to look up as we were navigating the end of the crane. He was quick to shout up at us, "*Hey, you kids get down from there immediately!*" I wasted no time and began moving rapidly down the narrow triangular tunnel. When I arrived at the vertical portion of the crane, I made my way as fast as I could scaling down the ladder. You tend to move much quicker when your adrenline kicks in, realizing you're in trouble.

Ed was following close behind me, as we descended down the ladder back to the building itself. The sun was down and the building was much darker than the crane had been. We had no desire to get caught and were convinced that the construction manager who hollered at us was looking for us.

We realized that the construction company only bothered to light up the fourth floor of the building, which was the place where they stored their construction tools at night. We hid on the fifth floor, waiting for the right time to make our move.

I grew anxious and whispered to Ed, "*I think we should make a run for it and get out of here.*" He responded, "*No, we haven't waited long enough.*" Rather than argue, I made my move and began creeping across the floor to have a peek down the empty elevator shaft. I only made it a few steps, when I accidently kicked a small metal pipe. The pipe rolled across the floor, making a noise that was easy to hear.

Immediately after I kicked the pipe, a bright flashlight shined in my direction. The man holding the light hollered, "*Freeze, I have a gun pointed in your direction. Come toward me with your hands where I can see them.*" I figured that the man must have been a paid security guard or a cop if he had a gun, although I wondered if he was bluffing. Ed came out of hiding and the two of us moved toward the light.

He shined the light in the direction of a set of stairs and told us to start walking. As we followed his instructions, he followed closely be-hind us and guided us to the ground level. When we finally reached the ground below, he escorted us to the trailer where we first spotted him. It was clear when we were in the light, that he'd been bluffing about the gun.

He asked us what we were doing on the crane and if we were trying to steal construction tools. We assured him that we meant no harm and merely wanted to check out the view from the end of the crane. He seemed to buy our story, which was in fact true. We had no intention of stealing anything. However, he didn't want to let us go with a warning.

He gave us two choices, "*I can call the cops or drive you home to your parents' house. Which do you prefer?*" We opted for a ride to the parents' house, knowing that the police would end up calling our parents anyway. Why not skip one step in the process, go straight home and face the consequences? The man asked us our names and Ed responded quickly, "*My name is Steve and my parents are away. I've been staying at my friend's house.*" When he got to the word 'friend,' he motioned in my direction. At that point, the construction worker directed his attention to me.

Ed's crafty, fast-paced lie, put me in an awkward situation. After all, how could I say my real name if he had chosen a false one? How would this play out when we arrived at my house? We were standing in front of the man, so there was no way to conspire or agree upon a tale. I had to play off of Ed, so I did.

"*My name is Ted and Steve is staying at my house for the week.*" The man responded, "*Alright, let's go, I don't have all night,*" as he pointed at his truck. We headed in that direction, and I hopped in first. I was in the center, Ed in the passenger seat, and the construction manager climbed in to drive. He started up the engine and asked, "*Where are we headed?*" I pointed right out of the parking lot and said, "*You will want to take a left on Soapstone Drive.*" Not having time to hatch a plan, I simply directed him toward my actual house.

I was growing nervous as we got closer to my home and decided to have our driver turn right. Once he turned on Clipstone Lane, he asked, "*Which house is it?*" as he motored along slowly in that quiet neighborhood. I had him make another right turn onto Red Clover Court. Now my choices were limited. As I rapidly surveyed seven short driveways, our chauffeur inquired, "*Which one?*" I pointed to the one in the direct center of the court and he pulled into the driveway.

He threw the gear into park and we climbed out of the truck. The construction manager remained in his vehicle and lowered the window. He said, "*Go get your dad, so I can speak with him.*" I replied, "*Yes, sir,*" as Ed and I walked toward the front door.

We caught sight of a large family eating dinner in the kitchen. They were visible through the large bay window as we walked toward the front door. The man seated at the head of the table had clearly noticed the truck parked in his driveway. We watched as he stood up to make his way to the front door. I whispered to Ed, "*When the man opens the front door, you run to the right around the house and I'll run left. Head into the woods behind their house as quickly as you can, and call me when you get home.*" There was no time to consider other options, as the moment I finished sharing my plan with Ed, the door abruptly opened. My heart raced although my feet outran it. Ed followed suit. Before the door opened enough to see the man's face, we were gone!

I have no idea if the truck driver attempted to chase us or if he remained frozen inside his truck, confused by our unanticipated departure. I didn't dare turn around to ponder either man's reaction. I just knew I'd better disappear into the dark woods, before they had time to consider a plan.

I suppose Ed did the same on the opposite side of the house. We were not strangers to a good chase, and prided ourselves on rarely getting caught. Adrenaline provides additional fuel for speed, and moving fast was critical in situations like that. Ed called me about 20 minutes later, and we were both relieved that neither of us had been caught. I'd been in situations when one person getting caught meant that everyone would eventually get caught. It wasn't enough for only one person to escape.

While we weren't able to dine that evening on a full pizza buffet, we did have quite an adventure climbing the crane. The antics surrounding our escape were just as exciting! Our minds were at ease, although our stomachs were empty. I'm sure we both managed to find some leftovers. That would describe a typical day in my friendship with Ed.

A number of people who are aware of our trips to San Diego have asked, "*What was so special about your friendship with Ed that you have been willing to search for him on the opposite side of the country?*" I suppose three answers come to mind. For starters, we had countless adventures like the crane climbing I just mentioned, or crossing the Potomac River near Great Falls Park, as I shared earlier in the book. Facing life-threatening and adrenaline-charged situations tends to create a close bond between people. Our friendship ran deep as a result.

The second reason has to do with our encounter in Anaheim, California in November of 2013. When Ed made the effort to travel all the way from San Diego up to Anaheim to be with us, I knew he had something he wanted to share. When he expressed his desire to change his life and make a new start, I knew something was happening in Ed's life that I should be attentive to. He went so far as to ask for my help and even asked me to pray with him. Every dynamic in that encounter was significant to me. While I shared about his visit in 2013 earlier in the book, I failed to mention that without Ed's plea for help, I'm not so sure I would have felt the same conviction to search for him. As you know, Ed never made the trip to Ghana that he promised in the summer of 2014, but I was unable to shake his cry for help. His interaction with Sandra and me on that particular trip is the second factor that caused me to pursue Ed on this journey.

(Left to right: Will & Ed at Embassy Suites Hotel in Anaheim)

The third reason for pursuing my friend Ed, has been my desire to live by what Jesus said are the greatest two commands (*found in Luke 10:27*). I desire to love God completely and to love others the way that I would want to be loved if I were in their place. As a result, the question that has motivated me throughout this entire process has been, "*If I was in his shoes, how would I want to be loved?*" The answer was obvious in my mind, I would want someone to come looking for me. I certainly wouldn't want to be forgotten.

As a matter of fact, that's the same question I asked when we met Whitey, and Israel and Juan and countless others. That principle has guided my friendship with Ed, as well as each one of these trips to California and to Hawaii. I find that every now and then, I need to stop to consider 'why' I'm doing what I'm doing. The reason 'why' serves as the primary motivation for the 'what' and the 'how.'

Our memorable adventures, Ed's candid request for help back in Anaheim, together with the conviction that I should love my friend the way I'd want to be loved if the roles were reversed, all served as motivation for me to search for him. Consequently, they also served as a motivation for me to carry on the pursuit. Despite Ed's unwilling desire to make a change, I recognized the value that John Costello noted, saying the mission had become, "*Bigger than Ed.*"

In hindsight, I had no clue that that one encounter would inspire me to actually live on the streets. If you would have told me back in 2014, that six years from that time I would be living homeless two weeks each year, and that Ed no longer lived in San Diego, I'd think you were tweaking.

Who besides God would have known the turns this journey would take, and the ones that would remain before us? It's probably for the best that God doesn't reveal too much of our future, or perhaps we wouldn't make some of the decisions that we make. However, having said that, I wouldn't want to trade this experience for anything. When we take risks in life and step out of our comfort zone and daily routine, we often grow. Perhaps that's why the Bible says, "*Without faith it's im-*

possible to please God," (Hebrews 11:6). Oftentimes, when we take risks we're more apt to trust in God, especially when the challenge is greater than we are.

In the summer of 1982, after my sophomore year of high school, I recall an afternoon when Ed and I were seated in a theater, waiting for the movie previews to begin. Once the film was underway, we were glued to the screen. We were watching the movie "First Blood." Who knew that this was part one of the Rambo franchise that would lead to five total movies, released over a 37-year span? I recall the movie having a significant impact on the two of us. I honestly believe that if there had been a military recruiter outside of the theater that evening, he would have had our signatures on contracts, eager to enlist. The following day we invented a game we referred to as *"War Games."*

In the 1980s, the city of Reston had acres and acres of forest area. The game we invented involved one of us heading deep into the woods and hiding, while the other person would wait five minutes before searching for the other person. Before you get the idea that we were playing "hide and seek," let me add that "War Games" involved hunting for the person to kill them. A "kill" consisted of hitting the person with a tennis ball, a stick or rock, before getting hit by the other player who was in hiding. We took turns being the hunter and the hunted. Paintball hadn't been invented yet, so this was the next best thing.

I recall one particular game in which I ran into the woods to hide and wait for Ed to look for me. I decided to climb a tree that stood in close proximity to the trail we used to navigate the woods. I climbed about fifteen feet up the tree and waited for Ed to walk down the path next to where I was hiding. Beside the tree that I climbed stood a holly tree that was about 12 feet tall. If you are unfamiliar with holly trees, they grow wide with branches filled with small green leaves, each possessing small thorn-like points. From my vantage point perched on a limb above the holly tree, it looked quite bushy. The holly tree beneath me triggered an idea from a scene in "First Blood."

I recalled John Rambo, (Sylvester Stallone) being chased by some crooked cops. He found himself pinned down on the side of a cliff.

When he realized he was surrounded, Rambo chose to jump off the cliff. Just to the right of the cliff there was a tall bushy Pine tree, which he jumped on to help cushion his fall. I imagined that the holly tree would work in a similar fashion, cushioning my fall, as I caught Ed off guard. I imagined making the jump when he got close to the tree, so I could hit him with the stick that I was holding in my hand. It seemed like an easy win and he wouldn't expect me to leap from a tree above.

Ed came walking up the trail just as I predicted. As he neared the holly tree, I remained frozen still, until the precise moment that I decided it was time to leap. I did so in stealth form, leaping from the limb spread-eagled as though I had a parachute to slow my fall. I did not. When my body connected with the holly tree beneath me, the center of the tree bent under my weight. My guess is that after the approximate seven-foot top portion of the tree had slowed my fall, the tree snapped in half, leaving the lower stronger portion, which pressed firmly in the side of my waist. The force of the tree connecting with my hip caused my entire body to flip right back over in the opposite direction. I was left on my back, facing the sky in the center of the trail. I landed hard, and was disoriented by the unexpected flip onto my back.

Shocked by the incident, my reflexes were slower than I'd hoped and as I gathered my wits, Ed hit me with a stick and announced, *"You're dead, I win!"* Let's just say that things didn't quite play out in the way that I'd imagined. If I had paid closer attention to the scene from *"First Blood"* which inspired my jump, perhaps I would have thought twice. After Rambo's jump in the movie, his arm tore open. The Green Beret character had to stitch up his own wounded arm. Ed and I thought that scene in the movie was very cool. However, when I took the leap, I ended up with a fairly nice bruise and an injured hip, not to mention my bruised ego.

I hadn't stopped to consider every possible scenario before jumping. Risk assessment is a funny thing; you never quite know what may happen when risk is involved. Ed and I rarely paused to consider potential risks. Perhaps I'd been inspired by the lyrics of the popular 1980's Van

Halen song "*Jump?*" After all, the song repeats the phrase, "*Might as well jump,*" more than once.

My choice to pursue my childhood friend who'd become homeless involved a decision to 'jump.' Many of the biggest decisions we make in life require a "jump." It requires faith to take a leap. I suppose we have to stop to consider "*what*" and "*who*" are worth jumping for? How would you answer those two questions?

Jumping oftentimes involves a risk as well as an associated cost. I'd decided that not only was pursuing my friend worth my time and the effort to make the jump, but so were the many new homeless friends that I'd made along the way. Frequently a jump doesn't turn out in the way we planned or imagined, and yet, it can be filled with blessings we never considered. As the journey continued, so did my resolve which caused me to say again and again, "*I might as well jump!*" Once you're convinced and willing to make the jump, you need only decide where and when. I recognized that it was time for another jump back to Maui, so I sat down with Sandra to determine the when.

Chapter 16
Ed & Owen

In February of 2018, I returned to San Diego for another round, joined by Ben Skriloff, who had been a participant on the previous trip. We were accompanied by rookies who were both closer to my age: John Morales and Semisi Tipeni. This was the first actual homeless trip that Steve Bowman didn't join me on. While he agreed that returning to San Diego was important, we did not agree on the frequency. He promised to participate on one trip each year, but our previous trip had taken place only five months earlier and he wanted a break. It made sense to me. The four of us had an eventful week caring for the homeless, but it wasn't the same without Steve.

It was a privilege reconnecting with Paul and Tom and the usual suspects. The week went by in a flash, and after returning home, I decided to make a change. We had always made two trips each year to San Diego, but after finding Ed in Maui, it felt like a lot to continue with the same routine in addition to a Hawaii trip. I decided to make one trip each summer to reconnect with Ed in Maui, and one trip every January to live on the streets of San Diego. After making the decision to change up the trip rhythm, I began planning trip ten, back to Maui.

Six months later, on August 29, 2018, we made our way back to Maui. Our team of seven was made up entirely of family members, except for one additional person. Sandra and I brought our two youngest daughters Capri and Skye, while my in-laws came to help with the kids while we searched for Ed. Our added member was Eric Locklear. He'd been on trip eight to San Diego and informed me that he wanted to join us on our hunt for Ed. Remember, Eric also knew Ed from high school, so he was no stranger to him.

Adjusting to a six-hour time change when traveling from east to west is never easy. That reality is only compounded when traveling with two young children under the age of five. For starters, even if your kids are used to waking up at 8:00 a.m., that's 2:00 a.m. Maui time. The kids managed to sleep until 10:00 a.m. (East Coast time) on the first morning, although that is 4:00 a.m. (Hawaii Time) when the two were ready to start their day. The only problem with that was the fact that everything was closed, and the sun hadn't yet risen. We managed to find a television channel with 24/7 cartoons on and a grocery store with all night hours.

Eric was not due to arrive until lunchtime, so Sandra and I decided to leave our girls with her parents and head over to Paia for a 6:00 a.m. coffee. We were hopeful that perhaps we might run into Ed, although there were no sightings that morning. We walked the town and refamiliarized ourselves with the layout of the bohemian beach town. We killed time playing the part of tourists, before heading to the airport to retrieve Eric. His flight arrived as scheduled. We drove him back to the hotel to discuss our game plan and check on the girls.

Knowing that Ed rarely travels anywhere without his bike, I brought mine along for the trip. It would have been easier to rent a bike in town, but I was hoping that Ed might be interested in servicing mine during our visit. Remembering that Donnie's shop gives Ed five dollars per bike to clean them up, and being aware of Ed's knowledge about servicing bikes, I was looking for another opportunity to connect with my old friend.

In addition to refinishing furniture, Ed was an avid cyclist. He is mechanically-minded, handy at restoring antiques, and able to maintain bicycles. On my previous trip, I met with Ed's friend Stephanie back in San Diego. She had been keeping a few of his belongings, and when she heard that I had found him, she sent them my way. I brought an old wallet of his, which still contained his California state driver's license in it as well. I hoped that perhaps my bike or his wallet and driver's license might help me reconnect.

As we discussed the game plan, Sandra agreed to drive Eric and me across the island, 22 miles from where we were staying in Wailea, to Donnie's shop in Paia. I'd reassembled my bike after travel, and Eric rented one from Donnie's shop. We were ready to make our rounds looking for Ed via bike rather than on foot. We checked in with Donnie at the bike shop to find out if there had been any changes in Ed's routine or behavior. In fact, I kept up with him throughout the year. I would periodically check in to find out how my friend was holding up. Donnie was an amazing support to Ed and a contact for me. I'd always pass along the updates to Ed's family, as a matter of courtesy.

Donnie told us that Ed traveled almost everywhere on his bike, and that we'd most likely pass him cycling through town. The bike plan was also helpful, since we had only rented one car. I figured Sandra, along with her parents and the kids may need the vehicle to get around. Eric and I planned to make the trek back to Wailea before sundown on our bikes. According to Google Maps, the 22 mile ride takes the average cyclist an hour and 49 minutes from one side of the island to the other.

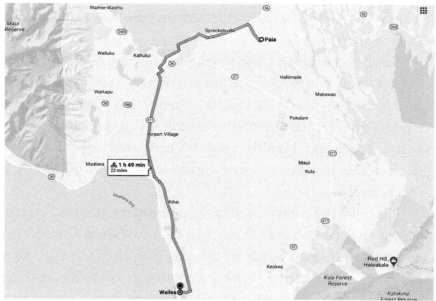

(Our daily bike ride in Maui)

After we rented a bike for Eric, got our update from Donnie and said goodbye to Sandra, we were ready to hit the streets. Eric appreciated the opportunity to meet the guys working at Maui Cyclery before we took off. I can't say enough positive things about the way they've cared for Ed while he lived homeless in their town. We made a few initial passes down the main streets in Paia, when Eric confessed being incredibly hungry. His flight didn't serve anything other than a small bag of pretzels, and we hadn't slowed down to eat since we picked him up. We parked our bikes back at Donnie's shop and crossed the street to get some lunch.

There are a couple of great restaurants near the main T-junction, which is the center of Paia. The intersection of Baldwin Avenue and Hana Highway is a tourist magnet, since everyone drives that route when exploring the famous "Road to Hana." We got an outdoor table at the corner Mexican resturant known as Milagros Food Company. Our table provided front row seats to keep an eye on everyone passing through town. We continued the search from our table-side stakeout, as we ordered up some delicious fish tacos and the local Kona Brewing Company lager.

Lunch was a fantastic opportunity to catch up. Life in northern Virginia seems to move at a pace that makes moments like that few and far between. I suppose living in close proximity to our Nation's Capital can have that effect on surrounding cities. Eric shared about his family, work and faith, and I did the same. It's been encouraging for me to watch the change in Eric's life ever since he showed up on the doorsteps of our church.

Eric seems to possess the ability to cut through pretense and express himself with openness and honesty. I find this attribute to be refreshing in a world where most people are extemely guarded. While Eric's faith had grown, he remained the same straight shooter that he'd been when he showed up at the church and told me his reasons for not trusting church people.

As we conversed, our eyes were constantly scanning the intersection in front of us for any sign of our friend Ed. After a relaxed, extended lunch hour, we paid our bill and crossed the intersection to retrieve our bikes. It was time to mount the cycles and bike up Baldwin Avenue to scout for Ed and work off the calories we had just ingested.

Baldwin Avenue posseses a steep incline and is quite narrow. It provided a challenging workout for a couple of 52-year old men who weren't used to riding daily as Ed was. We decided to head from Paia straight up the mountain. We dropped the bikes into the lower, easier gears and made the best of it. Our ascent was slow, but we steadily continued climbing the hill. You could tell that we both became winded, since we stopped chatting to conserve every breath for the oxygen required to continue moving.

I thought back to my trip one year earlier when I chased Ed on foot up the same hill. I was confused when he had been able to outrun me at that time, despite the fact that he was an addict. Donnie mentioned Ed riding his bike every day up this steep hill, which made a lot more sense concerning his cardio conditioning, regardless of his continued drug use.

We reached the small town of Makawao at the top of Baldwin, and then biked the side streets hoping to spot our friend. After covering a lot of pavement, we decided to head back down the hill to Paia. Cycling down Baldwin Avenue was a blast, although we had to use our brakes frequently, trying not to lose control. When we arrived back in Paia we biked through the town hoping to locate Ed. After spending another hour searching, we realized that we had better start our 22 mile trek back to Wailea if we wanted to make it before sunset. My legs were fairly spent, and the six hour time change was also a factor. I imagine Eric must have been even more exhausted, since he'd traveled earlier that same day.

(Riding behind Eric on Hana Highway in Kahului)

I was excited to see the family and be able to take a break from cycling. When you're not used to cycling, the seat or saddle can cause a sore backside. Lily, my mother-in-law, had made some spaghetti bolognese with garlic bread, and we were ready to "carb up." Her supper, along with a glass of red wine, was enough to knock me out for the night. We were spent and ready to call it an early night. Eric was only able to get a few days off of work, so he was keen to resume the search again early the following morning.

Our hotel in Wailea included a full breakfast, so we took advantage of that before saddling up once again on our bicycles. I could tell that Eric was eager to hit the road and get back to Paia. The idea of the 22 mile trek made my butt hurt just thinking about it. I was sipping my coffee slowly, as a way of procrastinating the trek ahead.

Sitting across the table at the hotel restaurant, Eric made a few statements that caught my attention. He said, *"I've been praying this morning and the Lord made it clear to me that I'm going to find Ed today.*" He didn't say "*We are going to find Ed,*" his comments were specific to himself. Eric followed that comment up by adding, "*I feel strongly that God wants me to share a few things with Ed, which I intend to do when I find him.*" I was processing his comments and thinking, "*Why didn't I get a word from God like Eric?*" At the same time, I was inspired by the confidence of his faith. Eric was telling me with absolute certainty his objective which he felt had come directly from God. This is the same guy who showed up at my church a year earlier and told me that he wasn't sure if he believed in God, and definitely didn't trust in the word of churchgoers. What accounted for such a drastic change? Although the journey's focus was to locate Ed, I was once again reminded that the impact was much wider. Eric Locklear was evidence of that reality.

As I sat in silence, considering my friend's faith-filled words, he added one more comment. "*I'm going to head out now, but I think you should relax and enjoy time with your family.*" Knowing my personality, I knew I was prone to spend the entire week on my bike searching for Ed. This was the first trip in which we brought multiple family members along. I agreed with his comments and said, "*I'll head out in about an hour and call you when I reach Paia.*" With that, Eric and I took a few moments to pray together and then he mounted his bike and was off.

I returned to the hotel room to invite our little girls, Capri and Skye, to go to the pool. Sandra seemed surprised that I hadn't left with Eric, yet was excited to join me and the girls in the pool. I told her about Eric's remarks, which served as an encouragement. While I have a sincere belief in God, I've never heard His audible voice. I oftentimes get a sense in my spirit of things I believe He wants me to do, and yet I was moved by Eric's confident words, expressing total trust in his mission for the day. As promised, I jumped on my bicycle an hour later and began the long trek to Paia.

The ride from Wailea to Paia is much better than the reverse direction. There is a long portion of the route on Piilani Highway that is almost all downhill. The name changes to Maui Veteran's Highway at about the halfway point. I enjoyed the cool breeze as I descended on the highway from Wailea. It isn't until you reach the old abandoned sugar cane factory that you have to cycle a slight incline.

I turned right on Hansen Road and began peddling harder. Just after passing the historic factory, my phone rang. I pulled off to the side to take the call. I had my phone mounted on my handlebars, so I could see that the incoming call was from Eric. I was hoping to hear some positive news about Ed, but figured he wanted to know my estimated time of arrival. As I pulled off the road and answered the call, he had my complete attention when I heard him say, "*I found Ed!*" I moved my bike a bit farther from the curb to focus intently on what he was saying.

Before Eric could continue I asked, "*Is he with you now?*" Eric replied, "*No, I met him on a street corner and we had a wonderful conversation. When we finished chatting he said that he had to get going.*" I was mad at myself for not setting out earlier, but wondered if it may have been better for Eric to have some one-on-one time with Ed without me present. I said, "*I'm about 20 minutes away and will bike faster to meet you in town.*" Eric responded, "*Take your time, he's long gone by now.*"

Just as I was about to end the call, Eric surprised me with even more information. He asked, "*Do you want to know who else I ran into?*" "*No, who?*" I inquired. He said, "*I ran into the actor Owen Wilson. Apparently he has a home here.*" If I wasn't jealous before, I certainly was after he shared the news of his brush with a celebrity. I responded, "*Alright, I'm leaving now, see ya soon!*" With that I secured my phone back on the mount, and hopped back on my bike. My frustration with myself served as fuel as I peddled like mad.

I moved rapidly up Hansen Road toward the town of Paia, replaying everything I'd just heard from Eric. I thought, "*That's not fair, he got to see Ed and Owen. I didn't get to see anyone. I'll begin searching for Owen while I'm here, as well.*" My jealous train of thought was what you might expect from a middle school kid. I'm just being honest that while I was happy for Eric?, I was also a bit envious. Regardless of my mixed motives, the adrenaline coursing through my veins helped me make great time.

(Left to right: Donnie Arnoult & Owen Wilson in Paia)

When I arrived in town I swung by Donnie's shop and told him what Eric had shared with me. Donnie said, "*Yeah, I saw Ed this morning too.*" "*No kidding, so everyone but me?,* " was the thought that I kept to myself. I also told Donnie about Eric meeting Owen Wilson. Donnie added, "*Oh yeah, he has a home here. He and I are friends and go cycling sometimes.*" "*Of course you do,*" I thought.

I thanked Donnie for the update and headed outside to meet up with Eric. It was about lunchtime so we found a place to park the bikes and decided on a different restaurant. We settled on the Paia Fish

Market, which provided visibility of the primary town intersection. We ordered lunch at the counter, then slid into some benches with a direct line of sight on the pedestrian traffic.

I was anxious to hear the details of Eric's interaction with Ed and also with Owen. He told me that he simply said *"Hello"* to Owen, but his conversation with Ed was remarkable. Eric ran into Ed at an intersection in Paia. He approached Ed, not completely sure if he would remember Eric from high school.

Eric said, *"Hey Ed, I'm not sure if you remember me but I'm Eric Locklear and we were on the same wrestling team at South Lakes High School in Reston, Virginia."* Ed did in fact remember him, so he proceeded to share what he felt God had placed on his heart to say. Keep in mind, Eric told me that he was convinced God wanted him to see Ed and to share something very specific. Eric also told me that God made him aware that he would see Ed on that specific day. If I'd been somewhat skeptical of Eric's ability to discern God's voice, that was gone at this point. He had my complete attention and continued to share about his encounter with Ed.

When Eric had Ed's full attention, he said, *"I wanted you to know that you have changed my entire life."* Ed listened intently as Eric continued, *"I heard about Will and other individuals who had gone looking for you and discovered that they had been willing to live homeless to find you. That caused a curiosity in me which led me to church. I found out about Jesus and His love for me, which has impacted my life, as well as the lives of my entire family. I felt compelled by God to travel to Maui to say 'thank you for indirectly changing my life.'"*

Eric mentioned that Ed was speechless for a brief moment, after which he managed to say, *"Well, that's good to hear."* He also let Ed know that he is missed and loved by friends and family back at home. He mentioned that I was back in town with Sandra and hoped to see him as well. Ed thanked Eric for coming to Maui, but communicated his desire to maintain a distance from past acquaintances. He was courteous, although after they finished their exchange, Ed was ready to bolt. Eric watched as he took off down the road on his bike.

Eric was content having had an interaction with Ed. As he had informed me earlier that morning, Eric had been able to deliver the message that he felt compelled by God to share. We took a moment to thank God for His faithfulness in answering Eric's prayer and said a blessing for our food that finally arrived.

After lunch Eric made the comment, "*I'm not so sure we'll see Ed again today. Now that he's aware we're all here, he may go into hiding.*" Eric made his second accurate prediction of the day. Although we searched the area on our bikes after lunch, Ed was nowhere to be found for the remainder of the day. Coming to grips with our failed search attempt, we decided to begin our two hour ride back to Wailea. The trek seemed a bit more strenuous on day two. Perhaps my discouragement played a part. We were thrilled after climbing the final hill and catching sight of our hotel.

(Left to right: Will & Eric on Piilani Highway)

As I mentioned earlier, due to Eric's work schedule he was only able to stay for three days and needed to fly back east the following day. We biked back to Paia early the following morning, to search one last time, before he had to make his way to the airport. Eric returned his rental bike to Donnie's shop around noon, after our search yielded no results. We'd been unable to locate Ed, although Eric was satisfied. He hopped on an island bus headed for the airport, and we said goodbye. His trip had been a success and he needed to get back to work. Sandra drove the rental car over to Paia, and we picked up where Eric and I had left off.

We met a local homeless man by the name of Kai. Kai was familiar with Ed and talked a bit about their friendship. He described their interaction as a mixture of friendly and not so friendly communication. Donnie had mentioned that Ed was more of a loner, who preferred to talk to people in the local shops, while disassociating himself from the other homeless men and women of the community.

Neither Sandra nor I had eaten lunch, so we decided to invite Kai to eat with us. He said, 'yes,' while his answer revealed obvious excitement. We settled into the Paia Fish Market for some fish tacos and a chance to learn more about Kai. He was kind enough to share a bit of his story with us, while we all enjoyed the fresh seafood.

(Left to right: Sandra, Kai & Will at the Paia Fish Market)

Sandra and I hiked up and down the same exact streets that we'd marched on only one year earlier. We had to call it quits early that afternoon, since we had plans with our family that evening. We made reservations for the six of us to enjoy a traditional Hawaiian luau that evening. Sandra's parents and the girls loved it! Capri and Skye thought that Disney's Moana had come to life. The memorable family time was just what we needed to lift our spirits. I had begun to get a bit discouraged since we only had one more full day to locate Ed. While I was thrilled that Eric had his prayer answered, I was praying fervently to see Ed at least once before leaving.

Sandra and I decided to get an early start the following morning. Never fully adjusting to the Hawaiian time made early mornings no problem at all. After all, why bother adjusting to a six hour variance, when we were scheduled to travel home a day later?

We parked our rental in the public parking lot and made our way to the café next door to Donnie's bike shop: The Paia Bay Coffee Bar. We ran into Kai once again at the café and purchased him a cup of coffee to start his day. We were unsure what to expect, but planned to stay in town all day long, or at least until we had a chance to see Ed. While I felt confident that we would run into him that day, I wasn't willing to state it with the same confidence as my friend Eric.

After an hour at the coffee shop with no sign of Ed, we wandered over to Maui Cyclery next door. Sandra said that she was going to search the street while I checked the parking area next to the bike shop. When I turned the corner, there was Ed on the ground changing his bike tire. I was shocked and began walking toward him. I spoke first and asked him how he was doing. He replied, *"I'm well but as I mentioned last year, I'm not interested in reconnecting with people from my past."*

Ignoring his comment, I replied, *"I brought you your wallet."* I removed it from my pocket to hold it up for him to see. Ed responded, *"I don't want any charity."* I answered, *"It's not charity. Look at it, it's your wallet that you left with Stephanie Wilson back in San Diego."* Ed looked up at the wallet in my hand and recognizing, it he leaned forward and said, "*In that case, I'll take it!*" He snatched it from my hand and walked in the direction of his bike.

(Ed changing tire outside of Maui Cyclery)

I continued, "*Ed, I won't bother you any longer but I want you to know that I love you. I plan to return here once each year to remind you of that and to see if you need any help.*" Ed listened and then replied, "*I love you too Will, thank you.*" And with that he walked around the building toward the street. Wanting to give him his space, I went into the store and spoke with one of the employees by the name of Hank. I had no clue where Sandra had ended up.

About five minutes later, Ed still hadn't returned and neither had Sandra. I decided to venture out and look for her. I hit the sidewalk out front, along Hana Highway. I caught sight of her headed in my direction and she had a big grin on her face. I was curious and asked, "*Did you see*

Ed?" She replied, "*Yes, I did. Did you?*" I said, "*Yes,*" at which point we were both itching to hear about the other person's interaction with Ed.

It was obvious that Ed wanted some space, so we walked in the direction of the parking lot to retrieve our rental vehicle. Once in the car, I figured we could talk as we drove around the area. I started up the engine and headed through town toward Turtle Beach. We spotted Ed hiding between two buildings, looking back toward the bike shop. I hollered out the window, "*See you later Ed!*" I wanted to be sure that he saw us leaving, so he could return to his bike without worrying. I don't understand the logic behind the paranoia of a meth user, but it certainly was real to him. We parked at Ho'okipa Beach Park, which always seems to have its share of protected sea turtles lounging on the sand. The locals refer to the place as 'Turtle Beach.' I turned off the engine, and we got out of the vehicle to share the details surrounding our encounters with Ed.

I told Sandra about Ed taking the wallet, and our complete exchange. She seemed surprised that I promised Ed that we'd return once each year to let him know that he is loved. I was unsure why my statement shocked her, until she told me about her interaction with him. She began, "*Ed must have just walked away from your conversation with him, when he ran into me.*" She continued, "*I was walking on the sidewalk when all of the sudden I looked left and Ed was walking beside me, clutching his wallet. When I noticed that it was him, I said, 'Hi Ed, do you remember me, Will's wife Sandra?'*" He replied, "*Of course, we spoke last year when you were here.*"

Sandra said that Ed seemed startled after realizing that he'd walked right up beside her, so he picked up his pace in an attempt to get ahead. That made it difficult for Sandra to keep up, so she decided to pray. She said, "*I offered a prayer to God and asked, 'What should I say to Ed? Please give me wisdom.'*" Just after uttering her prayer, a plan began to form in her mind, so she acted.

Sandra addressed Ed now that he was a few paces ahead, "*Ed, it's difficult for me to keep up with you, would you mind holding my hand so I can keep pace?*" Without fully thinking it through, Ed responded,

"*Sure,*" as he paused for her to catch up. He took her by the hand, and they began walking together. Imagine trying to lose someone and then stopping to take hold of their hand. It hardly makes sense and would make it difficult to escape. God's way of thinking often trumps logic, and Sandra confessed that the idea came as the result of her prayer.

As they walked hand in hand down the sidewalk, Sandra spoke softly, asking God to give her the words. She continued, "*We love you Ed, and that's the reason we've returned.*" Then she promised, "*Will and I will continue to return here every year to let you know that you are loved and that we care about you.*" Without knowing that I'd just promised Ed the exact same thing, she felt compelled to make the same promise. That was the reason she was surprised when I told her what I had spoken to Ed.

After speaking those words to Ed, she invited him to join us for dinner. We had dinner reservations later that evening at Mama's Fish House, but figured that we could squeeze him in. It was our final night in Maui and we wanted it to be special. Ed thanked Sandra for the invitation and for her promise, although he declined the dinner invitation.

Ed let go of Sandra's hand and said, "*I really need to get going.*" She replied, "*If you won't join us this year, how about next year?*" Ed said, "*Alright, I'll join you two for dinner next year.*" As Ed turned to leave, Sandra asked, "*Can I at least get a hug?*" He responded, "*Of course,*" then he hugged her and gave her a kiss on the cheek, before saying "*Goodbye*" and crossing the street. We were both thrilled that we'd been able to see Ed, despite his unwillingneess to join us for dinner.

That evening we had an unbelievable meal at Mama's Fish House. It was the perfect way to spend our final night in Maui. We sat at the table reminiscing and retelling the stories of four years invested in searching for Ed. Some of the memories had us laughing, while others such as Jose's bear, and his horrific death, brought tears.

We were both grateful to God for granting us each an opportunity to engage with Ed before our trip home. The fact that both of us had separately promised Ed that we'd return to Maui on an annual basis, gave us hope for a different response on a future year. I commented, *"I'm so glad Ed got lost in such a beautiful place."* Sandra smiled as we savored the moments on our last evening in Maui.

On our way home that evening, we happened to drive right past Ed who was out for an evening bike ride. There was some evening tourist traffic which slowed us down to the same pace as Ed. Sandra put her window down and I shouted, *"Hey Ed, It was great to see you! We're leaving in the morning, so we'll see ya next year. We love you!"* Ed shouted back, *"I love you too."* It was a treat to have a final goodbye as we drove through Paia, back to Wailea. We had an early flight the following morning and still had packing to do. While Ed was unwilling to connect on a deeper level, at least he knew that he was loved. Sandra commented to me, *"He'd better keep his promise for dinner next year!"* I hoped he'd remember that when we returned.

(Ed biking through Paia on our final night)

Chapter 17

Fork in the Road

I completely expected Ed to join us on our medical trip to Ghana in May of 2014. After all, he was the one begging to join the trip, expressing his desire to help the less fortunate. I'd offered to raise all of the necessary funds to make his trip possible and he thanked me profusely. Then we hit a fork in the road. Ed headed left toward life on the street, while I went in the planned direction toward Tamale, Ghana.

When we had our emotional exchange on Baldwin Avenue in August of 2017, I reminded Ed of his expressed desire to serve the less fortunate. I even let him know that Stephanie had sent me his updated passport when she sent me his driver's license. I would pray from time to time, begging God, "*Please restore Ed to a healthy state and allow him to realize his vision. Let him serve those who are in a difficult place and discover his purpose in the process.*" That would certainly be miraculous!

I thought, "*If and when Ed returns home, I want to hear all about his journey.*" I wanted to hear how he made it to Maui, where he'd camped and hidden all those years and how he'd managed to survive.

In a similar fashion, I wanted to share about the effort made on his behalf. I wanted him to know how much he is loved and where the forks in the road had taken me. There would be so much to catch up on, and I prayed that one day we'd have that opportunity.

I encountered numerous unexpected forks and turns in the road, during our first 14 homeless trips. In other words, I often imagined that circumstances would play out in a particular manner, when something entirely out of the ordinary would occur. Every time the journey began to feel predictable, we'd encounter an unpredictable turn in the road. I began to wonder when the roads might intersect and when the worlds would collide. Just as my encounter with Ed back in November of 2013 served as a catalyst for the entire mission, I had another significant encounter at around the same period of time. The incident was not with a high school friend, nor did it occur in a hotel back in Anaheim, California. My other encounter was with a complete stranger in a grocery store at three in the morning.

I happened to be shopping for my family in the middle of the night. Sandra and I had a matter of hours to get my older kids situated before we were scheduled to fly to Spain the following day. I was stocking up on food and other essential items at the Harris Teeter Grocery store, which happened to maintain all-night hours. I liked the fact that it felt as though I was the only shopper in the store. I was making good time filling my cart with the items on my list.

I was headed down the cereal aisle when an employee restocking shelves said 'hello.' He seemed eager to talk with someone, which made sense in the store that felt like a ghost town. I introduced myself and asked where he was from. When he replied, "*Ghana,*" I told him that I was leading a trip to Ghana the following month. He asked, "*Where in Ghana are you going?*" When I answered, "*Tamale,*" he about lost his mind. He announced, "*That's where I'm from! I would be happy to tell you all about my country!*" I appreciated his enthusiasm even if I was a bit startled by his level of excitement.

His name was Naporo, but people call him 'Nap.' Before I was able to resume my shopping, he exclaimed, "*I'd like to meet with you and tell you all about my country before your trip!*" I replied, "*That would be helpful,*" so we exchanged contact information and set a date.

When the day arrived, Nap was joined by his friend Justice. He called the day before and asked, "*Would you mind if my friend comes with me?; he is also from Tamale and works with me at Harris Teeter.*" I told him that it wasn't a problem. We had a wondeful meal getting to know Nap and Justice and learning more about the country of Ghana. In addition, we came to discover that they were both Muslims. Sandra and I had just completed training called "Common Ground," which was meant to equip us how to work well with Muslims and understand their faith. It couldn't have been timed more perfectly.

It boggled my mind that two men who worked in a shop within one mile of my home were from the city located just over 5,000 miles away. I was coordinating a team to volunteer at a camp with over 400 children. The mind-boggling part, was the fact that the place I was working was less than a mile from where Nap and Justice lived. What are the odds?

Just before they left our home that evening, they asked if we might bring a couple of laptop computers to their families in Tamale. We agreed and told them the deadline for bringing the laptops over before our travel date. They showed up at our home the evening before we were set to make the trip. Imagine our surprise when we opened the front door and saw Nap and Justice dragging two large suitcases.

The bags each appeared to be jam-packed, most likely filled to the maximum weight capacity. Their idea of "a couple of laptops" was not what I had imagined. I invited Nap and Justice into our home and they entered dragging the two heavy pieces of luggage.

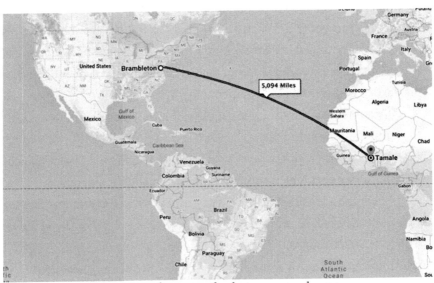

(The span of 5,094 miles between my home
and Tamale, Ghana, courtesy of Google Maps)

How would you respond if you were in my place? Consider two Muslim men who you only just met, asking you to take two completely packed suitcases on an overseas flight. To put the situation in a different context, the incident took place just ten years after the September 11, 2001 terrorist attack on the United States. The idea of carrying two fully packed suitcases on a plane for our new friends made us nervous.

I asked if we could look at the contents of the two bags. Nap and Justice were quick to agree and opened both bags, emptying the contents onto our living room floor. They spread out the items of clothing, medicine and diapers across the floor for us to inspect. I was so moved by these two immigrant men who'd been separated from their families by more than 5,000 miles. When I saw the contents, most of which were obviously for small children, I agreed to carry their luggage and deliver the bags to their families.

My reason for saying 'yes' was precisely the same reason that I chose to search for Ed. While I do not share the same faith as Nap and Justice, I do what I can to live out my own faith. As I mentioned earlier, for me, that entails a willingness to love God completely and to love my neighbor as I love myself. Applying the "golden rule," caused me to think differently, "*If I were an immigrant working in a foreign country and separated from my family, how would I want to be loved?*" That same logic and line of thinking inspired me to go looking for Ed on the streets of San Diego, and eventually to live homeless.

In this scenario, it motivated me to carry the bags of the men whom I had met in my local grocery store and deliver them to their families in Tamale, Ghana. Two days later, my wife and I were in the back of an old beat-up Nissan Pathfinder, traveling toward Nap's community. Sandra whispered, "*Is this dangerous?*" "*Of course not,*" I responded, "*We are helping them connect with their son.*" I spoke with confidence, although I had my suspicions. After all, I'd never been to a completely Muslim village. The feeling that we were both out of our comfort zones was compounded by the fact that we were also the only white-skinned people for miles. It was all part of the adventure.

Nap's family welcomed us gladly, although we had to communicate with the help of an interpreter. The primary language in Tamale is

Dagbani. We followed the cultural cues, so as not to inadvertantly disrespect their culture. The entire family and community turned out to greet us, before we were ushered into a large mud hut to meet the village chief. Who knew that Nap's dad was the village chief? The exchange moved us both and before we left, Nap's father said, "*I would like you to serve as Nap's father while he is in your country.*" It was an incredibly memorable occasion and has led to more than I have time to share.

That first interaction also had an impact on our relationship with Nap and Justice when we returned home. We met more friends from Ghana during that time period. Some worked in the grocery store, others at Home Depot, in restaurants and other places that we frequented. Everytime we told them that we'd visited Ghana we ended up inviting them to dinner, along with Nap and Justice. Before long, we had dinner about every six weeks, an event that we referred to as "Ghana Night." We would invite every local person who we'd met from Ghana. One evening we had more than 20 show up, and we enjoyed hearing their stories. Every single person we met possessed sincere gratitude to God. It was refreshing.

When November rolled around, we hosted a large Thanksgiving meal for our friends from Ghana. We included a brief history of the holiday and invited each person to share one thing that he or she was thankful for. One of our Ghanaian friends by the name of Bawa said, "*I've lived in the United States for five years and this is the first time that I've actually been invited into an American's home for a meal, and treated like family.*" We felt blessed to know these friends. I was saddened by the fact that Ed had neglected his opportunity to serve in their communities back in May of 2014. I hoped that one day Ed might have the desire to serve alongside us in Ghana or another country where we work. Time would tell.

As our friendship grew with Nap and Justice, we always enjoyed seeing them when we were out shopping for groceries. On one particular day trip, I ran into Justice restocking packages in the freezer aisle. For some reason I asked, "*What do you do for vacation?*" He looked puzzled and responded, "*I work two jobs and send almost all my money back to my family in Ghana. When I get extra days off I sleep.*" I hadn't considered my friend's situation until he shared his perspective with me.

As I stood there considering his comments, he asked me a question, "*What do you and your family do with vacation time?*" We had a scheduled trip to Disney World in Orlando, Florida, so I replied, "*We're going to Disney.*" The look of confusion returned to his face and he inquired, "*What's a Disney?*" I was thinking, "*That's improper English, my friend. You may ask, 'Where is Disney?' or 'What do you do at Disney?' but not, 'What's a Disney?'*" Try explaining Disney World to someone who's park experience is limited to a swing set. I did my best, explaining the concept of an amusment park atmosphere, but this only added to his confusion. I was pressed for time and closed out the conversation to resume my shopping.

Over the course of the next week I had difficulty shaking Justice's question, "*What's a Disney?*" I prayed about the situation and then approached my wife with a question. "*Don't think I'm crazy, but what do you think about the idea of bringing Nap and Justice on our famliy vacation to Disney World?*" Sandra asked, "Would they stay in our hotel room?" I responded, "*No, we will get them their own room and also purchase their flights. I'm not sure they have ever been to a large playground, let alone an amusement park. Let's love them by treating them as members of our family while they are separated from theirs.*" Because I've got a caring wife, she agreed and so I invited Nap and Justice to join us on our family vacation. They both seemed thrilled and sent me images of their driver's licenses so I was able to purchase their plane tickets. We were moving into uncharted waters inviting African Muslim immigrants on our family vacation, but it just seemed right to love them the way we would want to be loved if the roles were reversed.

When the week finally arrived, it was moving and memorable. Their level of gratitude was off the charts! Everything we did, from the parks to basic meals, both Nap and Justice would thank us profusely. When they exited certain rides at Disney, they were so overcome with appreciation that they would hug every single person in our family.

The looks on their faces said it all, whenever they would lay their eyes on something unimaginable. When we entered Disney's Animal Kingdom, I remember vividly their comments when they caught a glimpse of the gigantic replica of the Baobab Tree. Nap blurted out, *"Wow, how old is that tree? I've never seen one grow so large!"* I responded, *"It's a fake tree."* He and Justice replied, *"No, that cannot be true. Who would make an imitation tree that is so large?"* We had to break the news to them that Americans are known to do such a thing. I warned them that they would see a lot of strange things in the days that followed, so prepare to expand your minds.

(Left to right: Courtney, Sandra, Justice, Hailey, Nap & Will)

When we got closer to the tree, we were able to show them the hidden animal carvings and the fact that it was made of plastic. They finally realized that we were telling the truth. However, when they posted the photos of themselves in front of the enormous tree, their famliy members posed the same questions that they had asked us. They told us that when they let their friends and famliy know that the tree was a fake, no one back in Ghana believed them. Go figure.

The week was unforgettable and impacted our family so deeply that for the years following that trip, we made a tradition of inviting other immigrant friends from Ghana to join us on our family vacations. There's something special about watching people experience the unimaginable in a context of being included as family. We felt equally blessed by the experience. After four years of establishing this tradition with our friends from Africa, I felt led to mix it up. It was time for the worlds to collide and the roads that had drifted apart, to merge back together.

In chapter 14, I wrote about our 8th trip to San Diego. I mentioned my homeless friend Paul Arnold, who confessed to me that he had been battling depression. Paul was part of the group we referred to as the "upper-class homeless." To us that meant that they lived in a vehicle, rather than camping outside. They had protection from certain elements associated with sleeping under the stars, or clouds depending on the weather.

While Paul had chosen to live homeless to help others on the streets, his seven years had begun to take its toll. Paul felt that the majority of those he'd helped had begun to fall into the same predictable pattern. Although many whom he'd invested in demonstrated short-term change, most reverted to familiar self-destructive habits that haunted their past.

Seeing the cycle repeated over and over led to his discouragement. When Paul confessed to feeling low, I recall telling him that if he was the only reason we showed up on that particular week, then the entire trip was worth it. Paul wept when we conveyed the value we felt for him.

After returning home in September of 2017, I continued to think about the struggle that Paul had shared so candidly. I wondered if there was anything we could do in addition to praying for him. That's when the idea occurred to me to invite Paul on our family vacation, as we'd done with our immigrant friends from Ghana.

Sandra and I had recently been discussing which of our African friends to invite on vacation that particular year, although we hadn't made up our minds yet. I asked Sandra, *"What do you think about mixing it up this year and inviting one of our homeless friends from San Diego instead?"* I mentioned Paul's situation and figured that he could use a break to lift his spirits. She agreed so I gave him a call.

After I shared the idea and invitation with my friend Paul, he caught me off guard with his question. *"Will we be serving those who have been impacted by Hurricane Maria while we're in Florida?"* I replied, *"No, we'll be relaxing on vacation. Is serving those impacted by the hurricane something that you'd like to do?"* He answered, *"Absolutely!"* I replied, *"Let me call you back later."* My mental gears were turning.

Hurricane Maria had wreaked havoc in late September of that year, with some of the worse damage occuring in Puerto Rico. We were moved by the images that we saw on the news, and wanted to do something tangible to help. We began planning a hurricane relief trip to the island over Thanksgiving break that November. Sandra and I coordinated our efforts with a partner in Puerto Rico, while we recruited a team of volunteers to join us and serve as boots on the ground.

I wasn't sure if Paul needed a passport to travel and didn't want to promise something I couldn't deliver. After realizing that Paul only needed a valid driver's license to travel, I called him back. I asked him if he wanted to join us in Puerto Rico over Thanksgiving break for our hurricane relief trip. He seemed thrilled and said, *"Yes,"* without hesitation. I asked him to send me a picture of his driver's license, so I could purchase his plane ticket.

Once I had Paul's itinerary, I called him to apologize about his unfortunate layover. The only reasonable flight I could find required him to fly from San Diego to Newark, New Jersey and then on to San Juan, Puerto Rico. The problem was that his layover was an all-night in the Jersey airport.

When I apologized he asked, *"Are they going to kick me out of the airport?"* I said, *"Absolutely not, you have a plane ticket. You just have to wait there overnight.*" He responded, "*Why is that a problem, I have a warm place to stay and a roof over my head.*" The perspective of a man who's lived on the streets is far more grateful than most people who we book travel for. The average person requests the least amount of inconvenience and financial burden. It was a pleasure to have Paul join our team, and I appreciated his attitude.

Our hurricane relief team brought water filters which we delivered to communities in the epicenter of where the catastrophic storm struck. Much of the regular drinking water supply had been contaminated by the hurricane, so the filters met a significant practical need. We also purchased a large number of bed mattresses to deliver, since a vast number of the roof tops blew completely off. Although many of the roofs had been repaired, countless bed mattresses had been soaked for prolonged periods of time. The initial rain and residual moisture permanently ruined the beds due to water damage and mold. Paul was an integral part of the team that week, serving those who were in dire need.

Imagine offering a homeless person an all-expense paid vacation, to relax in sunny Florida. How many do you think would say 'no' to the offer? Of the group that turned down the offer, how many do you suppose would say, "*No thanks, I'd rather help someone who is worse off than me. Can you serve hurricane victims?*" That's essentially what Paul said, and more importantly, what he did. As I said previously, there is no one-size-fits-all homeless person. Paul is not an addict or a lazy bum. He is one more face that people pass on the streets, and may be a victim of stereo-typing. In truth, he's a man who lives in his 1998 Ford Ranger, and serves other homeless men and women who are worse off, as a manner of serving God.

(Left to right: Will, Carlos & Paul in Puerto Rico)

Paul represents just one of the friends that we made while searching for my childhood friend Ed. There are many more. As we have continued to travel to San Diego to be a blessing to the homeless and those who serve them, it doesn't always work like that. What I mean to say is, on numerous occasions, the trip participants wind up being the recipient of the blessing, rather than the other way around. Just because we travel west to help others doesn't guarantee that the roles won't be reversed.

On my 9th trip to serve on the streets of San Diego, I was joined by three other men. One of them, by the name of John Morales, had been walking through a difficult crisis at home. The second, a Samoan named Semisi Tipeni, had recently lost his job. The third recruit was a college-aged student named Ben, who was trying to figure out what to do with his life. All three men seemed to be at some sort of crossroads in life, and yet they all felt the desire to serve in San Diego, regardless of their situations.

There are times when leaving our everyday surroundings and perceived problems can actually help rather than hinder. I'm not advocating the concept of running away from our problems. However, getting a fresh perspective by serving those who are worse off can be a cathartic experience. Just as Paul decided to serve the victims of Hurricane Maria despite his own struggles back in San Diego, John, Semisi and Ben experienced the same phenomenon traveling in the opposite direction.

John Morales and I were walking down the Arena Boulevard area in San Diego, when I spotted an old friend. Steve and I had met her on trip two, along with her friend Joaquin. On trip five, our entire group had prayed with her when she confessed that she was struggling. It was a pleasure to see here again.

Her actual name is Candace, although she goes by the street name of "Gypsy." She appeared excited to run into us, although she also looked a bit shaken. I asked her if everything was alright and she asked, *"Have you heard what happened to Joaquin?"* Joaquin Tuttle had been with Gypsy when we first met. We got acquainted after a large group of homeless people ran for cover in a serious downpour. The entire group, along with Steve, Brian and myself, were confined to a gazebo at Mariner's Point. It proved to create a captive audience situation which allowed us the opportunity to become familiar with Candace and Joaquin.

(Joaquin Tuttle)

285

At the end of that same week, Joaquin helped me and Steve deliver pizzas to many of our homeless friends at Ocean Beach. Then she shared the heartbreaking details of his death, informing us that he had been murdered earlier that year. Joaquin celebrated his 40th birthday not long before the incident. His 29-year old murderer, Cameron Parker, apparently struggled with rage. I was broken up to hear the news, reminded as I had been when Jose was murdered, that life doesn't seem to hold the same value on the street. It caused me to worry for Ed and I wondered about the characters whom he was forced to interact with on the streets.

I recalled Joaquin proudly sharing his passion for building custom bicycles. He had started a shop called "Real Hard Bikes," and took a great deal of pride in his work. When you meet individuals on the street with real ambition, it's inspiring. In addition, Joaquin was the kind of guy who liked to help others, as we saw when he helped us deliver pizzas to our homeless friends in Ocean Beach. The news of his death was a real tragedy.

Before sharing the exact details, Candace laughed as she recalled all of us stuck under the gazebo for 90 minutes. She also brought up the memory of our team praying with her, after she complained of severe back pain. Candace said, *"My back has been better ever since and I have fond memories of your mom. Please tell her that I said, 'hello.'"*

I asked her how she was holding up and she replied, *"Not well. Almost everyone I've called 'friend' out here has either robbed me, burned me, lied to me, used me or abused me."* She commented, *"A small portion of those you meet out here are actually trustworthy and kind, but you have to be careful who you choose to trust among the other 95%. I try to be kind and hope that they might treat me that way in return."* I asked, *"If it's that bad, why do you stay? Why not head back to Culpeper, Virginia, where you came from?"* She responded, *"I'm not sure where I would go and I'm not so sure I'm ready to return."* I appreciated her openness and was saddened by her suffering, and the tragic news of Joaquin's death.

(Left to right: Will, Candace & John)

John and I took the time to pray with Candace before she had to leave. She expressed her gratitude for our willingness to return to the streets year after year. The entire interaction made an impression on John. He began to rethink his situation back home. Hearing about Joaquin and being reminded of the fragility of life, John was rethinking his own crisis back at home.

As the two of us walked toward Pacific Beach to meet up with Ben and Semisi, John asked, *"Would you mind if I went home early? I think I need to deal with a situation that I left back in Virginia."* I responded, *"Of course, go home and do what you need to do. Life is about relationships and what good is it for you to help people out here, when there are other people at home who need you?"* When John flew home in the middle of the week, the rest of us completely understood. In a strange way, serving on the streets had served as a reminder to John of what truly matters in life.

Later that week, Semisi and I ran into another woman, who also went by the name of Candace. She's an older African-American woman, who seems to know every single individual in the Pacific Beach homeless community. If she doesn't know you, then she's apt to be suspicious of you until she hears your story. Candace treated me and the individuals on our teams as outsiders on our early trips. At some point she heard the reason for our trips, and has welcomed us with open arms ever since.

When I saw Candace at the Mission Bay lunchtime meal, she approached me and asked, "*Well, you gonna introduce me to your team?*" She recognized Ben from a previous trip, so I introduced her to Semisi. Candace took one look at him and said, "*Now wait a minute, this one is struggling!*" Candace wasn't a woman to keep her thoughts to herself. When she took a close glance at Semisi's face, she could sense something was wrong.

She wasted no time and approached him. Candace transitioned from her abrupt, confrontational introduction to a warm maternal tone as she stepped in his direction. She was eye-to-eye with Semisi and whispered, "*Come on honey, tell me what's wrong.*" With no pretense or safe-guarding, Semisi shared openly concerning his job loss and other struggles back home. Candace took on a bit of a southern accent as she said, "*That's not right, honey. Let me pray for ya, 'cuz the Lord wants to bring healing and give you a job!*"

With that said, Candace placed one hand on Semisi's chest and rested her right hand on his shoulder. She began to plead with God loudly, right there on the spot. She had no concern for anyone in the park as she focused her complete attention on interceding for Semisi. "*Lord Jesus, help my brother Semisi! Hear his pain and heal his heart. Grant him a job, Lord Jesus. Restore his dignity, Lord Jesus. Provide for his family, Lord Jesus and fill him with the Holy Ghost power to change his life!*"

As Candace continued beseeching the Almighty with all her heart, Semisi began to weep. It was an incredibly inspiring situation to witness. Somehow the roles had reversed. The one who'd come to minister to others had become the broken man who needed ministering. And caring mother Candace was ready and willing to provide the love and presence that Semisi desperately needed.

(Left to right: Semisi & Candace)

What occurred to me on this journey was the reality that we often feel inclined to head in a particular direction. When the route we take runs into a fork in the road, we have to make choices. If we wrestle with the desire to be in control and stay the course, we may miss an added blessing along the way.

While we came to serve others in San Diego, certain situations and circumstances turned the tables. When I tried to do some fast shopping in the middle of the night, my fork in the road led to the blessing of meeting Nap. Who would have imagined that allowing that interaction to lead to dinner, would also allow me to serve Nap and his friend Justice, and that they would join us on a family vacation, which would eventually lead to an invitation to our homeless friend Paul?

While I imagined Paul joining us on our family vacation in Florida, the path in the road he selected led him to join our hurricane relief trip in Puerto Rico. What I had imagined was a simple road to San Diego, making one trip to bring my friend home, had become a full-blown adventure. Without the forks in the road and willingness to love others as though they were Ed, I would have truly missed out. Like the ripple effect of tossing a single stone in the water, I'm privileged to watch in amazement as the concentric circles continue expanding outward, and enriching my life.

Chapter 18
Come to Your Senses

How do you rate the success of a venture to find your homeless friend? What are the metrics you use to know if the journey has truly paid off? I've had several people ask me during my first six trips if I would conclude the journey once I discovered where Ed was located. I didn't embark on this quest to simply figure out where my friend was living. When someone you care about goes missing, you want to make sure they're not in harm's way. It would have been different if I found Ed healthy and happy and living in a home somewhere, and he told me to 'bug off.' If I knew he was doing well, yet no longer wanted to continue a friendship, I'd be hurt but I'd also respect his wishes.

When you realize that a close friend or family member is addicted to a substance that alters their sense of reality and compromises their health, you still do what you can to help. While the first miracle we prayed for was discovering where Ed was hiding, the second had to do with Ed coming home, even figuratively speaking.

Ed would say things to Donnie and other employees of Maui Cyclery, such as, "*I wonder if Will and Sandra are working undercover with the CIA?*" He questioned if the CIA was trying to send him secret messages in the local Maui newspaper. His behavior had become similar to a person suffering with schizophrenia, which is also characteristic of a tweaker who is addicted to methamphetamine. While we had been fortunate to realize the first miracle of locating Ed, we were still concerned for his safety and well-being. We wanted to persevere and pray that God might grant us the second miracle by helping Ed come home. It would take a miracle to open his eyes so he might realize that his delusional thinking was nowhere close to reality.

When Sandra and I spoke with Ed on trip seven in Maui, he mentioned what he referred to as an intervention. He spoke about a time in the summer of 2014, when his mom and two other friends came to check on him at his shop on Hancock Street in San Diego. Ed mentioned a pending eviction due to unpaid bills. His belief was that those who said they loved him had actually conspired with his landlord and the CIA to have him tossed out on the street. When Ed convinced himself that there was a conspiracy against him, concocted by family members and a government agency, there was no changing his mind, and he left for the streets.

That same sort of illogical and suspicious way of thinking is common for certain drug users. Severe paranoia can influence how they perceive reality, as well as whether or not they are willing to trust anyone. It didn't matter what anyone said to Ed, his mind was made up concerning people from his past, and his continued drug use only served to reinforce his delusions.

After our second trip to Maui with Eric Locklear, Ed's sister Diane decided that she would give it a shot. Now that we knew where Ed was living and spending his days, she chose to fly to Maui with one of her daughters, and hopefully make contact with Ed. We wondered if Ed had perhaps decided to cut off certain people from his past, but not everyone. Ed and his older sister Diane had always shared a close relationship. They'd spent time together back in 2013, which had been extremely positive. We all prayed that Diane and her daughter might receive a different reception than the one we'd experienced during our two attempts.

I shared with her all of the details of our exchanges with her brother, to prepare her for what she might expect. I let Donnie know that they were coming and hoped to connect with Ed. Ed's parents and big brother were also hopeful as they made their travel plans. Everyone waited anxiously to hear how Ed might respond to an encounter with his sister and his niece.

Diane was successful in locating Ed at the Paia Bay Coffee Bar next door to Maui Cyclery. When she spotted Ed, she began to move in his direction. Ed noticed his sister and said, *"You don't see me, I'm not here."* Diane responded, *"But I am here."* He gave the two of them a hug and a kiss on the cheek before riding away on his bike in a heavy downpour. While we were thrilled that they'd been able to at least make contact with their brother/uncle, yet it was obviously not the outcome that everyone was hoping for.

In our minds, the fact that Ed ran from his sister the way he had from us, served as confirmation that he was unwilling to reconnect with anyone from his past. Regardless of how close you may've been with Ed before he began his life on the streets, he demonstrated no desire to reconnect. As long as Ed was convinced that he'd suffered a painful "*intervention*" (as he called it) in the conspiracy between the government and his friends and his family, he would maintain his distance. His belief was not in line with reality, but there seemed no way to convince him otherwise.

On my third homeless trip to San Diego, Steve and AG and I met a man by the name of Richard. Shortly after meeting him, we witnessed him making drug exchanges with homeless individuals at Mariner's Point Park. When we first met him, we were annoyed by his part in the drug trade. We viewed him with disdain, as the enemy who kept numerous individuals addicted to their mind-altering substances. I was aware that the chemicals he provided only served to perpetuate wrong thinking that kept people like my friend Ed enslaved to life on the streets. I wondered who Ed's pushers were.

On our fifth trip we saw Richard again. I spent some time talking with him, when it occurred to me that dealers need help like anybody else. Certainly, Richard was somebody's Ed. I wondered who he was connected to and who he thought of as family.

When speaking with him at a park near Mission Bay, Richard mentioned a certain situation which he blamed for landing him on the streets. He recalled serving a brief stint in prison. With bitterness in his tone, he said, "*I trusted a no-good lawyer to help me get out of jail, and instead of helping, he swindled me out of my money and my home!*" He mentioned losing his primary residence, his marriage and his children. The anger in his voice was toxic even though the incident took place

293

years earlier. He used a few other expletives when describing the attorney, but I'll spare you the details.

I offered to pray with Richard and he declined. Then I offered to pray for the daughter he'd mentioned only moments earlier. He softened up and said, "*Yes, please. I haven't seen her in years since my ex-wife turned her against me.*" I offered a prayer for his estranged relationship with his daughter and he seemed grateful.

(Left to right: Richard in background at Mission Bay & Steve)

From that day forward, every time I saw Richard, he'd approach me to chat. He seemed to be a loner and kept to himself for the most part. On one particular day he approached me at the lunchtime meal at Mariner's Point. Out of the blue he commented, "*Did I tell you that my brother is famous and that he played on the PGA Tour years ago?*" "*No, you didn't, tell me about him,*" I replied. Richard bragged about his brother and spoke with sorrow in his voice at losing contact with him.

Then he added, "*I'm not lying, why don't you look him up? His name is Barry Jaeckel.*" He walked away after making that final comment. I did a speedy web search on my phone and verified what he'd shared with me. I read the brief article that popped up as a result of my search. Then I strolled back to Richard to show him what I discovered about his brother Barry. He commented with pride, "*Yep, that's my brother. I told you I wasn't lying.*" I wondered how his brother Barry felt about Richard, and the reason for their distance.

As was our tradition, I invited him to dinner on the final Friday of that week. He seemed thrilled beyond measure and thanked me profusely. I gave him the name of the Italian restaurant to meet us at, along with the time to meet us that Friday night. He said, "*No Sh#! I'll be there!*" I was encouraged that he'd decided to join us. However, when Friday rolled around, he was a no-show.

Before our sixth trip I did a little more research and discovered that while Richard had shared with me about his famous brother Barry, he neglected to tell me about his father whom he was named after. In fact, Richard's father was far more famous than his brother Barry, the pro golfer. His father, Richard Jaeckel, had key roles in such movies as: "*The Sands of Iwo Jima*" with John Wayne, "*The Gun Fighter*" with Gregory Peck, "*The Dirty Dozen,*" and several other well-known, box office hits. His sons, Richard and Barry, had grown up in Hollywood among the stars. Who would have guessed that by seeing Richard in a line among the other homeless men and women of San Diego?

(Richard Jaeckel, Sr., Metro-Goldwyn Mayer, Copyright 1973)

295

On my sixth trip to San Diego, I happened to run into Richard again. I asked, "*We missed you at dinner before we left back in September. What happened? I hoped you were all right.*" He replied, "*I got thinking about it and I didn't want to owe you anything.*" I responded, "*I offered the dinner as my treat and was happy to pick up the check.*" Without hesitation he replied, "*Nothing's free in this life. You always owe people and I don't want to owe anyone anything.*"

Richard's mindset and belief didn't allow him the opportunity to receive from me without believing that there were strings attached to the offer. Our past can distort our willingness and ability to trust others in the present and the future. If you've been betrayed by someone you thought you could believe, then you may be slow to trust anyone else. After all, the situation that Richard constantly brought up concerned the crooked lawyer who had betrayed him and ruined his life.

Wanting to change the subject, I mentioned that I discovered his father was the famous actor Richard Jaeckel. As though I had somehow hit a major social speedbump, his entire demeanor changed. He distanced himself from me when he realized I'd discovered something about his past that he hadn't personally divulged. He gave me a brief response while avoiding eye contact, "*Yes, he was.*" He spoke those three words as he began walking away. He kept his distance from me on the remainder of that trip, even though we saw him at several of the meals. It was obvious I'd crossed a line that he hadn't invited me to cross, a social transgression that sent him running.

I wondered if Richard and Ed are both examples of wrong thinking that impedes their ability to move forward in life. How can you build trust with men who believe that you have ulterior motives? While Richard kept a safe distance, I'd still say 'hello' when I'd see him. He would say 'hi' before walking away. He wasn't completely rude, yet his body language said, "*Back off!*"

On my 8th trip to San Diego, I approached Richard at one of the Pacific Beach meals to say 'hello.' Usually if he hadn't seen me in half a year, he would inquire about our search for Ed before distancing himself. On that particular occasion I let him know that we actually found Ed one month earlier. He seemed surprised which piqued his curiosity.

He asked, "*Did you come right back to see him again?*" I surprised him when I mentioned that we found Ed in Maui. Richard inquired, "*How the hell did he get from California to Hawaii. And why are you guys back here if your friend is in Maui?*" I let him know that while the mission began for Ed, there were a number of friends we'd made during our six trips to San Diego, who we wanted to see. He said, "*You guys are wasting your time - the people on these streets are losers!*" With that said, he began to walk away as he mumbled, "*It was good to see you. I'm happy you found your friend.*"

Although he warmed up a bit when he heard we'd found Ed, he maintained his distance. I asked him how he'd been doing, and the most he was willing to share was, "Fine." After that brief exchange, Richard returned to the way he'd acted toward me before I asked him about his father. My efforts began to repair the relational bridge that had been damaged. I wondered if his final comment exclaiming that, "*People on the streets are losers,*" reflected the way he felt about himself, the way he thought about others, or both?

I continued to connect with Richard on subsequent trips. Before my 12th trip, I came up with a new idea, hoping it might establish more trust. I searched on E-Bay for some sort of golf paraphernalia that contained an image of his brother Barry. I was able to find a card with Barry Jaeckel's golf information on it, similar to a baseball card. It was reasonably priced, so I purchased it before our trip. It arrived in a sturdy plastic collector's case. I wrapped it up and took it with me on the trip.

I happened to run into Richard on our second day during our lunch at Mariner's Point. I approached him and said, "*I brought you a late Christmas gift.*" Our 12th trip was in January of 2019, so I added, "*Sorry it's a month late.*" He looked surprised, but accepted the gift and unwrapped it. When he laid eyes on his brother's golf card, he looked up at me and said, "*This is my brother!*" I responded, "*Yes, it is.*" And then all of a sudden, as if someone reminded him that he wasn't allowed to receive gifts, since there may be unspoken expectations attached, he said, "*I can't take this, it's yours, keep it!*" I replied, "*Barry's not my brother, I don't want it. Besides, I brought it for you as a Christmas gift. Do you still celebrate Christmas here on the streets?*" He smirked and said, "*I suppose so, thanks.*" I replied, "*You're welcome.*"

We seemed to gain some ground in our friendship after I gave Richard the collection card with his brother's photo on it. For whatever reason, on our 14th trip in January of 2020, I seemed to run into Richard almost every day. We had some great conversations throughout the week. At one point, I decided to invite Richard to dinner once again. "*How would you like to join our team for dinner on our final night in San Diego later this week?*" To my surprise, he responded, "*Sure, what the hell, why not?*" I gave him the time and location for our team dinner and he agreed to meet up. On that particular trip, he actually showed up.

Our team had selected an Italian restaurant known as Buca di Beppo, in the popular Gas Lamp District. The restaurant serves family style portions to share, so it was perfect for our team to conclude the week and invite a few of our San Diego friends. When I entered the restaurant, Richard was nowhere in sight. I arrived about ten minutes ahead of our group to be sure I wouldn't miss him. When I found him, he was seated at the bar. He confessed arriving 45 minutes early to get himself acclimated. I realized after chatting with him briefly that perhaps "acclimated" was code for swallowing down a bit of liquid courage. As I mentioned earlier, he is a bit of a loner and an introvert. I understood that joining our team for dinner was forcing him out of his comfort zone, so perhaps the early bar visit helped.

(Left to right: Will & Richard Jaeckel at Buca di Beppo)

Richard and I joined the rest of the group after chatting briefly at the bar, while he gulped down his vodka tonic. He selected a seat at the far end of our group table, so I joined him. Once we settled in, I asked him if he might be willing to share more about his life. He seemed relaxed enough and was more than happy to do so.

Richard spoke of growing up in Hollywood, watching his dad on the historic film sets. He mentioned that his father would often bring him and his younger brother Barry to watch the movies as they were being made. His father earned his fame, starring in 35+ movies, as well as television programs.

His tone became warmer and sad, when he spoke of his dad's painful bout with cancer and agonizing death in 1997. Speaking of his father's death triggered something in him. He abruptly returned to expressing his rage toward the lawyer, who had taken advantage of him.

I listened patiently, but as the evening rolled on, my mind began to wonder. I grew curious. It sounded as though Richard had been living on the streets for more than ten years. I inquired, *"Since I met you five years earlier, I've heard you express anger at the man who you believe robbed you of your home. What's kept you from moving on with your life, getting a job and perhaps purchasing a new home?"* My question caused him to pause and then he answered, *"That man owes me, but our society is crooked and won't make him pay!"* Richard's anger boiled hot, as he repeated his corrupt attorney's offenses, as though I'd forgotten them.

While I attempted to encourage him and invited him to seriously consider the idea of moving forward, he was content to vent his anger and blame others for his ship-wrecked life. It seemed as though his mindset had paralyzed him, and he'd become content to remain in that place for the past ten years.

I thought about the power of holding a grudge and allowing bitterness to invade our way of thinking. Richard's inability or perhaps unwillingness to move on, appeared to be connected to his choice to blame others for his plight. I've no idea if Richard's version of the dishonest lawyer was as straight-forward as he claimed, or if there was much more to the story. Often times when we grow bitter, we fail to see things from a wider perspective. That unwillingness can paralyze us if we're not careful.

When we spoke with Ed, he seemed to hold a similar grudge toward people who he accused of being involved in what he referred to as the 'intervention.' While living on the streets, we've tried to encourage as many people as we possibly could. An individual's mindset plays a significant part in their willingness to receive help and move forward. While I've listened to hundreds of life stories from friends on the street, many have wounds or someone to blame for their situation. Very few are willing to own a portion of the responsibility and move on.

In truth, there are countless humans like Kyle, from an earlier trip, who've suffered abuse and horrific treatment from those who should have loved them. While they are unable to change their past, healing is possible. Unfortunately, most choose to either medicate as Kyle had done, eating pills from his own vomit, or remaining bitter and paralyzed, as Richard seemed to prefer. Neither medication nor grudge holding seems to get us very far in the long run.

On my 9th trip I met Mike. Our group was in Mission Bay one morning, when Mike Drumright said 'hello.' I hadn't seen him before, although he told me that he'd been homeless in the area for quite some time. He was eager to chat, as we killed time before the lunch meal arrived. Mike asked me what we were doing there and I shared briefly about our situation. Then I asked Mike about his life. Before he could answer my question, he said, "*Let me first say that what you're doing for your friend is incredible! I wish I had friends and family like you all.*" I thanked him and asked what his friends and family were like, if not like us. He sat quietly before answering my question. I'm not sure if he was trying to decide on what answer to give me or whether to respond at all. After an extended pause he shared with tremendous candor.

(Left to right: Will & Mike Drumright at Mission Bay)

301

Mike began, "*To tell you the truth, I have a good family, but they've given up on me because I've let them down too many times. None of them believe my word anymore.*" I interjected, "*Why's that?*" He continued, "*Because I've made promises over and over again, which I'm unable to keep. I honestly mean well, and express honest intentions, yet I can't seem to stay away from booze and drugs. I do pretty well when I'm broke, but when my monthly pension check arrives, I can feel an inner voice down deep saying, 'You need to get high.' There have been times when I've resisted for a short while, but I can't be trusted with money.*" Then he added, "*When I'm broke and sober, I'm a good guy.*"

Mike's level of vulnerability was refreshing. He shared with no false pretense, nor did he claim to be a victim. Perhaps he'd been sizing me up before deciding to level with me. After chatting for about 20 minutes, Mike asked me if I would pray with him. After we spent a minute or two praying, Mike asked, "*Would you mind if we exchanged phone numbers?*" I said, "*Not at all,*" so we did.

On our final night that week, we invited Mike to join our team for dinner downtown. When he met us in Little Italy, he expressed his gratitude over and over for our willingness to include him. He was also grateful for our desire to hear his story. While Richard blamed others for his struggle in life, Mike only blamed himself. I asked Mike, "*How can we help you?*" His response shocked me, "*You can't help me, because I know I can't do it.*" How can you help someone who's given up on themselves? Where do you start with an individual who doesn't believe they are capable of kicking a drug addiction?

It would seem to me that an admission of needing help, coupled with a strong desire to be free, would be a great place to start. I wondered if Ed would express the same sad defeated mindset that Mike had shared? Can you help someone who has given up believing in themselves? Did Ed have any desire to be free from his addiction?

On our 11th trip to San Diego, I recall standing outside of Saint Vincent's while we waited to be admitted into the cafeteria. It was day one of that particular week, when I happened to meet Jerry. We were both standing in line for the lunch meal, when we struck up a conversation. I asked Jerry how long he'd been on the streets and how he managed to survive.

Our discussion lasted as we walked the line through the buffet, and continued at the table. As we sat down and placed our trays in front of us, I asked Jerry, "*What's your biggest struggle out here?*" Over the course of lunch, Jerry shared with me about his lifelong bout with diabetes. He said, "*It's brutal but that's not my most significant struggle.*" I replied, "*What is?*" Jerry continued, "*I have a drug problem that's impossible for me to kick.*" I replied, "*It sounds as though you've made a few attempts to stop?*" He responded, "*More than I can count.*" I could hear the sense of defeat and discouragement in his words. My heart went out to him. Similar to Mike, Jerry was willing to admit his problem, and yet he'd thrown in the towel and abandoned any belief in himself.

We finished up lunch and stepped outside into the sunshine. I offered to pray with Jerry and he replied, "*Yes, please.*" I placed my hand on his shoulder and began to ask God if He might restore hope to my friend Jerry. I prayed for his battle with diabetes and begged God to lift his spirits. Jerry began to weep while I prayed. When we concluded the prayer, Jerry was clearly moved and gave me a hug. He thanked me for sharing a lunch meal and more importantly, for listening to his story.

I said, "*When you give up hope, you need to surround yourself with people who can remain hopeful for you.*" He responded, "*There ain't many people like that 'round these days.*" I wished I lived closer to San Diego so I could meet with Jerry on a regular basis. Certainly, there are people willing to be present in his life and offer consistent encouragement, right? I began to consider my role in Ed's life, what would it look like if Ed made it home and needed encouragement? Can offering hope and steady encouragement make a difference for an addict? I wanted to learn how to help an addict stay the course and beat a long-term drug habit. I prayed that I'd get the chance if my friend ever miraculously returned home.

(Left to right: Will & Jerry at Saint Vincent's)

In January of 2020, I ran into Jerry once more. He was at the same meal at Father Joe's Kitchen, a ministry of Saint Vincent's Catholic Church. Jerry seemed surprised by the fact that I remembered his name. I was eager to catch up and get an update on his life. He said that he was hanging in there, yet still battling diabetes and addiction. I asked, *"Have you found any support base of friends who share your struggle, such as Narcotics Anonymous?"* He shook his head *"Nope,"* with a look of shame in his eyes. I'm not so sure that anyone can overcome a serious war on addiction without the help of others.

I had no intention of shaming Jerry, I just wanted to hear how he was progressing. He thanked me for saying 'hello,' and told me that he hoped to see me again soon. As he left the cafeteria, my mind drifted to the story of the prodigal son. When Jesus spoke of the loving father waiting at home for his lost son, he did not say that the father was responsible for bringing his adult son home. In fact, Jesus said that when the son was at his lowest point, he "came to his senses," (Luke 15:17). In other words, the son had a sudden change of heart, and desired to return home. Until the lost son decided that he wanted to return, no one could move forward, despite how much his father loved him. I began to pray that Ed might *"come to his senses."*

Chapter 19
JD Alive and Free

When making new friends on the streets we learned to keep our ears open for people who actually wanted help. As I mentioned earlier, Ed had rejected our help, although he was willing to speak with me briefly. In addition to keeping an eye out for those who wanted help, we also paid attention to people's attitudes. Positive attitudes on the street tend to stand out because they're not quite as common as the negative ones. Remaining positive and optimistic is exemplified in our blind friend Tom, who we have never heard make a single complaint. When you meet someone like him, it's difficult not to have your spirit lifted. I suppose that's how I felt when I first met JD.

On the same day that I met Jerry at St. Vincent's lunchtime meal, a unique individual caught my attention. Standing in line, just behind my friend Steve Bowman, was a man in his early 40's. The man began complaining loudly and cursing about having to wait in line. He whined about the local government, the churches and the police. Steve and I had grown accustomed to that sort of rant, so we were unfazed. What caught us off guard was the reaction of the beefy 50-year old standing behind him.

At a glance I thought he would have made an effective bouncer at a local pub. He'd also been listening to the man fussing, who was sandwiched between the three of us. Apparently, he grew tired of hearing it and decided to confront the obnoxious complainer.

I still recall what he said. "*Hey man, you gotta stop complaining. Every day is a gift from God! You should consider all we've got to be grateful for!*" The loud mouth redirected his attention toward the man who was rebuking him. He carried on, "*I spent 17 years in prison and I'm grateful for every day that I'm free. We have our health, the sun shining above and there are incredible people here who are serving us lunch today, so let's show a little courtesy.*" The man who'd been complaining

306

had no response. Perhaps he piped down when he noticed the enormous size of the man confronting him.

The man encouraging a spirit of gratitude added, "*The District Attorney put me away for writing bad checks, although I ain't complaining. I figure I got away with armed robbery, which they never connected me to, so I suppose I deserved the time.*" Steve and I listened intently and when the pep talk was over, I said to Steve, "*I need to meet that guy.*" He agreed, although the moment didn't feel right to insert ourselves into their exchange.

After lunch and my chat with Jerry that I referenced in the previous chapter, I happened to run right into the optimistic preacher. I saw him on his way out of Father Joe's kitchen and said, "*Excuse me, but I overheard you talking before lunch and expressing your positive perspective. My name is Will and I just wanted to say that I really appreciated what you had to say.*" He smiled and replied, "*Aw thanks man, I meant every word of it. My name is JD.*" And with that he extended his hand in my direction. We shook hands and took a few minutes getting acquainted.

I shared our reason for living homeless on that given week and asked JD if he had always been that positive. He said, "*Not at all man, in fact, I went to jail because I was so full of hate at that time in my life. That kind of attitude usually leads to trouble. At one point in prison, I decided that I'd had enough and met a different crew of guys. They introduced me to God and my attitude began to change. When I got out of jail, these people at Saint Vincent's and Father Joe's Village taught me how to speak properly, how to have self-respect and helped me turn my life around. I'm eternally grateful to the people working here, which is the reason I couldn't sit back and listen to that guy complain.*"

I thanked JD for sharing and introduced him to Steve. Since we make a habit of inviting a few people to dinner on the final night of each homeless week, I invited JD to join us on that particular Friday. He was grateful but said, "*Sorry man, I'm working into the evening this Friday so I won't be able to join you.*" We found an alternative plan and invited him to join us for breakfast one morning. JD mentioned a diner that he liked which happened to be close to a construction site where he'd been working. We set the date and time and exchanged phone numbers.

Similar to our friend Paul, JD was what we refer to as "upper class homeless," since he was living in his car at that time. He mentioned the work he was doing and once again sang the praises of Father Joe's workers who'd helped him land a job. I asked him if there was anything we could pray for and he responded, *"Yeah man, thanks for asking. My wife is presently in a drug rehab facility and needs to stay clean for a full 90 days. Her name is Pita."* We prayed right there on the spot, and JD thanked us profusely for taking the time to listen and pray. It was difficult to believe that he'd been the angry man who he described earlier in his life. Change is inspirational! I wondered how Ed might respond to a guy like JD, if he had heard the same speech that we witnessed in line that day.

We looked forward to meeting up with him later in the week. Our introduction to JD took place on my 11th trip in this homeless adventure. I had returned in mid-September of 2018, accompanied by Steve Bowman, Georgia McGowan and Andrew Beall. Andrew was the only rookie in the bunch. He had formerly been a drug addict, which allowed him to adapt to the culture and engage those on the streets with firsthand knowledge of their struggle.

(Left to right: Steve, Georgia, Will & Andrew)

The four of us covered a lot of ground but also encountered an obstacle on our first evening. We discovered that there were no evening meals on that particular night. I called my friend Paul Arnold to see if he had a recommendation. He said, *"Actually, I've begun receiving a monthly Social Security check, so why don't you let me treat your team?"* We appreciated his generosity and met him in a parking lot at the corner of Sports Arena Boulevard and West Point Loma Boulevard. From there he escorted us to a local buffet restaurant, called Souplantation. It was situated in the same parking lot as Denny's. Steve and I were all too familiar with that Denny's, since we'd held a stakeout there one night, hoping Ed might walk in on trip two. It was also the same restaurant where we slept in a corner booth during a cold night on trip three, when AG had joined us. By trip 11, we'd become extremely familiar with the area.

When we exited the restaurant, Paul mentioned seeing a woman who'd been standing in the bushes before we entered for dinner. She happened to be there when we left so he offered her his leftovers. She gladly accepted the food and seemed out of place standing in the bushes. I'd been working with a human trafficking organization back in Virginia, and the woman seemed to carry some of the characteristics of someone being trafficked.

We even watched a man come and check up on her and then return to what he was doing. The entire situation seemed suspicious. I asked Georgia if she might be willing to engage the woman and inquire if she was in trouble. She did, and discovered that the woman's name was Alexandra and she confessed that she was in trouble. Georgia offered to meet her for lunch the following day and Alexandra jumped at the offer. We prayed for her that evening and wondered what her backstory was. We hoped that she would show up for the lunch meeting with Georgia.

The next day, Alexandra not only showed up, but she confessed to being tied up in a dangerous traffic ring. Georgia called me and I was able to coordinate a safe house with our friends from Northern Virginia Human Trafficking Initiative. When I made Georgia aware, she offered

Alexandra a one-way plane ticket back to the east coast, to help her es-cape her situation. Steve purchased a flight for her that same day, and he accompanied the two ladies to the airport in San Diego.

Andrew and I walked the streets of San Diego meeting more home-less friends, while Steve and Georgia took an Uber ride to the airport with Alexandra. They spent the entire afternoon with her, hearing more of her story while they waited for her flight. She mentioned having a daughter and being so appreciative of their help. When they were about 90 minutes out from the flight time, they said a prayer and farewell to Alexandra before they watched her head to her gate through the security check point. She didn't have a cell phone, but they gave her a list of numbers and told her to borrow someone's phone in the airport if she ran into trouble.

(Alexandra saying "Farewell" at the airport)

Among the names on the list, was Kay Duffield's number. Kay is the director of the Northern Virginia Human Trafficking Initiative and planned to pick Alexandra up when she landed in Washington, D.C. When Georgia and Steve met up with Andrew and me for dinner, they were ecstatic, having been able to assist in Alexandra's rescue. That situ-ation made the entire week worth the trip.

At around 6:00 a.m. the following morning, we received a heart-breaking text from Kay, who'd been waiting at Dulles Airport to receive Alexandra. Kay said, "*Alexandra messaged me in the middle of the night to say that she couldn't leave. She apologized for her change of heart and never showed up this morning at the airport.*" Our celebration over her freedom was short- lived, since for whatever reason, she was unwilling or unable to get on that plane. We had no phone number for her and the text she sent to Kay mentioned that it was coming from a borrowed cell phone.

While we were broken over the situation, we didn't give up on Alexandra. We returned twice each day to the place where we'd originally met her in front of Souplantation. Although we hoped she might return, she never did.

On the day we returned to the airport to depart, Steve and I went to the United Airlines Customer Service office to find out if she used the ticket credit to fly elsewhere. Since Steve had purchased the ticket with his credit card, he was able to get some answers. He had retained a copy of the ticket with her last name: Mazzant. The United agent helping us searched frantically for the ticket. We watched her eyes as they scanned the screen that we were unable to see. Then she said, "*It seems that she was issued a refund for the ticket.*" Steve and I commented, "*I guess she played us to get the money from the ticket.*" The United agent corrected our inaccurate assumption and said, "*No sir, it appears that she made sure that the credit went back to your credit card, so you were not charged for the ticket.*" We were saddened by the fact that she never made it to freedom and moved by Alexandra's willingness to make sure that Steve was issued a refund before she left the airport.

There are so many on the streets, and each has a story, just as Ed has a backstory. It's easy for us to pass a homeless man or woman and assume that they are lazy and unwilling to work or addicted to drugs or alcohol, when in fact every homeless individual has their own unique story. I've been moved by the countless stories that I've been privileged to hear over the course of 14 trips, and we have no plan to stop going.

I've often prayed that if Ed is unwilling to connect with people from his past, that perhaps God would send someone to love and help him who had no ties to his past life. I'm grateful to God for providing Donnie at Maui Cyclery to care for Ed and be a consistent person in his life. His relationship with Ed, as well as the other employees from his shop who look out for him, have been a life saver! Just to have a point of contact to keep us updated on Ed's condition has been a blessing. We prayed that God would send someone like Donnie into Alexandra's life to follow up where we left off. God only knows why she left the airport that day.

On Thursday morning, we met up with JD for breakfast. He showed up on time at the diner he'd selected. We had a wonderful breakfast with him and got to hear more of his story. It was encouraging to be around someone as positive as JD after the emotional hit we'd experienced with Alexandra's situation. He greeted our team with the same bursting gratitude and optimism that he possessed when we met him three days earlier.

JD shared more about his wife Pita and her recovery. He said, *"I'd really like her to meet you guys. When do you plan to return here?"* Steve and I exchanged glances, since we'd been kicking around the idea of when we should return. For whatever reason I said, *"I think we will be returning in early January."* I had requests from a number of college students who were interested in joining us for a trip. We had developed a pattern of returning to San Diego every September and February, although that pattern wasn't conducive for university students who were in school. I considered moving the winter trip to an earlier date to accommodate the requests. JD replied, *"That would be awesome, since I want you all to meet Pita. And, she gets out of treatment in December, so the timing is perfect!"*

(Left to right: Steve, Will, JD, Andrew & Georgia)

As I inquired about Pita, JD shared about her history of battling drug addiction. He added, "I want the best for my wife and when she gets out of treatment, I'd like to renew our wedding vows and dedicate our marriage to God." Then he turned in my direction and asked, "Would you be willing to officiate a service like that when you come back?" I responded, "Sure, I'm flattered you asked. We can make that happen. Let me give it some thought and get back to you."

Our team was headed toward Old Town, since the Thursday night meal was held in Presidio Park. We invited JD to meet us at the meal and gave him the necessary information and details. He offered to drive us in the direction of Old Town San Diego, but when he began removing items from his car, he quickly realized that there wasn't enough room for our crew. When you live in your car, your entire life's belongings tend to take up a lot of space. He was embarrassed and began apologizing. We assured him that it wasn't a problem and thanked him for his thoughtful offer. We gathered around him to have a final prayer before heading east up the road. After the prayer, he looked straight at me and said, "I'm really looking forward to the service in January when you meet my wife!" "Of course, me too." I replied. I gave him a hug and we were on our way.

(JD outside of the diner by his car)

That afternoon I received a phone call. The previous summer I'd led our annual medical mission trip to serve in Honduras. During that time, I shared in front of a church a bit about our team and what our non-profit does throughout the year. One woman by the name of Julie Meisterlin approached me after the service and told me that she and her family lived in San Diego. She said, "*We are very interested in serving the homeless community next time you return to the area.*" I'd forgotten to call her, although she noticed our posts on Facebook and called me. She inquired, "*I saw on Facebook that you're in town with a team, and we'd like to help.*" I told her about the evening meal at Presidio Park. I said, "*I know it's short notice, but if you can volunteer this evening, there's an opportunity.*" She took down the details and replied, "*Fantastic, we'll see you tonight!*" I love the way God provides opportunities in life that weave a tapestry of relationships, that would never happen if I kept to myself.

That evening we arrived just as the sun was setting. Julie approached me to say "hello" and she introduced me to her daughter Carly and her friend Sierra. What made that particular weekly meal unique, was the fact that the host church was located in Ramona, about 20 miles away from Presidio Park. Rather than make the hungry homeless come to them, they serve the friends from the street on their turf. Since the meals were held outdoors, they were subject to the elements. On that evening, it was cold and dark.

(Left to right: Sierra, Will & Carly at Presidio Park Dinner)

The team hosting often begins by playing some live worship songs followed by a preacher who delivers a message, as the homeless assemble for the dinner. While I appreciate the church's efforts to feed the hungry, my personal preference would be to preach after the meal, so that people have a choice as to whether or not they want to stay and listen to a sermon. I'd rather have individuals decide if they want to listen, as opposed to a captive audience. I don't say that as a criticism of the host church, as I'm very appreciative that they have been feeding our hungry teams for years now, every Thursday evening.

Just after I finished catching up with Julie, a woman approached me. Her name is Sherrie Day and she pastors at that particular church. She asked, "*Are you the pastor who lives homeless a couple times a year and invited Julie and her daughter to serve this evening?*" I replied, "*Yep, that's me.*" She continued, "*Fantastic, our scheduled preacher was unable to make it tonight, so I'd like you to bring the Word.*" "*Bring the Word,*" is church slang, which is another way of asking, "*Can you preach a message for us?*" I stood there stunned by her request, having no desire to preach in that instance.

After giving Sherrie's offer a moment of thought I responded, "*Actually, I'm here to love the homeless and am not really feeling much like preaching this evening.*" As though she'd been unable to hear what I just said, she placed her hand on my chest and began to pray, "*Lord give my brother a Word for the crowd this evening. Amen!*" At the conclusion of her brief and poignant prayer she exclaimed, "*OK, the Lord's going to give you a Word, you've got this. I'll call you up when it's time.*" And with that, she spun around and walked away. I thought to myself, "*What just happened?*" I uttered a silent prayer to God, "*Lord, you know I have no desire to preach to my homeless friends this evening, so please put some words in my mouth, 'cause I got nothing!*" I'm not sure if you've ever been asked to do something that you didn't feel excited about. That's precisely how I felt, and so I invited God to do the miraculous since I wasn't feeling up to the task.

I joined Steve where he was standing on the hill. He was waiting for the music to begin playing, and said, "*This is when they always have that guy preach, I wish they'd ask you some time.*" I looked at him without telling him what had just transpired and replied, "*Yep.*" About ten minutes later Pastor Sharon approached the microphone and introduced me as a visiting East Coast preacher who had been living homeless to find his missing friend. With that, Steve looked at me, "*What?!*" I smiled his direction before walking up front to grab the microphone. As I mentioned, I had nothing in mind to share, but God granted my prayer and the words filled my mind. I began by saying that this was my 11th trip searching for my homeless friend who I'd discovered was a meth addict. I am used to asking questions when I speak to interact with the crowd so I said, "*How many tweakers are in the crowd this evening?*" A few hollered out in response. Not behavior I was trying to encourage, but I appreciated the honesty. The audience appeared to be listening intently. I told them a few highlights of my journey, such as Crazy Ted challenging me to live homeless. I shared about young Kyle eating pills out of his own vomit, because he was desperate to medicate the pain of his past. I commented, "*I wonder how many of you listening tonight have been trying to medicate the pain from your past?*" The crowd fell silent.

I told them about my search for Ed and the privilege it has been to meet so many incredible friends on the streets and hear their stories. Some homeless guy on the hill shouted, "*Right on man!*" I carried on. I made the comment that every person we meet is someone else's 'Ed.' I asked, "*Is there anyone at home wondering where you are?*" Again, the hill of homeless listeners grew quiet.

I mentioned being awakened by police officers and other homeless people and someone shouted, "*I've been there!*" Then I said, "*On my 7th trip I located my friend Ed.*" A number of the homeless began to applaud. I continued, "*But my friend Ed told me that he wasn't ready for help.*" Then I asked the question, "*Are you ready for help this evening?*" In the midst of the silence I sensed God's Spirit was getting through. Then I confessed, "*I discovered that my friend doesn't live in San Diego anymore, he relocated to Maui. So, you might wonder, 'Why did we return here if Ed is in Hawaii?'*" With every spectator fully attentive, I stated, "*We returned because you matter to God and you matter to us.*"

I shared a bit more about their value and the importance of never giving up. I told them that the people serving from the church in Ramona are present to help if you want it, but they can't read your minds. You have to ask for help, something my friend Ed is not yet willing to do. I led them in prayer as we closed out the service and opened up the meal.

Something in the atmosphere had changed. One homeless gentleman who'd been moved by the words spoken approached me after my prayer. He said, "*Hey man, your team is welcome to come sleep with my crew. We camp out in an area close to the riverbed.*" I thanked him for his kind offer but said, "*We have a place where we've been camping, but thanks for the offer.*"

A man by the name of Les Reading approached me and said, "*I've been volunteering with the homeless for over 20 years and I have never witnessed anything like what happened here this evening. I've never seen our street friends so attentive. I want you to know that every time you're in San Diego, we will reserve the pulpit for you to preach.*" Les obviously hadn't heard what I told Sharon, when I said that I had no desire to preach. Les asked me how long our team would be in town. I let him know we were scheduled to depart on Saturday morning. He asked if he could take our team out to dinner the following evening. We made plans to meet Les for some delicious Mexican food the following evening in Old Town.

I invited a friend by the name of Magda, whom I met the previous year while she was serving our dinner at the Catholic Church in Pacific Beach. Magda is from Poland and let me know how much she enjoys serving others. When she heard what we do with our non-profit, she signed up to join us on a mission trip serving orphans in Limatambo, Peru in the summer of 2017. Both Magda and Paul joined our last meal in San Diego, courtesy of Les Reading.

As I chatted with Les over dinner to get to know him better, I was struck by his generosity. I'm not simply referring to his willingness to treat our team to dinner, but something he offered to Magda, whom he'd only just met. Les asked Magda about her life dreams and she responded, *"I've always wanted a sailboat that I could live on and sail around the world."* His response to Magda's dream was enough to cause my jaw to drop. Les said, *"What if I gave you a sailboat?"* She responded, *"Excuse me?"* He continued, *"In all seriousness, a business partner and I own a boat that you can sleep on and sail around the globe if you have your license. We are tired of paying the slip fees to keep it anchored and rarely use it. You can give it a whirl and if you are willing to assume the fees and ownership, we'll donate it to you."*

Magda was clearly stunned by his incredibly generous offer and thanked him profusely. While they discussed the particulars, I was waiting for Les to ask me what my dream was, and hopeful that he and his business partner owned some beach front property that also went unused. In all honesty, I was thrilled for Magda and inspired by my new friend's generosity.

(Left to right: Steve, Will, Magda, Paul, Georgia, Andrew & Les)

When the dessert arrived, I told Les about meeting JD and his incredibly positive attitude. He had been unable to join us that evening due to work, but I shared JD's request with Les. "*We plan to return to San Diego during the first week of 2019, so what if we throw a New Year's Eve party for the homeless at Presidio Park and work JD's marriage renewal ceremony into the mix?*" Les seemed excited about the idea and promised to do the necessary legwork to see if he could make it happen. I figured he was the man to get the job done, after all, I wasn't asking for a yacht!

Les's question caused me to ponder if Ed still has any dreams. Many lose hope when living in the streets. If an individual has been out too long, it can have that effect. I wondered how Ed would have answered Les's question if he'd been present that evening. I hoped time would tell, and prayed God might move in his heart.

Chapter 20
Murder at Midnight

I want to be hopeful, how about you? When I ask a homeless individual to share their story with me, I sincerely hope that what they're sharing with me is true. I try not to second- guess, although there are times when I've checked the details of particular stories to verify them for myself. On our 12ᵗʰ trip in early January of 2019, we had a fairly large group of trip participants. Steve invited both of his daughters, Kara and Holly. He even recruited a guy by the name of Clay, who was dating his daughter Kara at the time. I believe he wanted to find out what Clay was made of, since the streets have a way of revealing someone's character.

On one particular day that week, we were walking through Old Town San Diego when I met a man who told me that he was the brother of George Harrison of the Beatles. I must admit that he looked a bit like him and was carrying an acoustic guitar and sporting a beard. However, as we walked away, I made a quick web search of George Harrison's family to reveal the fact that George didn't have a brother by the name of "Carl." If he had, then I'd be telling you about how I met one of the Beatles' brothers in San Diego.

When you realize you're being lied to or played, it's important to not take it personally. Walking the streets of San Diego, I wanted to treat every man and woman that I met with dignity, offering them the benefit of the doubt. While my friend Ed never lied to me when we encountered him over those two summers, it still hurt to have him reject our help. Steve and I had worked in advance to prepare our team for the streets, also prepping for our unique celebration with JD and his wife Pita.

Les had worked with his church in Ramona to reserve the gymnasium in Presidio Park, so that we could host a New Year's Eve party with our homeless friends that wasn't weather-dependent. We had recruited a stellar team to walk the streets of San Diego, in addition to two friends whom I'd invited as musical guests for the party. JD was thrilled that the plan had come to fruition, although he mentioned that his wife was extremely nervous. We hit the streets early with our team on Monday morning, December 31. We were ready to ring in the New Year with our friends at the Presidio Park gymnasium where we planned to rendezvous at 4:30 p.m.

Everyone rallied that afternoon at the gymnasium to make sure we were prepared for the meal, the music and the service. It was a bit of a thrill to be undertaking a new endeavor. While I enjoyed the traditions that had developed over time, it was exciting to do something fresh, like a New Year's Eve party.

(Left to right: Enzo, Will, Melanie, Georgia, Holly, Steve, Kara, Peter, Randy, Clay, Hawley, JD & Pita)

JD called me to say that he was running late. I let him know that we'd reserved a local hotel room for Pita and him for the night. After all, I didn't want them sleeping in his car after celebrating years of marriage and the big event. I told JD to take his time and freshen up at the hotel with Pita, while the rest of us helped Les' church prepare for the dinner that evening. Les was on point. He had the sound system set up, his volunteers ready to serve, and a tasty meal prepared for our guests. I felt we were ready, although that didn't prevent me from recruiting more volunteers.

On my flight to California the day earlier, I struck up a conversation with my United Airlines flight attendant. Her name was Janet Castellanos and I happened to ask her about her New Year's Eve plans. She said that she didn't have much going on, but she planned to hang out with her brother Julio and his friend Adrian Delgado. Then she asked me about my plans and I told her that we were throwing a New Year's Eve party for the homeless in Presidio Park. When Janet heard my plans she said, "*I always wanted to do something like that to serve those in need.*" I immediately responded, "*Well, why don't you do it with us?*" She looked as though the thought hadn't crossed her mind. I gave Janet all the details, including my phone number. She said, "*If I can talk Julio and Adrian into it, then we'll see you at Presidio Park tomorrow evening.*" Sure enough, they showed up and were an integral part of the team, serving the hungry who attended the festive party.

(Left to right: Adrian, Julio, Janet & Will)

The meal was amazing, and my friends Melanie and Enzo played background music while people enjoyed their meal and pleasant conversations. Our team spread out at tables among the homeless to engage in conversations and offer hope when possible. JD and Pita arrived late, but had a chance to grab a plate of food before we began the service. It was my first-time meeting Pita, and I could tell that she was nervous.

Alternatively, JD seemed ecstatic about such an event that he'd envisioned when we met four months earlier. It was obvious that JD loved Pita and did his best to remain sensitive to her feelings. I sat with JD and Pita as they ate, and talked through the ceremony one last time to see if they wanted to make any final changes. When the final song concluded, I stepped up front to take the microphone and welcome our guests.

Our homeless friends seemed thrilled to have this out of the ordinary celebration and applauded the church volunteers who made it happen. I made a few introductions, including my flight attendant Janet, her brother Julio and his friend Adrian. After thanking the volunteers and our hosts, I invited JD and Pita up to the front.

(Left to right: Will, Pita & JD)

I made the audience aware of their marriage commitment and desire to put God in the center of their lives. They confessed struggles and said, *"We need God to make it forward as a couple and in order to remain drug-free,"* a message that resonated with our spectators that evening. A few of our homeless friends in the audience were tearful at the occasion. All in all, it was a memorable evening, certainly unlike any New Year's Eve event that I had ever been part of.

After the final song had been sung, we hung around to have conversations with those who lingered. JD and Pita thanked us, but seemed anxious to get back to their hotel. When you live in a car, you are especially appreciative of a full room for the night. Anyone on our team who wasn't engaged in conversation with our street friends helped Les' team clean up the gymnasium. It was an unforgettable evening! I'm grateful to Les and to Hope Christian Fellowship for cooking, serving and partnering together to pull off such an amazing service.

Our two musicians, Melanie and Enzo, were headed home, so that left nine of us on the streets. Once we finished cleaning up, our team hiked to what we began to refer to as the "Pine Needle Motel." We'd grown accustomed to the small crop of Pine Trees across the street from Sea World, so we hiked there to set up camp. The group did well on their first night camping, although our second night was a different story.

Perhaps we'd grown too comfortable in that space, which allowed us to sleep so soundly. In the middle of the night, two homeless men, along with their Pitbull walked right up on us as we slept. It was about 3:00 a.m., when our surprise visitors arrived. The larger of the two was holding a baseball bat and a flashlight, while the other held the Pitbull's leash. I woke, and then I heard the question, *"What the hell is going on here?"* All I could see was the bright flashlight being shone in my eyes. My first assumption was that it was a cop, since that seemed to be their pattern, when we'd been awakened by police on past trips.

I leaned back to take a look beyond the glare of the flashlight and realized that it was a couple of homeless men. They appeared to be armed and ready to rob unsuspecting individuals who were sleeping on the street. What they didn't anticipate was a group of nine people. Intimidated by our numbers, the leader of the two hollered, "*What is this, some sort of love fest?*" I responded, "*Maybe so, what do you want?*" He replied, "*Nothing man,*" and with that, the men took their dog and walked away.

It's difficult attempting to fall back to sleep when your adrenaline gets pumping like that, in the middle of the night. They clearly hadn't anticipated the size of our group. My guess is that if there had only been two of three of us, then there might have been trouble. People don't tend to wake strangers in the middle of the night while wielding a baseball bat, with the intention of making new friends. The Pitbull added more muscle to their team. I was thankful for the group and God's protection.

While we've never been harmed during our 14 trips, we've certainly been in harm's way. I give God the credit for our safety and by no means believe that living on the streets is a safe endeavor. I wondered how many times Ed has faced danger while living on his own? Traveling as a loner puts you at a greater risk. I hoped to ask him one day.

We had an eventful week with the team and I was inspired by each member's commitment to love those whom we encountered on the streets. When I returned home, I kept in close contact with JD and Pita to find out how they were progressing. A month later we had a family vacation planned for Disney. Sandra's parents had a time share in Orlando, Florida, and they were generous enough to let us to use it.

As I mentioned in chapter 17, we usually invite our friends who have migrated from Africa with us on an annual vacation. However, on that particular year, we decided to invite JD and Pita to join us. Sandra and I thought it could be sort of an anniversary-honeymoon type vacation to get them out of their car for a week. When I pitched the idea to JD, he said "Yes," without hesitation. He texted me an image of his driver's license, as well as Pita's, so I could purchase their plane tickets and a room at our timeshare hotel. Sandra is extremely resourceful and applied for free Disney passes each year via our non-profit. Disney generously donated four passes for each of our trips, which we'd been able to use for our guests from Ghana, and for JD and Pita in 2019.

They arrived in Orlando late one afternoon, so I shuttled them back to our hotel to help them get checked in. JD was like a little kid going to Disney for the first time, whereas Pita was a bit more reserved. I felt as though I was getting to know JD fairly well after spending time with him in San Diego on two trips. However, we'd only met Pita at the ceremony, since she had been in treatment on our previous visit. We allowed them a day to relax and settle in and told them to get well-rested, since we had plans to take them to Disney park the following day. We met them for breakfast in the morning and Pita was a bit more at ease and willing to engage. Perhaps she'd been tired from her travels?

(Left to right: JD, Pita, Lily, Skye, Will, Capri, Hailey, Sarah & Sandra)

We had an incredible day riding rides, eating food and enjoying some laughs. JD has an extremely warm personality and managed to connect with everyone we'd brought along. My mother-in-law Lily was with us, three of our daughters: Hailey, Capri, and Skye, as well as my niece Sarah. After the long day park-hopping, we went back to the hotel and took the girls to the pool. JD joined us, while Pita rested in their room.

I asked JD if she was all right. He replied, "*She's never experienced people loving her like this, so she is very suspicious. She asked me on the flight to Florida if I thought you all planned to murder us.*" I considered what he shared with me concerning his wife. It was difficult to understand why anyone would ever think like that. I wondered what Pita had experienced in her life to assign such dark motives to our Disney invitation. I began to pray that she might feel loved and be able to enjoy herself rather than remaining distant and guarded. She did join us for dinner later that evening and spent the following day at the Magic Kingdom.

We began to notice Pita opening up more as the week progressed. She seemed to connect with Sandra and was comfortable talking about her grown children back in California. The day in the park brought smiles as the walls continued to drop. There was a visible difference in their openness as a couple, perhaps a result of Goofy and Mickey showing up.

(Left to Right: Goofy, Pita, JD & Mickey at Disney)

Pita mentioned what it had been like for her to grow up in Mexico, and she connected with my mother-in-law who is from Argentina. Perhaps being able to speak in Spanish was also helpful, since all three women were fluent, including my wife. That allowed JD and I more time to discuss his construction work and future plans.

On the following day, we spent the morning around the pool and then took our guests to Target to do some shopping. We let them know if they needed any clothes or items before returning to California the following day, that we'd be happy to purchase them. We'd been taking photos of JD and Pita all week at the parks and also brought images from their wedding renewal service. We were killing time at Target while all of the photos developed, so we could surprise them with an album before they returned.

While we were waiting, JD approached me to say that Pita needed the keys to our rental vehicle and wanted to go sit in the car. I wasn't sure if she was feeling tired or under the weather, but we still had about 10 minutes until the photos would be ready so I gave her the keys.

Once all of the photos were developed, we purchased the album and took everything to assemble back at the hotel. Pita had been waiting patiently in the car and told us that she just needed time to rest. She was tired and needed a break, although JD shared a different version of the story back at the hotel.

JD and I took a brief walk at the hotel when he announced, "*I'm so mad at Pita!*" "*Why's that?*" I asked. He continued, "*Because she was shoplifting when we were at the store, and that's the reason she wanted to go to the car so abruptly.*" I stood there a minute trying to understand what he'd just told me. "*Why would she shoplift when we offered to purchase anything that you two needed?*" He responded, "*She doesn't know you guys like I do. She believes that if you get us something, then we'll owe you something in return.*" His comments concerning Pita's way of thinking were consistent with her previous comment in transit, fearful that we might kill them. They also reminded me of my friend in San Diego, Richard Jaeckel. I wondered how many people must have taken advantage of Pita in order to make her so distrusting. It made me sad after we'd spent the week together, that some level of trust hadn't yet been established.

I left the matter for JD to sort out with his wife, since we merely wanted to bless them as a couple in hopes of getting them off on the right track. JD also mentioned that Pita wanted to return to her drug use. He commented, *"If she does that again, I'm afraid that I'll need to leave her. We can't survive another bout with drugs."* Bringing two homeless friends from the streets of San Diego to Disney certainly had a few unexpected turns. It wasn't really what we'd been accustomed to with our friends from Ghana; we were hoping it would be a blessing to them as they made a new start.

They were due to fly back to California the following morning, so we focused on enjoying one final dinner with them. After dinner we presented them with the photo album and a card, to remember the service when they renewed their marriage vows and pictures we'd taken during the week in Florida. Pita seemed surprised and extremely appreciative of the keepsake album. She sat on the sofa in our hotel room, slowly paging through the book and admiring the images and the moments they represented.

Pita actually teared up as she offered us repeated thanks. JD was grateful as well and told us what an unforgettable week it had been for the both of them. The couple retired to their room shortly after, to get packed up for their trip early the following morning. They had an extremely early flight so I scheduled them an Uber ride to the airport. I met them in the lobby to say farewell. The rest of the family said their goodbyes the previous evening after dinner, since the departure was so early. We had some time together while we waited for their ride to arrive, so I decided to speak openly with both of them. I said, *"Pita and JD, we want to help you both in whatever ways we can. However, that entails being open and honest with one another."* JD had given me the liberty to offer Pita help with her drug habit, so I decided to bring up the subject before they departed. Pita looked seriously annoyed at her husband for sharing her baggage without her knowing. She responded by saying, *"Sure, I'd like some help, but I also have a question. Did JD tell you about his drug habit as well, or was he only willing to share about mine? It's true that I battle addiction, although JD is equally guilty when it comes to using drugs!"*

I sat across the table from the couple in the hotel lobby, stunned by Pita's big reveal. While JD had shared openly about his wife's addiction since Steve and I first met him back at Saint Vinnie's, he'd never once admitted to sharing her struggle. I felt somehow betrayed. I felt the sting which made the moment before their departure tangibly awkward. After a pregnant pause, I responded, *"Of course, JD's drug problem. There's that too, right JD?"* He glanced my direction, but looked like a kid who'd just been nabbed with his hand buried deep in the cookie jar. His eye contact was only momentary, but it said enough.

As a parent of six kids, it brought back moments when I've caught my own children doing something, they knew they weren't supposed to do. The shame on his face was obvious, although I had no desire to shame my friend. I asked, *"Would you mind if I pray for the two of you before your car arrives?"* The offer seemed to somewhat break the tension, so I extended my hands and the three of us held hands as we sat around that table. I pleaded with God to help my friends kick their drug addiction. With the same desire that I have for my friend Ed to find freedom from the deadly snare of methamphetamine, I begged God to shatter their chains. The driver showed up a moment after we said *"amen."* I helped them with their bags and gave both a warm hug before they climbed into the backseat.

As I walked back into the hotel, I was saddened by our closing interaction and was still thinking about the revelation. Pita's candor about her husband caused me to rethink everything he'd shared with me. Were there more things that he'd neglected to share? The moment Steve and I met JD he had no idea we were listening to him while he did his best to encourage the angry man in line. I felt strongly that JD was sincerely the man whom he'd presented himself to be; he'd simply neglected to share vulnerability about his own demons and struggles. Perhaps he thought that if we knew the truth then we might not help him. I suppose to some extent, we all try to put on our best side. JD sent me a text from the airport apologizing for not telling me sooner. I responded, "*No worries my friend, but I can't help you if you're not willing to be honest. I love you brother.*" He responded, "*I love you too Will, thanks for everything!*"

We kept in touch after JD returned to San Diego. He'd call from time to time, and told me that he was doing better with his struggle. One evening he called me and seemed frantic. He said, "*Will, I need your help! I've lost my keys and I need to be somewhere and I've no idea what to do.*" I replied, "*JD, I can't help you if I'm not on the West Coast; why don't you try calling Les.*" I had introduced the two of them at the ceremony on New Year's Eve, so they were acquainted. It seemed like a good idea, so I made sure he had the correct number and left the two of them to sort it out.

The following day Les called me to say, "*I'm finished helping JD!*" Shocked by his statement, I inquired about what transpired on the previous evening. Les continued, "*When I arrived at the address that JD had given me, he was a mess! JD was high on meth and had torn his entire dashboard apart attempting to hotwire his car, after losing his keys. He was angry and impatient, although I had driven 30 minutes to help him. I questioned his actions and he admitted being high. I called an emergency mechanic and even paid for a locksmith to sort out his key issue. While we waited for the technician to arrive, JD turned angry and threatened me. I did what I could do to help him, but I wanted you to know that I'm done.*" I completely understood Les' decision and the need to set some healthy boundaries with JD going forward.

Why is it that we humans seem to possess a divide in our personalities, waxing between good and evil, selfless and selfish desires? Similar to Robert Louis Stevenson's book, "The Strange Case of Dr. Jekyll and Mr. Hyde," an individual can be incredibly kind when sober and yet when under the influence of a substance, they can become a monster. I called JD the following day to let him know that Les and I had spoken, and to see how he was doing. He acted as though nothing had happened. I'm not sure whether JD blacked out and forgot a portion of the previous evening or if he was pretending that everything was fine. I encouraged him to find a narcotics anonymous group to join. He thanked me for calling, but clearly didn't want to talk about substance abuse. JD was polite, but after that call, he remained fairly distant for a time.

Three months later around 3:00 a.m. on June 22, 2019, I received a phone call. When you receive a call at that hour, you can almost always assume that someone's in trouble. I answered in groggy tone, "*Hello?*" I tried to comprehend who was on the other end of the call and what was wrong. It was a woman's voice and she seemed desperate. I asked, "*Who is this?*" She said, "*Will, this is Pita. I'm sorry to call you at midnight,*" (she didn't realize that meant 3:00 a.m. East Coast time). She continued, "*JD's in trouble!*" I replied, "*What kind of trouble?*" She replied, "*The cops picked him up for murder. I don't think he did it but he's in jail now.*"

"*What do you want me to do?*" I inquired. She said, "*I don't know, I just thought perhaps you'd know a lawyer or could at least have your church pray.*" I responded, "*We will pray but I don't know any lawyers in San Diego. Do what you can to find out more information, and call me back tomorrow.*" Pita agreed to do so. I prayed with her before she hung up.

Sandra awoke when she heard me talking. She asked, "*Who was that on the phone?*" I quickly filled her in on the details and then said, "*Let's chat about it in the morning.*" She responded, "*Oh no, that's awful! All right, we can talk tomorrow.*" We both turned to go back to sleep, but my mind was racing, which made sleep difficult.

I pondered the idea of helping my homeless friends. I wondered, "*Is it possible to truly help anyone on the streets?*" I considered Ed, Kyle, JD, Richard, Candace, Paul and so many others. What are the factors that allow you to actually help someone in need? My mind returned to the passage in Luke chapter 15. Clearly an addict has to "come to their senses," before they can get help or return home.

I became convinced that I was unable to help JD, Ed, or any of the others if they lacked two attributes. For me, "coming to our senses," requires a willingness to recognize our need for help and to seek it out; and secondly, to be completely honest and open about their issues. Regardless of how badly we may want to rescue another individual, we can't help someone who doesn't want help and who is unwilling to be 100% open about their struggle. I fell asleep that night asking God to bring both JD and Ed to their senses. I was asking God for a miracle, as only He can do.

Chapter 21
Round Three in Maui

Two weeks before departing for round three in Maui, Sandra and I were enjoying dinner on our back patio with a few close friends. One by the name of Dustin Holliday asked me for an update concerning Ed. I shared with Dustin and his wife Lisa the latest details, including our pending trip. Dustin called me a day or so later with a proposition. He said, *"I'm not trying to force my way onto your family vacation, but Lisa and I have been trying to figure out where to spend our time off from work this summer. We heard you share about your trip to Hawaii the other night, and figured that you may want some company when you go searching for Ed. If you two are all right with it, we'll make plans and book a different hotel in Maui so that you're not in this alone."* I replied, *"That's a thoughtful offer, let me chat with Sandra and get back to you."* She liked the idea as well, so I responded to Dustin and he booked their trip.

Truth be told, Dustin had planned to join me on my very first trip to San Diego back in 2015. Due to a family emergency he was unable to make the trip, which is the reason I went solo on my very first manhunt for Ed. Only God knew Dustin would be unable to join me on the front end of this mission, yet join me years later on trip 13.

On August 12, 2019, we flew our family to Maui. Our crew on that particular trip, consisted of Sandra and her mother Lily, as well as three of our daughters: Hailey, Capri and Skye. Lily came to assist with Capri and Skye who were ages 5 and 3 at the time. Hailey was excited to join the Ed venture, since her older sister Courtney had lived homeless with me on trip five to San Diego. We booked a place back in Wailea again, 22 miles from Paia. I wanted to give Ed his space and figured that we could bike to the other side of the island, as I'd done the previous year with Eric.

We went to Paia to rent bikes from Donnie back at Maui Cyclery. I was thrilled to catch up with him in person. He told me that he'd seen Ed in town earlier that day. He got us outfitted with two bikes, since my daughter Hailey said that she wanted to join me cycling on some of the days. Hailey turned 18 during our week in Maui, so we wanted to make the trip memorable.

Dustin and Lisa had arrived a day ahead of us and took some time to explore the island. I spent our first two days riding with my daughter Hailey and searching for Ed. On our second day in Maui, Sandra, Hailey and I drove over to Paia, while Lily stayed back at the hotel pool with Capri and Skye. Sandra was looking forward to seeing Ed, since he'd promised to join our family for dinner when we returned.

I encouraged Sandra not to get her hopes up, stating, "*I think Ed just said that to keep us from pestering him.*" She replied, "*He told me that he'd join our family for dinner, and I believe that he will.*" I desperately wanted Sandra to be right, but didn't want to experience more disappointment.

We stopped by Donnie's bike shop to say "*hello*" before heading next door for coffee. Just as I began chatting with Donnie, he said, "*There's Ed,*" as he motioned directly behind me. Ed had biked up to the back lot behind Donnie's shop and was filling his tires with air. I headed outside to engage him. Realizing that Ed could take off at a moment's notice, I approached him cautiously and said, "*Hey Ed, how've you been doing?*" He responded, "*I have no complaints, but as I told you last year, I can't hang out with people from my past.*" While I hoped he had changed his mind, I was emotionally prepared for his response on my third year visiting him. I replied, "*I understand and have no plans to bother you. Can I get a hug?*" He responded, "*Of course,*" and I gave my old friend a big hug. I'd been hoping that Sandra was right, but Ed seemed to have the same mindset as the previous two years we'd visited him. I told him that I looked forward to seeing him over the course of the week, if he had a change of heart.

When I walked back to Maui Cyclery, Sandra headed straight out to the parking lot to greet Ed. I stood inside with Donnie, watching through the window. If body language was any indication, it looked as though Ed was giving Sandra an excuse for being unable to have dinner with our family, despite his promise. They exchanged words for a few minutes and then my daughter Hailey said, "*Can I meet Ed.*" I figured that it may be wise for us to head out to the parking lot, since Sandra's face looked discouraged by their exchange. I replied, "*Sure, let's go!*" Hailey followed me out and I introduced her to Ed.

Ed was very sweet to her and took a minute to greet her. After the introduction Ed announced that he'd better get going. I offered him a coffee next door but he declined. We watched as he mounted his bike and peddled swiftly out of the parking lot. I could tell that Sandra was saddened by Ed's response, so I suggested that we all head over to the coffee shop to decompress.

(Left to right: Sandra & Ed outside of Maui Cyclery)

We placed our order at the Paia Bay Coffee Bar and took a seat while we waited for our order. Sandra confessed her disappointment and I echoed her sentiment. Hailey asked if this had been the same reaction that we'd received in previous years. We answered her questions and talked about the days of old when Ed and I used to be best friends. Hailey asked me to share a story from our early years, so I obliged. The first story that came to mind involved our years hunting snakes. Ed and I shared an unpopular love for snakes. We spent countless Saturdays scouring creek beds, flipping rocks and walking through fields in search of reptiles.

We also enjoyed going downtown to the Washington National Zoo. The park was free and we had no problem killing a day observing animals throughout the vast landscape in our Nation's Capital. On one particular day we were in the reptile house and decided to knock on a door marked, "*No Trespassing, Authorized Personnel Only.*" When the man behind the door found the two of us waiting as the door swung open, he inquired, "*What can I do for you?*" I replied, "*Would it be possible to get a tour behind the scenes? My friend and I are aspiring herpetologists.*" A "*herpetologist*" is a scientist who studies reptiles and amphibians. The zoological employee's eyes lit up, as though he wasn't used to receiving requests like that. He responded in the affirmative and said, "*Sure, come on in!*" We were thrilled about the opportunity and followed the scientist back into the lab.

The herpetologist showed us his trade with pride. He milked a Diamondback Rattle Snake before our eyes. "Milking" a venomous snake entails holding the dangerous serpent behind the neck and forcing its mouth open to reveal its fangs. The expert then hooks the snake's fangs over the edge of a glass cup and moves the snake until droplets of poison are excreted from his front teeth. The venom is used to make an antivenom, which can be used to bring healing to a future victim of a snakebite inflicted by that species.

Ed and I were thoroughly impressed and asked our guide if he had ever been bitten. He replied, "*Not by this actual snake, but by others, yes.*" He added, "*When one of us has to work daily with a particular venomous breed, we take the antivenom as a precaution, since the odds of a bite are highly probable.*" Ed asked, "*What about non-venomous snakes?*"

Without hesitation the expert responded, *"Of course, we get bit almost every day."* I asked, *"What do you do when you're bit?"* As though it really wasn't a big deal he replied, *"You simply shake it off!"* Long before Taylor Swift released her 2014 hit single *"Shake it Off,"* our herpetologist friend recommended the technique.

When Ed and I returned home that evening, we'd been inspired by the expert who was kind enough to grant us a tour. It just so happened that I'd captured an Eastern Black Racer on a recent fishing trip. I had been cautious about handling that breed of snake based on what I read in the North American Field Guide of Reptiles and Amphibians.

The description of the Black Racer said, *"This species does not like to be handled and bites readily."* While the guide warned against handling this species, Ed and I thought the description made our snake the perfect sample to attempt the "shake it off" technique. Usually when we caught a snake in the wild, we would handle it with gloves. Once a snake realized that biting our gloves didn't deter its captor, it would cease from using its bite as a defense mechanism. After reading the description of the Eastern Black Racer, we were fairly sure that the glove taming strategy was not going to work on that snake. However, we'd never considered the "shake it off" approach.

As we stood above the aquarium that held the long sleek reptile, we peered through the screen lid. I said, *"Why don't you go first and give it a try?"* Ed responded by popping the lid off the cage and plunging his arm into the tank. The snake was approximately two feet in length and Ed grabbed it at the center to remove it. As he lifted the racer out, it turned its head toward Ed's hand and gave him a bite. He hollered, *"Ouch!"* I asked him if he was all right, as I noticed two small marks on his skin where the snake's teeth made contact. He replied, *"I suppose."* To which I encouraged him with the advice of the zoological expert, *"Just shake it off."* As I mentioned, most snakes cease from biting when they realize that their captor is not bothered. However, this was not the case with our Black Racer. Realizing that Ed was unwilling to put him down, the snake turned toward Ed's hand and struck again.

When the Racer bit Ed for a second time, it latched its mouth on Ed's right hand, between his thumb and index finger. Ed began to shout in pain, so I told him once again to "shake it off." He raised his voice and exclaimed, "*I can't, it's teeth are digging into my skin. Get it off me!*" I began laughing out loud at the situation as I did my best to lift the front of the snake's mouth off of Ed's hand to loosen its grip. I finally managed to remove the snake and tossed it back into the aquarium. Ed looked at me and said defiantly, "*Your turn!*"

After witnessing the entire ordeal and seeing the blood on Ed's hand, I said, "*No thanks, I don't want to be a herpetologist any more. Those guys are nuts!*" Needless to say, my friend was not pleased that I was unwilling to attempt the new technique as he had done. Can you blame me after watching how the snake responded? I talked Ed into letting the snake go free and that was the end of the matter.

With our history of climbing cranes, crossing rivers, catching snakes and numerous other antics, I wondered if the Ed I'd grown up was somewhere under the surface, waiting to come out. Had the impact of the drugs made his mind so paranoid that he was unable to trust a childhood friend? It was difficult for me to make sense of it and I missed the Ed who I'd grown up with.

Sandra, Hailey and I sat in the café sipping our hot drinks and laughing about the old stories. A little while later, Sandra headed back to the hotel to check on Lily and the girls. Hailey and I began the 22-mile trek back across the island. I told her that the ride wasn't very difficult, but she hardly agreed with me, especially on the portions of the ride that contain a few steep hills. We powered through it, which actually gave me an outlet for my frustrations in having Ed reject a third year of repeated attempts to connect. I wondered what held him back.

(Left to right: Will & Hailey in Maui)

The following day, Hailey decided to stay back at the hotel and enjoy some rest and relaxation. Dustin rented a bike from Donnie's shop and met me at our hotel in Wailea. I gave him an update concerning our encounter with Ed the previous day. Dustin had been a police officer in Fairfax County, Virginia some years earlier, so he had a way of looking at situations differently. I appreciated his insight and willingness to join me on the ride. Dustin had been through his share of bumps in life and yet he managed to maintain a positive outlook. We swapped stories over the course of the 90-minute ride, which helped take our focus off the difficult segments. When we arrived in Paia, we took a break and grabbed some lunch at the same restaurant where Eric and I sat one year earlier. I wondered if we might run into Owen Wilson as Eric had done.

After lunch, Dustin and I walked through Donnie's shop to say hello to the guys who were working. We decided to ride straight up Baldwin

Avenue, the same road where I'd chased after Ed when I first discovered his whereabouts two years earlier. As I pumped the peddles and continued my ascent, I began to second guess myself. I wondered if my efforts only served to frustrate my old friend. While he told us that he didn't want to reconnect on a deeper level, I felt strongly that most of his decisions were influenced by his drug use. I thought back to the Ed pleading with me for help in 2013, as he expressed his desire to make a change in life. Could that much have changed in six years? Certainly, the Ed who wanted to make a change was still buried in there somewhere. I just hoped it wasn't too late for him to shake the paranoia and get free from the drugs.

Dustin and I worked those bikes for about an hour, making the six-mile climb to a town called Makawao. We took a brief break to have a drink and discuss the trip. As we sat on the front porch of the Casanova Italian Restaurant and Deli, Dustin offered a question for me to consider. He asked, "*What's the definition of insanity?*" I wasn't sure where he was headed with his question, so I played along and responded, "*Keep doing the same thing and expect different results.*" He definitely had a point he wanted to make and continued, "*So this is your third summer coming out to connect with Ed and his response each year seems to follow the same annual pattern, right?*" I agreed and asked, "*What's your point?*" He carried on, "*What would it look like if you changed up the pattern? What if you and Sandra came for a longer trip next year and instead of pursuing him, you stayed in Paia and bumped into him on a daily basis, simply saying 'hello' and going about your business. I wonder if his paranoia would begin to subside and he might let his guard down if he realized that you aren't out to get him.*" His questions got my mental gears turning. He certainly had a point.

(Left to right: Will & Dustin on Baldwin Avenue)

After spending some time kicking around ideas and brainstorming strategy, we decided to begin our descent. While climbing the six-mile hill took about an hour, heading straight down took no time at all. The only effort required from us was steering and knowing when to apply the brakes. We enjoyed the view, the wind in our faces and the simple job of coasting.

We decided to pay more attention to the woods on the way down Baldwin Avenue, hoping to spot Ed's actual campsite. We reasoned that Ed must be camping in the woods somewhere directly uphill from Paia, so we took the time to search on the way back down. I couldn't imagine Ed making that strenuous climb on a daily basis. We passed a park, two churches and a school, as well as some scattered homes. When we got a bit closer to the area where we believed Ed might be living, we slowed the bikes down to make a thorough search. I spotted a dilapidated cinderblock wall that looked as though it was the ruins of an old home. We set our bikes on the edge of Baldwin Avenue and briefly explored the site.

There stood a single wall in the woods about 25 yards from the road. On the backside of the wall, facing a large pineapple field, there was a tent and clothes line. Dustin noticed a few of Ed's shirts hanging up and it was clear that this was indeed his campsite and home. We were whispering quietly and kept our distance. We decided not to go any further. Neither of us wanted to disturb Ed or cause him any undue stress. I was afraid that if he felt threatened by the fact that we'd discovered where he lives, he might pack up and go on the run again. We wanted to respect his space so we remounted our bikes and headed down the remainder of the hill leading back into Paia.

It was near the close of the week, so we returned the rental bikes, said goodbye to Donnie and called Sandra to pick us up. Dustin and his wife Lisa were scheduled to fly home the following day, so we had dinner with them before they departed. We were grateful for their willingness to join us on the journey. The four of us spent the evening discussing more ideas concerning an extended return in 2020.

(Left to right: Lisa & Dustin Holliday in Maui)

I realized that September 2020 marked my 30-year anniversary, since I'd begun serving in ministry and non-profit work. I'd never taken an extended break in the 30 years since I began, so we considered a sabbatical in Maui. It seemed like perfect timing for us to be able to return to Maui as Dustin had suggested. We were inspired by our time with Dustin and Lisa and filled with new hope of rebuilding trust with Ed.

The following evening, we took Hailey out to celebrate her 18th birthday at Mama's Fish House. It was a beautiful evening and an incredible meal. That was the perfect way to end the trip and dream about what was to come.

(Left to right: Skye, Hailey, Lily, Capri, Sandra & Will)

I have tried to remain hopeful over the course of this journey. Dustin had sparked an idea by reminding me about the definition of insanity. I certainly had no desire to continue repeating the same trip each year, with the exact same results. I believe in a God who is alive and has the power to change lives, no matter how far gone they may appear. I'm living proof that He also offers grace to messed-up people like me. Boarding our flight east the following day, my spirit was renewed and hope had been restored. While Ed had reneged on his promise to join our family for dinner; there was always next year.

Chapter 22
Living in a '98 Ford Ranger

It all began when Ed expressed his desire to join us on one of our mission trips to a foreign country, to serve those in need. He told me that he wanted to make an impact on the less fortunate. I told him to get his passport updated and nine months later, Ed was living on the streets. While he never joined us on a trip, Sandra and I have continued leading excursions to serve those in need since we met back in 2006. In May of 2018, we led a trip with university students who served alongside a church in Siena, Italy, while we recruited a second team to care for the homeless in Genova, Italy. We have an Italian partner by the name of Daniele Marzano, who does incredible work with those living on the streets in Genova.

(Left to right: Evan, Bethany, Jesse, Will, Ben & Randy in Siena)

The team I was leading in Siena had been invited into a local high school to help teach English classes to Italian students. Each participant from our university team took turns sharing a bit of their background with the classroom, speaking slowly in English. The Italian students could ask them questions about their lives, as they practiced their English vocabulary and pronunciation. A few of our students from the U.S.A. shared about their faith in God, as well as other facets of their lives. We spent an entire day in the classroom doing the same presentation for different classes, as they rotated on the hour. It was a wonderful opportunity to teach language and culture and the education was mutual.

Two days after the language class, I asked Maria, (the English teacher of the Italian school), how she felt the lesson went. She replied, "*The students loved it, however, a teacher from our school heard that a few students shared openly about their faith in God, and she was angry about that.*" I responded, "*What's her name and what subject does she teach?*" Maria answered, "*Her name is Grazia and she teaches Spanish. Why do you want to know that?*" I said, "*I just wonder if we can bless her in some way. Please let Grazia know that my wife Sandra is a native Spanish speaker and would be happy to come teach a lesson in her classroom, if that would be helpful.*" Maria agreed to pass the message along, unsure what Grazia would think of the offer. Apparently, she appreciated it, since Maria called me back to schedule Sandra for a day of Spanish lessons later that week.

Sandra ended up teaching Spanish all day long in Grazia's classroom. Not only did it go well, but Sandra told me that Grazia was interested in having our non-profit arrange a trip for the Italian students to study Spanish in Uruguay. Sandra told Grazia that her late grandparents owned property in Colonia-Valdense, Uruguay, and that it would be the perfect place to hold a language camp. I was excited that things had gone so well. However, I wondered how many students would actually be interested in a language camp in Uruguay. In November of 2019, 43 students and three adult leaders traveled from Italy to Uruguay to spend 11 days with us. Among the many things we needed to accommodate such a large group was lots of help in the kitchen.

Shortly before welcoming the 46 Italians to Uruguay, we realized that we were still short-staffed. When attempting to recruit potential volunteers, I was striking out. In addition to the pending Italian group planning to join us, we had planned to host a group of adult leaders on the week after the Italians departed. Essentially, we were looking for a couple more volunteers who on very short notice would be willing to wash dishes for three weeks. My friend Paul Arnold, from the streets of San Diego came to mind. I called him to see if he was interested in joining our service team. Without hesitation, Paul said, "*I'd love to help out where needed!*" We purchased Paul's ticket and were thrilled that he would be joining us in Uruguay. I only wished I could make a similar phone call to Ed in Maui to have him join us as well.

(Paul serving Italians in Uruguay – backrow center with beard)

Paul was a tremendous help cooking and cleaning up for our Italian guests, as well as for the leaders from Latin America whom we served on the following week. During our time organizing the Spanish immersion camp for the Italians, we decided to organize a brief program for the students each evening after dinner. The entertainment included some participation games, followed by a brief message containing a character lesson. I decided to teach the lessons using real life examples from the streets of San Diego. The stories seemed like a good idea to keep their attention and connect each story to a character value. For example, when I shared about my decision to go searching for my friend Ed, I asked the Italian students, "*Do you have any friends who would go looking for you, or any friends who you would go looking for?*" My intention was to utilize the stories so they might consider peer pressure, life choices and values that truly matter.

On one particular evening late in the week, I made the comment, "*While my friend Ed hasn't chosen to receive our help, we have been able to impact others along the journey.*" With Paul's permission I shared, "*As a matter of fact, one man who had been living in his truck and confessed battling thoughts of depression and suicide, flew with us to Puerto Rico to serve hurricane victims. He said that serving others had helped to lift his spirits, and served as an anti-depressant. That is part of the reason we invited him to serve you this week. I'm not sure if any of you knew that our friend Paul who has been cooking and cleaning for you all week has been living on the streets for seven years?*" At that point, I motioned to Paul who was seated along a wall near the kitchen. Every Italian student looked in his direction in shock that the worker they had been chatting with all week was in fact homeless.

I didn't realize until I motioned toward Paul that he had begun to cry as I shared his story. When the students looked at Paul's face, many were moved with emotion. I concluded by saying, "*Perhaps some of you students have battled depression. Have you ever considered the idea of serving others as an exercise that could help bring you out of a slump?*" I let them know that if any of them wanted to speak further with Paul, he would be available for the remainder of their trip.

When I wrapped up the message time, there was a tangible feeling in the room, that everyone had been inspired by Paul's life and situation. Perhaps you've been in a space when a crowd is moved with emotion and there's a moment of awkwardness when people are unsure how to respond. In the midst of that brief period of tension, one 17-year-old teenager walked straight up to Paul and embraced him. I could see that her decision was cathartic for both of them, although I was unsure of her backstory. While that show of compassion came unexpectedly, what followed was an even bigger surprise. Inspired by her example, about 15 students gathered and formed an impromptu receiving line behind her. Each student waited their turn to hug Paul and offer a few words of encouragement. The emotion in the room was palpable.

Paul and I spent many late nights during those three weeks discussing his life. On one particular evening, Paul mentioned his looming battle with depression and the reality that what he'd shared with me on my 8th trip was still an issue. He told me that the trip to Puerto Rico had served to encourage him and let me know that he was enjoying his time in Uruguay. He confessed that he'd become discouraged in San Diego, feeling that many of the people he'd helped seemed to return to their addictions and struggles. He began to wonder if he was making any difference at all. I invited Paul to join our family back in Virginia for the week of Thanksgiving following our time in Uruguay. Paul said *"I'd enjoy that very much,"* so we made the appropriate flight arrangements so he could share the holiday with our family in Virginia.

During the weekend after Thanksgiving, Paul visited our church. I had a God-inspired idea on my heart, and decided to run it by a few friends. Realizing that Paul had shown signs of improvement during our time in Uruguay, I wondered how we might continue that trend. I thought, *"What if we could give Paul a year off the streets by asking 12 families to host him in their homes during the coming year?"* I was unsure how people would feel about the proposition, so I bounced the idea off of a few families. When I had eight homes lined up, starting with my own, I figured that the other four would fall into place later.

During that Sunday while Paul was visiting from California, I decided to make the offer right there in church. Paul was seated in the front row that evening so I looked straight at him and said, *"Paul, you mentioned that life had become difficult in San Diego, and your desire for a break. Our church would like to offer you a year off of the streets for free, with a different home to live in every month in 2020. What do you think?"* Before I finished making the offer and announcing the complete details, Paul's eyes welled up with tears. When I finished describing the offer, he was full-on weeping, as were a few friends in church that evening whose hearts were moved by the occasion.

Although Paul accepted our offer, he still had a scheduled fight back to California the following day. He wanted to return to San Diego to say goodbye to many of his friends there, gather his belongings and to begin the slow trek across country in his 1998 Ford Ranger. And so, he did.

Paul provided us with regular updates as he prepared to depart East. When he began the 2,667-mile road trip, he would drive as far as he was comfortable on a given day, and then provide us with 24-hour check-ins. We kept up with his itinerary as he rolled east toward Virginia. Paul managed to follow a safer southern route, since he was traveling in mid-December. His plan was to begin at our home and stay until early January, which meant we were able to host Paul for Christmas. Capri and Skye thought he had the perfect long white beard to play Santa Claus. In all seriousness, we were glad he had accepted our offer and yet unsure of all that it would entail.

(Paul encountered the frosty air halfway across country)

We were somewhat concerned about Paul's 1998 Ford Ranger surviving the journey. He assured me he would get the oil changed before the trek and seemed fairly confident of his truck's reliability. Imagine living in your car for seven years so that your vehicle is no longer just an automobile, but more of a home to you. It would no doubt change your perspective of the vehicle, which I tried to keep in mind when making suggestions about Paul's truck.

We were thrilled when he finally arrived and our girls were excited that "Uncle Paul" would be joining us for Christmas. He seemed fairly excited to be in a room and mentioned appreciating the comfortable bed during his three weeks in Uruguay. Readjusting to sleeping in his truck after that bed made it all the more difficult for him to return to life in his truck during his brief stint in San Diego. I suppose living for years in a warm climate like Southern California added to the shock of sleeping in a truck coated with winter frost. All the more reason to welcome a warm bedroom indoors.

Our two youngest daughters, Capri and Skye, enjoyed having Paul as an additional member of our household. Our church welcomed Paul as part of the family as well. They'd been so supportive of our trips to San Diego and Maui, to the extent that many of the attendees had joined me on different ventures there. I put out the word that I still needed a few more volunteer families to host Paul for the months that were open. Within two weeks-time, we were able to get every month in 2020 accounted for. It takes an unbelievable bunch of people to open their homes to a man who just moved off the streets. It's one thing to have someone stay for a night or two. It's quite another to invite a stranger to join your family for an entire month.

I wanted to do something special for Paul to make him feel welcome. Realizing how important his truck was to him, as it had been his home for seven years, I plotted a truck makeover. I suggested to Paul that we take it in to my mechanic for an oil change. In reality, I'd asked a friend who is a mechanic to give Paul's truck a thorough inspection and to repair whatever was needed. We rallied people from the church who expressed a desire to contribute toward the effort. We had a generous group of friends get behind the endeavor, so we decided to have the truck painted and the dents repaired. There had been a broken taillight and some significant dents that required attention.

The difficult part was making excuses to Paul for the reason a simple oil change was taking so long. I told him that the mechanic was doing a required state inspection and repairing a few small things as necessary. After completing the work in a two-week time span, a family brought Paul to lunch and then swung by the church where we'd orchestrated a surprise party. We invited everyone who'd contributed to the truck makeover to celebrate with Paul. When he walked through the doors, we all shouted *"Happy Truck Day, Paul!"*

(Paul's Truck makeover celebration cake)

As everyone greeted him in the church foyer, I texted a friend who'd been waiting to drive Paul's truck around front. He rolled up right on cue, so Paul could see his new- looking 1998 red Ford Ranger. We definitely caught him off guard. We also had the interior cleaned and detailed. His face revealed the pleasant shock. The crowd of friends present to surprise Paul helped him feel loved and appreciated. Someone picked up a cake and drinks to make the party all the merrier. I ordered a red toy truck as a cake decoration and also for Paul to keep to remember the occasion. Our hope was that he would feel loved and accepted by the community of new friends in his life. The power of acceptance is extremely significant for someone who is battling self-doubt and depression.

(Paul celebrating his freshly made-over 1998 Ford Ranger)

Paul enjoyed being part of the community, although life was about to take a series of unexpected turns that would shift our focus. Everything changed in a matter of months! We got through the truck makeover party in February of 2020. Who knew that the entire planet was about to face a global pandemic? When the Coronavirus swept the country and the world, I began to wonder if things would ever return to normal. Our plans to return to Maui for five weeks in 2020 were cancelled, due to a state-wide mandate from the Governor of Hawaii. All of our usual summer trips had to be cancelled or postponed, and I began to feel discouraged. Then I came down with COVID-19!

On May 13, 2020, I concluded my final chapter of a book I'd been writing called, *"Along the Way."* I decided to lay down and rest a few minutes at the end of the day, feeling unusually exhausted. Sandra took my temperature and realized that I had a fever. We were planning to celebrate her birthday the following day, but no one would dare come to our home at the mention of a fever. Instead, I went to my doctor's office to get tested for the Coronavirus. One day later, my doctor called to say that I'd tested positive. The following day, Sandra and the kids became ill with the virus as well. So much for five weeks in Maui, even if the travel ban had been lifted.

Approximately two weeks later, we were resting at a home on Smith Mountain Lake in southwest Virginia, when I received a text from Donnie. The date was June 3rd, when Donnie said, *"There's been a bike accident involving a homeless person, but I don't yet have all the details. The homeless person was taken via helicopter to the hospital and I'm trying to verify if it was Ed."* Needless to say, Sandra and I began praying for Ed's safety, although I refrained from calling his family. I didn't want to worry them in the event that Ed wasn't the cyclist in the accident, or if the news took a morbid twist.

The following day, Donnie called me to confirm that the cyclist in the accident was indeed Ed. He'd been taken via helicopter to Queen's Medical Center in Honolulu, Hawaii. Donnie confirmed that he was alive and being treated, although he was unable to visit Ed since he'd been relocated to the island of Oahu. I wondered what this meant for Ed and how serious his accident had been. Would the hospital be able to dry him out long enough to help him think straight? I thought, *"If Ed walks out of the hospital now, he'll be lost on an entirely different island where he doesn't know anyone."* I worried about Ed's situation, which was clearly out of my control. I prayed and asked God to use this serious turn of events to move in Ed's life. I wondered if I was going to need to schedule a homeless trip to the island of Oahu in the near future.

While that was going on in Oahu, Paul was left navigating home changes each single month, despite the pandemic. He seemed very positive about living with different families and mentioned the need to make certain adjustments each month based on the particular family he was living with. Every family carries its own subculture and way of doing life. Some families had small children, like my own, whereas, others had older kids and a few were empty nesters. There were families who eat dinner together and some that don't. There were families with set lists of chores and others that pay for a cleaning service. A few homes had pets while others did not. Certain families were late-nighters, while others were early-risers. Imagine Paul making adjustments every single month. He never complained; on the contrary, he seemed grateful for the opportunity.

Paul began to serve with a ministry from our church known as *"Bridge Feeds."* Volunteers make regular pickups at local restaurants which generously donate surplus food. We sort the food each Monday morning and then distribute it to families in need, in the late afternoon. Paul became a vital part of that weekly endeavor, making regular restaurant pickups, as well as sorting and distributing the food to families in need.

(Left to right: Gaby Ramirez & Paul cleaning at Bridge Feeds)

When I asked Paul about his other expectations for the year, such as work for pay, he didn't show interest beyond volunteering. He receives a modest Social Security check each month, which he has often used to bless others. When the U.S. Government sent stimulus checks to help alleviate financial stress related to the COVID-19 virus, Paul repurposed his check to support a college student, raising funds to serve overseas. What I've come to learn about my friend Paul is that he's not lazy, nor is he greedy. On the contrary, he's generous with what little he receives and helps out whenever he sees a specific need. He simply wanted a break from the streets and a place to belong.

When I asked Paul about his future plans, he responded nonchalantly, "*I've no idea, but I'm sure God will make it clear when I need to know.*" I appreciated Paul's candid answer about his own expectations. I wondered what expectations I might have of Ed if he were to return home. I'd want Ed to be drug-free and to get healthy, although I'd still love my friend if he was unable to do those things. I prayed for a breakthrough, knowing Ed was receiving treatment in a hospital back in Oahu. What would happen next? Only God knew.

Chapter 23
Prison & Trip 14

In January of 2020, we returned to San Diego with a team of ten participants. There was at least one unique nuance that we had never undertaken on a previous trip. I'm referring to our prison visit to meet with JD Terrell. He was incarcerated among thousands of other men at a border prison south of San Diego. I decided to pay him a visit and to take a couple of people with me.

(Will, Peter, Steve, Emile, Bill, Brian, Kara, Betsy, Hawley & Maria)

JD was detained in the George Bailey Detention Center, situated on the border of California and Mexico. Steve and Kara had both met JD on previous trips, so they were the obvious choice to come with me to the facility. We hopped in an Uber car that Thursday, to make our scheduled meeting time. I'd called ahead to make the visitation appointment at which time they informed me what we could bring, as well as what had to be left behind. We were not allowed to take any photos in the jail area once we were past the prison guards in the reception area.

We walked down a long corridor with colored paint strips on the floor. The attending guard instructed us to follow one designated color line all the way to the specific visitation area, where we would meet JD. We walked thousands of feet of hallway, following the orange line as we'd been told. We finally arrived at a door marked "*Prisoner Visitation.*"

There were a number of warnings and procedural reminders posted on the door to read before we entered. Inside, there was a large room which contained a center area, constructed with thick bulletproof glass. Along the clear glass walls there were different assigned seating areas, each marked with a designated number. We were directed to follow the orange line to the specific room and then to take a seat at window number three. We sat down and had been told by a guard behind the glass that JD would join us shortly. We waited, as the guard ushered JD up to the window and told us that we had ten minutes.

(Left to right: JD & Will at St. Vinnie's cafeteria on trip 12)

JD's hair had been shaven and he was wearing a jumpsuit, as you'd expect if you've ever watched a prison movie. He looked a bit slimmer than he'd looked when he was with us in Orlando. Apparently, the prison guards told him that he had visitors, although they hadn't told him who the guests were. The look on his face contained a mixture of surprise and shame. He stared through the glass and then motioned for me to pick up a phone on my side of the glass. He did the same as we each took our seats on opposite sides of the glass. He said, *"Hey Will, thanks for coming man."* I reintroduced JD to Steve and Kara, since he looked surprised by our visit. I didn't want him to feel embarrassed if he couldn't remember their names. I had already sent JD a letter and a couple of books, before we visited that day. He was quick to thank me for the letters and books. After our initial greeting, JD took a long pause and I could see that he was trying to find the words. I wondered what was going on in his head.

When JD spoke up, I could hear by his voice that he was struggling to keep it together. He said, *"I'm so embarrassed that you guys had to come and see me like this in prison."* There was a fresh bruise around his eye and I asked him if things had gotten rough behind bars. He said, *"Yes, they have. I requested to be placed in solitary confinement since I was being pressured to join one of the gangs in here."* Then he whispered to me through the glass, even though we were both holding phone receivers to hear one another, *"I can't do this again, Will."* His voice cracked with emotion. My mind went back to the moment I met JD in front of Father Joe's Village and he spoke of being released after serving 17 years behind bars. He said, *"It's not like you think, I didn't do everything they accused me of."* I responded, *"JD, even if you did, we would be here to visit you, so you don't have to convince us of anything."* He added, *"I'm so ashamed. I'm sorry you and Steve had to come all this way with his daughter."* We assured him that it was all right, we didn't mind coming. I asked him how he was holding up. JD gave us a brief summary of his time behind bars, which didn't sound pleasant.

I asked him how we might be able to help. He replied, "*Your coming here is more than you'll ever realize, so thank you!*" We offered to pray with him and he responded, "*Will you please?*" When I began to pray for JD, he pressed his hand against the glass and I did the same on the opposite side. As I offered a prayer up for my friend he began to weep. When I concluded, I simply handed the phone receiver to Steve and he picked up where I left off. When Steve said "amen", Kara took the phone and prayed for JD. By the time all three of us were finished, the four of us each had streams of tears running down our cheeks.

The emotion felt was tangible and when we turned to leave, JD sprang to his feet and moved toward the glass. Looking in my direction he said, "*Wait Will!*" I turned back in his direction to face the glass and he lifted his hand again to the glass. I did the same and while I couldn't hear his audible voice through the thick glass without the phone receiver, he hollered, "*I love you all, thanks for coming.*" We told him we loved him as well and with that, the guard removed him from the visitation area.

The three of us were speechless as we retraced our tracks out of the prison, along the same orange line. When we exited the prison, I opened my Uber app and requested a ride back to San Diego. We waited out front, although none of us felt much like talking. I was thinking of my friend JD back in his small solitary confinement cell, hoping he would be okay. I purposed in my mind to send him a letter as soon as we returned to the hotel later in the week. Steve and Kara promised to do the same.

I wanted to help my friend JD, although there wasn't much anyone could do. I planned to continue praying for him and writing. He mentioned that his court case was scheduled for the summer of 2020, so he had at least six months to wait for sentencing. JD gave me the name of the lawyer and told me that I was welcome to call the guy if I wanted to discuss his case. I wasn't sure what difference that would make but took note of the attorney's name in the event that I wanted an update.

(Left to right: Steve, Kara & Will at George Bailey Detention Facility)

We caught a ride to a hospital in the downtown area, where we heard that our blind friend Tom Williams was a patient. Another kind friend from the streets by the name of Jeff Horn had picked up where Paul had left off. He had been looking out for Tom, who became ill and had to be hospitalized. We searched two different hospitals with no luck. After striking out on our third attempt, we made our way to the Old Town area to meet up with the rest of our team.

A good friend of mine by the name of Brian Silvestri mentioned how the trip had begun to impact his thinking. He said, *"I'm a businessman and I've always looked at the homeless as a lazy bunch who simply needed to find jobs."* He continued, *"Over the course of this week, I've come to realize that there is no one-size-fits-all homeless person, and that each individual has their own unique story."* He seemed grateful for his new revelation and I wondered how many people think in a similar fashion. I'm grateful to my friend Ed for opening my eyes to the homeless; a world I never would have entered apart from this experience.

I had no idea that Ed would be a patient in Oahu at Queen's Medical Center six months later. Donnie had some luck connecting with a doctor at that hospital, since the medical staff needed Ed's history. All Donnie was able to discover was that Ed had been a difficult patient, which they said is normal for an addict going cold turkey off of a strong substance like methamphetamine. Through one of Donnie's law enforcement contacts, he discovered that Ed's accident did not involve a car or another bike. Ed had a serious crash on his own bicycle while riding way too fast, high on drugs.

I contacted Ed's family to bring them up to speed on his situation and whereabouts. Ed's sister Diane has a medical background, and decided to contact the professionals at Queen's Medical Center. The nurse who took her call was unable to disclose too much information due to HIPPA privacy laws, however, she verified that Ed was indeed detoxing from the heavy presence of chemicals in his bloodstream. Ed was fairly banged up with a broken hip, lacerations on his arm and stiches in his scalp. Ed was not wearing a helmet when he took the fall.

I decided to contact Peter Arnade. Peter is a professor and dean at the University of Hawaii in Honolulu, so he was the only local person I could think of to make contact with Ed. Ed had done a great deal of furniture restoration work for Peter, when the Arnade family lived in San Diego. Of course, that was years earlier when Ed had his restoration business located on Hancock Street. Due to COVID-19, Peter was unable to visit Ed in the hospital, although he did make a phone call.

Surprisingly, Ed took Peter's phone call and never thought to ask him how he knew about the accident. Perhaps when you battle paranoia and believe the CIA is following you, one assumes that the agency knows everything. Ed told Peter that he wanted to talk with him. He mentioned being in pain from his accident and handed the phone back to the nurse. Peter learned that while there had been drugs found in Ed's bloodstream at the time of the accident, there were no charges against him. That meant Ed could walk out of the hospital whenever he felt well enough. In addition, the hospital wouldn't pay to get Ed back to Maui, which meant that we could have a problem when Ed was ready to be released. My hope was that the medical center would keep him for as long as possible, to help his mind return to clearer thinking.

Worrying about what might possibly happen can lead to discouragement. I was worried for JD after leaving our prison visit. JD sounded borderline suicidal. I hoped he could hang on since he hadn't even received his sentencing. One source of encouragement for me, when I faced days like that on the street, was to connect with some of the stellar volunteers who served the homeless on a regular basis.

On my third trip, I met a Catholic priest who was pushing a broom to clean up. He was not wearing his collar that would have signified he was a priest. Instead, he wore a sweatshirt and jeans and was busy cleaning floors. Being involved in Protestant ministry, I'm happy to meet Catholic friends committed to the same cause. Serving the less fortunate provides an area of common ground to focus on where we agree, rather than dividing us. I'd rather build relational bridges than burn them down.

The priest's name was Father Joe Coffey and he took a sincere interest in our cause. In fact, when I sent him an annual newsletter describing our work, Father Joe sent me a generous contribution. On my 9th trip to San Diego, he took me and John Morales to lunch at Hodad's in Ocean Beach. If you haven't had a burger from Hodad's, you don't know what you are missing. On my 12th trip, he invited me, Steve and Georgia to lunch at his home where he personally cooked us a tasty meal in his kitchen.

Father Joe Coffey served as a military chaplain and told us that he'd been reassigned to serve in Japan. Shortly after that assignment, he was promoted as a bishop with oversight of the largest diocese in the world; the entire United States Armed Forces ministry branch. These trips have allowed me to meet some unforgettable people like Bishop Joe. There have been moments during the journey when a conversation with someone like Father Joe has made all the difference.

(Left to right: Georgia, Father Joe, Will & Steve)

A week after we returned home from trip 14, I received a letter from JD. He expressed how appreciative he was that we'd come all the way to the border prison and made time for a visit. After expressing his gratitude, he confessed something I was unaware of. JD said, "*When you and Steve and Kara stopped by for a visit, I was recovering from a prison brawl and had spent a week in solitary confinement. I had requested the move as a matter of personal protection and yet I was battling discouragement. I had plans to end my life sometime within the next 24 hours. However, you all showed up to see me and it made a huge difference. After you three talked with me and prayed for me, my spirit soared. I decided not to take my life. You have no idea how perfect your timing was. I believe if you had come one day later, I wouldn't have been alive, so thank you.*" He said a number of other things, but requested that our entire church continue praying for him as he prepared to stand trial.

I shared the news with our church and invited others to pray for JD. In addition, a few individuals asked for JD's address and began writing him in prison. Some friends sent him books, and others drafted letters to provide encouragement. In early June, JD wrote to tell me that he'd written a full confession to the district attorney regarding his part in the murder of the homeless man. He'd taken responsibility for his actions, although he hadn't intended to kill the man. JD told me in the same letter that he got involved in a prison Bible study and began to experience more freedom behind bars than he ever had on the outside. He seemed at peace with God, himself and others, which encouraged me greatly.

JD asked me about Steve and Kara. I sent him a reply to let him know that Kara had become engaged to Clay Whitley, the boyfriend whom she brought to San Diego on the trip when we met him. They had even asked me to officiate their wedding. Kara wrote JD as well and the numerous pen pals lifted his spirits even more. Two months later, I received a letter from a man by the name of Ruben Ruiz. Ruben wrote, "*You don't know me, but I met JD Terrell in prison and he gave me a copy of your book, "Along the Way." I wanted to thank you for what you wrote in that book and for impacting JD's life. JD has made a tremendous influence on me and my faith.*" Although I'd never met Ruben, it did my heart good to hear that despite JD's dire situation, he was making a positive impact in prison.

Certain drugs can enslave a human as much as any thick prison wall. Ed and JD were examples of that reality. While Ed's imprisonment to crystal methamphetamine was the catalyst for his serious bike accident and illogical paranoia, JD had begun to experience true freedom apart from drugs, while locked behind bars.

I was beginning to feel a sense of enslavement related to the Coronavirus. Contracting the virus as a family limited our lives for a couple of weeks, but the world-wide impact was paralyzing. While the initial impact impeded our plans to visit Maui for an extended period of time, the continued travel restrictions wouldn't allow us to visit Ed in the hospital. All we could do from home was pray and ask God to release Ed from the bondage of drugs that had altered his way of thinking.

I was optimistic that Peter would have some positive engagements with Ed, since Donnie was no longer on the same island. Back in Virginia we held onto the hope that God would use Ed's bike accident as a catalyst for positive change, just as He'd used JD's prison circumstances to bring about freedom. God has a way of using the worst "crap" in life as fertilizer to produce some of life's most amazing fruit. Only God can do such a thing. We were left to wait and watch and hope for what was to come.

Chapter 24
The Prodigal Returns

Donnie and I continued to communicate, while Peter was calling Ed at the hospital each day. Between the two of them in direct communications with Queen's Medical Centre, we learned that Ed's injuries were serious. In addition to breaking his pelvis, he had also damaged his shoulder. We were all hoping that the hospital might be able to keep Ed in their care, while he continued to detoxify from the drugs. While we were thrilled to hear that Ed was alive despite his serious accident, we were hoping that the situation would also serve to bring healing to his mind.

(Left to right: Will & Donnie at Maui Cyclery in Paia)

Donnie had been an incredible support to Ed throughout the entire process. Taking into account Ed's addiction to Methamphetamine, and his random bouts of delusional thinking, he wasn't always easy for

Donnie to manage. While there were days when Ed could clean bikes and help around the shop, there were other occasions when he would show up mentally out of sorts. Ed's mindset and moods paralleled his drug use. On June 5th, Donnie messaged me to say that Ed was experiencing some serious symptoms related to his drug withdrawal. He displayed irrational behavior and fits of rage, making him a difficult patient to treat. I was afraid that the hospital might be tempted to turn him out on the street.

As Ed's body adjusted to the lack of substance, he was also dealing with pain associated with a broken hip and fractured shoulder. The nurses told his sister Diane that he had been difficult to work with. In one of Ed's worst moments, he actually tried to strangle the attending doctor. Ed was apparently concerned that he would never be able to ride his bike again. However, when the physician exclaimed, "*You will ride again,*" Ed let go and apologized for his reaction. While Peter was trying to connect with Ed on the phone, he was still unable to visit in person due to the Coronavirus.

Ed's behavior had been erratic, which made me wonder if his risk of flight was elevated. While we waited and wondered about Ed's state of mind, we were thrilled as each day passed. Hearing that he was still present in the hospital and had survived another day without using drugs or running away, was worth celebrating. We continued to pray that his mind would recover enough for him to make smart choices without his irrational paranoia kicking in.

Peter genuinely cared about Ed and had learned about Ed's drug addiction back in San Diego. There'd been a kitchen cabinet job that Ed hadn't finished in Peter's home, and Peter went looking for him. He caught Ed using drugs back at his shop. Feeling tremendous shame, Ed returned to the jobsite and finished the job for Peter. After the job had been completed, he began taking Ed out for meals, seeking to help Ed get free from the addiction. Peter and his family relocated to the University of Hawaii about the time that Ed hit the streets. I'd spoken with Peter back in 2017 when I found Ed in Maui. After Ed was admitted at Queen's Medical Center in Honolulu, Peter was the perfect person to continue following up with Ed.

It was as though the baton of looking after Ed had passed from Donnie to Peter in the first two weeks of June. Whenever the hospital wanted to speak with a family representative, Diane would field the calls. Peter discovered that the hospital was ready to transfer Ed to a half-way house after approximately 10 days. Apparently, that was the normal protocol for a local homeless person who was in recovery, when no family is present to pick them up. The medical professionals felt that his hip, shoulder and other various wounds no longer needed their care, so they had him relocated.

Peter called Ed at the new facility and discovered that Ed was not at all fond of the place. He was anxious to get out. Peter was unsure what to tell Ed, since we all assumed that the half-way house would a better situation to keep Ed clean while he was recovering from his injuries and staying clean. Every day we ran the risk that Ed might bounce to the streets, although the fact that he was on an unfamiliar island made that option a lot less appealing. Afterall, Ed couldn't simply return to his campsite in Paia. At least he had a bed and three-square meals if he stayed put. Peter did his best to encourage Ed to stick with the plan while his body healed.

Ed's mom called Peter to get an update on his condition and state of mind. Everyone was hopeful that the detoxification period might be an answer to prayer and help Ed return to his senses. On June 14, 2020, I received a text message that changed the entire trajectory of my journey to search for my childhood friend, Ed. The message was from Mrs. Pelzner and it read, "*I just spoke with Ed and he told me that he's ready to come home.*" I was in the middle of a meeting when I received the text. There was no way I'd be able to focus on the meeting after reading the news. I wondered what on earth would cause Ed to have a change of heart and speak to his mom about his potential return? I desperately needed to know, so I excused myself from the meeting and found a quiet place to call Ed's mom.

Apparently, when Peter spoke with Mrs. Pelzner, she requested the direct phone number to Ed's room. She was anxious to speak with her son, whom she hadn't seen since early October of 2014. Approximately six years later, Ed spoke with his mom, 11 days after his bike accident. It was during that conversation that he expressed his desire to return home. I asked her to relay the conversation and she did.

She confessed that when Ed answered the phone, she didn't recognize his voice on the other end of the line. She asked to speak with her son, Ed Pelzner. To which Ed responded, "*This is Ed.*" She said, "*No, I need to speak with my son, Ed Pelzner.*" I'm not sure if she simply couldn't imagine truly speaking with him or if his voice somehow sounded different than what she remembered. Ed insisted, "*Mom, this is your son, Ed Pelzner!*" She continued, "*Oh, well it didn't sound like you.*" Then the two of them spent some time chatting about the details of the accident and the injuries he had sustained. Of course, any mom would want to know how her son was doing, first and foremost. Once he expressed an interest to return home, she told him that she would work on the details and get back to him.

After speaking with Mrs. Pelzner on the phone, we were both thrilled beyond words about Ed's change of heart. While this had been a miraculous turn of events, we realized that there were still a few major hurdles to overcome. Hurdle number one had to do with the reality of restrictions related to COVID-19. No one could travel to visit Ed or travel with him as a co-passenger. Hurdle number two was related to Ed's erratic behavior. We were unsure if Ed would maintain the frame of mind he displayed when speaking with his mom on the phone. He had expressed his desire to leave decisions about the treatment facility to Peter and Mrs. Pelzner, so we hoped he would hang in there long enough for us to organize his return.

We discovered a third hurdle when we researched flight itineraries and realized that there were no direct flights from Oahu to the Washington, D.C. area. That meant that Ed would need to navigate at least one layover in an unknown airport somewhere between Hawaii and the East Coast. This may not have been a problem under normal circumstances. However, taking into account Ed's broken hip, his history of drug use and living off the grid for six years, we didn't want to take any unnecessary risks during his travel. The final significant hurdle was the reality that Ed didn't possess any current legal identification papers required for his travel home. How frustrating is that? Ed finally expresses his desire and willingness to return home, and yet we couldn't seem to make it happen.

I'd begun to imagine Ed growing frustrated in the treatment facility with no money and only the blood-soaked shirt and shorts he was wearing when he arrived at the hospital. I figured we only had a matter of days before Ed would be tempted to wander out on to the streets of Honolulu. Would our future homeless trips need to be extended to Oahu? I was emotionally exhausted and wondered if my present hopes would be short-lived. After making 14 trips I certainly had no intention of giving up at that moment, but I prayed earnestly for my friend's return. I did my best to focus on the hurdles that I could assist with and offer those out of my control to God.

Back in November of 2013, when I asked Ed to acquire a new U.S. passport to join us on our trip to Ghana, he promised to do so. While he never sent me his passport to obtain a travel visa, I never knew if he had so much as submitted the paperwork. I'd discovered that Ed's friend Stephanie had his renewed U.S. passport in a storage box back in San Diego. She had sent it to me along with his expired driver's license, after I located Ed on trip seven. While I had given Ed his driver's license with his old wallet on our second trip to Maui, I had retained his passport for such a time as this.

Before attempting to ship Ed's passport to Peter, I contacted Donnie back in Maui. Donnie knew where Ed's encampment was in the woods off Baldwin Avenue, the same place that Dustin and I had biked to on the previous summer. Donnie agreed to make a trip to Ed's campsite to search for any possible form of legal identification. We waited for him to get back to us and when he did, he reported that he was unable to find any form of ID among Ed's belongings. Donnie was also kind enough to bag up the remainder of Ed's possessions before another homeless wanderer had an opportunity to steal it.

After hearing from Donnie that there was no identification to be found, I reminded Mrs. Pelzner that I had Ed's passport. Since Ed obtained his passport after we met in November, it was not going to expire until ten years later, January 2024. I've kept it in a fireproof safe in my home, in the miraculous chance that Ed might decide to come home and to take a mission trip as we planned seven years earlier. I quickly retrieved Ed's passport from the safe and overnighted it via Fed Ex to Peter in Oahu.

Meanwhile, Mrs. Pelzner purchased a flight for Ed that was a redeye, scheduled to depart the following day. She booked his departure from Honolulu on Wednesday evening, June 17th, with a layover in San Francisco the following morning. Ed had to change gates only once, and was scheduled to land at Washington Dulles International Airport around 3:30 p.m. on June 18th. Peter let me know once he'd successfully received the Fed Ex package containing Ed's passport. He was ready and willing to pick up Ed from the halfway house and deliver him to the airport in Honolulu, along with his legal identification.

One more potential wrinkle in the plan was the fact that Ed didn't have a cell phone. In other words, if Ed ran into any problems along the way, he had no way to let anyone know. We were all anxious about his travels and invited friends from our churches to pray for this tremendous answer to prayer and the final leg of the journey. We were excited, but he wasn't home yet. As they say, *"Don't count your chickens before they hatch."*

Mrs. Pelzner and I coordinated our efforts to put together a plan that involved Ed coming home in the quickest and most direct route. Neither of us wanted to miss out on this opportunity after Ed spoke the words, *"It's time to come home, I'm ready."* There was still the nagging thought, shared by Mrs. Pelzner and me, *"What if Ed changes his mind?"* This possibility created a sense of urgency to act quickly while

Ed desired to return home. We'd done everything in our power to create a safe and semi-direct route home. The rest was in Ed's hands, so we offered up more prayers and waited to hear from Peter. While Peter had Ed's passport in hand, he was scheduled to oversee the first leg of Ed's journey. He was planning to pick him up and deliver him to the airport with his passport.

As Ed's travel day was upon us, I wasn't sure where Ed stood with me. While his mom said that he'd been kind to her on the phone, I didn't want to assume that his good will would extend to others. Since 2017 Sandra and I had visited Ed in Maui for three summers in a row and each time he'd made it clear that he wasn't ready to reengage with anyone from his past. My hope was that his newfound openness with his mom might extend to us as well. It was hard for me to believe that it would happen, since I'd experienced a distant, combative version of Ed for three consecutive years.

My curiosity got the better of me, so I decided to call Peter. I wanted to find out if he had an idea about Ed's attitude toward me. I phoned Peter on the Wednesday evening of Ed's scheduled departure. Peter confirmed that he was scheduled to take Ed to the airport around 8:30 p.m. later that evening, so he could be present for his 10:30 p.m. departure. Keep in mind, Ed had no luggage or belongings to check, just the clothes on his back, so two hours was more than enough time for Ed to find his way to his departing gate.

I thanked Peter for his willingness to transport Ed and for playing such a critical role since we'd discovered that Ed was in the hospital. Then I got up the courage to ask the question that was plaguing my mind, "*Hey, when you speak with Ed, would you mind bringing my name up to see how he responds and feels about me?*" Peter replied, "*I already know what he thinks about you, since your name came up earlier today.*" My heart started racing, nervous about what Peter might say next. I dared to ask, "*And how does Ed feel about me now?*" To my surprise Peter replied, "*When your name came up earlier, Ed asked, 'Do you think Will can forgive me for keeping my distance from him all these years? He has been a great friend to me, so I hope he doesn't hold any resentment against me.'"* Tears filled my eyes as I absorbed Peter's words, which came as a complete shock. *"Wow, Ed said that?"* I inquired with a sense of disbelief. *"Yes, he did."* I was moved with emotion and thanked Peter for sharing that precious news.

I decided to take yet one more risk, in light of Ed's comments to Peter. *"Would you mind giving me the direct line to Ed's room?"* *"Of course!"* Peter responded, before passing it along. I thanked him and asked him to keep me posted once he dropped Ed off at the airport later that evening. He agreed and I hung up the phone. I sat paralyzed in my chair, unsure of what Ed might actually say if I was to call him. I'd been on this venture for six years at that point, so the entire situation felt all too surreal. I was feeling like you do before making a call about a job interview, that you've been waiting years for, and yet you're incredibly anxious because you don't want to get your hopes up. There is always the chance that you don't get the job, or in my case, the chance that Ed would tell me once again to back off. Or perhaps you've had to call a doctor about test results that could be either catastrophic or a reason to celebrate. Both of those scenarios might help explain how I was feeling. I experienced an inner turmoil, knowing that 14 trips brought me to this phone call. How would Ed respond? I dialed the phone to find out.

I said a quick prayer as I dialed the last set of numbers. The phone rang twice before anyone picked up. I heard a voice I recognized all too well on the other end of the line, *"This is Ed."* *"Hello Ed, this is your old friend Will Cravens. How are you doing?"* Ed responded immediately, *"I'm so glad you called, I'm well. Did Peter give you my number?"* *"Yes, he did, and I understand you're coming home tomorrow?"* Ed continued with excitement in his voice, *"Yes I am, will you be at the airport?"* I replied without hesitation, *"If you want me to I will. Sandra and I would love to be there to welcome you."* Ed replied, *"By all means, if it's not too much trouble. I'm excited to see you both and have so much to tell you!"* Is this the same Ed from Maui? I wondered. Have you ever prayed prayers that deep down you weren't so sure would ever be answered?

Perhaps a mustard seed-size faith is enough, if it keeps you from giving up?

Ed apologized for not being friendlier when we'd seen him each summer in Maui. Then he added, "*I hope you know that it wasn't personal. I'd decided to break off all contact with people from my past, but I'm ready to come back now.*" It was hard to believe the words I was hearing. I wondered what accounted for Ed's change of mind and demeanor? It was like talking to an entirely different human than the one we'd encountered in Maui the last three summers. What had God done in that accident scenario to bring about such a significant change? I wasn't complaining by any stretch of the imagination. I was full of awe and gratitude to God for this unbelievable miracle. We chatted a bit more before ending the call. As I was about to hang up on my end, Ed added, "*Hey Will, I love you dude, and I can't wait to see you tomorrow!*" I responded, "*I love you too Ed. We'll see you tomorrow at the airport, so travel safe.*"

When the call ended, I sat in my chair and replayed the entire conversation in my mind. I wondered about what it would look like to help Ed break his addiction to methamphetamine. I had no clue how to assist him in ending his self-destructive cycle and dependence on meth. I realized that I'd better become a fast learner, since he would be home in less than 24 hours. There was also the issue of Ed moving back into his parent's home. His mom was 88 and his father, was a World War II veteran of 94 years. Rather than contemplate everything that could potentially go wrong, my spirit lifted at the idea of Ed actually returning home. As the excitement mounted, I raced up the stairs and woke Sandra, who was already asleep. "*You'll never guess who I just spoke with on the phone?*" Her face contained a mixed expression of curiosity and annoyance, after being abruptly awakened from her slumber. With frustration in her tone she played along, "*I don't know, who?*" I wasted no time responding, "*Ed!*" The news jolted her from her drowsy state, "*Your homeless friend Ed?*" She asked in shock. "*Yes, my homeless friend who we have been praying and searching for over the last six years!*" She sat up ready to hear more.

I filled her in on my conversation with Peter, which led me to ask for Ed's number. I shared the details of my discussion with Ed, and let her know that we'd been invited to meet him at the airport. We sat there for a minute in silence, soaking it all in. Our emotions were attempting to keep up with what our minds had heard. Perhaps our brain processes quicker than our heart? There were so many questions prompted by Ed's decision to return home. We talked about what his recovery might look like, how he'd manage traveling alone, what would living with two senior citizens be like, and more. Imagine being an empty-nester for the last 34 years, and then having your recovering addict son move home. What would that be like? We were soon to find out.

The questions flooding our minds had no end, which made getting to sleep a bit tricky that evening. We decided to pray together and offer our concerns back to God. After all, we both sensed that He was the One behind this miraculous turn of events. Certainly, He had answers to the questions we'd only begun to consider. We thanked Him for the events that were transpiring. We prayed for Ed's safe travel through the night and for his restoration of mind and freedom from drugs. We offered up some prayers for Ed's family, certainly for his parents who were in for a significant change. When we concluded our prayer, Sandra drifted quickly back to sleep, which wasn't quite as easy for me.

I recall saying to Steve Bowman on a number of our homeless trips, *"This journey will be a series of three miracles. Miracle one will be God allowing us to locate Ed, which seemed like a needle in a haystack, with one missing homeless man among 13,000 others. The second miracle would be Ed's willingness to come home or get help with his addiction. And the third and final miracle would be Ed's freedom from drugs and the restoration of his mind."* We had been grateful to experience miracle one on trip seven, when we located Ed in Maui. The road to locate him had been anything but easy, yet we experienced God's hand directing us the entire way. And after seven more trips, Ed called to say that he was ready to return home. We were thrilled to be on the eve of miracle number two, after 14 trips. The entire process inspired me to pray all the more for miracle number three! Surely if the Living God was willing to accomplish the first two miracles, why would He stop short of the third? Time would tell.

The following day, Sandra and I were present at Dulles Airport, along with Ed's parents, another high school friend of Ed's named Mason, and one of their neighbors, named Todd. Mr. Pelzner waited in the car since he had trouble walking. Mason, Todd and Mrs. Pelzner joined Sandra and me in the airport baggage claim area.

Since Ed traveled without a cell phone, we weren't completely sure that we'd see him at the gate, when his flight arrived. Due to the Coronavirus, Peter was unable to walk Ed through the airport to see him off. That meant there was a slight possibility that Ed never boarded his flight in Oahu. In addition, Ed could have gotten lost in San Francisco during his layover earlier that morning. I'd already begun to wonder if I would need to schedule a homeless trip to search for Ed in San Francisco, which has a much larger street population. As we stood waiting at Dulles International Airport, I certainly hoped that wasn't the case. Why does waiting in a situation riddled with unfortunate possibilities seem to make time feel as though it is moving at a slower pace? The five of us stood staring at the security doors, all hoping to catch a glimpse of Ed's face.

We saw a crowd of passengers making their way through the double doors into the baggage claim area. I asked one man if he'd arrived from San Francisco, to which he replied, "*Yes, I did.*" I thanked him as we searched with greater intensity, scanning every single face that made its way through those doors. A few minutes later, as the crowd began to thin out, we noticed a tall figure hobbling through the doors using a cane. Sure enough, it was Ed making his way toward us. His facial expression appeared just as excited to see us, as we were to see him.

Ed greeted his mom with a hug and a kiss, although she was nervous given the contagious Coronavirus at the time. Ed's friend Mason offered his greetings, as did Ed's neighbor Todd. Sandra and I waited our turn, then gave him a warm hug and welcomed him home. It's difficult to find the words to capture the emotion felt by all of us in that significant moment of time. As I had guessed, Ed had absolutely no luggage to retrieve, so we simply headed for the car. Most of the homeless travel light, a lesson that those of us living in homes can learn from. However, Ed literally arrived with a crutch and the clothes on his back. Since Ed had been rushed to a hospital on a different island 15 days earlier, he never returned to his campsite or had a moment to bring any belongings. And so, after a warm greeting, we made our way to his parents' car. I noticed that Ed appeared to be experiencing some pain, so I grabbed a wheel chair and offered him a ride. He was all too happy to take a seat.

(Left to right: Ed's mom in background, Ed & Will at Dulles Airport)

Ed's dad, who'd been waiting in the car, exited the vehicle when he saw his son coming. We watched as they embraced and laughed together. Mr. and Mrs. Pelzner were anxious to take their long-lost son out to dinner to celebrate the occasion. I told Mrs. Pelzner that our church was planning a special service that coming Sunday to welcome Ed home.

I knew that Steve Bowman was anxious to finally meet Ed, as were many others who'd made trips to California to search for him. I asked a friend of mine by the name of John Zoller, if we could borrow his church's large outdoor pavilion. We needed a space like that to host a special service to celebrate the return of my lost friend. John gladly said, "*Yes!*" and so we made plans to welcome the prodigal home, four days after his return. I also knew that Ed's sister Diane was in transit from Colorado, with her husband Doug. Diane was excited to see her little brother face-to-face, and was driving across country to make it happen. While Ed had only just arrived home, the party was about to begin!

Chapter 25

A Homecoming Celebration

On Saturday, June 20th, I swung by the Pelzners' home to pick Ed up for dinner. Ed had promised Sandra that he would have dinner with our family back in Maui in 2018. Although he reneged on the promise when we returned to Paia in 2019, Ed told Sandra at the airport two days earlier, "*I'm ready to have that family dinner now, if you still want it.*" Sandra's face lit up with a smile and we made plans for Saturday evening. On the way back from Ed's parents' house, I decided to mix it up a bit. I told Ed about my friend Steve Bowman. I mentioned that he'd been willing to make nine homeless trips on Ed's account, and that he attended our rival high school in Herndon, Virginia. Ed seemed interested, so I continued, "*In fact, Steve's daughter Holly made one trip, and his daughter Kara made two.*" With that, Ed was clearly moved by this family's efforts, although they'd never met. Then I asked, "*So, do you want to meet them?*" Without hesitation, Ed replied, "*By all means!*"

I called the Bowman family to let them know that I was bringing a surprise visitor to their home. Steve's wife Lisa said, "*We're headed out to dinner and don't have much time.*" Then I added, "*Even if the guest is my homeless friend Ed?*" Lisa inquired, "*Are you kidding?*" "*No ma'm, I'll see you in five minutes.*" We headed straight over, so they could finally meet face-to-face. Steve and Lisa had planned to travel to Maui during the same time that Sandra and I hoped to be there in the summer of 2020. However, COVID-19 cancelled their plans as well as ours. Although we'd imagined the Bowmans would finally meet Ed in Paia, God had intervened and allowed them to meet Ed in their own home.

Lisa must have sent Steve out to the driveway, because he was waiting for us when we arrived. Ed and I exited my truck and I made the introductions. Steve was beside himself as Ed thanked him for all of his efforts searching on his behalf. He even thanked Steve for caring for other homeless people on the streets. Steve replied, *"It was completely worth it and I'd do it all over again if I was given the opportunity. I'm a better man for it."* I was simply a spectator to their meeting, as I noticed Steve's daughters watching from the window. I made a comment about seeing them, and Steve asked Ed, *"Would you mind meeting my daughters? They've both lived on the streets of San Diego and would love to meet you."* Ed replied, *"Of course not, I'd love to meet them!"* With that, the girls and Lisa, all came out to connect with Ed. Their exchange was moving and I snapped a photo of the Bowman family with Ed. I reminded them about Ed's homecoming party the following evening and they said, *"We wouldn't dare miss it. We'll see you then!"* From the Bowman's house, we drove Ed to my home to have dinner with my family, the dinner date that we'd been waiting for since 2017.

(Left to right: Holly, Ed, Kara, Steve & Lisa)

We arrived at my house, where Sandra was getting dinner ready. We had invited my mom, who was like a second mother to Ed when we were growing up. Ed was so grateful to everyone for dinner, for opening our home and for welcoming him at the airport. When the meal was ready, we sat down to eat and Ed asked, "*Would you mind if I said the blessing?*" We responded in unison, "*Of course not,*" and so he did. It was an unforgettable evening and of course, Sandra was thrilled that Ed had kept his promise.

Sunday, June 21st was the big day. I invited every individual who'd ever come with us to search for Ed and who'd participated on the homeless trips. We met under the large outdoor pavilion that Pastor John Zoller had kindly provided for the occasion. There was plenty of free-flowing air to assuage fears of the Coronavirus.

My inspiration for the party that afternoon came from the same Bible passage which inspired me to leave the safety of the "99" for the "1." Jesus actually told three stories in Luke chapter 15, to communicate how God feels about those whom society often looks down upon. In that account, it was the religious leaders of His day, who were standing in judgement of those they deemed outcasts. The third and most well-known of the three stories, was that of the prodigal son.

Jesus told the story of a son who asked his father for his share of the inheritance, and then abandoned his family. The son squandered his father's money on wine, women and parties, until he had no money left. With no money left and no friends who stuck around to help, he was forced to slop pigs for a living. That job was considered incredibly demeaning, since pigs are unclean animals to Jews and Muslims alike. One particular day, when he was feeding the pigs, he'd become so hungry that he considered eating the food in the trough where he was slopping the pigs. Just before taking his first bite, the son "*came to his senses.*" Rather than eat the pig slop, he decided to return home and beg for his father's forgiveness. He thought, "*Perhaps my dad will have mercy and hire me on as a servant. Even his servants eat better than this.*"

When his father saw his son in the distance, he ran to meet him. Rather than cursing him, punishing or shaming him, he threw his arms around his son and embraced him! He did not hire him on as a servant.

Instead, he gave his son a ring for his finger, a jacket for his back and sandals for his feet. Those items signified the father accepting his son back into the family. The incredibly moving act of love from the father toward the son was Jesus' way of communicating the way God loves us, even when we stray far from Him. I hoped to borrow those ideas for the service to celebrate the return of my friend Ed.

In addition, the father from the account of the prodigal son killed the fatted calf and threw an extravagant party for his son who'd been lost. While I didn't provide any veal that evening, we did hire a Mexican food truck with some pretty tasty tacos. Others from our church who had been praying for Ed during his six years of wandering, also showed up to celebrate. Ed's sister Diane and her husband Doug, who drove the farthest for the occasion, were present. In addition, a few friends from our high school days even surprised us with their attendance.

(Left to right: Doug (Ed's brother-in-law), Ed & his sister Diane)

We kicked off the party with some live music, followed by two guests whom I'd invited to share up front about the impact of this journey on their lives. Steve Bowman went first. He recalled our very first trip living on the streets, weathering the rain and walking miles in search of Ed. In the midst of Steve's speech, Ed hollered out, *"Thank you Steve, I love you!"* Steve responded, *"I love you too, Ed, and I would do it all over again."* Steve went on to speak of the impact that the nine trips have made on his life, his family and his faith. He was moved to tears, as were many in the audience that evening.

(Steve Bowman sharing at Ed's homecoming party)

After Steve, I invited Eric Locklear to the front to share publicly. Eric spoke of knowing the two of us in high school and being on the same wrestling team as Ed. He mentioned how his life had been radically impacted for the positive, as the result of this adventure. Eric mentioned showing up for church as a response to his wife Carolee telling him about the homeless trips she saw posted on Facebook. While he'd entered the journey as a skeptic, Eric soon after became 100% committed.

It wasn't long before he was on a homeless trip with us in San Diego, followed by a bike trip to meet Ed (*and Owen*) in Maui. His entire life and family had been changed in the process, which Eric shared openly about at Ed's celebration. Ed expressed the same gratitude to Eric during his speech, as he'd done for Steve.

Before I took the microphone, my friend Erik Palmer sang the song "*Reckless Love*" by Cory Asbury. If you're unfamiliar with the tune, I suggest you download it, as the lyrics were a dead perfect fit with the mood and message of the evening. Just as Erik finished singing, I took the stage and began by thanking everyone for joining us. I offered special thanks to those who'd taken a trip with us to San Diego or Maui, and mentioned each person by name, rattling through the list of more than 40 participants over the course all 14 trips. I mentioned the reason I'd taken on this mission by simply answering one question, "*How would I want to be loved, if the roles had been reversed? I certainly wouldn't want to be forgotten. Who would?*" I'm constantly challenged by what it means to love another human the way that I would want to be loved if I were in their shoes.

I did a little crowd participation and asked everyone who had lived homeless with us on a trip to San Diego to please stand up. As they remained standing, I asked everyone who'd made a trip to Maui with us to please stand up. Then I said, "*If you have ever prayed for Ed Pelzner on this journey, then please stand up.*" With more than half of the guests standing, I motioned to Ed and asked my friend, "*Hey Ed, do you see these people standing?*" With a shaky, emotionally charged voice he responded, "*Yes.*" Then I said, "*Look at them, they love you and so do I, and you are not alone in this. We are here to support you!*" I told everyone who was standing that they could be seated and then I invited Ed to the front of the pavilion. He made his way slowly up front with the use of his cane. Keep in mind, he'd only been home for three days, and this was 18 days after his accident.

When Ed arrived up front, he stood to my right and I told him the story of Jesus caring about oppressed and messed up people, like us. I mentioned Jesus standing up for people whom the religious leaders of his day looked down upon. I told him the illustration of the lost sheep, the lost coin and the lost son, from Luke chapter 15. I added that Jesus was making a point regarding communicating the type of grace that God has for people like us. He also wanted to communicate the lack of grace and acceptance that the religious priests of his day had shown toward those whom he had been socializing with. Jesus was willing to stick up for the outcasts of his day.

Then I told Ed about the son who left his father and dishonored his family. Despite his son not deserving anything else, his father had welcomed him back into the family. I wanted to personalize that for Ed, so I held up a ring. I gave it to Ed and said, "*This is for you.*" I did the same with a brand-new pair of sandals that Ed had mentioned wanting. In addition, I pulled out a sweatshirt that I'd purchased in San Diego during one of our trips to search for Ed. It was a Rip Curl brand sweatshirt and had the California bear symbol on the front. It also had the Rip Curl slogan "*Live the Search.*" I told Ed that these three items, similar to the jacket, ring and sandals in Jesus' story of the prodigal son, signify that he belongs and that we would not hold his past decisions against him. Ed muttered an emotional "*thank you,*" as he received his new gifts and continued listening.

I added, "'*Live the Search' means something different to me than it does to Rip Curl. To me, 'Live the Search' means that we never stop going after those who are lost. 'Live the Search' entails that we always have an eye out for those who are struggling and in need of our encouragement. We should maintain a life that has open arms for those who are lost and waiting for someone to come searching for them. 'Live the Search' should be seen in our lifestyle, not a posture relegated to one or two mission trips per year. And while we celebrate your return, the search is not over. It's not over, because there are more people like you and me who are still lost and waiting for us to 'Live the Search.'*" Ed listened and nodded as he was clearly overwhelmed with emotion. He had difficulty maintaining eye contact, as he ingested the words and love surrounding him.

(Handing Ed his new Rip Curl, "Live the Search" sweatshirt)

Lastly, I said "*It will take a village to help Ed beat his drug addiction once and for all. If you're willing to stand with Ed as he fights this final battle and we ask God for help, to see the third and final miracle of Ed becoming drug-free, will you please come join us up front?*" A large number of friends joined us up front, where they laid hands on Ed and prayed for him. Among the 20 or so people who were praying up front for Ed, was my friend Paul Arnold from San Diego. He had been living with families in our community for half a year at that point, and it warmed my heart to see Paul praying for Ed.

(Group praying for Ed at the close of homecoming service)

At the close of the formal part of our presentation and prayer for Ed, we played more music, ate amazing food and celebrated his return. I invited every person who had ever been on a homeless trip with us to come and have their photo taken with Ed. It was like an unforgettable reunion, although we were missing a few who'd been unable to make it. Many of the people were meeting each other for the very first time, since there were so many separate trips. It felt that each past trip participant had formed a family-like bond from living in the same street trenches, even though we hadn't all experienced it on the same particular week.

(Some of the homeless trip participants, present for Ed's Homecoming)

To me the past participants felt like brothers and sisters, whose actions had done more to keep me in the fight then they could imagine. I told Sandra later that evening, *"This was by far the highlight of my 30 years of doing non-profit work and ministry!"* It was like a party that I hoped would not end. I looked around that pavilion at the faces impacted. I considered the amount of lives touched along the way, those in San Diego, in Maui, in the pavilion that evening and those who cheered us on via social media platforms. The impact continues even now, as you read this incredible account of a modern-day miracle. I'm so grateful to God that He didn't grant my prayer request and allow me to find Ed on trip one; imagine what I would've missed!

Ed returned to our home that evening for a sleepover. Keeping in mind that Ed's parents were in their 80s and 90s, we wanted to give them regular breaks, as they were bearing the brunt of responsibility for Ed's recovery. As I said, "It's going to take a village." For that reason, we passed around a sign-up sheet that evening for those who wanted to volunteer time with Ed in the coming days, weeks and months ahead. I attempted to recruit a team of people willing to stand with Ed. From what I'd been reading about recovery from methamphetamine, it takes approximately two years off the drug to see significant transformation. Understanding that it was going to require a team willing to walk with Ed, I figured, "*Why not recruit as soon as possible, while I have a caring audience?*"

(Ed & Will at the Homecoming Celebration)

When we got Ed back to our home, he was beside himself. He couldn't stop telling Sandra and I enough about how much the evening had meant to him and how much he loved and appreciated everyone. For me, it was still incredibly surreal. When you search for someone, hoping and praying for their recovery one day, it's a sheer miracle if and when your prayers are realized. Ed hadn't been home for a week, and it hadn't completely sunk in that he was actually present and wanted to change. We were also unsure what to expect of the overnight in our home. Meth can do some damage to a user's brain, often causing symptoms very similar to schizophrenia. Ed shared about his mental struggles and mentioned hearing voices over the course of his six years on the streets, while he was tweaking.

We had so many questions for Ed and yet we didn't want to overwhelm him. His demeanor was simple and appreciative beyond what you can imagine. Certain things that we've become accustomed to, such as using Amazon's Alexa to play music or tell you the weather, were things that startled Ed. Imagine living without electronics for six or seven years. Consider how much has changed in our culture over that time; it's mind-boggling. Ed missed certain music and movie references. When we took him around town on a walk, he literally said, "*Hi, how are you?*" to nearly every single person we passed on the sidewalk. He did that on a walk through our Nation's Capital in Washington, D.C. and people were startled by his friendliness. We felt as though we were hosting "*Buddy the Elf*," as opposed to a homeless friend. He was so full of joy and gratitude.

I'd been racking my brain to think of something fun and memorable I would do with Ed to help build some new memories. Given the restrictions associated with COVID-19, not to mention Ed's inability to move around without pain due to his fractured pelvis, I came up with the idea of fishing. I figured I could hire a boat on the Chesapeake Bay and Ed could sit down on the boat and fish. Ed was thrilled about the idea, and the weather was perfect. I invited Eric Locklear along and figured we'd make a day of it on that following Monday.

Ed was still on cloud nine, reliving and discussing the events from his homecoming party the previous evening. As we drove toward the

Chesapeake Bay in Maryland, I also enjoyed catching up with Eric. We were unsure if we'd be lucky with the fish, but it didn't matter at all, because this was a recreational day with three old friends that I would've never imagined having.

As it turned out, we were lucky. The captain we hired took us to a spot on the bay where the fish were biting and we had an unforgettable time. Of course, the new, happy, appreciative version of Ed thanked the captain and first mate every time we hooked a fish. At one point after catching his third Rockfish, Ed turned to the captain and said, "*I love you man, thanks for being such a cool guy!*" Sensing the awkwardness of the moment, I asked the captain, "*Are you used to receiving comments like that?*" He responded, "*Not at all man, people usually cuss me out if they don't think they've caught enough fish. Your friend is welcome on my boat any time!*" I certainly agreed and thanked God for Ed's return and unbelievably positive attitude.

(Eric, Ed & Will fishing on the Chesapeake Bay)

393

Our day was unforgettable! We packed up our fresh fileted fish on ice, then found a local seafood restaurant to grab dinner. We wanted to savor the last moments of our outing before making the trek home.

When I dropped Ed off back at his parents' home, I reviewed his schedule with Mrs. Pelzner. I already had a list of people signed up to take Ed out for a meal or activity every single day for the coming month. That group of incredible volunteers helped extend daily support to Ed through the first three months of his recovery. In addition, Sandra and I coordinated at least one overnight each week for Ed, to help give his parents a break. Eric and Carolee Locklear decided to do the same, which helped share the responsibility of his recovery. Ed's mom and dad seemed to appreciate the support, as did Ed.

Not only have we been blessed to know some fantastic individuals and families who showed their support of Ed, but one very generous couple expressed their interest in purchasing Ed a bicycle. Ed mentioned missing his time biking, and we had been waiting for his hip to recover enough to make that possible. When that was the case, I contacted Donnie back at Maui Cyclery, knowing that sort of choice fell into his expertise. Donnie recommended a nice new bike from a company in Tennessee that makes titanium frame bikes. We surprised Ed with the bike and Donnie generously outfitted Ed with a load of extras to make his biking experience a little more satisfying. We sent him a picture of Ed wearing his new kit, while modeling it on his new ride, so Donnie could showcase Ed's transformation at the shop. Most people who frequent Maui Cyclery in Paia, know Ed. That includes Owen Wilson, whom Eric and Ed were both able to meet. If you happen to visit Donnie's shop, thank him for his part, since it was no small part of Ed's journey.

(Ed on his new titanium bike with kit from Donnie at Maui Cyclery)

I suppose I could go on and on with tremendous stories of Ed's restoration and recovery, but we're still in the early days and Ed just celebrated four months of drug-free living. We have our eyes set on the goal of helping him make it to the two-year mark, and witness what other miracles God has in store for Ed. His big dream at present is to take a mission trip with us to work on an orphanage with our partners in Limatambo, Peru. We are simply waiting for the borders to reopen without the restrictions associated with the Coronavirus. Of course, Steve Bowman has informed me that if Ed is going to serve, then he wants to join the trip as well. Eric Locklear echoed the same desire, as did Ed's sister Diane. I'm sure we'll have many more recruits on board before the trip is underway.

(Ed a bit emotional when we celebrated 90-days drug-free)

And so, the adventure continues. Ed is determined to remain substance-free, and he certainly has a crew of people behind him to help, any way they can. He's begun taking on a few odd jobs to earn some money for the Peru trip. In addition, he volunteers weekly helping pack food for families who can't afford to eat based on what they earn. It's the same ministry that Paul Arnold volunteers with every week (*Bridge Feeds*).

One day recently, Ed expressed his desire to stay in Peru and serve at the orphanage for an entire three months or longer. He wants to stay on after the short-term team departs. We realized that we cannot simply leave Ed in a foreign country to serve with our orphanage partner on his own. We were wondering who might be able to assist Ed as he explores that dream. Paul said, "*If Ed's on board then so am I!*" Imagine that, two homeless guys from San Diego, serving side-by-side at an orphanage to help impoverished kids in a foreign country. Only God can make stuff like that happen. I am excited to watch it unfold when the borders re-open.

Many people have asked me questions regarding Ed's own perspective and survival over the course of his six years on the street. I've entertained some of the same questions, including his journey from San Diego to Maui. I recently spent four hours with Ed on a road trip from Virginia Beach back to northern Virginia and decided to use the time to interview Ed about his experience. The next chapter is my best effort of recording Ed's own version of the story. You won't want to miss it!

Chapter 26

The Other Side of the Story

As is commonly said, *"There are two sides to every story."* While the crux of this book is my version of what transpired during our homeless journey, you may have wondered about Ed's side of the story. Well, you're not alone. In fact, I can't tell you how many nights Steve and I would ponder and discuss Ed's decisions and whereabouts while we were camping under the stars on the streets of San Diego. We wondered where Ed was and what he was doing. I would say, *"If Ed ever comes around, I've got some questions to ask him."* So now that Ed's around, that's precisely what I did.

On a recent four-hour road trip with just the two of us in the car, I decided to pick Ed's brain and have him share his story. I let him know that our interview was for the conclusion of this book. Ed was all too excited to get started and said, *"I want this story to be told."* I hit the voice memo recorder on my phone and the following details are from our conversation on September 4, 2020.

His story began six years earlier, in late September of 2014. Ed told me that he'd been in a stage of regression. In his own words he said, *"I was slipping. The drugs and the entire situation had become too much for me to handle. I believe that my mom had been speaking with Rex Huffman, the landlord who managed my warehouse shop space."* Ed said that his mother showed up at his shop on a particular day late that September. He conveyed that she appeared to be fairly broken up. According to Ed, his mom entered the shop and expressed her desire to go out for a meal with him. He told her that he had some work to finish, but sensed that something wasn't right.

Ed confessed feeling a level of betrayal when his mom mentioned Rex, his landlord. Keep in mind, this is Ed's take of the situation. Any concerned mother who tries to contact her son, who in turn doesn't bother responding to her calls from across the country, is going to get worried. When she showed up to help, Ed confessed that he felt intruded upon. Ed also mentioned two old friends named Mason and Brett, who showed up at his door that same week. He believed that they were working in connection with his mom, and that they'd conspired with his landlord to have him ejected from his wood shop. Having spoken with Mason and Brett, they were simply two concerned friends who knew that Ed was in a bad place, and they wanted to help. Regardless, Ed saw this as some kind of unwarranted intervention, which he wanted nothing to do with.

Ed told Mason and Brett that he needed to go get his hair cut, when in reality, he simply wanted to leave and avoid any confrontation or conflict. He returned to spy on them and saw them packing up his things and changing the lock on his shop door. Ed was being evicted for not paying his rent and his landlord Rex had already given him an extended grace period. When Ed hadn't responded to Rex's request for overdue payments, and not wanting to call the cops, he phoned Ed's parents on the East Coast. Mrs. Pelzner requested the help of some of Ed's friends, not knowing how he might respond to the pending eviction.

Ed expressed that he felt hurt by the entire way that things were managed. I asked him, "*How do you wish they had handled the difficult situation if it happened all over again?*" He replied, "*I wish they'd stayed out of my business and allowed me to crash and get evicted.*" I asked Ed how he thought he might have responded if things had happened as he wished.

He transitioned from my question and instead of answering, he told me about a time when he'd been thrown out of Boy Scouts. When I asked the reason for his being kicked out of the Scouts, he replied, "*I'd taken an arrow and wrapped the end in toilet paper, then I dipped it in charcoal lighter and lit the end on fire. I shot the arrow at a tent and it burned to the ground. There was no one in the tent, but it was enough to get me ejected.*" Then he answered my question, saying, "*I handled being* cut from the Boy Scouts without a problem, and I would've handled my eviction with no problem as well."

Ed carried on, "*When I was in the Boy Scouts, we learned a bit about how to save a drowning victim. Our instructor commented that the person assisting the one who's in danger is also at risk of being drowned by the panicking victim. It's important to understand the risks involved to both people, in the way that a flight attendant always tells you to, 'Put your mask on before attempting to assist others.'*" I asked, "*How does that relate to your mom and friends coming to help you in San Diego?*" Ed replied, "*There's a relationship between the person helping someone and the person being helped. I believe that element was lacking in my situation, since I was excluded from their obviously preconceived plan.*"

As the person conducting the interview, I was merely trying to understand his mindset. I wanted to know what Ed was thinking when he decided to take to the streets. I'm not pointing blame at either side. I know that Ed's mom, Brett and Mason, and all love Ed and went to San Diego in September of 2014 with one sole intent of helping Ed. While Ed perceived their presence as an intrusion, he viewed the events which transpired as an unwelcomed "intervention." Ed confessed that his reason for breaking ties with all past relationships was based on his understanding of that particular week. He views that incident as the catalyst for his decision to live homeless. I'm sure his mom and friends would see it differently. However, when you are dealing with a drug addict, perception is often not in alignment with reality. Regardless, that was the situation that launched Ed onto the streets on October 3, 2014. His mom called me to share about Ed's choice, when she returned home from California.

Ed confessed that he had begun hearing voices in his head while he was living alone in his shop. The voices began to haunt him before he was ever evicted. He added, "*When I saw my friends changing the lock on my shop door, I never turned back, nor did I contact Rex my landlord.*" I asked Ed where he went from there and he mentioned meeting a homeless guy that same day, down in the Robb Field area near Ocean Beach.

He recalled, "*I didn't want to blame my situation on someone else, so I let it run its course and rolled with it.*" He was unable to recall the man's name, although Ed remembered that he was from Colorado. His new homeless friend had a bike with a child seat mounted on the back. The man had two small dogs, which he'd trained to ride in the child's seat. The two became fast friends and Ed began sleeping at Robb Field, which happened to be the park where Steve, Brian and I slept on our first homeless trip.

When I asked Ed how he survived and was able to find food, he responded, "*I got fairly good with sticky fingers. I would steal hamburgers and steaks from a grocery store called Ralph's. Although, when I was about three weeks into the homeless thing, I freaked out! I had a hard time keeping my shit together, so I told my homeless friend on the bike to call for help. He made a call and a cop showed up to meet us at Robb Field.*"

The cop found Ed in the midst of a panic attack and said, "*Don't freak out on me, I'm here to help.*" Ed felt the weight of what he referred to as a "life-changing situation." He said that over the course of the first few weeks he'd continued to replay the memory of his mom and friends showing up at his shop. When the reality of living on the streets with no money and no belongings caught up with him, it was more than he could handle mentally and emotionally. The police officer took Ed to the psychiatric hospital on Rosecrans Street and made the medical staff aware of Ed's meltdown. You may recall that Gumby met a police officer on trip six, who told him that he'd escorted Ed to a mental hospital when he found him having a breakdown.

Ed mentioned an intake nurse, who calmed him down and said, "*You know what we want from you? Nothing but for you to hang out and speak to a doctor who will be here tomorrow.*" Ed was assigned to a bedroom and met with the physician the following day. After Ed was given a psychiatric workup, the doctor assigned him to a crisis house that was run by a non-profit known as Charter Oaks. Ed was relocated to the shelter in downtown San Diego following his assessment. He found the staff to be very supportive of his situation. Ed described the Charter Oaks Foundation as a place staffed with caring people. He recalled that everyone who entered was only allowed to stay for a maximum of ten days.

Ed described his ten days as a very organized program in which you were encouraged to get involved with the staff, who were trained to diagnose your situation and provide help. The people there were seeking to put each individual on a path with the right plan, tailored to their specific situation. At the end of ten days of evaluation, Ed was sent to the Alpha Project Shelter. In 2015, the shelter was only open during the winter months between November and February. Ed entered the Alpha Project shelter sometime in November of 2014, and began to get acquainted with the staff.

Ed became emotional when speaking about the workers from the Alpha Project. He remembers the staff as being incredibly kind to him. Most of the staff was comprised of previous addicts and homeless people, who had been success stories. They had stayed the course and completed their program, and now served as coaches. Ed mentioned that their facility was known as a "wet tent." This meant that the shelter wouldn't throw a participant out of the shelter if they smelled like alcohol. While they could eject an individual with a bad attitude, or someone who created problems, they leaned more on the side of grace. It was clear that they genuinely wanted to help participants, and were not looking for opportunities to send people back to the streets.

The staff at the Alpha Project worked hard to assist every individual. Their case workers helped each occupant develop a plan for their improvement. Ed recalled one man who worked at the Alpha Project who expressed his belief in him. He said that his support had been so meaningful that Ed wrote a letter to their office in Mission Hills to express his gratitude. He was grateful for the investment they'd made in his life, from the day he arrived at the Alpha Project.

Ed became teary-eyed when sharing and added, *"I'm embarrassed that I can't remember his name. I recall that he was from Mexico and wore a baseball cap, and he was incredibly kind."* Ed learned that the Alpha Project was seeking additional funding, about seven million dollars needed to acquire their own building. Ed was invited by the staff to a town hall meeting with the San Diego City Council. He was honored to be one of the program participants, with the privilege of sharing before City Council members Marti Emerald and Donna Frye.

During the last week of January 2015, the Alpha Project began placing people in other housing, since their seasonal occupancy was soon to close. They assigned Ed to the Salvation Army Centre City Corps, a shelter located on 825 7th Avenue in downtown San Diego. Ed recalled being greeted at the door by an older black gentleman, who acted as a sort of drill sergeant for new recruits. Ed and a few others were assembled into a room, where they were presented with an orientation to the shelter. The sergeant provided a complete list of rules and expectations that had to be followed if a participant wanted to stay.

The leader spoke firmly, *"Gentlemen, you won't be doing any drugs here, I assure you! You'll be clean in this shelter and you're going to learn to develop a resume and get a job! I see some of you slumping over in your chairs. I need you to sit up straight right now and demonstrate respect with your posture. Tomorrow we will get started, so get unpacked and get some rest, because we won't tolerate any excuses."* After the orientation concluded, that same leader singled Ed out and invited him to his office. Ed recalled fondly, *"For some reason, he was kind to me and told me that he liked me and wanted to help me succeed. He was extremely cool."* I asked Ed if he was still using drugs at the time he entered the Salvation Army shelter. He responded, *"No, but not because I didn't want to. I was just out of money and it's not like your pusher is giving anyone free bags because he likes you. One way to get clean is to run out of money and that will get you straight in a hurry."*

While Ed was residing in downtown shelters in San Diego, he confessed a certain habit he'd developed during that time. Ed enjoyed exploring the high-end hotels and ducking into their lobbies to locate and use their hot tubs. After checking into the Salvation Army shelter and seeing 24 men packed into a single room on 12 bunks, Ed was not very excited. He selected a mattress on the top bunk to leave his things, then left to purchase some food. While he was staying at the Alpha Project, the staff helped him register to receive food stamps, also known as the EBT (Electronic Balance Transfer). Ed qualified to receive $350 a month in EBT food credit, which he was grateful for. He went shopping with his food stamps, labeled his food with his name, then packed it away in the Salvation Army pantry. Ed stashed his clothes in a closet near his bunk and set out for the evening. He wanted to explore some of the local hotel hot tubs on North Harbor Drive.

On Friday, January 30th, 2015, Ed targeted the Manchester Grand Hyatt Hotel on 1 Market Place in downtown San Diego. He commented, "*I really liked the hot tubs in their twin towers.*" On that particular evening, Ed chatted with a guy he met in the hot tub. For some reason, he told the man that his sister lived in Parker, Colorado. That man happened to be from Parker as well, which led to deeper conversation. The man asked Ed, "*Are you going to the Steve Miller Band Concert later this evening.*" Ed asked where the concert would be held. The Parker resident responded, "*Right here in this hotel, for the final evening of the Ameritrade convention. That's the reason I'm here as an employee.*" Then he asked Ed if he was with one of the vendors. Ed responded honestly, "*I live here in San Diego. I just come here because I like the hotel hot tubs.*" The guy replied, "*Well you should come to the concert, since it's casual attire and there will be complimentary food and drinks.*" Who was Ed to say no? He decided to take full advantage of the offer.

Ed wandered into the area set aside for the concert. He noticed some of the technicians setting up for the band. As he stood near the stage, a woman approached him and asked him what his story was. She happened to be a roadie for Steve Miller Band. She was working hard and commented, "*Steve likes his shows to go as planned, and is a bit of a perfectionist.*" She was very friendly and welcomed him, saying, "*I hope you enjoy the show.*" No one asked Ed to present identification or to display an entrance badge. Meanwhile, Ed helped himself to the delicious food and free drinks. He said that the band played all of the Steve Miller Band's classic hits and sounded incredible. Ed knew that while the Alpha Project required everyone to be in by 8 p.m., the curfew at the Salvation Army shelter was midnight. He had no intention of being late on his first night, but planned to cut it as close as possible. After all, it wasn't every day that one stumbles into such an event.

When Ed approached the shelter at around ten to midnight, the man working the front door commented, "*You reek of alcohol!*" He made Ed take a breathalyzer and when Ed failed it, he commented, "*Alright buddy, you're out of here. Pack up your stuff and hit the road!*" He escorted Ed into the room to gather his belongings amongst the room full of 23 sleeping men. Ed was quick to pack up his stuff and roll out with his backpack jammed full of his clothing. Although he still had food in the pantry, the man told him that he'd have to return the following day to retrieve it. At that point Ed had been homeless for approximately four months and mentioned that he'd learned to travel light.

Ed strolled across the street to an open parking lot, where he spent the night under the stars. He mentioned meeting a guy in the parking lot who offered him a beer. Ed commented, "*Alcohol is not my poison. I wrestle with speed, (methamphetamine). What happened to me at the Salvation Army that evening needed to happen. They're a great organization and I knew that I broke their rules. I deserved to be thrown out and I knew it.*" Ed jumped ahead in the timeline and mentioned meeting a man by the name of Mark Saxon, who works with the Salvation Army in Maui. Mark was a Desert Storm veteran who had himself been homeless before working with the Salvation Army in Hawaii. Ed added, "*Mark's a pastor and he's a great guy. I like the Salvation Army and even applied to work with them, although I didn't get the job.*" Ed was clearly not bitter about getting bounced.

I asked Ed about his drug habit during that time. He replied, "*During that time, I wasn't actively searching for drugs, nor was I trying*

405

to avoid them. I was simply trying to make something work out with housing and wanted to get back on my feet." The following day, Ed awoke in the downtown parking lot. He headed back over to the Alpha Project to see if he might be able to get back in, after being bounced from the Salvation Army. They told him they could potentially find him a bed if he was willing to wait. Ed slept outside for three more nights until a spare mattress became available. Ed recalled purchasing food the previous afternoon with his EBT. He confessed that there had been times that he and others would trade EBT points and food to score some methamphetamine. When that was the case, he would make up for his lack of food by attending one of the church-sponsored meals, that our teams had grown accustomed to. Ed expressed his appreciation for the Government program that supplied his food, and speculated that the EBT program lowers crime rates. He reasoned that homeless individuals with full stomachs are less likely to rob others as a matter of survival.

After three nights on the streets, the Alpha Project told Ed that they had a spare bed. The staffer manning the front door, known as "Shorty," recognized Ed when he returned. The first thing he said was, *"You need to drop and give me 20 man!"* Without hesitation, Ed dropped and did 20 push-ups. Shorty added, *"You're welcome to return, but you better not disappoint me."* Ed promised to play by the rules as he walked past Shorty. Ed commented, *"I wouldn't mind working at Alpha Project one day."*

During the month of February 2015, when Ed returned to the Alpha Project, he frequented the San Diego Library to read about the latest bikes, cyclists and races. When Ed learned that Lance Armstrong used drugs to compete, he liked him all the more as a fellow bike enthusiast and chemical user. Ed mentioned using the Neil Good Day Center that was connected to the Alpha Project. He recalled one of the men working at the front gate saying, *"Hey Ed, there was a guy who came by here looking for you this week."* Ed wondered if the man was referring to either Mason or me. In fact, I made my first trip searching for Ed between February 9 – 13, 2015. I visited the Neil Good Day Center downtown during that week, so that man was referring to me. We must have missed each other by a matter of days.

Since the Alpha Project was scheduled to close for the spring at the end of February, they reassigned people to shelters in the surrounding area. Ed was relocated to a shelter in Carlsbad, California, 35 miles north of downtown San Diego. The name of the Catholic run shelter was "La Posada de Guadalupe." Ed mentioned seeing Deborah Szekely's name on one of the walls, commemorating significant financial contributors toward that particular shelter. Ed had done some work for her when he ran his business, refinishing furniture in her home. He spoke fondly of the shelter and the staff there, and specifically mentioned an older black gentleman by the name of Charles, although Ed referred to him as Chuck. Ed said that he and Chuck became fast friends, during the approximate three months that he lived there.

In late February, before the Alpha Project closed its doors for the season, Ed made a special connection. He was walking toward the hotels of Harbor Drive to do some hot- tubbing, when he noticed a large sailing yacht. What caught his eye was the group of men working hard refinishing the deck. Since that had been Ed's area of expertise, he made a comment to them concerning their work.

A man by the name of Daniel, from South Africa, asked, "*Do you know something about refinishing wood?*" Ed responded, "*Yes, I do.*" Daniel asked him some technical questions about the job. Ed's response clearly demonstrated his knowledge. Daniel was impressed and turned to the captain and asked, "*Hey captain, what do you think about hiring this guy?*" As a result, Ed was offered a job on the spot, which he willingly accepted. That decision meant that Ed had to catch the early train to downtown San Diego from Carlsbad, five days a week.

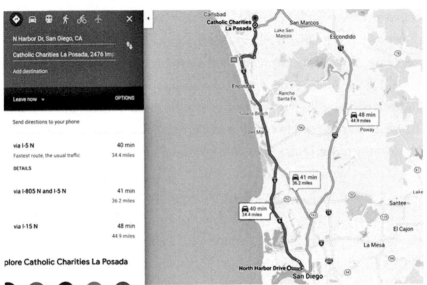

(Ed's 35-mile commute to work in San Diego)
Courtesy Google Maps

The 185-foot topsail schooner was built in 2010. The captain of the ship was a man by the name of Jim Thom. Jim was an experienced captain from England with his wife and two children as passengers on board. In addition to Daniel, a third key crew member was Para from Spain. Ed was taken with the beauty of the ship and began working the following week. He adapted quickly to his new daily 35-mile commute via train. He did confess boarding the rail twice each day without paying the fare, and boasted, *"They only caught me once, although I rode for free during the three months that I worked onboard the yacht."*

Ed recalled feeling an immediate affinity with Daniel. Their friendship gave Ed a level of comfort with his new boss, which led him to share openly about his road to the streets and battle with methamphetamine. Without judgement, Ed was accepted onboard. Once Daniel and Captain Thom recognized his level of skill refinishing wood, they began to consult Ed, asking his opinion on different projects below deck. Ed helped refinish wood throughout the entire vessel. He even painted the ship's anchor. Ed took a great deal of pride working on such a magnificent schooner.

(The 2010 Atlantic, 185-foot Schooner)

Ed recalled a certain man who worked on the ship, who didn't care for him. He often challenged Ed's work, as well as his advice. The antagonist appeared to be jealous after Ed won the captain and first mate over with his skill set. While that man didn't like Ed, he hired a friend by the name of Eric, who did. Ed remembered a kind woman who worked below deck and cooked for the entire crew. He said, "*I wanted to thank her for cooking for me while I worked onboard for those three months, so I purchased her a box of chocolates with my EBT. I did that the day before I left for Maui.*" Ed added, "*I believe I saw her a couple of years later in Maui at a grocery store. She noticed me and took my photo, although that may have been the drugs messing with my mind.*"

When Ed first began working onboard the Atlantic, he heard them playing the song "Totally Wired" by The Fall. He didn't believe in coincidence and saw that as a sign. He reasoned, "*They liked the same music as me and I wrestled with getting wired on meth, so their meeting that day had not happened by accident.*" Ed stopped and asked, "*Do you think the Lord opened that door of opportunity for me, even though I was battling drugs?*" Before I could respond he answered his own question, "*I do!*" He mentioned having to make the long commute at the end of each long day. Ed would make his way to the train station, sneak on board the train, and travel north back to Carlsbad.

Ed said, "*I made a friend at the shelter in Carlsbad, by the name of Enrique. He was a nice guy from Mexico and we got along well.*" He added, "*In addition to Enrique and Chuck, I enjoyed the social aspect of my connections at La Posada de Guadalupe.*"

(Courtyard of La Posada de Guadalupe Shelter)

Ed recalled one particular evening when he arrived at the shelter with the smell of alcohol on his breath. While he didn't drink as much as the night when he returned to the shelter at Salvation Army, he had polished off more than one beer. The guard standing watch on that particular night wanted to have Ed ejected from the shelter. He made Ed wait by the door while he located an older gentleman who was in charge. When that man arrived at the door and heard the accusation against Ed, he shocked Ed by what he said to the security guard. "*You know what we are going to do about this? Absolutely nothing. We're going to allow him grace and welcome him back in for another chance.*" With that said, the older man opened the door and allowed Ed to shuffle past and make his way to his bedroom. Ed became emotional when recounting that specific incident.

For approximately three months, Ed worked hard refinishing wood, staining the upper deck, painting and doing other odds and ends on board the Atlantic. He realized that the massive yacht was due to set sail for Alaska in late May, which left him with a choice to make. Ed had enjoyed working on the ship and hatched a plan to do similar work elsewhere. He heard from a local captain that there was a bustling seaport in Oahu, Hawaii, so he decided to head in that direction.

He'd been saving money while working on the Atlantic, and ventured out to the airport via train with his friend Chuck from the Guadalupe shelter. Ed spoke with a woman at the American Airlines counter concerning his ticket options. For some reason, a ticket to Oahu at that time was approximately $1,500. While Ed stood at the counter contemplating such a high cost, the employee from American said, "*I can get you a one-way ticket to Maui for $200 if you leave next week.*" Ed liked that price much better and made the purchase. He commented that his friend Chuck became very sad after Ed actually purchased his ticket. Perhaps he thought that Ed might change his mind and not actually go through with it. The feeling was much more somber on the train ride back to Carlsbad after Ed made the purchase. The two men enjoyed dinner together that evening, knowing that Ed had a week left before his departure.

(Chuck from the La Posada de Guadalupe Shelter)

As Ed mentioned to Sandra and me when we saw him on trip seven, he confessed, "*I thought the state of Hawaii was just one big island. I figured I could take a bus from Maui to Honolulu. I guess I should have paid closer attention in Geography class back in high school.*" He was in for a geographical revelation when he arrived to Maui the following week. In the meantime, Ed had one final week left to finish work on board the Atlantic and say goodbye to his friends.

Captain Jim Thom was not the type of man to joke around. He once commented to Ed that if all of the ropes hanging from the three large masts and sails were laid out flat, they would measure approximately seven miles in length. Attempting to joke with the captain, Ed said, "*I suppose all those ropes are unnecessary if the ship sinks on your way to Alaska.*" Captain Jim got very serious and said, "*We never joke about a ship sinking, it's not a laughing matter.*" Ed realized he'd crossed a line and apologized.

Ed mentioned a friend he'd made on board by the name of Louie. Louie had served as a deckhand for many years and apparently neglected his dental hygiene. As a result, he had to make numerous appointments to address the decay while they were in port. Ed commented, "*The crystal meth had done its share of damage on my own mouth, so I was careful never to joke with Louie about his poor oral hygiene. I was interested when I saw the difference it made, and was jealous, wanting to have my clean smile back.*"

Another aspect of the crew on the Atlantic that stood out to Ed was the sheer talent that each man possessed. He was impressed by the fact that every crew member could tie any knot, sew the sails, repair mechanical breaks and be ready to trim the sails to brace for a storm. He realized his time working on board was coming to a close and it was an emotional time for him as they prepared to depart for Alaska. His own flight was scheduled to fly to Maui approximately one week before their departure, so the timing was perfect. He had been enjoying his new friendships and weekly routine, as he managed life between the shelter in Carlsbad and work on board the Atlantic. The life that had begun to feel comfortable and familiar over those three months was about to come to a screeching halt.

Ed mentioned grieving his departure from the shelter in Carlsbad and spent extra time with his friend Chuck, when he could. Chuck gave Ed a nice wooden box as a gift. Ed recalled another habit that he'd developed over the course of those three months. He mentioned exploring the large library in downtown San Diego. His favorite subject in the periodicals was cycling. He'd been following the Tour of Spain (The Volta), also known as "*La Volta a Catalunya.*" He enjoyed collecting newspaper articles and notes about the races, which he kept in the box that Chuck had given him. Ed's favorite cyclist was a man by the name of Alberto Contador, known as "El Pistolero" (The Pistol). Ed commented that his shipmate Para, was from Spain. Para was also a fan of El Pistolero, so the two enjoyed discussing the races. When Ed was saying his goodbyes later that week, he gave the box full of cycling articles to Para. While he appreciated the gift box from Chuck, he chose to pass it on so he could travel light to Maui.

Ed reconnected with an old friend by the name of Judy Hartley. They had become friends in San Diego before Ed took to the streets and he wanted to let her know that he would soon be gone. Judy is actually the daughter of the famous producer of the Carol Burnett show, Joe Hamilton. Before Joe married Carol, he was married to a woman by the name of Gloria Hartley. Judy is the youngest of their eight children and a step-daughter of Carol Burnett. Ed said that he'd been introduced to Judy by a mutual friend many years earlier. He and Judy used to frequent a pub with a pool hall and seemed to get along well. Their relationship was strictly platonic, and it was clear that Ed valued their friendship. Ed recalled having dinner with his friend Judy the evening before his departure. She even drove him to the airport the next day, to see him off.

Ed purchased a canvas backpack from the Army-Navy Surplus Store to stuff all of his earthly belongings into. He went to pay his respects to the crew of the Atlantic just before departing. His close friend Daniel from South Africa took one final stroll with Ed on the deck of that magnificent schooner. He became very serious as he addressed Ed, saying, "*Whatever you do, don't screw up your life on meth. If you're not careful, it'll kill you.*" Ed grew very emotional when retelling me that part of his story. He commented, "*Daniel truly liked me and he believed in me. Can you believe that? That guy meant so much to me.*" It was a heartfelt farewell between Ed and the crew, but it was time to press on.

Judy got Ed to the San Diego International Airport on time for his flight and he was Maui-bound. He departed the San Diego area around late May or early June of 2015. With that said, we missed him entirely on trips two – six. Anyone who told us that they'd seen him, was sadly mistaken. We did run into a number of men who looked similar to Ed and even met a few who shared the same first name. I'd like to give those people the benefit of the doubt, and believe we experienced a lot of mistaken identity.

Meanwhile, Ed arrived in Maui with no plan of action and nobody to pick him up from the airport. Although he'd saved up a decent amount of cash working on board the Atlantic, he wasn't sure how to spend it. Ed recalled walking out of the Maui airport and making his way to the Queen Kaahumanu Center to catch a local bus. Unsure of where he was headed and not seeing the city of Honolulu listed as an option, Ed's eyes were drawn to a town called Lahaina on the west side of the Island. He recalled, "*I had no clue where to go, but I always enjoyed the Lahaina Beach House Bar on the boardwalk in Pacific Beach, so Lahaina, Maui was my choice.*" With that sense of logic, Ed purchased a one-way bus ticket and headed toward Lahaina.

He spent his first couple of weeks staying at a hostel in Lahaina. He met a guy by the name of Chris Trovolone, who was a local. Ed rented a room from a woman by the name of Sherry, and liked the atmosphere in Lahaina. He became friends with Sherry's son J.J., who referred to himself as "*the King of the West Side.*" J.J. was not into the drug scene, but enjoyed his fair share of vodka. Chris was a fellow drug user and left one of his hypodermic needles in the back of J.J.'s car. When J.J.'s mother Sherry found the needle and accused her son, J.J. told her that it was Chris' bag, not his. In turn, Chris blamed Ed and told her that Ed had left the needle in his bag. Ed had begun doing odd jobs for Sherry on the multiple hostels that she managed, and the accusation didn't help foster trust.

Ed realized that he was blowing through his savings way too fast at the hostel, and was interested in finding some lower cost housing. There were two homeless shelters in Maui, one in Kahului near the airport and the nicer one in Lahaina. Ed attempted to secure a room at the shelter in Lahaina and applied for more permanent housing. He discovered that it may take approximately six months before he could get admitted into their general housing program, so he tried to get settled in the local shelter.

Ed became friends with another man by the name of Daniel. He referred to Daniel as *"a speed freak from Portland Oregon."* Daniel had jumped bail and flown to Maui to avoid the pending charges in Oregon. He asked Ed, *"Can you get clean?"* He added, *"If we want to get admitted into the shelter, we have to pass their drug test."* Ed mentioned purchasing what he referred to as a "piss cleaner." Unfamiliar with the term, I asked Ed what a piss cleaner was. He replied, *"A piss cleaner is fake urine and you pour it into the cup when someone administers a drug test. The synthetic urine can be purchased at a head or smoke shop. With a drug habit, it's important to learn different techniques to beat the system."* Apparently, Daniel passed his test and was accepted into the shelter. However, he got tossed out soon after, when he failed a random drug test one evening as he entered the shelter.

Ed got to know the man who ran the shelter in Lahaina. His name was Wayne and he liked Ed. Ed confessed being very nervous about taking the test with Wayne and mentioned strapping the bag of synthetic urine to his leg. I asked if that was to hide it and he replied, *"Yes, but it's was also to make sure that the piss cleaner warmed up to my body temperature, since handing over a cup of cool urine is a dead giveaway."* Ed recalled that when Wayne gave him the test to take, he stood just a few feet behind him and waited. That required some careful deception on Ed's part, but he managed to pull it off without getting caught.

Once he handed the cup to Wayne, Ed watched as the caretaker dipped the chemical tester into the cup and stared at Ed's face. He felt like it was a poker game, as the man looked intently at Ed, attempting to read his reaction. As Wayne did his best to evaluate Ed's expression, he tried to discern if he was lying. Apparently, Ed passed the test and when Daniel got bounced, Ed was immediately assigned to a different room. He had to reside with a few strangers.

Ed used free cell phones to communicate while he was there. The homeless refer to the free smart phones as "Obama phones," credited to the president for passing the bill which gave them the phones during his time in office. He mentioned that someone stole his phone while he was living amongst the strangers in the room. He added that the Obama phones were loved by the homeless. One of the primary reasons his friends appreciated them was that they provided free access to pornography. Ed said, "*In addition to the access to pornography, many of the homeless use them to make drug deals.*" He was amazed that they were paid for with U.S. tax dollars. I'm fairly confident that the United States Government did not have drugs and pornography in mind when they passed the bill, providing homeless individuals with free cell phones.

Daniel told Ed that he knew who stole his phone and tried his best to get it back for him. Daniel and Ed shared a meth pipe, which he described as a glass pipe with little tiny hole on top. Ed said that you can purchase them from any head or smoke shop. The code word to request one is to ask for an "incense burner." Any employee working in a smoke shop will know that you're asking about a meth pipe. Even though Daniel got ejected from the shelter, the two remained close friends and got high together on a regular basis. Ed commented that their shared habit created a strong bond between the two of them. He added, "*Daniel wasn't a fan of using needles, but I had no problem with 'slamming,' the street term used for injecting drugs.*"

During Ed's first year in Lahaina, he'd moved from the hostel to the shelter, and was awaiting his acceptance in permanent housing. He recalled that after his roommate Daniel tested dirty, Daniel grew tired of running and hiding. He decided to return to Portland, Oregon to face the charges held against him there. Shortly after Daniel departed for Oregon, Ed was accepted into the permanent low income housing. In addition, Ed had been looking for some new ways to make money, and it was about that time that he met Leo.

Leo was a Tongan from the South Pacific. He invited Ed to join his weekly labor force that was responsible for raising enormous tents every Thursday. Working with Leo also included work on Sundays, when those same tents had to be disassembled. The tents served as a temporary roof for a craft fair, which showcased local wares to visiting tourists. Ed remembered that the labor-intensive work took approximately three or four men to raise a single tent in approximately three hours. It was tiring work.

In addition, laborers had to earn Leo's respect. Ed recalled a particular day when Leo told him to raise the center pole by himself. Ed struggled for quite a while as Leo berated him and told him that he was too weak to do the job. After countless unsuccessful attempts, Ed confessed that he was simply not strong enough. Leo mocked him for being too weak. When Ed sat down in defeat, he watched as Leo walked to each of the four corners of the tent, loosened the ties on each pole and then raised the center pole with ease. Leo had set Ed up with an impossible task, since no one can raise the center pole when the corner poles are strapped down tightly. Without loosening the straps, Leo knew it couldn't be done. Ed saw that as a test of character, after which time, Leo treated him kindly as part of the team.

Just as Ed had earned Leo's respect, Ed developed an equal amount of respect for Leo. He was from a Samoan Island and had previously spent time in prison. Ed commented that Leo was not a drug user. He remarked that Leo was a family man and his parents also lived on the island. Leo's father was a professional wood carver. Ed got emotional as he remembered a day when Leo accidently crushed his hand with a hammer, while raising a tent. Ed wanted to help Leo get to the hospital, but Leo barked at him, "*Ed get back to work and raise that tent!*" Ed did as he was told, but didn't like seeing Leo in pain.

Over time, the two became friends. Leo offered, "*My sister owns this tent business and it's difficult work. Would you like to work with my dad raising smaller street-side tents for his carving business?*" Ed knew that Leo's offer was an honor and an upgrade, so he accepted it with gratitude.

The following week, Ed began working with Leo's dad in Kaanapali. He got to know Leo's father well. He quickly learned the daily routine of setting up the small sidewalk tents, providing shade for the wood carvings and shoppers. Ed enjoyed chatting with Leo's dad. Ed recalled with a smirk, "*Leo's dad made predictions about potential buyers when he spotted a group of tourists headed in our direction from the cruise ships.*" Ed remembered, "Leo's dad would say something like, '*See that woman in the large floral hat?' She's going to buy a large wood sculpture today. And the man in the khakis with the sky-blue golf shirt, he's definitely going to make a purchase.*'" When the crowd reached the tents, Ed watched in amazement as the old artist transformed into a savvy salesman. "*Aloha, ma'm. Can I show you an authentic Hawaiian wood carving, found only on the Island of Maui...?*" Ed was taken with the sweet man's charm, as were many of the tourists. Leo's father demonstrated his talents as a gifted artist and likeable salesman, two traits that come in handy on an island like Maui.

After living in Lahaina for approximately seven months, Ed was approved for permanent housing. Daniel had just left for the mainland, when Ed met Lars. Lars was a smart young guy from Northern California, although he had family in Oahu. Lars was not a drug user. Instead, Ed commented that Lars was extremely interested in God. They built a friendship living in the same residence, and spent time discussing random topics such as Chinchillas being killed for their furs. Lars also had a Netflix account, so the two got hooked binge watching the series known as "Narcos." Narcos is a dramatized series about real life DEA agents chasing the notorious Colombian drug-lord, Pablo Escobar. In fact, one of the primary DEA agents that the series is based on (agent Steve Murphy), attended the same church as I did in northern Virginia. Ed remembered enjoying the show since it covered a different aspect of the drug scene that had been such a significant part of his life.

When the tourist season subsided and business was slow, Ed got a short-term job working at the annual Maui Invitational Basketball Tournament, held annually at the Lahaina Civic Center. While he worked each day at the Civic Center, he was also getting settled in at the permanent housing. There were two bedrooms in the house Ed had been assigned to. Lars was in one room and Ed was in another room with a different roommate. Ed said that the pressure associated with living in the house started to get to him. Some of the other residents Ed knew got evicted when random drug tests were administered. Ed began to fear getting caught during such a test, and hated the constant pressure. His drug habit had grown with his steady flow of income and he had no desire of giving it up. Rather than live with the looming fear of eviction, he decided to move to Paia. He'd been living in Lahaina for close to a year, and felt that it was time to move on. When I asked Ed his reason for choosing Paia, he responded, "*The girls were better looking there.*"

Ed commented, "*I decided one day that living in permanent housing was far too orthodox for me, so I informed the landlord that I was moving out.*" At that time, Ed owned a bicycle which he'd purchased on Craigslist. He used his friend Chris' Craigslist account to make the transaction. Chris was the same guy who had falsely accused Ed of leaving a needle in J.J.'s car. When Ed used his Craigslist account, Chris tried to extort some money from Ed for the use of his computer. Ed was ready to go. He packed up all of his earthly belongings and stuffed them into a single backpack. He mounted his bike and left for Paia in the summer of 2016.

Ed found a place in Paia referred to as "Middles." He purchased a tent, which became his home on a beach there. He said, "*I discovered*

Paia after I heard Lars mention it. He used to visit Paia when we lived in Lahaina. I was ready for a change with zero drug testing, and figured that Paia would be the place." Ed hadn't actually lived on the streets for quite some time. He had successfully managed to find shelters, hostels and low-income housing, since his mental breakdown in Robb Field Park back in the fall of 2014. He was ready to return to the freedom of the streets and embrace homelessness.

Ed mentioned that his transition to living alone, coupled with his increase in drug use, led to hearing more voices. The voices were similar to the ones that plagued him when he lived alone back in his woodshop in San Diego. He wasn't fully convinced that the voices he was hearing in his head were related to his methamphetamine habit. Ed commented, "*Some of those voices began to torment me.*"

Rather than blame the chemicals he was smoking, Ed came to believe that the voices in his head were related to a federally funded program which targeted homeless addicts. He mentioned that the frequency of voices he heard elevated when he was alone in his tent. When I inquired as to why he believed that they increased after he left the permanent residence, he replied, "*It's because I was living in a federally funded housing facility and those controlling the voices didn't want to get exposed.*" It's difficult to reason with an addict who believes that the CIA is behind every strange idea that enters their brain.

Ed mentioned that he didn't move to Paia quite as abruptly as conveyed. He spent a few months in between his time in Lahaina and Paia, living in the Kahului area. Kahului is a little more populated with locals than Paia. Ed got connected at the Family Life Center in Kahului and spoke fondly of a man there by the name of Pastor Dan. Ed described Pastor Dan as a kind, long-haired man, who drove a classic VW bus and cared for the homeless community. He recalled a particular day when he opened up with Dan and shared his personal story. Ed turned to me and asked, "*Do you know what Pastor Dan did when I finished sharing?*" I replied, "*No Ed, what did he do?*" He responded as he was visibly moved by the memory, "*He wept. Can you believe that?*"

Then Ed exclaimed with deep emotion, *"He actually cared about me."* Ed teared up and took a break from sharing his story.

Recalling those who had cared for him in Maui, Ed also mentioned a kind Salvation Army worker by the name of Mark Saxon. He had commented earlier about his appreciation of Mark when he shared the story of getting bounced for drinking at the Salvation Army shelter in downtown San Diego. Ed was trying to convey that people were very kind to him throughout his journey living on the streets. He added, *"One day I hope to give back and help others the way that they helped me."* I looked straight at Ed and commented, *"I believe you will my friend. God didn't rescue you from your situation for no reason."*

When Sandra and I went to Maui looking for Ed in August of 2017, we had received a tip that Ed had been seen hanging around the Family Life Center and Salvation Army in Kahului. That is actually where we searched in addition to the bike shops. Apparently, we were not far off. Although by the time we showed up, Ed was primarily residing in a tent back in Paia.

When I asked Ed his reason for finally making the move from Kahului to Paia, he mentioned getting numerous flat tires in downtown Kahului. There was a type of local thorn that wreaked havoc on his bike tires and he couldn't afford to keep purchasing new ones. Ed mentioned pushing his bike into Pastor Dan's church parking lot one afternoon with another flat tire. He recalled meeting a very kind man who was exiting the church building as Ed arrived. The man asked Ed what he needed and Ed replied, *"I have a flat tire."* Once again, Ed was moved with emotion recalling the memory of yet one more person who showed him kindness. He said, *"That guy took me to a bike shop and purchased me a new inner tube and a wrench that I needed to change the tire. He even let me keep the wrench. I'm so thankful for people like that guy who showed me kindness when I was struggling! I'm ready to give back the way that they gave to me."*

(The Family Life Center in Kahului)

Part of Ed's experience in Maui allowed him to meet a number of the local natives of the island. On another day when Ed was frustrated by the thorns piercing his tires, a local native shared a common belief about the origin of the thorns. He said, "*We believe that the white settlers originally planted the thorn bushes on our island to prevent native Hawaiians from living in the bush.*" Ed mentioned a few other locals who spoke with pride about their history. They commented in particular about the execution of British explorer Captain James Cooke, who made three trips to the Hawaiian Islands.

History teaches that the Hawaiians believed Captain Cooke had exploited their people. In response, his third return was met with opposition. The Hawaiian natives killed him on February 14, 1779. That sentiment seemed to carry over to white settlers and has perpetuated over the years. Although James Cooke was their primary example regarding how the natives felt about non-islanders, there are still some natives that have difficulty with settlers from the mainland. Ed believed that he'd earned the respect of the locals, the same way that he'd done with Leo.

Ed mentioned living in a tent for the remainder of his time on the island. Estimating that Ed left Lahaina in the spring of 2016, and spent a couple of months in Kahului, he would have landed in Paia around August of 2016. During his months in Kahului, Ed camped near the library, but when he moved to Paia, he began by camping on the beach. While Ed said that he trusted the island natives whom he'd befriended in Lahaina and Kahului, the beach population was made up of mainland homeless people. Ed mentioned being robbed on several occasions. It's difficult to lock a tent. He had bikes, clothes, food and other belongings stolen by other people living on the beach. He mentioned returning on one occasion to discover that his entire tent had been stolen.

Homeless people don't carry homeowner's insurance. When you lose your things or have them stolen, it's final. Learning where to camp, where to hide your things and who to trust, is important for survival on the streets. Our teams learned that same lesson on our numerous trips to San Diego. Developing street smarts is critical.

After numerous altercations and theft, Ed decided to move his campsite up Baldwin Avenue. Most homeless people don't wander up that steep road. Ed resided in that same location during the three summers that we visited Maui searching for him. As a way of making some money, Ed landed a job shortly after meeting some people in Paia. His first job in town was working as a dishwasher at the Flatbread Company. There was a manager at Flatbreads by the name of Nick who gave Ed a job.

While Nick was responsible for hiring him, Ed reported to A.J., his supervisor. Ed wasn't sure he'd last long working there. He said, "*I was the only white guy working in that kitchen, all of the other dishwashers were Hawaiian nationals. After getting to know them, we all got along well.*" Nick understood that Ed was homeless and generously offered him food on several occasions. Donnie's wife also worked at Flatbreads on a part-time basis. The restaurant was situated just around the corner from Maui Cyclery.

Ed got acquainted with Donnie when he relocated to Paia in 2016. Donnie remembered meeting Ed in San Diego at a time when Ed was doing some competitive cycling. They welcomed Ed warmly at Donnie's bike shop and gave him some part-time work. Ed was paid $5 per bike to wash them after renters returned them.

Ed developed a rhythm of life that he enjoyed on the island. Although his internal voices that haunted him were growing worse, he continued his meth habit. Ed's struggle to manage the voices led to his quitting his job at Flatbreads. He said, *"I just couldn't keep it together."* Donnie had patience with Ed, and when he got out of sorts, Donnie would tell Ed to take a break. There were times when Donnie would say, *"Ed, I need you to take a walk. You're spooking my customers."*

Ed mentioned one particular day when he woke feeling tormented by the voices. He recalled biking into Kahului from Paia to steal some alcohol from the Food Lion grocery store. On his way back to Paia, he got a flat tire. Ed chained his bike to a tree and began to walk back toward Paia. He continued drinking heavily, hoping that the alcohol and drug mixture might silence the voices that were plaguing him. He said that he drank enough booze that he blacked out for a good portion of the day.

Ed felt that he was losing his mind and began challenging cars in the middle of the road. He jumped in front of a few cars traveling around 40 miles per hour, daring them to hit him. Ed commented, *"I knew that if one struck me head on, it would silence the voices."* It was that very day that a social worker by the name of Ruth just happened to be behind the wheel of one of those cars. As a social worker, she knew that something was seriously wrong, so she pulled over to try and talk some sense into Ed. He screamed at her, so she headed back to her car.

She witnessed Ed jump in front of another oncoming car and when the vehicle hit the brakes, Ed began pounding on their hood. His anger was out of control, as was his obvious disregard for his life. Ruth called the cops and they showed up a short time later. Meanwhile, Ruth kept a close eye on Ed to provide the police with a detailed report. Her desire was to help him.

That situation took place in June of 2017, approximately two months before Sandra and I traveled to Maui. The police officers took

Ed to a local hospital, although they gave Ed's information to Ruth, in the event that she wanted to follow up. She did some research online, which is when she discovered the ABC News San Diego story about my search for Ed. She found a Google phone number that I had posted and called me. She wanted to make me aware of Ed's presence in Maui. She told me that she'd seen Ed at a local bike shop before, which helped Sandra and me target our search efforts on the island. She also mentioned the Family Life Center in Kahului.

Meanwhile, the police officers took Ed to the hospital in Maui. Ed remembered waking up in his hospital room and attempting to recall everything that had happened. He was missing one shoe and his shirt was torn. He tried to recall where exactly he had locked up his bike the previous day. Someone from the mental health department asked Ed a myriad of questions, trying to understand his break from reality. He did his best to answer their questions and tried to piece fragments of the previous day back together. Someone from the hospital drove him back to his tent on Baldwin Avenue. He found his bike the following day, chained up where he left it.

As Ed shared with me, I realized that this wasn't an isolated occurrence. During my second trip to Maui in the summer of 2018, Eric and I showed a photo of Ed to our waitress and asked if she'd seen him. She commented, "*Yeah, I saw that guy a week ago. He was riding his bike and challenged our car. He rode his bike straight at us and if we hadn't veered out of the way, we would have killed him.*" She commented, "*That guy has a death wish, he looked like he wanted us to hit him.*" I told Ed about our conversation with the waitress and he confessed, "*I've been battling those mental voices on and off during the entire three years that I've lived on my own. Although, they actually began back in the spring of 2014, when I was living alone in my shop on Hancock.*" That's about the time that Ed stopped returning my phone calls.

I asked Ed if he thought the voices were getting worse over the course of the past year, and he replied, "*Yes.*" Ed said, "*There's an internal war waging within my head. It feels as though my mind is the battleground where thoughts of good versus evil compete and challenge my life."* I asked Ed, *"In addition to challenging cars, have you attempted to take your life on other occasions?"* He replied, *"For sure! The first time I made an attempt was during the summer just before my mom came to San Diego and I was evicted. I'd been battling the same voices and grew exhausted. I took a long metal chain that I had in my shop, connected it to a dog collar and strapped the collar around my neck. Then I walked over to the railway bridge not far from my shop. I climbed the bridge to take my life. I attached the chain to the bridge and was just about to jump when a man came walking up the trail below with his dog. I didn't want to traumatize the guy so I returned to my shop."*

Ed went on to mention one more occasion that took place in late April of 2020, about two months before his bike accident in Paia. Ed told me that he climbed a Banyan tree located in the woods not far from his campsite on Baldwin Avenue. He was growing tired of the voices in his mind, which had become extremely negative. Ed hated the fact that they were constantly up and then down and wanted to put an end to them, once and for all. He tied a hangman's noose on the end of a length of rope and cinched it around his neck. Ed tied the other end of rope to the branch that he was seated on. He sat perched on the edge of the branch trying to muster up the where-with-all to jump.

Ed confessed, *"I figure that I was up on that branch for at least two hours. I was contemplating suicide and heard one voice that kept telling me to take the leap. At the same time, I heard another voice encouraging me not to jump. When I climbed back down a couple of hours later, the one voice accused me of being a coward for climbing down."*

It was difficult listening to my friend recount those stories. I wanted to cry and said, *"Ed, you're not a coward! You did the courageous thing by climbing down and facing life, rather than ending it."* I added, *"You need to learn which voices to listen to, the good versus the evil. Any voice that tells you to take your life is obviously evil, and you listened to the right voice in both scenarios. I thank God you listened to that voice and I believe that the hundreds of people who have been praying for you over* the past six years are able to see an answer to their prayers. It's a miracle that you're home with us, alive and well!" Ed replied, "I think you're right. I was curious when I woke in the hospital in Oahu after my bike accident. I wondered what was going on and why I'd been moved from one island to another. I suppose God spared my life more than once."

I agreed with Ed and believe that it's a miracle that he's back home, able to function in his right mind. I called Donnie about three weeks after Ed's return and asked, "What was the longest period of time you ever saw Ed acting completely normal during the last three years, while he lived in Paia?" Donnie replied, "There was a time when Ed had another bad bike accident. My wife and I helped him out and he was very appreciative. He acted completely normal for about eight hours." Then I asked, "So the fact that Ed is acting normal around all of us for three weeks is a big deal?" Donnie answered, "It's a miracle!" And I truly believe it!

I asked Ed what he thought about his situation and the circumstances leading to his return. He responded, "God definitely has something to do with this and with my story." Then I asked, "Do you think you'll be able to stay off meth and get involved helping others, as you've wanted to do for years?" Ed replied, "Oh, no doubt, for sure!" If God was willing to intervene and help us locate Ed, bring him home and clear up his mind, He can certainly complete Ed's restoration and help him realize his dreams! God is a miracle worker and my best friend Ed is a perfect example of that fact.

There is no human on the planet worth giving up on. I'm convinced that a good shepherd is always willing to go after the lost ones, even if the search puts us in harm's way. Individuals are worth the risk! At least God believes that. Do we?

Chapter 27

99 for What?

This journey began for me in October of 2014, when Ed first went missing. I had no clue about the twists, turns and tumbles that would be associated with my decision to embark on this adventure. All I knew was that my friend was missing and that if it had been me, I'd want someone to go searching. How would you feel if it had been you on the streets? I didn't stop to consider the potential danger or cost of the decision. I simply felt that it was the right thing to do. I was inspired by the way that Jesus cared for overlooked outcasts of his day, and I wanted to live life in a similar fashion. When Jesus was questioned about his decision to associate with the rabble, he had no problem defending either his choice or the people who the religious leaders judged harshly.

The concept of leaving comfort to search for another in harm's way resonated within me, when reading Luke chapter 15. Of course, I imagined that the one lost sheep was my friend Ed, and I had no idea there'd be more sheep I'd meet along the way. Life has a funny way of offering surprises when we're willing to take risks on another person's behalf. There was no guarantee that we'd ever locate Ed or that he would want to change after we found him. I'm convinced that the best things in life come when we remain persistent. It's imperative that we don't throw in the towel and quit, especially when circumstances don't move in the direction we desire. We can be equally tempted to give up when our desired results aren't realized in the time frame that we expect them to happen. Life is messy and negative circumstances shouldn't be allowed to undermine a decision made to help another individual.

I have no idea, even today, if my friend Ed will remain drug-free, nor can I control him. However, I can love Ed and support him on his journey. If Ed falls off the wagon and uses methamphetamine again, it wouldn't disqualify the journey and the investment that we've made in his life. Imagine only investing in people with whom you can guarantee a positive outcome. There are no humans like that. Every human, including you and me, is capable of making good and bad choices at any stage in our life. Demonstrating belief in another person whom others have given up on, is a powerful thing to do and worthy of the risk on our behalf. I'm not sure if you caught it in chapter 26, but every single time Ed conveyed the stories of individuals who believed in him, he got emotional. The power of believing in any individual whom others have given up on can serve as a catalyst for their change.

While I left the safety of the "99" for the "1" whom I imagined Ed to be, I never imagined all the others. My life is so much richer knowing Paul, JD, Donnie, Father Joe Coffey, Kyle, Candace, Tom and countless others. That list only scratches the surface of those I met on our trips out west. In addition to those relationships, I've been blessed beyond words by the sacrificial men and women who've been willing to camp on the streets, walk miles, go without food and risk harm to join me on this epic journey. I'm so incredibly grateful for Steve, Eric, Georgia, Brian, Sandra, AG, Maria, Kara, Laki, Peter, Betsy, and approximately 30 others who were willing to advance to the front lines and live in the trenches with me. I wouldn't trade a single trip, nor do I plan to stop going. I look forward to a day when Ed is well enough to join me on a street trip to help others.

Somewhere along the way, my original journey of 99 for "1," became 99 for "more." As one woman on Facebook remarked during our first homeless venture, *"Everyone you meet is another person's Ed."* That was tremendous advice which has served us well during this journey. A significant fork in the road was when we decided to return to San Diego after realizing that Ed was in Maui. Our choice to continue loving others on the streets of California, grew our hearts and took the mission in a much wider direction. I could've never imagined heading back to San Diego if I'd known Ed wasn't there; however, God expanded my heart for those whom I met on the streets while I was there.

While I learned a great deal about relationships and perseverance over the past six years since this began, the importance of "presence" was also an important factor. In other words, what would it have meant if my search had been limited to phone and online research? How about if I had paid a private investigator? In my opinion, there's no substitute for your presence with another person. Many hardworking parents wrestle with a balance of putting in long hours to provide for their families, and actually being with their children. There are parents, who have such limited time with their kids, that they seek to make up for the lack of presence by providing generous gifts and large homes. In the end, what do the presents mean if there is no personal presence? I'm not trying to drop a guilt trip on anyone. However, quality time and personal presence makes all the difference when communicating that we care.

In the same way that crazy Ted challenged me to live on the streets as a way of finding Ed, he was challenging me to do something radical as a manner of understanding the world that my friend was living in. There's no teacher like experience. Perhaps you've seen the TV program "Undercover Boss." While the show features managers and company owners who go undercover to find out how their employees are actually functioning behind the scenes, there's always a second revelation that takes place. At some point during the high-level manager's hours working as a grunt level worker incognito, they usually see through the eyes of their employees, who have been neglected. That eye-opening revelation often makes a significant impact between a company CEO and their employees. Ted's challenge to me certainly provided an education about the homeless, in addition to what it meant to care for them. The principle of being with people on their level and walking a few miles in their shoes is important in families, businesses and certainly when it comes to friendship.

As a parent, leader, pastor and president of a non-profit, I never want to ask someone to do something that I'm unwilling to do myself. I felt that Ted's challenge to live on the streets was for me, foundational to the entire journey. After I experienced my first week on the streets with Steve and Brian, I invited others. No one respects a military leader who sends his troops into battle, if he himself has no battle scars and prior experience in the field. I believe that my leadership in the field mattered, especially when others showed an interest in joining me.

Once I had a few trips under my belt, an odd thing began to occur. Someone would contact me and say something along these lines of, "*I met a homeless person the other day in Washington, DC. Would you mind if I gave them your phone number since you're the homeless guy?*" In a similar fashion, when my wife Sandra and I began working with local Muslims from Ghana, I'd receive calls from time to time saying, "*I met a local Muslim from Africa and I heard you and your wife have them over to your home for dinner, would you mind inviting them?*" On both counts I would have the same answer, "*If you met them, then you should invite them to your home for a meal.*" Wouldn't it be nice if we could simply delegate certain relationships that make us uncomfortable to others who are more familiar with that particular type of person? Of course, it would be easier, but it wouldn't be right.

If your child was lost on the streets, could you imagine asking someone else to search in your stead? If you were young enough and physically able, wouldn't you want to go? I believe that when Jesus commanded his followers to love God and love others the way that every human wants to be loved, he actually meant it. The mandate to love others as we would want to be cared for if the roles were reversed isn't a responsibility that we were meant to pawn off on another person. We grow in faith and character when we learn to love people who aren't like us, who don't think like us, who don't believe as we believe. We can't delegate love.

I believe that this journey has stretched me throughout every step of the process. The first area of growth required me to love Ed enough to risk my own health and well-being to go after him. I imagine that step as leaving the safety of the 99 for the 1. The second phase of this process, which facilitated growth was deciding to love people beyond my friend Ed. Making the decision to return to the streets of San Diego and care for people other than Ed, expanded the original vision from "one," to "more." While we searched for the "one," we grew to love the other individuals whom we met in the process. That added dynamic turned out to be a tremendous benefit, not a burden. Anyone can love their childhood friend, but loving a stranger on the streets takes something quite different. I needed to be pushed to that step, and in hindsight, I'm grateful that I was.

Lastly, I refer to the final stage on the learning curve which occurred over the course of those years as "99 for life." What I mean by that is the way we learned to treat people on the streets shouldn't be relegated exclusively to the streets. Nor should it be limited to two weekly trips in a given year. It was the same principle of applying the golden rule to Ed that I applied to my immigrant friends from Ghana. I simply asked the same question, "*If the roles were reversed, how would I want to be loved?*" While the answer to that question will vary, the question and principle remain the same.

When it came to Ed, I reasoned that I wouldn't ever want to be forgotten. When I put myself in his shoes, I knew that I'd want someone to look for me, so I did. When I asked how I might want to be treated if I were working in a foreign country, separated from my family, I had a different answer. I thought, "*If I were alone in a foreign country, I would want to be included by others and invited over.*" That line of thinking led to our Ghana nights and dinners with our new friends from our local grocery and do-it-yourself stores. My life is richer as a result of those relationships on both counts.

Another aspect of taking on the "99 for life" way of living, requires us to maintain that perspective, as we go about our daily routines. It should be organic. I mean that one doesn't need to travel to a distant land to live life on mission. If the mission includes loving God and loving others, we can make that part of our everyday lifestyle and character regardless of where we are.

I have a few friends who are atheists and they tell me that they prefer to implement the exercise of loving others, but skip the first command of loving God. How an individual chooses to love and who they choose to love is up to that individual. For me on a personal level, I find my inspiration to love others in the way that I believe God loves me sacrificially and without condition. I know that I have plenty of flaws and am far from perfect, and yet God still loves me, mistakes and all. Far be it from me to put limits and restrictions on who I love based on the mistakes of their past or their present.

I'm not sure about you, but I'm motivated to change when people around me know my raw life shortcomings, and yet they still believe in me. If we had embarked on this mission with restrictions concerning who we would love and serve based on their choices, the quest for Ed would have stopped when we discovered that he was an addict. The news saddened my heart, yet we never relented from our pursuit. If I love others the way that I want to be loved, then I would not want them to give up on me when they discover my faults.

Consequently, that's precisely how the Living God loves you and me. Jesus demonstrated that fact throughout his life, but one example compelled me on this journey. I was inspired by the way he went to bat for the rabble and outcasts that he was hanging out with in Luke chapter 15, verse one. I want to be more like that, even if the religious leaders or others judge me for the company that I keep. If that's the way that Jesus loved, then I can learn from his example.

As I write this final chapter, I've been planning a mission trip with Ed to work with orphans in Peru. When I asked Ed about his future hopes and dreams, he responded, "*I want to help others who are in trouble, the way that God put people on my path to assist me.*" He acknowledged many people who he met throughout his struggle, as sent by God to guide and protect him. He added, "*Will, I believe that I never went through with my suicide attempts because God was protecting me and He heard everyone's prayers.*" He's grateful to be alive and well, and expresses his desire daily to remain drug-free.

When I asked Ed how long he plans to serve in Peru, he replied, "*As long as they will allow me to stay.*" I let him know that a person without a visa can stay for three months at the orphanage. Ed added, "*Then three months it is!*" I was nervous about his answer, wondering who could stay with Ed to serve for three months. After praying about it, I decided to ask Paul Arnold what he thought of Ed's request. Paul spent some time thinking and praying about the idea and called me back the following day. He said, "*After praying about Ed and Peru, I've decided that I want to go and serve alongside him for the three months.*" We are planning to start that trip in late January of 2021, if the borders are open to the USA and COVID-19 restrictions lifted. Imagine that, our two homeless friends from San Diego and Maui, serving orphans side-by-side in Peru. It's incredible!

(Left to right: Paul Arnold & Ed Pelzner)

Just as Ed was closing in on 100 days of sobriety from drugs, he asked me an unexpected question. "*Hey Will, would you mind if I got a matching tattoo to the '99 for 1' that you have on your right arm?*" He reasoned, "*It makes sense, since I'm the '1' that you went searching for.*" I responded, "*I wouldn't mind at all Ed, in fact I'd be flattered.*" And so, we located a local tattoo artist, and Ed added to his ink.

The vision to value those who are lost, leaving comfort to search for them, is always a worthy cause. I see that reminder daily on my right arm. Realizing that I'll probably encounter a person who feels lost and in need of love on any given day, I consider it a privilege when I find those opportunities within my normal life routine. "99 for Life" entails that I consider what it means to love those on my path in the way that I'd want to be loved if I were in their place. Now Ed has the same daily reminder on his arm. What if we all lived that way, without the tattoo as a reminder? We can't make the world or government leaders mandate such an exercise, nor can we delegate that responsibility. However, we can decide to live in such a way. Imagine if we did. What about you?

(Ed & Will displaying matching ink: "99 for 1")

About the Author

Will Cravens is the President of Endurance Leadership, Inc., a non-profit whose mission is to train leaders that will impact the world. He and his wife Sandra help coordinate and lead life-changing trips around the globe through the organization's trip branch: Leadership Excursions.

Will is a professional communicator, speaking regularly for businesses, conferences, churches and other organizations. To book him for a speaking engagement, contact Endurance Leadership at: LeadershipExcursions@gmail.com

Will is also the lead pastor of Bridge Community Church, located in Ashburn, Virginia.

Twitter: @wcravens
Facebook: will.cravens1
Trip Website: leadershipexcursions.org

#99for1
Facebook: 99-For-1
Website: 99for1story.com

Made in the USA
Middletown, DE
20 September 2021